Introduction to Data Structures in C

Introduction to Data Structures in C

ASHOK N. KAMTHANE
Assistant Professor, Department of Electronics and Telecommunication
Shri Guru Gobind Singhji Institute of Engineering and Technology
Nanded, Maharashtra, INDIA

Pearson

Original edition, entitled *Intro to Data Structure in C*, 1 by Kamthane, published by Pearson Education Ltd.,

ISBN 9788131713921

First Impression, *2007*
Eighteenth Impression, 2023
Nineteenth Impression, 2024

Published by Pearson India Education Services Pvt. Ltd, CIN: U72200TN2005PTC057128.

Head Office: 1st Floor, Berger Tower, Plot No. C-001A/2, Sector 16B, Noida - 201 301, Uttar Pradesh, India.
Registered Office: Featherlite, 'The Address' 5th Floor, Survey No 203/10B, 200 Ft MMRD Road, Zamin Pallavaram, Chennai – 600 044.
Website: in.pearson.com; Email: companysecretary.india@pearson.com

Printed in India at Repro India Limited

To my beloved wife
Surekha Ashok Kamthane

Preface

This book is an introduction to all popular data structures, and their implementation with the C language. It is planned for beginners who would like to learn the subject through programs. We have therefore included a large number of programs along with their theories. It is hoped that the book will be of immense help to graduate and postgraduate students of engineering, science, and computer application. It can be used as a text-cum-reference book by students of BE, MCA, BCA, M.Sc. and B.Sc. courses, and also by students pursuing courses such as O, A, B, and C levels conducted by the DOEACC Society.

This book covers abstract concepts of data structures and describes how these theories are useful in problem-solving. Chapter 1 introduces the reader to the fundamentals of C language. It covers data types, structures, unions, algorithms, iterations and concepts of data structures.

Chapter 2 deals with arrays. It covers one-, two- and multidimensional arrays and contains numerous examples. It also covers row major and column major arrays. Pointers and arrays are also described at the end of the chapter.

Chapter 3 deals with recursion, which is a powerful and important concept in programming. Recursion plays a pivotal role in implementation of algorithmic solutions with minimum code. Direct and indirect recursive are explained through programs, and popular examples such as the Tower of Hanoi are also covered in the chapter.

Another building block of data structures is stack, which is described in Chapter 4. Terminologies of stack, pictorial representation of stack, push and pop operations and applications are discussed in the chapter. In addition, operations such as insertion and deletion of elements in a stack are explained with the help of examples. Evaluation of postfix expression and infix to postfix expressions are also given at the end of the chapter.

Queue, another linear data structure, is explained in Chapter 5. Representation of queue, insertion and deletion of an element in a queue, its static and dynamic implementation, and its applications are covered in the chapter. In addition, circular, deque and priority queues are explained. Ascending and descending priority queues are also discussed at the end of the chapter.

Chapter 6 discusses linked list, another significant element of data structures. Operations such as traversing a list, searching and retrieving an element from a list are described in this chapter. Types of linked lists, single, double and circular linked list are also described.

The most important topic presented on storage of data is memory. Chapter 7 discusses all the fundamental concepts of memory: how efficiently memory is managed by an operating system, how space is allocated by the operating system to the different programs and how storage allocation and de-allocation of memory are done. Buddy, binary buddy and compaction techniques are illustrated in this chapter.

One of the non-linear data structures, tree, is explained in Chapter 8. Basic terms used in binary tree are described at the beginning of the chapter. Topics such as binary tree, complete binary tree, extended binary tree, traversal in tree, threshold binary tree, balanced tree and B+ are all covered in this chapter.

Chapter 9 is devoted to graph. It deals with the basic terminologies of graph, representation of graph, traversals in graph, spanning tree, etc.

Chapter 10 discusses various searching techniques such as linear, binary, hashing, mid-division, mid-square, folding and length-dependent methods. Attention has also been paid on establishing the efficiency of some searching methods.

Chapter 11 is devoted to sorting methods. Various sorting techniques such as selection insertion, bubble, tree, merge, heap sot methods have been elaborated with programs. Partition exchange and radix sort methods have been discussed and supported with programming examples.

Utmost care has been taken in bringing out this book, and it is hoped that the book will serve the requirements of those for whom it is intended. However, it is possible that a few errors might have managed to evade the watchful eye. The author will be grateful to the readers for bringing these errors to his notice and also for their valuable suggestions for improving the quality of the book. The author can be reached at kamthanean@yahoo.com

ASHOK N. KAMTHANE

Acknowledgements

I am indebted to Mr S. Ramamurthi, president of Subhram Trust, Bangalore, for conferring upon me the Samaja Seva Bhushan Award 2004 for technical book writing from Maharashtra region. It is indeed a matter of great pride that Mr T. N. Chaturvedi, Governor of Karnataka, had felicitated me on the occasion. I am also thankful to Mr Suryakant Bidwai and Mr Satish Banglore of Phoenix Software for their inspiration and support.

I am thankful to the members of Vasavi Club of Nanded, especially Mr Prabhakar Nilawar, Dr Naresh Rayewar, Mr Lakshman Rewanwar, Mr Prashant Moralwar, Mr Rajesh Kotalwar, Mr Ramchandra Modi and Sanjay Kachawar for their encouragement and support.

I wholeheartedly express my deep sense of gratitude to the Minister for Higher and Technical Education, Mr Dilip Walse-Patil, who complimented my previous books.

I would like to express my sincere gratitude to the members of the board of governors of our institute, honourable chairman Mr Baba Kalyani (Chairman of Bharat Forge, Pune) and Prof. N. B. Pasalkar, Director of Technical Education, Maharashtra, for their encouragement and support. I am also thankful to the other board members, Prof. T. R. Sonatkke (Director), Prof. Narayan Khedkar, Prof. Vijay Ghate, Mr Kamlesh Pande, and Mr Dimri V. for their whole-hearted support and encouragement. I am also indebted to Mr S. R. Chandak of Bharat Forge for precious guidance and to Dr M. B. Kinhalkar, former Home Minister of Maharashtra, Dr J. G. Wadekar, and Dr V. A. Hambire for complimenting me for writing this book.

I am also grateful to Prof. B. M. Naik, former principal of S.G.G.S. Institute, Nanded, who has been a source of inspiration throughout my life.

I am thankful to all my colleagues, close relatives, well-wishers and students who complimented me and helped me during the preparation of this book. My thanks goes to Prof. S. G. Kahalekar, Dr P. D. Jadhav, Dr P. Pramanik, Dr P. S. Charpe, Dr D. S. Choudhary, Dr B. M. Dabde, Dr R. S. Bichkar, Dr Y. V. Joshi, Dr D. D. Doye, Prof. R. K. Chavan, Prof. J. V. Aghav, Dr U. V. Kulkarni, Dr S. N. Talbar, Dr S. P. Kallurkar, Dr V. M. Nandedkar, Dr A. U. Digraskar, Dr R. S. Holambe, Dr B. M.Patre, Dr R. C. Thool, Dr R. R. Manthalkar, Dr L. M. Waghmare, Dr R. H. Chille, Dr S. V. Bonde, Mr Gonde A. B., Prof. N. G. Megde, Mr J. V. L. Venkatesh, Ms S. S. Kandhare, Ms Kamble Usha, Mr P. S. Nalawade, Mr S. S. Hatkar, Mr Narayan Patil, Mr A. V. Nandedkar, Mr P. B. Londhe, Mr Trupti Deshmukh, Mr Sanjay Sarda, Miss Agrawal, Dr A. S. Sontakke, Dr P. T. Patil, Mr Bacchewar Deepak, Mr P. G. Jadhav and Mr A. I. Tamboli of my college who provided valuable suggestions in writing the book. I am thankful to my friends, Prof. S. L. Kotgire and Prof. Balaji Bacchewar for their suggestions and help, and to Mr M. M. Jahagirdar, Mr Medabalmewar, Mr Buddhewar L. M., Mr Buddhewar K. M., Mr D. V. Deshpande,

Mr Kokne S. R., Damkondawar M, Mr R. D. Yeramwar, Mr Tumma S R, Mr Dhanmane and Mr S. R. Mana for supporting me while writing the book.

My special thanks go to Mr Santosh S. Partani, Mr Moreshwar Deshmukh and Mr Santosh Kotgaonkar for the earnest efforts made during preparation of this book. They pointed me critical issues in the book. Their thorough reviewing of topics and modifications suggested by them in the programs were a great helping in writing this book. Without their involvement, this book would not have been possible. I thank once again to them for efforts in typing the book.

I am thankful to all the students, faculty, non-teaching staff of this college and other friends who have directly or indirectly helped me in this book project.

Thanks are also due to my wife Surekha who provided moral support at all times during the preparation of the book. Finally, yet importantly, my sons Amol, Amit, and daughter Sangita were also a great help to me all the times. I thank all of them.

About the Author

ASHOK NAMDEV KAMTHANE obtained his M.E. (Electronics) degree in first class from S.G.G.S. College of Engineering and Technology, Nanded. He was a meritorious student throughout his academic career, and has bagged a number of prizes for his works. He carried out his M.E. (Electronics) dissertation work at the Bhabha Atomic Research Centre, Trombay, and was associated with the development of hardware and software using 8051 (8-bit microcontroller) on Acoustic Transceiver System required in submarines. He worked for some time at Meltron, Mumbai, and then moved on to teaching, with which he is actively associated for the last 21 years. He has been teaching undergraduate and postgraduate students in engineering, and has also guided a number of students at various levels. He headed the Department of Computer, Electronics and Information Technology at S.G.S.S. Institute, Nanded, for a few years. Currently, he is Assistant Professor in Electronics and Telecommunication at the same institute. For his active role in organizing state- and national-level exhibitions, he has been felicitated on many occasions. He has published a number of technical papers at national and international conferences.

Contents

Chapter 1

Introduction to Data Structures

Chapter Outline

1.1 INTRODUCTION

Humans use different languages to communicate data and information with each other. Besides, thoughts and feelings can also be communicated to others using language. The newspaper, television and other media use different languages for communication of data/information. In all occupations, language plays a vital role. In fact, with the help of languages humans interact with each other.

Data is represented in the form of text or numbers or in the form of figures, tables, graphs, pictures, etc. The data can be stored in physical devices such as note books and in memory as string, number, characters, etc. A computer language is incomplete without data.

Information is derived from data. The following information can be drawn if data is provided:

- Per capita income
- Average population of the states
- Average temperature of the city
- Price index
- Performance of cricketers

Fig. 1.1 illustrates how information can be drawn from data.

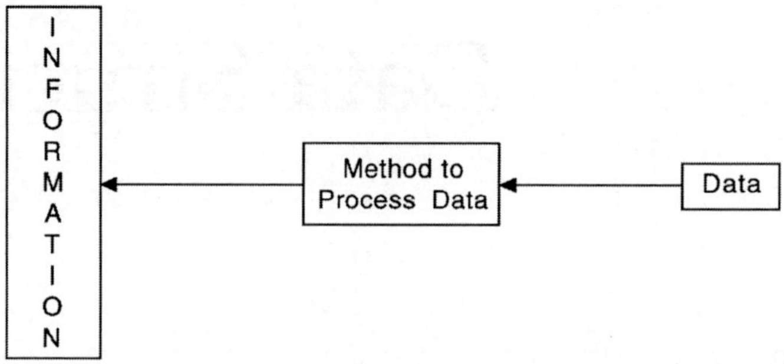

Figure 1.1 Relation between data and information

1. Everyday newspapers are delivered to our houses by the service man. It may be *The Times of India* or the *Indian Express*, and some other local language newspapers such as *Lokmat* and *Janjagruti*. The cost of each newspaper is different. How many papers have been received can be recorded in a notebook. This task is needed for calculating the total bill at the end of the month. The data here are the names of the newspapers, the dates on which they have been received and the cost of each. This data is needed to calculate the monthly or fortnightly bill. The total bill for the English newspapers as well as for the other papers can be calculated and analysed. One can draw different kinds of inferences such as whether the family is spending money on English newspapers or not and if so, how much. Does the family have educated members? Is the amount incurred on newspapers more than that on food? Data provided can be analysed for extracting different types of information.
2. Information about any human can be expressed with his/her name, age, gender, phone number, city, etc., and can be stored in the form of a table, which is as shown in Table 1.1.

Table 1.1 Information about a particular human

Information details	*Data*
Name	Satish
Gender	Male
Age	23
Phone	23234507
City	Pune

3. Consider the Fig. 1.2. *A* and *B* are two stations and distance between them is 100 km by train. The distance between them is certainly more if travelled by road and shorter by plane. Here, the distance between the two stations can be indicated by connecting two cities by train, road, or air. The distances, both relative and absolute, between the cities are nothing but the data. This information helps a person to decide the mode of travel from station *A* to *B*. One can decide to go by train or bus depending upon the need, urgency and convenience. It should be clear now that data and information are not the same.

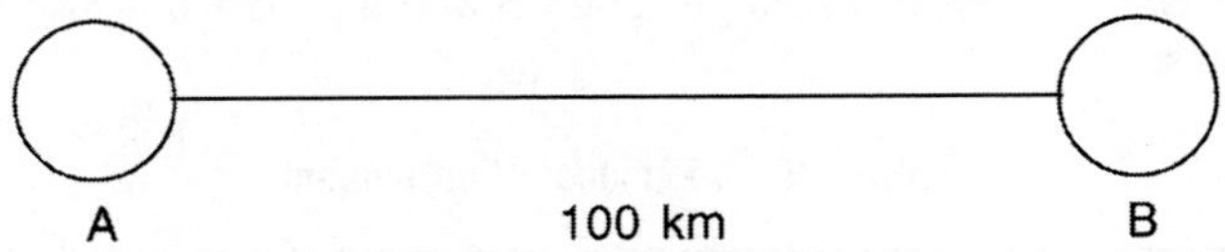

Figure 1.2 Distance representation

4. From the score of an individual cricket player we can draw information. Suppose, data consisting of the runs scored by a player in one-day cricket matches are provided. From the given data, the following information can be retrieved:
    1. Total runs scored
    2. Highest score
    3. Lowest score
    4. Average
    5. Best performance
    6. Strike rate
    7. Number of sixes
    8. Number of fours
    9. Number of forward shots
    10. Runs due to wide balls.

Information helps planners/analysts to make decisions. In this chapter, we are going to discuss application of data and information related to the computer.

1.1.1 Information in Computer

A computer is an electronic programmable device that manipulates information presented in the form of data. Computer science is mainly related to the study of data structures and their applications. The student of computer science should be aware of how data is manipulated in a system and the methods for utilization of data. It is, therefore, very essential to study the concepts of data organization and manipulation.

Data *"Data is nothing but a collection of numbers, alphabets and symbols combined to represent information."*

Data stands for value or group of values. Table 1.2 describes the common data types used in the computer.

Table 1.2 Data and its description

Data	Description
587	Numeric data
25/24/2002	Date formatted data
C PLUS PLUS	Character data

Entity An entity possesses some attributes and some values can be allocated to it. For example, a student is an entity of a college. The probable properties and the corresponding values are as follows:

Table 1.3 Information about student

Entity: Student				
Information	Name	Birth date	Gender	Course
Assigned Values	Harsha	01.03.1982	M	Data Structures

Every student in a college is an entity with different attributes. Sets of attributes are known as *domain*. Domains refer to possible values of a particular property. For example, the gender property can be assigned with values M or F.

1.2 DATA AND INFORMATION

The study of computer science deals with storage, retrieval, handling and organization of information. Information is generated in every sphere of life. For example, information about business transactions, or a student's performance in an examination, can be stored in the computer memory. The same information can be retrieved, modified, and restored. The total marks of a student can be obtained by adding the marks scored in all subjects. Similarly, the average percentage of marks can be computed and student performance can be monitored and evaluated using different factors such as total marks, average marks, highest score, and lowest score.

Information is symbolic representation. It has some useful meaning that helps us in making good judgments.

1.3 OVERVIEW OF DATA STRUCTURES

Data structures are a method of representing of logical relationships between individual data elements related to the solution of a given problem. Data structures are the most convenient way to handle data of different types including abstract data type for a known problem. For example, the characteristics of a house can be represented by the house name, house number, location, number of floors, number of rooms on each floor, kind of fencing to the house—either with brick walls or wire, electrification—either underground or open, whether a balcony has been provided or not, etc. One can use a variety of data types to represent these data elements while solving a problem with the help of computer language such as char, int, boolean type, etc. Figure 1.3 shows the various fields of house. For example, with the help of computer the characteristics of a house can be represented: *the number of floors of a house* can be given with either *int* or *char type*. The house number, the number of rooms in it can be declared with the same type, provided that the data is within the limits of the range of data type. In C language, the char data type works perfectly as integer data in the range from –128 to 127 and as unsigned char from 0 to 255. Sometimes, selection of data type is important. Just as, for example, if we are going to fence the house should we use brick or wire. Here, the brick wall may be expensive. Likewise, if we are using signed int instead of char to store a positive number (number of floors) we are wasting one byte of the system. Hence, here char is appropriate, which occupies only one byte.

Electrification should be declared with char data type. Like the above example, in the practical application of data structures, to create data structures some components are involved directly or indirectly to build the system. In other words, data structures are a structured set of variables associated with one another in different ways, co-operatively defining components of the system.

The components of data can be organized and records can be maintained. Further, the record formation leads to the development of abstract data type and database systems.

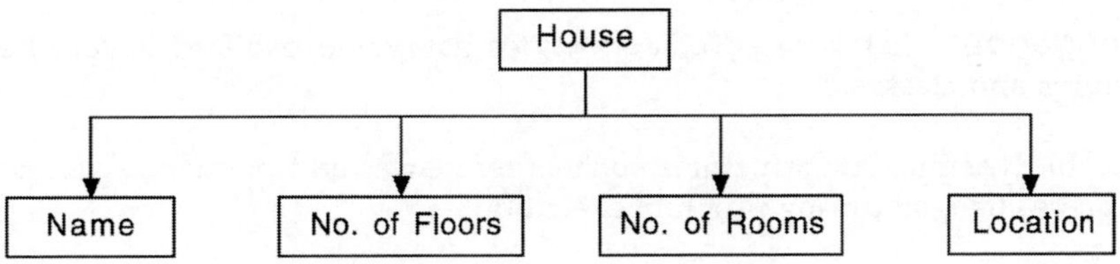

Figure 1.3 Information about a house

In data structures, we also have to decide on the storage, retrieval and operation that should be carried out between logically related items. For example, the data must be stored in memory in computer-understandable format, i.e. 0 and 1 and the data stored must be retrieved in human-understandable format, i.e. ASCII. In order to transform data various operations have to be performed.

1.4 TYPES OF DATA STRUCTURES

A data structure is a structured set of variables associated with one another in different ways, co-operatively defining components in the system and capable of being operated upon in the program. As stated earlier, the following operations are done on data structures:

1. Data organisation or clubbing
2. Accessing technique
3. Manipulating selections for information.

Data structures are the basis of programming tools and the choice of data structures should provide the following:

1. The data structures should satisfactorily represent the relationship between data elements.

2. The data structures should be easy so that the programmer can easily process the data.

Data structures have been classified in several ways. Different authors classify it differently. Fig. 1.4 (a) shows different types of data structures. Besides these data structures some other data structures such as lattice, Petri nets, neural nets, semantic nets, search graphs, etc., can also be used. The reader can see Figs. 1.4(a) and (b) for all data structures.

Linear In linear data structures, values are arranged in linear fashion. Arrays, linked lists, stacks and queues are examples of linear data structures in which values are stored in a sequence.

Non-Linear This type is opposite to linear. The data values in this structure are not arranged in order. Tree, graph, table and sets are examples of non-linear data structures.

Homogenous In this type of data structures, values of the same types of data are stored, as in an array.

Non-homogenous In this type of data structures, data values of different types are grouped, as in structures and classes.

Dynamic In dynamic data structures such as references and pointers, size and memory locations can be changed during program execution.

Static Static keyword in C is used to initialize the variable to 0 (NULL). The value of a static variable remains in the memory throughout the program. Value of static variable persists. In C++ member functions are also declared as static and such functions are called as static functions and can be invoked directly.

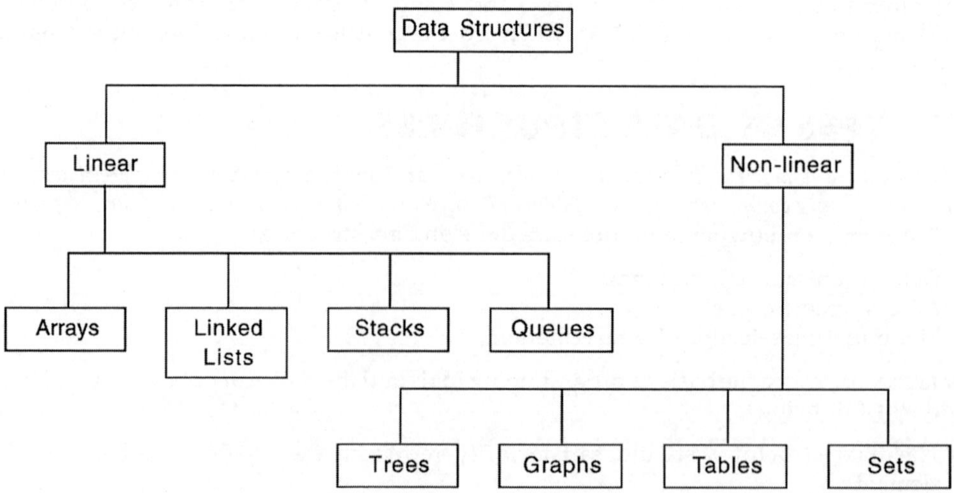

Figure 1.4 (a) Types of data structures

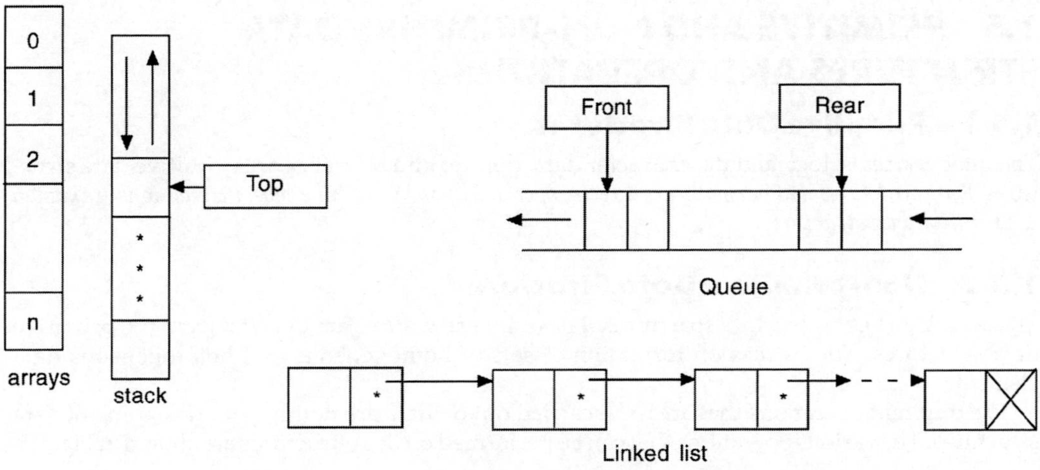

1. Linear data structures

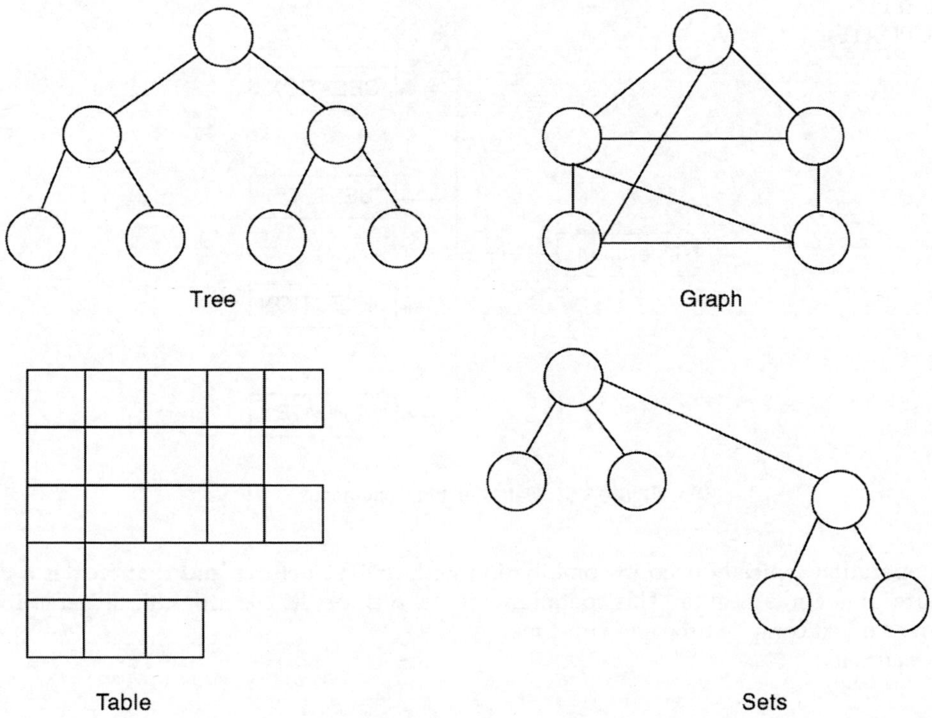

2. Non-linear data structures

Figure 1.4(b) Linear and non-linear data structures

1.5 PRIMITIVE AND NON-PRIMITIVE DATA STRUCTURES AND OPERATIONS

1.5.1 Primitive Data Structures

The integers, reals, logical data, character data, pointer and reference are primitive data structures. *Data structures that normally are directly operated upon by machine-level instructions are known as primitive data structures.*

1.5.2 Non-primitive Data Structures

These are more complex data structures. These data structures are derived from the primitive data structures. They stress on formation of sets of homogeneous and heterogeneous data elements.

The different operations that are to be carried out on data are nothing but designing of data structures. The various operations that can be performed on data structures are shown in Fig. 1.5.

1. CREATE
2. DESTROY
3. SELECT
4. UPDATE

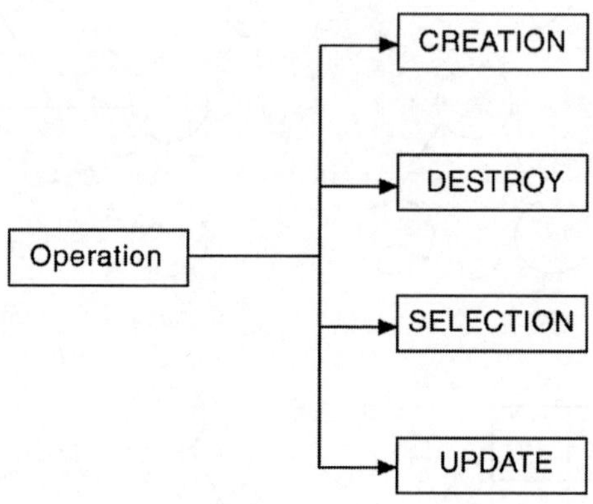

Figure 1.5 Data structures operations

An operation typically used in combination with data structures and that creates a data structure is known as creation. This operation reserves memory for the program elements. It can be carried out at compile time and run-time.

For example,

```
int x;
```

Here, variable x is declared and memory is allocated to it.

Another operation giving the balancing effect of a creation operation is *destroying* operation, which destroys the data structures. The destroy operation is not an essential operation. When the program execution ends, the data structure is automatically destroyed and the memory allocated is eventually de-allocated. C++ allows the destructor member function to destroy the object. In C *free ()* function is used to free the memory. Languages like Java have a built-in mechanism, called garbage collection, to free the memory.

The most commonly used operation linked with data structures is *selection*, which is used by programmers to access the data within data structures. The selection relationship depends upon *yes/no*. This operation updates or alters data. The other three operations associated with selections are:

1. Sorting
2. Searching
3. Merging

Searching operations are used to seek a particular element in the data structures. Sorting is used to arrange all the elements of data structures in the given order: either ascending or descending. There is a separate chapter on sorting and searching in this book. Merging is an operation that joins two sorted lists.

An iteration relationship is nothing but a repetitive execution of statements. For example, if we want to perform any calculation several times then iteration, in which a block of statements is repetitively executed, is useful.

One more operation used in combination with data structures is *update* operation. This operation changes data of data structures. An assignment operation is a good example of update operation.

For example,

```
int x=2;
```

Here, 2 is assigned to x.

```
x=4;
```

Again, 4 is reassigned to x. The value of x now is 4 because 2 is automatically replaced by 4, i.e. updated.

1.6 BINARY AND DECIMAL INTEGERS

Data is expressed in terms of 0 and 1 known as bits. Different number systems are used to represent numbers. For example, decimal, octal and hexadecimal number systems, can be used. The decimal system uses ten different symbols from 0 to 9, octal uses 0 to 7, hexadecimal from 0 to 9 and further from A to F. We can convert from one number system to another. To convert a decimal number to binary, the double dabble method is used. In this method, the decimal number is divided by 2 and remainders are listed in reverse direction. The binary number obtained from this method is the equivalent of the decimal. For example, the binary 111 is nothing but decimal 7. In the binary number system, every bit has its own weight. The least significant bit has 2^0 weight. Weight position is calculated to the power of 2. The right-most bit of a binary number has a value of 1, which is represented as 2^0. The next bit position has value 2^1 and so on and the values for further bits can be calculated. In other words, weights are assigned to each bit in binary. The weights from the least significant bits are 1,2,4,8----.

For example, the equivalent binary representation of 5 is 101. This is explained as follows:

$1 \times 2^2 + 0 \times 2^1 + 1 \times 2^0$
$4 + 0 + 1 = 5$

The power of two (weights) and binary bits are multiplied and the sum of all multiplications is taken to give the equivalent decimal number. There are two commonly used methods for representing negative binary numbers; they are as described in the following sections.

1.6.1 One's Complement

In this method, a positive integer is converted to negative by changing each bit to its opposite value. For example, the binary number 0101 represents 5 and its complement is 1010.

1.6.2 Two's Complement

In this method, 1 is added to the representation of one's complement. For example, 7 is represented as 0111 with an unsigned number. With two's complement, the number 7 becomes 1001 (One's complement of 0111 = 1000 and 1 is added at its least significant position giving a result of 1001).

1.6.3 Binary Coded Decimals

In addition to the binary number system, the programmer can also use decimal numbers. For example, a string of bits can be used to represent integers in the decimal number system. The decimal number from 0 to 9 can be represented using only a four-bit combination. Table 1.4 shows the decimal number and their equivalent binary digits.

A string of bits can be broken randomly into separate groups of four bits. Each group represents a digit. For example, the bit string 01100010 can be separated into two strings 0110 and 0010. The first string indicates six and the second two. The complete string represents 62. This method of representation is called as *binary coded decimal*.

Table 1.4 Four bits and equivalent decimal number

Decimal number	*Binary-coded decimal code* (8421)
0	0000
1	0001
2	0010
3	0011
4	0100
5	0101
6	0110
7	0111
8	1000
9	1001

1.6.4 Integers

We know what integers are and are aware of the arithmetic operations performed with them such as addition, subtraction, multiplication, and division. Integer-type data plays an important role in calculation. A counting of the number of objects can be shown by integers. The amount in a bank account, the number of students in a class and number of keys on a keyboard-all this information can be expressed in integers.

The traditional method of writing negative numbers is to put a sign symbol before the number. This method is called as *sign and magnitude method* and is commonly used in several computers to represent signed numbers. Normally, the sign is shown at the first or left-most bit of the binary number representation. In addition, the magnitude part appears followed by the sign.

The left-most bit is only for indicating the sign, but it does not have any weight as in an unsigned number system. In other words, a bit string beginning with zero shows a positive number whereas a bit string beginning with one indicates a negative number, if numbers are to be represented in a signed format.

Table 1.5 Sign bit

Number	*Sign Bit*	*Magnitude*
+7	0	00...0111
-6	1	10...0110

In the Table 1.5, 0 and 1 are used to represent positive and negative numbers. An integer shown with its sign is known as a signed integer. There are two types of signed integers: a) positive signed integer b) negative signed integer. We studied that these signs are represented in memory by 0 and 1 as shown in Table 1.5. The sign bit is always written as the leftmost bit. While storing signed numbers, the system reserves the leftmost bit for representation of the sign.

Positive signed integers are shown in the form called the signed magnitude form. In this style, in the leftmost bit, the sign is shown by 0 and magnitude is shown in the matching binary form.

For example,
+7 is shown by 0111
Negative signed numbers are shown in one of the following forms:

1. Signed – magnitude form
2. Signed – 1's complement form
3. Signed – 2's complement form

In the signed magnitude form method, 1 shows the sign of the number and magnitude is shown by the corresponding binary form.

Example
–7 is shown as 1111 signed number
–7 is shown as 1,000 in one's complement format
–7 is shown as 1001 in two's complement format
Table 1.6 shows the various ways of representing binary and negative numbers.

Table 1.6 Binary, Negative numbers in signed format and 1's complement of negative numbers

Decimal	Binary	Decimal	Signed numbers	1's Complement
+0	0000	–0	1000	1111
+1	0001	–1	1001	1110
+2	0010	–2	1010	1101
+3	0011	–3	1011	1100
+4	0100	–4	1100	1011
+5	0101	–5	1101	1010
+6	0110	–6	1110	1001
+7	0111	–7	1111	1000

In Table 1.6 positive and negative numbers are shown. Signed numbers and signed –1's complements of negative numbers are also shown in the said figure. The sign is shown by 1 and the magnitude is shown in the 1's complement form.

–7 is shown as 1,000.

In the signed–2's complement form, the sign of the number is shown by 1 and the magnitude is shown in the 2's complement form. The 2's complement of a number is the addition of 1's complement of the particular number and 1.

Table 1.7 shows 2's complement of the numbers.

2's complement of –7 is shown as 1,001

Table 1.7 2's complement of numbers

Decimal	2's Complement	Decimal	2's Complement
+0	0000	0	1000
+1	0001	–1	1111
+2	0010	–2	1110
+3	0011	–3	1101
+4	0100	–4	1100
+5	0101	–5	1011
+6	0110	–6	1010
+7	0111	–7	1001

1.6.5 Real Numbers

A number having an integer part and a fractional part is called a real number. The real number 548.56 can be written as 5.4856 × 102 or 0.54856 × 103. This type of representation is called scientific representation. The floating-point notation is generally used by all computer systems to indicate real numbers. There are several notations or methods to represent real numbers. Each method is unique and has different characteristics.

The real number has two parts: mantissa and base. It is represented by a number called mantissa. The base portion is always raised to the number and it is called the exponent. The base is always fixed. The mantissa and exponent vary. Different values of mantissa and exponent give different real numbers. For example,

The base is 10; the number 221.98 would be 22198 × 10^{-2}. The mantissa is 22198, exponent is –2. The values can also be written as.22198 × 10^3, 221.98,221.98n × 10^0.

The benefit of floating-point notation is that it can be used to show numbers with small or large absolute values. The biggest number that can be represented is $2^{23-1} \times 10^{27}$. In addition, the smallest positive number is 10^{-128}. which no doubt is very small. The limit of precision on a computer is the number of significant binary digits in the mantissa.

Example 1.1

Write a program to declare float and double type values and display them.

Solution

```
# include <stdio.h>
# include <conio.h>

main()
{
   float f=31343412.123;
   double d=46481232.77;
   clrscr();
   printf (" f= %lg",f);
   printf ("\nd=%lg",d);
}
```

Explanation In this program the variables *f* of float and *d* of double type are declared and are initialized. The values are displayed using base and mantissa format.

```
OUTPUT

f= 3.13434e+07
d=4.64812e+07
```

1.6.6 Character String

In the past, computers were in fact used as calculators and only numeric data could be manipulated with them. In those days, computer programs were written in numeric form. Programming in numeric form was difficult. To overcome this limitation symbolic codes were defined to represent information as character data. The invention of character data led to the formation of mnemonics for use as address and in operation. Using mnemonics, assembly languages and various procedure-oriented languages were developed.

A character is stored in computer memory as a series of bits in succession. Unique bit patterns are assigned to every character in the character set. Fixed length bits can be controlled more efficiently than variable length bit sequences. For that reason, character sets are programmed in fixed length bit sequences.

Information contains all types of data, viz., numbers, characters, symbols, etc. Hence, it is not possible to represent information by only numeric data. Information such as names and book titles are required to be represented with characters. Thus, all non-numeric information is represented by a sequence of characters called strings.

For example, in some systems 00100110 is used to show the '$' symbol and different types of such bit patterns represent 'A', 'C', 'D' and so on. In different countries, the computer may have a few additional symbols. The character set can be created using fonts. The programmer can create different fonts according to the language and culture of the country.

We know that 8 bits are used to represent a character and 256 different characters can be shown using these unique bit combinations. Suppose, the string 1101001 is used to represent character 'A' and 0100001 is used to represent 'B', then the string "AB" can be shown by the bit string 11010010100001. We know that a string is sequence of a characters and a character string is shown by concatenation as the bit strings, which represent separate characters of the string. Examples of strings are illustrated in Chapter 2.

1.7 LOGICAL INFORMATION

Primitive data structures also include logical data, i.e. true or false. Only two logical constants, true and false are present. In C /C ++programming 0 is assumed as false and any non-zero value as true. In C++, a new data type *bool* is introduced to handle logical conditions.

Expressions containing logical variables are used with relational operators such as <, >, ==, = etc. The result of such expression is only true (1) or false (0). The result is returned by the expression.

The storage representation of logical values depends upon the compiler or interpreter used by the language to convert the source program to a machine code. Normally, one bit is enough to store logical information. In C/C++ it is possible to store information in bits. The following programs explain true and false values returned by expressions and storing data using bits.

Example 1.2

Write a program to display logical values returned by logical expressions.

Solution

```
# include <stdio.h>
# include <conio.h>

main()
{
   clrscr();
   printf ("False : %d\n", 3>5);
   printf ("True : %d",5>1);
}

OUTPUT
False : 0
True : 1
```

Explanation The two expressions are put in the *printf ()* statement. The first condition 3>5 is false; hence, the return value is 0. The second expression 5>1 returns 1, i.e. the expression is true. Consider the following program, which stores return values in bits using structure.

Example 1.3

Write a program to identify the entered IP address. Display its class, mask and last address.

Solution

```
# include<stdio.h>
# include <conio.h>

main ()
{

 int ip0,ip1,ip2,ip3;
 clrscr();

 printf("\nEnter the IP address:-");
 scanf("%d.%d.%d.%d",&ip0,&ip1,&ip2,&ip3);

 if(ip0 >= 1 && ip0<128)
 {
 printf("\nThe given IP address %d.%d.%d.%d is in class A",ip0,ip1,ip2,ip3);
 printf("\nMask for class A address = 255.0.0.0");
 printf("\nThe last address of class A = 127.255.255.255");
 }
 if(ip0>127 & ip0<192)
 {
 printf("\nThe given IP address %d.%d.%d.%d is in class B ",ip0,ip1,ip2,ip3);
 printf("\nMask for class B address = 255.255.0.0");
 printf("\nThe last address of class B = 191.255.255.255");
 }

if(ip0>191 & ip0<224)
{
 printf("\nThe given IP address %d.%d.%d.%d is in class C",ip0,ip1,ip2,ip3);
 printf("\nMask for class C address = 255.255.255.0");
 printf("\nThe last address of class C = 223.255.255.255");
}

if(ip0>223 & ip0<240)
 {
 printf("\nThe given IP address %d.%d.%d.%d is in class D",ip0,ip1,ip2,ip3);
 printf("\nThe last address of class D = 239.255.255.255");
 }

if(ip0>239 & ip0<248)
{
printf("\nThe given IP address %d.%d.%d.%d is in class E",ip0,ip1,ip2,ip3);
printf("\nThe last address of class E = 247.255.255.255");
}

}
```

Explanation In this program the IP address is stored in the *ip0, ip1, ip2* and *ip3* variables. For each class a separate if condition is used and the relevant values are displayed on the screen.

```
OUTPUT:

Enter the IP address:- 198.1.1.1

The given IP address 198.1.1.1 is in class C
Mask for class C address = 255.255.255.0
The last address of class C = 223.255.255.255
```

Example 1.4

Write a program to store logical values in bit using structure.

Solution

```
# include <stdio.h>
# include <conio.h>

main ()
{

struct bits
{
int state :1;
};

   struct bits a;
   a.state=13>5;
   clrscr();
   if (a.state==0) printf ("False");
   else printf ("True : %d",5>1);
}
```

Explanation In the structure bits, the number of bits given is to be used by the member of structure to store values. The value returned by the expression 13>5 are stored in variable state that stores the value in one bit. The *if* statement checks the value and the appropriate message is displayed.

```
OUTPUT

True: 1
```

1.8 STORAGE OF INFORMATION

The digital computers have two types of memory: operational memory and storage memory. The operational memory refers to CPU registers. The CPU registers are temporarily used to store values. The CPU contains registers called accumulators that contain the variables while arithmetic operations are performed. For example, when numbers are added the result is stored in AX register of the CPU. The following program explains this.

Example 1.5

Write a program to access value using CPU register.

Solution

```
# include <stdio.h>
# include <conio.h>
main()
{
 int x=10,y=2;
 clrscr();
 _AX=x*y;
 printf ("\n Multiplication of x and y is %d",_AX);
 _AX=x+y;
 printf ("\n Addition of x and y is %d",_AX);
}

OUTPUT

 Multiplication of x and y is 20
 Addition of x and y is 12
```

Explanation In this program, integer variable, x and y are declared and initialised with 10 and 2. The statement $x * y$ calculates the product and $x+y$ calculates the addition of the variables. The obtained result is stored in register *AX*. We print the value using pseudo variable *_AX*.

In addition, CPU registers are also used to store 'temporarily' program instructions and program control information, which is helpful in program execution. Therefore, registers are only used to hold data temporarily.

The storage type memory is used for permanent storage of data that can be retrieved at any time. Before performing an arithmetic operation, the value of a variable is stored in the memory unit and then transferred to the register. If the obtained result is to be stored in another variable, it is necessary to again transfer values from register to storage memory

When a program execution is started, instructions and data are stored in storage units. The whole storage unit of computer is called main memory. Information is an input to the storage unit.

1.9 HARDWARE AND SOFTWARE

The memory of the computer is nothing but a group of bits. The values 0 and 1 are called bits. The unit formed by bits is called value, i.e. a group of bits represents a value. A group of 8 bits is called byte. Many bytes when grouped together are called word. Every byte in a memory has a unique address. The address is useful to identify the byte and its contents. In C it is possible to access the byte address. The address is always numeric (unsigned integer) and a not-negative number. The address is also called memory location. The computer system has a built-in mechanism that handles and manipulates different types of bit patterns according to the object or variable that holds the value.

For example, the computer contains an instruction to multiply two binary numbers and place the obtained value in another memory location. The mechanism to perform such an operation should have the following steps:

1. Extract argument bit patterns from two given addresses.
2. Construct a third bit pattern showing an integer, which is a product of two binary integers.
3. The obtained result bit pattern is assigned to another memory location.

The computer hardware is bit oriented whereas software is byte oriented, i.e. the computer hardware is capable of interpreting the bit patterns at a specified memory location. This is what we discussed concerning an operation between two integers. In case two real values are given, the computer hardware will apply another built-in mechanism to handle this data type. As discussed earlier, to handle native data type, necessary routines are *in-built into* the hardware. The instruction identifies the data type by value or address. The values are assigned explicitly and addresses are allocated implicitly by the system.

Consider the following C/C++ statements.

```
int j=4, k=5,h;
float p=9.1, q = 5.5, r;
```

In the above statements, four variables are declared and memories in bytes are allocated to them. *j*, *k*, *p* and *q* are called variables or identifiers. The variable name is useful to store values. A variable is nothing but a name given to memory location. The values stored in *j* and *k* will be interpreted as integers whereas the values of *p* and *q* will be interpreted as float. The C/C++ compiler translates the source program to machine language (object code).

Consider the following statements:

```
h=j+k;
r=p+q;
```

The first statement performs addition of *j* and *k* integer variables and stores the result in *h*. In the second statement addition of *p* and *q* are stored in variable r.

The operator '+' is common. Operators such as +,*,-,/ are overloaded in such a way that they can be used with any data type to perform an operation. All these operators are generic, i.e. they can be used with all standard data types.

1. These operators perform operations with all data types.
2. These operators have different meaning depending on context. For example, the operator '*' can be used for multiplication as well as for pointer notation.

In high-level language, declaration of variable plays an important role. The declaration contains data type name followed by variable list. The variables are allocated memory according to the data type.

For example, integer variable requires two bytes; float variable requires four bytes, etc.

The first column contains the name of the data type. These names are reserved words known as keywords. The second column has the number of bytes required by a variable of data type. The number of bytes may vary in different systems. The third column contains a range of data types, i.e. lowest and highest limits of numbers that can be stored in variables of respective data type.

1.10 CONCEPT OF DATA TYPES

A data type is a term that refers to the type of data values that may be used for processing and computing.

The information stored in memory is in the form of bits 0 and 1. We can view the memory in human-understandable format with the help of data type. The type of computer hardware decides the data type and the range it supports. Range means the largest and smallest possible values that can be represented. Our goal is to study how a user can utilize the data type to represent information. We need not think about what the computer does internally.

Suppose that data types are independent of computer hardware, then unlimited data types can be built. A data type is nothing but an abstract concept designed using logical operators. After designing such data type and its supporting operations we can use the data type. The instructions regarding the operation related to data type can be given by hardware and software. The necessary instructions are built into the computer hardware as hardware implementation. When a program gives such instructions it is known as software implementation. The instructions given in the computer program interpret the bit patterns.

1.11 DATA TYPES IN C

Various data types are used in the C language. Variables are used for assigning integers, long integers, or characters, etc. We can differentiate between data types such as integer, real, logical, complex variables, etc.

C contains four standard data types. They are *int*, *float*, *char* and *double*. Almost in all computers, all the above four data types are local to computer hardware. We have already discussed how integers, floats and characters are stored in memory and their manipulation. A double variable is a double precision floating-point number.

In addition, there are three qualifiers applicable to *int*. They are *short*, *long* and *unsigned*. When a variable is declared unsigned, it can store only positive values. By default when a variable is declared as int, it is short int. Its range is –32,768 to 32,767. To store values above this range, a long qualifier is used and its range is –2147483648 to 2147483647. An unsigned integer is always an absolute value and follows arithmetic laws of module 2^n, where, n is the number of bits in an integer. The ranges of data types and number of bytes needed to store them are shown in Table 1.8.

Table 1.8 C data types

Data types	*No. of bytes*	*Range*
char	1	–128 to 127
unsigned char	1	0 to 255
signed char	1	–128 to 127
int	2	–32768 to 32767
unsigned int	2	0 to 65535
signed int	2	–32768 to 32767
short int	2	–32768 to 32767
unsigned short int	2	0 to 65535
signed short int	2	–32768 to 32767
long int	4	–2147483648 to 2147483647
signed long int	4	–2147483648 to 2147483647
unsigned long int	4	0 to 4294967295
float	4	3.4E–38 to 3.4E+38
double	8	1.7E–308 to 1.7E+308
long double	10	3.4E–4932 to 1.1E+4932
enum	2	–32768 to 32767

1.12 ABSTRACT DATA TYPES

In programming, a situation occurs when built-in data types are not enough to handle the complex data structures. It is the programmer's responsibility to create this special kind of data type. The programmer needs to define everything related to the data type such as how the data values are stored, the possible operations that can be carried out with the custom data type and that it must behave like a built-in type and not create any confusion while coding the program. Such custom data types are called Abstract data type. In C struct and in C++ struct/class keywords are used to create abstract data type.

For example, if the programmer wants to define date data type which is not available in C/C++, s/he can create it using struct or class. Only a declaration is not enough; it is also necessary to check whether the date is valid or invalid. This can be achieved by checking using different conditions. The following program explains the creation of date data type:

Example 1.6

Write a program to create abstract data type date.

Solution

```
# include <stdio.h>
# include <conio.h>

struct date
{
 int dd;
 int mm;
 int yy;
};

main ()
{
struct date d; // date is abstract data type
clrscr();
printf ("Enter date (dd mm yy) :");
scanf ("%d %d %d",&d.dd,&d.mm, &d.yy);
printf ("Date %d-%d-%d",d.dd,d.mm,d.yy);
}

OUTPUT

Enter date (dd/mm/yy): 08 12 2003
Date 08-12-2003
```

Explanation In this program, using *struct* keyword the date data type is declared. It contains three-integer variables *dd, mm* and *yy* to store date, month and year. Through scanf statement date, month and year is entered and it is displayed using *printf* statement.

1.13 POINTERS

A pointer is a link or reference to data structures. The most important characteristic of pointer is that it allows identical method of referencing any data structures, no matter of what complexity and type. The pointer can point to any data type character, *float*, *int*, etc., and the method of accessing elements are the same. A pointer also allows quick insertion and deletion of an item in a list. The linked list is discussed later in this book.

There are two techniques of accessing data structures.

1.13.1 Computed Address

In this technique the data structures can directly be accessed using an address. The address is calculated by the compiler or interpreter, which translates the source program to an object code.

1.13.2 Pointer Addressing

The C/C++ pointers are of this type, in which a memory address is assigned to a pointer variable. Depending upon the complexicity of data structures some operations are also required in this technique. However, this technique is time consuming.

A pointer is a memory variable that stores a memory address of another variable. It can have any name that is acceptable for other variables and it is declared in the same way as other variables. It is always denoted by '*'.

1. Pointers save memory space.
2. Execution time of a program is faster because address of variable can be accessed and read/write operation with addresses directly done.
3. Memory is used efficiently with pointers.
4. Pointers are used with data structures. They are very useful for representing arrays.

```
int *x;
float *y;
char *y;
```

1. In the first statement '*x*' is an integer pointer and it tells the compiler that it holds the address of an integer variable. The variable f is a float pointer and it can hold the address of only the float variable. The **y* is a character variable and holds the address of any character variable.
2. The indirection operator (*) is also called the deference operator. When a pointer is dereferenced, the pointer retrieves the value stored at that address.
3. The indirection operator (*) is used in two distinct ways with pointers, declaration and deference.
4. When the pointer is dereferenced, the indirection operator indicates that the value at that location stored in the pointer is to be accessed rather than address.
5. The '&' operator is an address operator and it gives the address of the variable. The '&' immediately preceding the variable returns the address of the variable.

Example 1.7

Write a program to demonstrate the use of a pointer.

Solution

```
# include <stdio.h>
# include <conio.h>
main ()
{
   int x=2;
   int *p;
   clrscr();
   p=&x;
   printf ("\n Address of x is = %u", &x);
   printf ("\n Value of x is = %d ",*p);
}
```

Explanation In this program, an integer variable *x* is declared and assigned with value 2. Also, integer *pointer *p* is declared and initialized with address of *x*. The first printf statement displays the address of *x*. The second statement displays the value of *x* using *pointer p*.

OUTPUT

```
Address of x is = 65524
Value of x is = 2
```

Arithmetic operations on pointer variables are also possible. Increase, decrease, prefix and postfix operations can be performed with the help of pointers.

The following operations are not possible with address:

1. Addition of two addresses (pointers).
2. Multiplication of two addresses or multiplication with a constant.
3. Division of address with a constant.

1.14 STRUCTURES IN C

In this topic, we will discuss C data structures called structures. A structures is a collection of one or more variables of different data types, grouped together under a single name and new custom data type formed. The individual variables are called member variables. By using structures, we can make a group of variables, arrays, pointers, etc. The new data type formed by the structures is independent of computer hardware and we already studied that when data type is independent of computer hardware, unlimited data types can be formed. Now, consider the following declaration of structure and program to understand the concept.

```
struct student
 {
 char name[20];
 int age;
 float wt;
 };
```

In this example, the structure student is declared by combining three standard data types. The structure name is called as tag name. Here, three data types can be accessed separately and hence they are not mixed.

Consider the following example,

Example 1.8

Write a program to demonstrate how structures are used to store and display data.

Solution

```
# include <stdio.h>
# include <conio.h>

struct student
{
    char *name;
    int age;
    float weight;
};

main()
{
    struct student s1;
    s1.name="Nilesh";
    s1.age=25;
    s1.weight=55;
    clrscr();
    printf ("\n Name = %s",s1.name);
    printf ("\n Age = %d",s1.age);
    printf ("\n Weight = %g",s1.weight);
}

OUTPUT

Name = Nilesh
Age = 25
Weight = 55
```

Explanation In this program, structure is defined and a custom data type is formed. Here, the program contains information regarding data type; hence, it is called software implementation.

```
struct student s1; // c style
```

Using the above statement, variables (objects) of structures data type student can be declared. *s1* is an object of structure data type. The dot (.) operator with variable is used to access individual variables and initialization and display of value can be done. When a structure is declared separate, memory is allocated to each variable according to its data type. The total size of the variable of struct type is the sum of bytes of all member variables. Using the operator *sizeof ()* we can demonstrate this. Consider the following program.

Example 1.9

Write a program to demonstrate that the size of structure variable is equal to the sum of sizes of member variables.

Solution

```
# include <stdio.h>
# include <conio.h>
main ()
{
struct data
{
char ch;
int in;
float fl;
};
struct data d;
clrscr();
printf ("\nSize of character ch = %d",sizeof(d.ch));
printf ("\nSize of integer in = %d",sizeof(d.in));
printf ("\nSize of float fl = %d",sizeof(d.fl));
printf ("\nSize of object d = %d",sizeof(d));
}
```

Explanation In this program structure data is declared with three standard data types: *char, int* and *float*. *d* is a variable of data type. Using *sizeof ()* operator size of every member, variable d is calculated and displayed. The size of variable *d* is the sum of the sizes of all members. The output gives a clear idea.

```
OUTPUT

Size of character ch = 1
Size of integer in = 2
Size of float fl = 4
Size of object d = 7
```

1.15 UNIONS

Union is a user defined data type very similar to structure. It contains members like structure but no separate memory is allocated to each member. The size of the largest element is detected and this much amount is allocated. Members of a union share common memory locations. The union data structure is useful to invoke BIOS and DOS services. An example follows:

Example 1.10

Write a program to demonstrate use of unions.

Solution

```
# include <stdio.h>
# include <conio.h>
# include <dos.h>
main ()
{
union REGS in,out;
int86(18,&in,&out);
```

Explanation In this program union is in use. *int86 ()* is a function. The value 18 is a service number. The function calculates the total size of memory and it is displayed by *printf ()* statement. While discussing types of data structures, we

```
clrscr();
printf ("\n Total memory = %d KB", out.x.ax);
}
```

OUTPUT

Total memory = 640 KB

discussed static data structures. Consider the following example of a static variable.

Example 1.11

Write program for displaying the size of the data type in union and the size of the object of the union.

Solution

```
# include <stdio.h>
# include <conio.h>
main ()
{
 union set
 {
    char x;
    int y;
    float z;
    long double a;
 };
    union set s1;
    clrscr();
    printf ("\nSize of character x = %d",sizeof(s1.x));
    printf ("\nSize of integer y = %d",sizeof(s1.y));
    printf ("\nSize of float z = %d",sizeof(s1.z));
    printf ("\nSize of long double a = %d",sizeof(s1.a));
    printf ("\nSize of object s1 = %d",sizeof(s1));
}
```

OUTPUT:

```
Size of character x = 1
Size of integer y = 2
Size of float z = 4
Size of long double a = 10
Size of object s1 = 10
```

Explanation In this program, union of the set is declared and *s1* is the object of the union set. The union set contains integer, character, float and long double data types. The program shows the size of all the data types but it shows the size of the object 10 because the long double has the size 10.

Example 1.12

Write a program to explain the use of a static variable.

Solution

```
# include <stdio.h>
# include <conio.h>
main ()
{
static int x;
clrscr();
x++;
printf (" x= %d",x);
}

OUTPUT
x=1
```

Explanation When variables are declared and not initialized, they contain garbage values. Hence, they cannot be used without initializing. When such variables are declared as static, they are initialized to zero and can directly be involved in an operation.

1.16 ALGORITHMS

An algorithm is a well-organized, pre-arranged and defined computational module that receives some value or set of values as input and provides a single or a set of values as output. These well-defined computational steps are arranged in sequence, which processes the given input into output. Algorithms are used to solve applications that are complex. An algorithm is said to be accurate and truthful only when it provides the exact wanted output, obviously, after implementation of algorithm into program.

1.16.1 Analysing Algorithm

When one writes an algorithm, it is essential to know how to analyse it. Analyzing an algorithm refers to calculating or guessing resources needful for the algorithm. Resources means computer memory, processing time, logic gates, etc. In all these factors, time is most important because the program developed should be fast in processing. The analysis can also be made by reading the algorithm for logical accuracy, tracing the algorithm, implementing it and checking it with some data and with a mathematical technique to confirm its accuracy.

Algorithms can also be expressed in a simple method that will help the user to put it into operation easily. However, this approach has a few drawbacks. It requires more space and time. It is very essential to consider the factors of time and space of an algorithm.

1.16.2 Rate of Growth

In practice, frequently it is not possible to act upon a simple analysis of an algorithm to conclude the execution time of an algorithm. The execution time depends upon the machine and its way of implementation.

Timing analysis depends upon the input required. To accurately carry the time analysis, it is also very essential to know the exact directives executed by the hardware and the execution time passed for each statement.

1.16.3 Space Requirement

The space or memory requirement of a program is the memory space required to execute the program. From the total allocated memory, a fixed portion occupies code, variable and space for data, etc. The space analysis is only made for the memory space to store data values. It does not include the space required for the algorithm itself. The memory space requirement can be calculated as follows:

s(p)=c+sp
c is constant
s(p) is space requirement
sp refers to instance attribute.

1.16.4 Time Requirement

It indicates the time required for execution of the program. The complete time T (p) is the total of time required for compiling and executing of the program. The compile time is not dependent on instance attribute.

Summary

1. A computer is an electronic device that manipulates information presented in the form of data.
2. The study of any characteristic in computer science means the study of storage, retrieval, manipulation and organization of information.
3. Information is symbolic representation. It has some useful meaning for us and allows us to make good judgements. Information is always expressed by data. Data is nothing but a collection of numbers, alphabets, symbols, etc., combined to represent information.
4. The integers, real, logical data, character data, pointer and reference are primitive data structures. Data structures that are normally directly operated upon by machine-level instructions are known as primitive data structures.
5. Operations that create data structures are known as creation.
6. Destroy operations destroy data structures.
7. The most commonly used operation linked with data structures is selection, which is used by programmers to access the data within data structures. Selection relationship depends upon yes/no.
8. The iteration relationship depends upon repetition.
9. A number that has only the integer part is called an integer number.
10. A number that has the integer part and the fractional part is called a real number.
11. Primitive data structures also include logical data, i.e. true or false. Only two logical constants—true and false—are present.
12. All non-numeric information is represented by a sequence of characters called strings.
13. The information stored in memory is in the form of bits 0 and 1. The information in the memory can be viewed and understood by humans with the help of data types. The type of computer hardware decides the data type and the range it supports. Range means the largest and smallest possible values that can be represented.
14. A pointer is a link or reference to data structures.
15. A pointer is a memory variable that stores a memory address of another variable. It can have any name that is valid for the other variable and it is declared in the same way as any other variable. It is always denoted by '*'.
16. A structure is a collection of one or more variables of different data types grouped together under a single name and new custom data type is formed.

17. An algorithm is a well-organized, pre-arranged, and defined computational module that receives some value or set of values as input and provides a single or a set of values as output.
18. Analyzing an algorithm refers to calculating or estimating the resources needed for the algorithm. Resources means computer memory, processing time, logic gates, etc.
19. The space or memory requirement of a program is the memory space required to execute the program. The execution time is dependent upon the machine and the way of implementation.

Exercises

A. Answer the following questions:
   1. What is a computer?
   2. What is information? Explain with a few examples.
   3. What is data? Explain with a few examples.
   4. Mention different types of data structures.
   5. Distinguish between structure and class.
   6. What are the functions of pointer and reference?
   7. Explain logical information. List the operators related to it.
   8. Explain the different operations related to data structures.
   9. Explain the concept of data type.
   10. Explain integers and real numbers.
   11. Explain algorithm and its types. (a) Searching (b) sorting.
   12. Explain algorithm with the factors time and space.
   13. What are the different data types available in C language? Explain with examples.

B. Attempt the following programs:
   1. Write a program to store logical values returned by an expression in individual bits.
   2. Write a program to perform addition of two variables using pointers and reference.
   3. Write a program to demonstrate the update of the operation of data structures with variables.
   4. Write a program to convert a decimal number to its binary equivalent.
   5. Write a program to create abstract data types.
   6. Write a program to get information about a student and display it on the screen by using structure.
   7. Write a program to add two numbers using structure.

C. Select the appropriate option for each of the following:
   1. An array is a ——— type of data structure.
      (a) linear (c) dynamic
      (b) non-linear (d) (a) and (b)
   2. Homogenous means ———.
      (a) values of the same type (c) (a) and (b)
      (b) having all equal values (d) dissimilar values
   3. Information is represented by ———.
      (a) data (c) numeral
      (b) characters (d) bits

4. In this method a positive integer is converted to negative by changing each bit to its opposite value.
   (a) one's complement (c) both (a) and (b)
   (b) two's complement (d) none of the above
5. The data type defined by the user is known as ———.
   (e) abstract data type (g) classic data type
   (f) built-in data type (h) none of the above
6. The keyword class or struct can be used to create ———.
   (a) abstract data type (c) logical data type
   (b) built-in data type (d) all of the above
7. The destructor performs the ——— operation.
   (a) destroy (c) selection
   (b) update (d) both (a) and (c)
8. An integer data type is ———.
   (a) primitive (c) (a) and (b)
   (b) non-linear (d) non-primitive

D. What will be the output of the following programs?

1.

```
# include <stdio.h>
# include <conio.h>
main ()
{
static int a;
clrscr();
printf (" %d",a++);
static int a;
clrscr();
printf (" %d",a++);
printf (" %d",a);
printf (" %d",a++);
printf (" %d",a);
}
```

2.

```
# include <stdio.h>
# include <conio.h>
main ()
{
struct abc
{
char c;
int i;
float f;
};
struct abc a;
clrscr();
printf ("\n%d",sizeof(a.c));
printf ("\n%d",sizeof(a.i));
printf ("\%d",sizeof(a.f));
printf ("\n%d",sizeof(a));
}
```

3.

```
# include  <stdio.h>
# include <conio.h>
main ()
{
union xyz
{
float c;
int   i;
double f;
};
union xyz w;
clrscr();
printf ("\n%d",sizeof(w.c));
printf ("\n%d",sizeof(w.i));
printf ("\%d",sizeof(w.f));
printf ("\n%d",sizeof(w));
}
```

4.

```
# include <stdio.h>
# include <conio.h>
main ()
{
int a=2;
float b=220.20;
clrscr();
printf ("\n %f %d",a,a);
printf ("\n %f %d",b,b);
}
```

5.

```
# include <stdio.h>
# include <conio.h>
main ()
{
int a=2,b=10,c=100;
a=b;
b=c;
clrscr();
printf ("\n%d %d %d",a,b,c);
}
```

6.

```
# include <stdio.h>
# include <conio.h>
main ()
{
char c='A';
b=c+2;
}
```

7.

```
# include <stdio.h>
# include <conio.h>
main ()
{
int a=2;
int *b;
clrscr();
a=&b;
printf ("\n %u", &a);
printf ("\n %d",*(&b));
printf ("\n %d",*b);
}
```

8.

```
# include <stdio.h>
# include <conio.h>
main ()
{
int a=2;
float b=10.02;
clrscr();
printf ("\n%f %d",b/a,b/a);
printf ("\%f %d",a/b,a/b);
}
```

9.

```
# include <stdio.h>
# include <conio.h>
main ()
{
char c='A';
clrscr();
printf ("\n%d %c",c,c);
}
```

10.

```
# include <stdio.h>
# include <conio.h>
main ()
{
int b=32767;
b++;
}
```

Chapter 2

Data Structures: Array

Chapter Outline

2.1 INTRODUCTION

Array means collection. An array is used to store elements of the same type. It is a very popular and useful data structure and stores data elements in contiguous locations. More than one element is arranged in sequence so it is also called a *composite data structure*. Array is a linear and homogenous data structure. Homogenous means that the same types of elements are stored in it. It can be combined with a non-homogenous structure and a complex data structure can be created. We know that an array of structure objects can also be useful. Array of any standard or custom data type can be declared. The array of character (strings) type works somewhat differently from the array of int, float, etc.

When we declare a variable for example,

```
int x;
```

The variable x is declared and a memory location of two bytes is allocated to it. Later, a single value can be stored in it as shown in Fig. 2.1.

```
x=4;
```

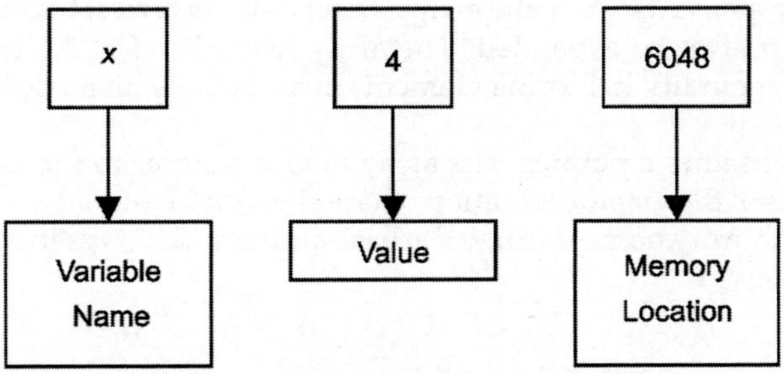

Figure 2.1 Variable, value and address

Every variable has a name, value and memory location. Hence, from the above, we can say that only one value can be stored in a variable.

2.1.1 Array Declaration and Initialization

To store more than one value, programming languages have an in-built data structure called array.

a) `int num[5];`

In the above declaration, an integer array of five elements is declared. Memory for 5 integers, i.e. 10 successive bytes are reserved for *num* array. To initialize a *num* array, the following syntax can be used:

b) `int num[5] = {1,2,4,2,5};`

In the above statement, all elements are initialized. It is also possible to initialize individual elements as follows:

```
num[0]=1;
num[1]=2;
num[2]=4;
num[3]=2;
num[4]=5;
```

The initialization can be done at compile time or dynamically at run time. The above is an example of compile-time initialization. In the statement (b) declaration and initialization is done at once. In such declaration, the number of elements (5) need not be mentioned in the []. The compiler automatically counts the values initialized and assumes the number of elements initialized as the array size.

In the above array, the element, *num* [0], i.e. 1 is the lowest bound and *num* [4], i.e. 5 is the upper element. In C, there is no bound checking. Hence, the programmer has to check it while accessing or storing elements. Once the array is declared, its lowest bound cannot be changed but the upper bound can be expanded. The array name itself is the constant pointer and, therefore, we cannot modify it. Storing elements in successive memory locations can expand the upper bound.

The array name itself is a pointer. The array *num* is pointer to the first element, i.e. *num* contains the address of the memory location where element 1 is stored as shown in Fig. 2.2. The address stored in the array name is called the base address. To access individual elements, the following syntax is used:

num[0] refers to the 1
num[1] refers to the 2
num[2] refers to the 4
num[3] refers to the 2
num[4] refers to the 5

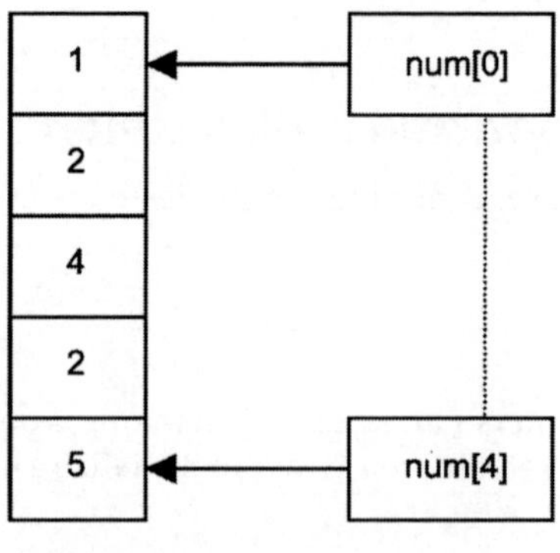

Figure 2.2 Arrays of integers

An array is a collection of elements of the same data type, stored in unique and contiguous memory locations.

2.1.2 Array Terminology

Size The number of elements or the array's capacity to store elements denotes the size, which is always mentioned in the bracket ([]).

Type Types refers to data type. It decides which type of element is stored in the array. It also instructs the compiler to reserve memory according to data type.

Base The address of the first element (0th) element is a base address. The array name itself stores the address of the first element.

Index The array name is used to refer to the array element. For example, in *num* [x], *num* is the array name and *x* is the index. The value of *x* begins from 0 onwards depending on the size of the array. The index value is always an integer value.

Range The index of an array, i.e. the value of *x* varies from the lower bound to the upper bound while writing or reading elements from an array. For example, for *num*[100] the range of the index is 0 to 99.

Word This indicates the space required for an element. In each memory location, a computer can store a data piece. The space occupied varies from machine to machine. If the size of the element is more than word (one byte) then it occupies two successive memory locations. The various data types such as integer, float, long, etc. needs more than one byte in memory.

2.2 CHARACTERSTICS OF ARRAYS

1. Array elements are stored in successive memory locations.

Example 2.1

Write a program to display array elements with their addresses.

Solution

```
# include <stdio.h>
# include <conio.h>

main ()
{
    int Num[5]={1,2,3,2,5};
    clrscr();

    printf ("\n Num[0] = %d Address: %u",Num[0],&Num[0]);
    printf ("\n Num[1] = %d Address: %u",Num[1],&Num[1]);
    printf ("\n Num[2] = %d Address: %u",Num[2],&Num[2]);
    printf ("\n Num[3] = %d Address: %u",Num[3],&Num[3]);
    printf ("\n Num[4] = %d Address: %u",Num[4],&Num[4]);
}
```

Explanation In the output of the program, elements and their addresses are displayed. Recall that integer requires two bytes in memory. The memory locations displayed have a difference of two. From the above program, it is clear that array elements are stored in successive memory locations. Fig. 2.3 shows the memory location and the values stored.

OUTPUT

```
Num[0] = 1 Address: 65516
Num[1] = 2 Address: 65518
Num[2] = 3 Address: 65520
Num[3] = 2 Address: 65522
Num[4] = 5 Address: 65524
```

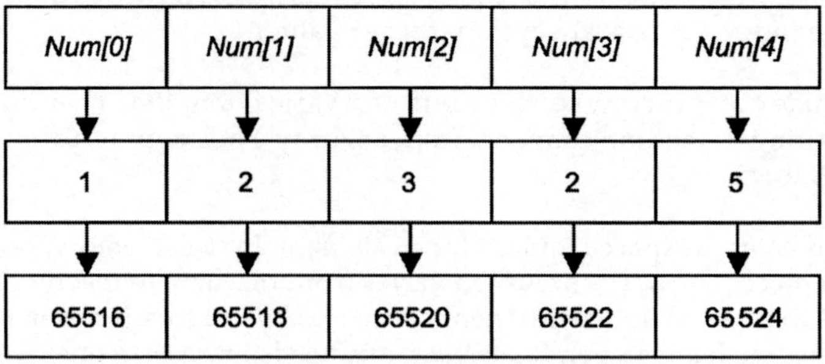

Figure 2.3 Storage of one-dimensional array

2. Once the array is declared, its lowest bound cannot be changed, but the upper bound can be expanded with the C++ compiler. The array name itself is a constant pointer and we cannot modify it. Therefore, the lowest bound of an array cannot be expanded.

Example 2.2

Write a program to demonstrate that the upper bound of an array can be expanded.

Solution

```
# include <stdio.h>
# include <conio.h>

main ()
{
   int Num[5]={1,2,3,2,5};
   Num[5]=6;
   clrscr();
   printf ("Num[5]=%d",Num[5]);
}
```

Explanation In this program array, *Num [5]* is declared with the array size 5 and it is initialized with five elements. In the next statement, the 6th element is also initialized and displayed. Hence, we can say that the upper bound of an array can be expanded. If you try this program with a C compiler, a run time error message will be displayed.

OUTPUT

```
Num[5]=6
```

3. We know that the array name itself is a pointer. Though it is a pointer, it does not need the '*' operator. The brackets [] automatically denote that the variable is a pointer.
4. All the elements of an array share the same name, and they are distinguished from one another with the help of the element number.
5. The amount of memory required for an array depends upon the data type and the number of elements.

Total bytes=sizeof (data type) * size of array

6. Operations such as insertion and deletion of element done with a list cannot be done with an array. Once an array is created, we cannot remove or insert memory locations. An element can be deleted or replaced but the memory location remains as it is.
7. When an array is declared and not initialized, it contains garbage values. If we declare an array as *static*, all elements are initialized to zero. However, the values of static type data persist and remain in the memory as long as the program executes. To overcome this problem, we initialize the first element of an array with zero or any other number. All the remaining elements are automatically initialized to zero, provided that the initialization is done in the declaration statement of array. The following program illustrates this:

Example 2.3

Write a program to initialize an array.

Solution

```
# include <stdio.h>
# include <conio.h>

main ()
{
   int Num[5]={0},j;
   clrscr();
   printf("The elements in array after initialization ");
   for (j=0;j<5;j++)
   printf ("\nNum[%d]=%d",j,Num[j]);
}
```

Explanation In this program an array, *Num [5]* is declared and the first element is initialized with zero. The compiler automatically initializes all the elements with zero. Using the for loop the contents of an array are displayed and we can see that all are zeros.

```
OUTPUT

The elements in an array after initialization
Num[0]=0
Num[1]=0
Num[2]=0
Num[3]=0
Num[4]=0
```

2.3 ONE-DIMENSIONAL ARRAYS

We have learnt how to declare, initialize and access the array elements. A one-dimensional array does not have any corresponding elements; it has only one row of elements. So far, the example we have discussed is of a one-dimensional array.

For example,

int *Num[5]*; // one dimensional array

In the following program we learn how to store and display values in the array during program execution.

Traversing The operation of displaying or listing all elements of an array is called traversing. The following program explains traversing with a one-dimensional array:

Example 2.4

Write a program to read and display the elements of an array.

Solution

```
# include <stdio.h>
# include <conio.h>

main ()
{
   int num[5],j;
   clrscr();
   printf ("\n Enter five elements: ");
   for (j=0;j<5;j++)
   scanf ("%d",&num[j]);
   printf ("\n Elements Address ");
   for (j=0;j<5;j++)
   printf ("\n%3d %10u ",num[j],&num[j]);
}
```

Explanation In this program, an array *num []* is declared. The first *for loop*, with the help of *scanf ()* statement, reads the elements and places in the array. The element position is indicated by the loop variable *j*. The same procedure is applied for displaying elements. The *printf ()* statement displays the elements and addresses on the screen. The %3d and the %10u is used to display the space.

```
OUTPUT

Enter five elements: 4 6 4 2 1

   Elements  Address
      4      65516
      6      65518
      4      65520
      2      65522
      1      65524
```

From Example 2.4 we can see that elements in a one-dimensional array are stored one after another in sequence in memory. In the array we can insert, delete, or add any element but we cannot insert or delete the memory location. We can change only the values.

2.4 OPERATION WITH ARRAYS

Fig. 2.4 shows operations frequently carried out with arrays.

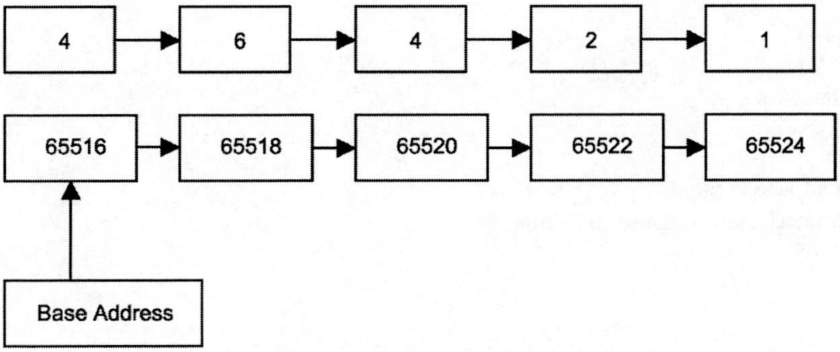

Figure 2.4 Elements in memory

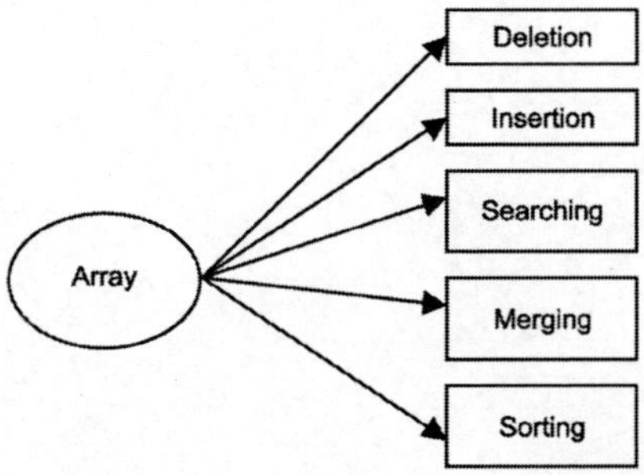

Figure 2.5 Operations with arrays

2.4.1 Deletion

This operation involves deleting specified elements from the array. Now, consider the following programs:

Example 2.5

Write a program to delete specified element from an array and rearrange the elements.

Solution

```
# include <stdio.h>
# include <conio.h>

main ()
{

int Num[20]={0},j,k,n,p,t;
clrscr();
printf ("\n Enter Number of elements: ");
scanf ("%d",&n);
printf ("\n Enter elements: ");
```

Explanation In this program, an array *Num [20]* is declared. The program asks for number of elements to be entered. The user has to enter the following input:

1. Number of elements to be entered and integers.
2. Element number to be erased from an array.

```
for (j=0;j<n;j++)
scanf ("%d",&Num[j]);
printf ("\n Elements are: ");

for (j=0;j<n;j++)
printf ("\n Num[j]=%d",Num[j]);
printf ("\n Enter element number to delete: ");
scanf ("%d",&p);
p—;

for (j=0;j<n;j++)
{
if (j>=p)
Num[j]=Num[j+1];
}

for (j=0;j<n;j++)
if (Num[j]!=0)
printf ("\nNum[j] = %d",Num[j]);
}
```

```
OUTPUT

Enter Number of elements: 5
Enter elements: 9 4 6 3 2

Elements are:
Num[j]=9
Num[j]=4
Num[j]=6
Num[j]=3
Num[j]=2
Enter element number to delete: 5

Num[j] = 9
Num[j] = 4
Num[j] = 6
Num[j] = 3
```

In the first for loop scanf statement reads the numbers from the keyboard and places it in the array. In the second for loop the array elements are displayed. After this for loop the number to be deleted is entered through the keyboard. In the third for loop the entered element is compared with all array elements. When match is found, the element is deleted and successive elements are pushed in their previous memory locations. The fourth for loop and printf statement display the elements of the array. You can see in the output that the third memory location is the same; only its contents are changed. See Fig. 2.6.

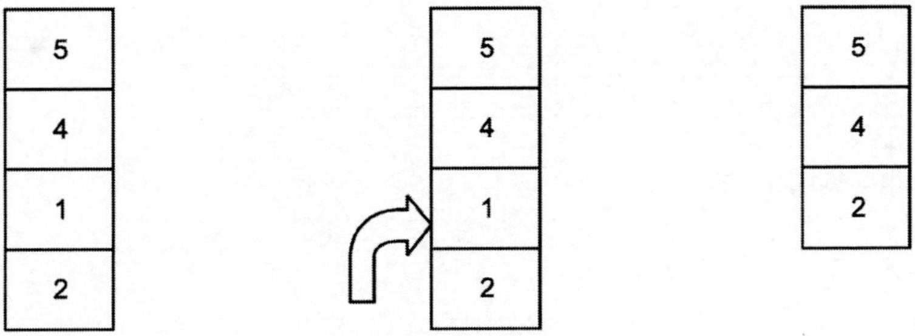

a. Original Array b. Shifting one element up c. After deletion

Figure 2.6 Deletion in steps

2.4.2 Insertion

This operation is used to insert an element at specified positions in an array. Consider the following program.

Example 2.6

Write a program to insert a element at a specified position in the array.

Solution

```
# include <stdio.h>
# include <conio.h>
main ()
{
int num[20]={0},j,k,n,p,t,s;
clrscr();
printf ("\n Enter number of elements: ");
scanf ("%d",&n);
printf ("\n Enter elements: ");

for (j=0;j<n;j++)
scanf ("%d",&num[j]);
printf ("\n Elements are: ");

for (j=0;j<n;j++)
printf ("\n num[j]: %d",num[j]);

printf ("\n Enter element and position to insert at: ");
scanf ("%d %d",&s,&p);
p—;
```

Explanation This program is somewhat like the previous program. Here, an element is inserted. The array elements are shifted to the next location, and at a specified position a space is created and the new element is inserted (Figures 2.7 (b) and 2.7 (c)). Here also, you can see that though we insert a new element, the memory location of the second element is the same (65482). Once again, it is proved that in an array operation, only the contents of memory can change but the actual address remains as it is. The address of the first element, i.e. *num [0]* (65480), is called the base address. This address can also be stored in another pointer and array elements can be accessed. The next program is illustrative in this regard.

```
    for (j=n;j!=p;j—)
    num[j]=num[j-1];
    num[j]=s;

for (j=0;j<=n;j++)
printf ("\n num[j] = %d",num[j]);
}
```

OUTPUT

```
 Enter number of elements: 5

 Enter elements: 1 2 3 4 5

 Elements are:
 num[j]: 1
 num[j]: 2
 num[j]: 3
 num[j]: 4
 num[j]: 5
 Enter element and position to insert at: 2 5

 num[j] = 1
 num[j] = 2
 num[j] = 3
 num[j] = 4
 num[j] = 2
 num[j] = 5
```

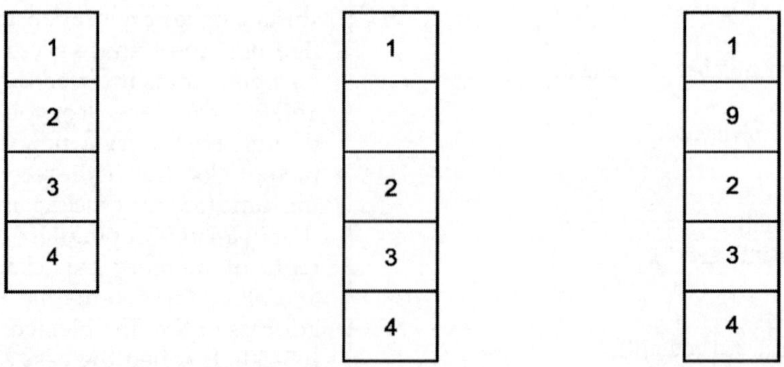

a. Original array   b. Insertion element (step 1)   c. after insertion

Figure 2.7 Insertion steps

Example 2.7

Write a program to display a one-dimensional array using an integer pointer.

Solution

```
# include <stdio.h>
# include <conio.h>
int main ()
{
int *p,num[5]={4,5,6,7,8},j;
clrscr();
p=num;
printf("Elements Address");
for (j=0;j<5;j++)
printf ("\n %3d %7u", *(p+j),(p+j));
}
```

OUTPUT

```
Elements    Address
   4        65516
   5        65518
   6        65520
   7        65522
   8        65524
```

Explanation In this program, an integer array *num []* is declared and initialized. In the same statement pointer **p* and integer variable *j* are declared. The base address is assigned to pointer *p*. While assigning the base address it is enough to write the name of the array. It is optional to write subscript number, i.e. *num [0][0]*. The for loop executes five times and the value of *j* varies from 0 to 4. The first time 0 is added to the base address and there is no change in the address. Hence, the 1st element is displayed. In the second iteration, one is added to the base address. It takes the next successive address and the 2nd element is displayed. The same procedure is continued and array elements are displayed. Fig. 2.8 shows what exactly takes place.

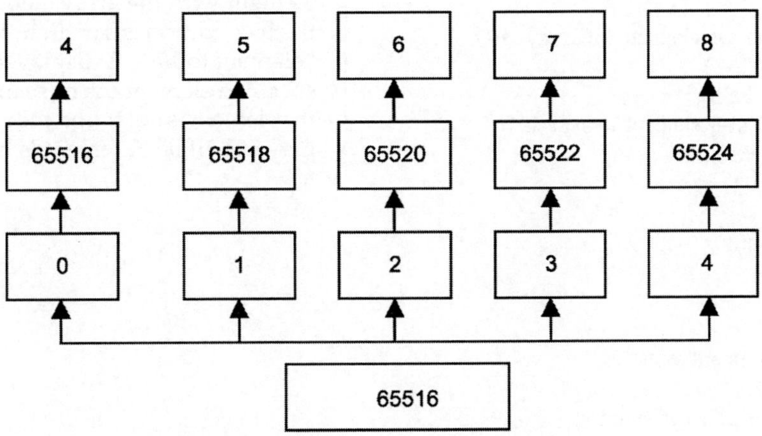

Figure 2.8 Accesses through base address

In the above figure, the first line of boxes contains values, the second contains memory addresses and the third contains loop variable values as used in the program. When the value of loop variable is added to the base address we get the successive memory addresses and the values stored in them can be displayed.

For example,

```
65516+0 = 65516, i.e. 4
65516+1= 65518, i.e. 5
```

and so on values can be retrieved.

2.4.3 Searching

The process of seeking specified elements in an array is called searching.

Example 2.8

Write a program to search for a specified element in an array.

Solution

```
# include <stdio.h>
# include <conio.h>

main ()
{
   int j=0,n;
   int x[10];
   clrscr();
   printf("Enter ten elements of array:\n");
   for(j=0;j<10;j++)
   scanf("%d",&x[j]);
   printf ("\n Enter element to search:");
   scanf("%d",&n);
   for (j=0;j<10;j++)
   {
      if (x[j]==n)
      break;
   }
   if(x[j]==n)
   printf("\n Element found");
   else
   printf("Element is not found");
}
```

Explanation In the above program, an integer array is declared and initialized with elements. The element which is to be searched is entered through the keyboard. Using while loop, all the elements are read. The if statement checks every element with the array elements. When the if condition is satisfied the, message "element found" is displayed. Thus, the specified element can be searched. When the element is not found the message displayed will be "Element is not found".

OUTPUT

```
Enter ten elements of array:
1 2 3 4 5 6 7 8 9 12

Enter element to search: 3

Element found
```

2.4.4 Merging

The merging of two arrays into a single one is an important operation. The easiest way of merging two arrays is first, to copy all elements of one array into a third one and then copy all elements of the second array also into the third one. We can also merge elements in an alternate order as shown in the following program. Figure 2.9 indicates the merging of two arrays. The following points should be taken into account.

1. Elements of one array can be appended to the end of the second array.
2. Elements of two arrays can be merged in an alternate order.
3. The size of the resulting array must be more than the size of two arrays.

Example 2.9

Write a program to merge two arrays into a third one. Display the contents of all the three arrays.

Solution

```
# include <stdio.h>
# include <conio.h>

main ()
{
   int j,h=0,k=0;
   int x[4]={1,2,3,4};
   int y[4]={5,6,7,8};
   int z[8];
   clrscr();

   printf ("\n Array X: ");
   for (j=0;j<4;j++)
   printf (" %d ",x[j]);
   printf ("\n Array Y: ");

   for (j=0;j<4;j++)
   printf (" %d ",y[j]);
   j=0;

while (j<8)
{
```

Explanation In the above program, three integer arrays are declared and initialized. The first two for loops are used to view the elements of array *x* and *z* by a transverse process. The while loop is used to execute until the condition is true. The 'if' statement checks the condition and accordingly if and else blocks are executed. These statements also fetch elements from both arrays and place them into array z. Fig. 2.9 illustrates the merging of two arrays.

```
    if (j%2==0)
    z[j]=x[k++];
    else
    z[j]=y[h++];
    j++;
}

printf ("\n Array Z: ");
for (j=0;j<8;j++)
printf (" %d ",z[j]);
}
```

OUTPUT

```
Array X: 1 2 3 4
Array Y: 5 6 7 8
Array Z: 1 5 2 6 3 7 4 8
```

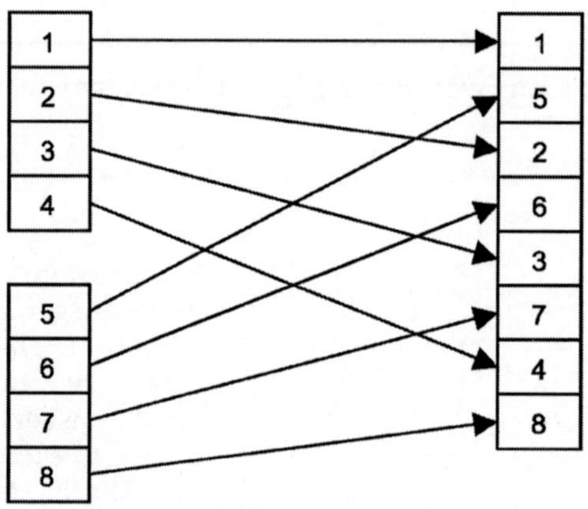

Figure 2.9 Merging two arrays

2.4.5 Sorting

Arranging elements in a specific order, either ascending or descending, is known as sorting. Sorting is a very important operation and compulsorily used in database application programs. Let us study the following program, which sorts an array of integers and stores them in another array.

Example 2.10

Write a program to enter integer elements and sort them in ascending order.

```
# include <stdio.h>
# include <conio.h>

main()
{
   int num[5],j,k,s=0;
   clrscr();
   printf ("\n Enter five Elements: ");

   for (j=0;j<5;j++)
   {
   scanf ("%d",&num[j]);
   s=s+num[j];
   }

   for (k=0;k<s;k++)
   {
      for (j=0;j<5;j++)
      {
      if (num[j]==k)
      printf (" %d ",num[j]);
      }
   }
}
```

OUTPUT

```
Enter five Elements: 5 8 9 7 2
2 5 7 8 9
```

Explanation In the above program, an integer array is declared and five numbers are entered. The sum of all the numbers is taken. Using nested loops every number of the array is compared from one to *s* (*s = sum of all numbers*). The *if* statement checks every array element with the value of *s* and displays the numbers in ascending order. Sorting can be done in various ways. The above sorting method is the simplest one.

2.5 TWO-DIMENSIONAL ARRAYS

Two-dimensional arrays can be thought of as rectangular display of elements with rows and columns. Consider the following example:

int *x[3][3];*

The two-dimensional array can be declared as above.

	Column 0	*Column 1*	*Column 2*
Row0	x[0][0]	x[0][1]	x[0][2]
Row1	x[1][0]	x[1][1]	x[1][2]
Row2	x[2][0]	x[2][1]	x[2][2]

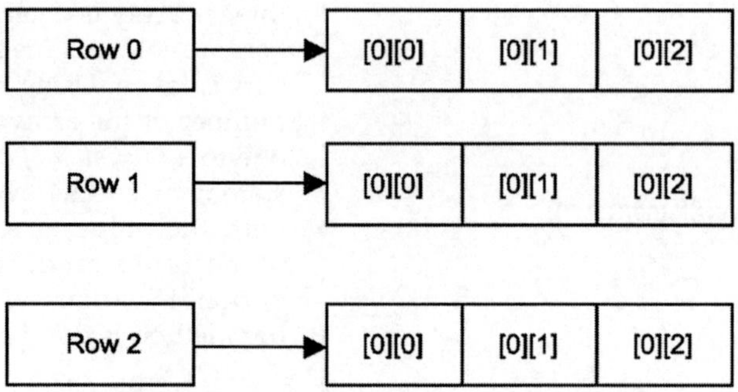

Figure 2.10 Array: element arrangement

The arrangement of array elements shown in Fig. 2.10 is only for the sake of understanding. Actually, the elements are stored in continuous memory locations.

A two-dimensional array is a collection of two one-dimensional arrays. The meaning of the first argument is in *x [3]*. [3] means the number of rows, i.e. number of one-dimensional arrays and the second argument indicates the number of elements. *x [0][0]* means the first element of the first row and column. Row number remains the same but column number changes. The number of rows and columns is called as the range of the array. A two-dimensional array clearly shows the difference between logical assumption and physical representation of data. The computer memory is linear and whatever may be the type of array—one, two or multi dimensional—it is stored in continuous memory locations. Fig. 2.11 explains the two-dimension array.

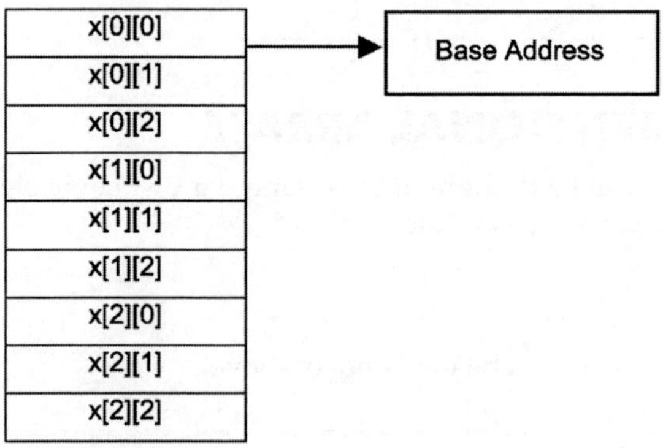

Figure 2.11 Storage of two-dimensional array

Example 2.11

Write a program to demonstrate the use of a two-dimensional array.

Solution

```
# include <stdio.h>
# include <conio.h>

main ()
{
   int i,j;
   int a[3][3]={1,2,3,4,5,6,7,8,9};
   clrscr();
   printf ("\n Array elements and address ");
   printf ("\n\t Col-0 Col-1 Col-2");
   printf ("\n\t ====== ====== ======");
   printf ("\nRow0");

   for (i=0;i<3;i++)
   {
      for (j=0;j<3;j++)
      printf (" %d [%u]",a[i][j],&a[i][j]);
      printf ("\nRow%d",i+1);
   }
   printf ("\r ");
}
```

```
OUTPUT

Array elements and address
          Col-0       Col-1      Col-2
         ====== ====== ======
Row0 1 [65508] 2 [65510] 3 [65512]
Row1 4 [65514] 5 [65516] 6 [65518]
Row2 7 [65520] 8 [65522] 9 [65524]
```

Explanation From this program's output, you can see that the memory addresses displayed are in sequence and it is true that elements of two-dimensional arrays are stored in successive memory locations. The one-dimensional array can be accessed using a single loop. However, for two-dimensional arrays, two loops are required for the row and column. The inner loop helps to access the row-wise elements and the outer loop changes the column number; just as a one-dimensional array base address can be stored in a pointer. Consider the following program.

Example 2.12

Write a program to assign the base address of a two-dimensional array to a pointer and display the elements.

Solution

```
# include <stdio.h>
# include <conio.h>

main ()
{
   int *p,num[2][2]={4,5,6,7},j;
   clrscr();
```

Explanation This program is the same as the last one. But the point to note here is that to store the base address of a two-dimensional array, it is not enough to mention the array; in addition, subscript number and address operation

```
    p=&num[0][0];
    printf("Elements Address");
    for (j=0;j<4;j++)
    printf("\n%3d %9u",*(p+j),(p+j));
}

OUTPUT
    Elements    Address
        4       65490
        5       65492
        6       65494
        7       65496
```

should also be mentioned. Only then will the compiler accept the statement; otherwise, the compiler flags an error message. For a one-dimensional array, an array name is sufficient, but onwards we have to mention the element number with the address operator.

2.5.1 Insert Operation with Two-dimensional Array

We have studied the example of insertion of element with a one-dimensional array. We are also aware how pointers can be used to access array elements. The following program gives you an idea of insert operations with a two-dimensional array.

Example 2.13

Write a program to illustrate an insert operation with a two-dimensional array.

Solution

```
# include <stdio.h>
# include <conio.h>

main ()
{
    int num[5][5]={0,0},j,*p,at,e,n;
    clrscr();
    printf ("\n Enter how many elements (<=25): ");
    scanf ("%d",&n);
    p=&num[0][0];

    for (j=0;j<n;j++)
    scanf ("%d",p++);
    p=&num[0][0]; printf ("\n");

    for (j=0;j<n;j++,p++)
    printf (" %d ",*p);

    printf ("\n Enter a number & position to insert: ");
    scanf ("%d %d",&e,&at);

    for (j=n;j>=at;j—)
```

Explanation In all types of array, one, two and three-dimensional elements are stored in the successive memory locations. A pointer can dereference to get successive memory location of memory. In this way, elements of the array can be accessed, changed or replaced. For all this, we require only the base address of the array that is to be assigned to a pointer.

```
    {
        *p=*(p-1);
        p-;
    }

    *p=e;
    p=&num[0][0];

    for (j=0;j<=n;j++,p++)
    printf (" %d ",*p);
}
```

```
OUTPUT

Enter how many elements (<=25): 5
1 2 3 4 5

1 2 3 4 5
Enter a number & position to insert: 8 3
1 2 8 3 4 5
```

Consider the statement *p=&num [0][0];* used to store base address (address of 0th element of the array) of an array. Later in this program the array is not accessed by its name and corresponding row column numbers. The total capacity of the array of storing elements is 25 as per the declaration. The user is asked to enter the number of elements he wants to enter. The entered value is stored in the variable *n* through the *scanf()* statement. Thus, by using *loops*, values are repetitively entered and displayed.

The user is again asked to enter a number and position in the array where the element is to be inserted. These values are stored in the variables (*scanf("%d %d",&e,&at);*), variables *e* & *at*.

```
for (j=n;j>=at;j—)
{
    *p=*(p-1);
    p—;
}
```

Using the *for loop* the elements are shifted to next position up to the value of the variable *"at"*.

When the loop ends, the entered element is assigned to * (**p=e;*). The ex- element is already shifted to the next position. Thus, finally the list of latest elements is displayed. The Fig. 2.12 (a) and (b) shows the insertion of element.

2.5.2 Delete Operation with Two-dimensional Array

Like insert operation delete operation can also be performed on an array. Consider the following program.

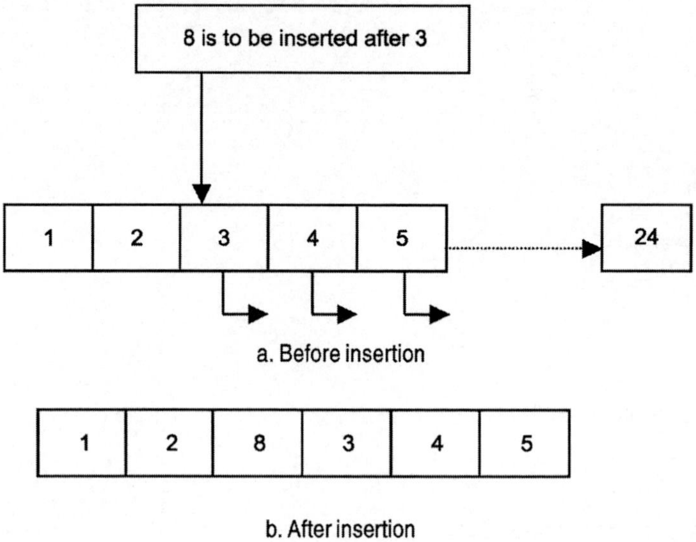

Figure 2.12 Insertion of element

Example 2.14

Write a program to demonstrate delete operation of element with two-dimensional array.

Solution

```
# include <stdio.h>
# include <conio.h>

main ()
{
   int num[5][5]={0,0},j,*p,at,e,n;
   clrscr();

   printf ("\n Enter how many elements (<=25): ");
   scanf ("%d",&n);
   p=&num[0][0];

   for (j=0;j<n;j++)
   scanf ("%d",p++);
   p=&num[0][0]; printf ("\n");

   for (j=0;j<n;j++,p++)
   printf (" %d",*p);

   printf ("\n Enter Element position to delete: ");
```

Explanation The method for obtaining base address and pointer arithmetic involved in the program is same as the last program. The element to be deleted is replaced with the next element. Thus, the entire elements are shifted to the previous location. Figs. 2.13 (a) and (b) describe the deletion of element.

```
    scanf("%d",&at);
    at - -;
    p=&num[0][0];
    p+=at;

    for(j=at;j<n;j++)
    {
       *p=*(p+1);
       p++;
    }

    *p=0;

    p=&num[0][0];

    while (*p!=0)
    {
    printf(" %d ",*p);
       p++;
    }
}
```

OUTPUT

```
Enter how many elements (<=25): 7
1 2 3 4 5 6 7

1 2 3 4 5 6 7
Enter Element position to delete: 5
1 2 3 4 6 7
```

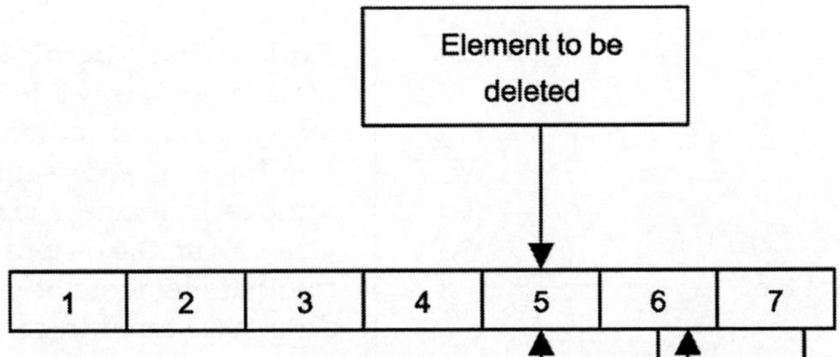

a. Before deletion

1	2	3	4	6	7

b. After deletion

Figure 2.13 Deletion of element

2.6 THREE- OR MULTI-DIMENSIONAL ARRAYS

A three-dimensional array can be thought of as array of arrays. Consider the following program:

```
int mat[3][3][3] =
      { 1,2,3,
          4,5,6,
          7,8,9,

          1,4,7,
          2,5,8,
          3,6,9,

          1,4,4,
          2,4,7,
          8,8,5};
```

Example 2.15

Write a program to demonstrate the use of three-dimensional array.

Solution

```
# include <stdio.h>
# include <conio.h>

main ()
{
   int a,b,c;
   int mat[3][3][3] ={ 1,2,3,
         4,5,6,
         7,8,9,
         1,4,7,
         2,5,8,
         3,6,9,
         1,4,4,
         2,4,7,
         8,8,5 };
```

Explanation In this example, a three-dimensional array is initialized. The three loops are used to access the elements. The logic of accessing the elements is same as in the case of two-dimensional array. From the output obtained, we can say that elements of multi-dimensional array are stored in continuous memory locations.

```
    clrscr();

  for (a=0;a<3;a++)
  {
    printf("\n");

    for (b=0;b<3;b++)
    {
      for (c=0;c<3;c++)
      printf ("%3d [%u] ",mat[a][b][c],&mat[a][b][c]);
      printf("\n");
    }
  }
}
```

OUTPUT

```
1 [65470] 2 [65472] 3 [65474]
4 [65476] 5 [65478] 6 [65480]
7 [65482] 8 [65484] 9 [65486]

1 [65488] 4 [65490] 7 [65492]
2 [65494] 5 [65496] 8 [65498]
3 [65500] 6 [65502] 9 [65504]

1 [65506] 4 [65508] 4 [65510]
2 [65512] 4 [65514] 7 [65516]
8 [65518] 8 [65520] 5 [65522]
```

2.7 STRINGS

The collection of characters, digits and symbols enclosed within quotation marks are called as strings. Strings are always declared as character array. Like other type of arrays, the elements of character array are also stored in continuous memory location. Each character occupies one byte in memory. One different thing about strings is that, the compiler automatically adds NULL ('\0') character at the end of the string. This character is used to detect the end of the string. The declaration of string can be done as follows. The Fig. 2.14 shows how the name is stored in the array.

char *name[6]*= "*KAMAL*";

K	A	M	A	L	'\0'

Figure 2.14 Storing name in array

While declaring character array the declaration of NULL character should be taken into account. Therefore, the above array is declared of 6 sizes out of which five characters are stored first, then NULL character is stored at the end.

Example 2.16

Write a program to declare, initialize character array and display the string.

Solution

```
# include <stdio.h>
# include <conio.h>

main ()
{
   char name[6]="kamal";
   clrscr();
   printf ("%s",name);
}

OUTPUT

Kamal
```

Explanation In this program a character array is declared and initialized with string *"kamal"*. Here, the array limit is declared for 6 characters and total six characters are stored including NULL character. Using *printf()* statement, string is displayed. Instead of 6 if limit is declared of 5, there is no place to insert NULL character and therefore the string will not be displayed properly.

Example 2.17

Write a program to encrypt a name and decrypt it.

Solution

```
# include <stdio.h>
# include <conio.h>
main ()
{
      char name[10],iname[10],dname[10];
      int i=0,y;
   clrscr();

   printf ("\nEnter the name:-");
   scanf("%s",name);
   while(name[i]!='\0')
   {
   iname[i]=name[i]+3;
   i++;
   }
   iname[i++]='\0';
   printf("\nThe encrypted name is:- %s",iname);
```

```
    i=0;
    while(iname[i]!='\0')
    {
    dname[i]=iname[i]-3;
    i++;
    }
    dname[i++]='\0';
    printf("\nThe decrypted name is:- %s",dname);

}
```

OUTPUT:

```
Enter the name:-amit

The encrypted name is:- dplw
The decrypted name is:- amit
```

Example 2.18

Write a program to display the string and determine end of the string by NULL character.

Solution

```
# include <stdio.h>
# include <conio.h>

main()
{
    char arr[]={'A','B','C','D','E','\0'};
    int j=0;
    clrscr();
    printf("Characters Address");
    while (arr[j]!='\0')
    {
    printf ("\n %3c %9u",arr[j],&arr[j]);
    j++;
    }

}
```

Explanation In this program a character array is declared and initialized. In the initialization, a NULL character is also initialized. The condition given in the while loop tests for NULL character. If it finds, the *while loop* is terminated, otherwise a character is displayed. We can also find that the characters are stored in successive memory locations.

OUTPUT

```
    Characters    Address
       A          65492
       B          65493
       C          65494
```

```
D          65495
E          65496
```

Example 2.19

Write a program to display ASCII numbers, corresponding characters, and its encryption.

Solution

Explanation In this program the first *for loop* is starting from 65 to 80 for displaying the corresponding ASCII numbers, its characters, and encrypted characters. Second *for loop* is used for the encryption of the string which is entered in *'name[]'*.

```
# include <stdio.h>
# include <conio.h>
# include <process.h>

main ()
{
   int i, p=65;
   char name[10];
   clrscr();
   printf ("\n Display the ASCII numbers, characters and encrypted characters:-");
   printf("\nASCII no. Characters Encrypted characters");
   for (p=65;p<=80;p++)
   printf( "\n%5d %10c %12c",p,p,p+3);

   printf ("\nEnter the string for encryption:- ");
   scanf("%s",name);

   printf ("The string after encryption:- ");
   for (i=0;i<10;i++)
   {
   if(name[i]=='\0')
   exit(1);

   printf("%c",name[i]+3);

   }
}
```

OUTPUT:

```
Display the ASCII numbers, characters and encrypted characters:-
   ASCII no.     Characters      Encrypted characters
      65              A                  D
      66              B                  E
      67              C                  F
      68              D                  G
      69              E                  H
```

```
70          F           I
71          G           J
72          H           K
73          I           L
74          J           M
75          K           N
76          L           O
77          M           P
78          N           Q
79          O           R
80          P           S
Enter the string for encryption:- apple
The string after encryption:- dssoh
```

Example 2.20

Write a program to enter the string for packet formation. Enter the size of the packet and display the contents of all packets.

Solution

```
# include<stdio.h>
# include <conio.h>

main ()
{

  char message[50];
  int f=0,i,np=0,pack;
  clrscr();

  printf("\nEnter the message:- ");
  scanf("%s",message);
  printf("Enter the size of packet:- ");
  scanf("%d",&pack);

  while(message[f]!='\0')
  {
  printf("\nPacket %d contains:- ",np+1);
  for(i=0;i<pack;i++,f++)
  {
  if(message[f]=='\0')
  break;
  printf("%c",message[f]);

  }
```

Explanation At first, the message without space is entered by the keyboard. Then, the packet size is to be specified. Fragmentation of data stream into packets is done with *while loop*. The end of the string is detected by using '\0'. While fragmentation, the characters are counted. On encountering '\0' character the *while loop* is stopped by *break* statement. At the end of the program the total packets are printed.

```
    printf(":- %d characters",i);
    np++;
    }
    printf("\nTotal packets:- %d",np);
}
```

```
OUTPUT:

Enter the message:- keepyourmindfreshforgoodprogramming
Enter the size of packet:- 5

Packet 1 contains:- keepy:- 5 characters
Packet 2 contains:- ourmi:- 5 characters
Packet 3 contains:- ndfre:- 5 characters
Packet 4 contains:- shfor:- 5 characters
Packet 5 contains:- goodp:- 5 characters
Packet 6 contains:- rogra:- 5 characters
Packet 7 contains:- mming:- 5 characters
Total packets:- 7
```

2.8 ARRAY OF STRUCTURES

We have already studied structure in the first chapter. We also know that array is a homogeneous data structure and structure is a non-homogenous data structure. By declaring an array of structure objects, we can make combination of data structure of different types. However, we cannot create an array of non-homogenous type as such an array will also be homogenous type. Because all the elements are of the same type, i.e. structure type. The following program explains array of structure.

Example 2.21

Write a program to read display data using array of structure.

Solution

```
# include <stdio.h>
# include <conio.h>

main ()
{
    struct item
    {
        int codeno;
        int price;
    };

    int j;
```

Explanation In this program, structure item is defined with two numeric fields, i.e. *codeno* and *price*. An array of structure item type *a[2]* is declared. Using for loop data read and displayed.

```
    struct item a[2];

    clrscr();

    printf ("\n Enter Codeno, Price\n ");

    for (j=0;j<2;j++)
    scanf ("%d %d",&a[j].codeno,&a[j].price);

    printf ("\n Codeno Price ");

    for (j=0;j<2;j++)
    printf ("\n %d %d",a[j].codeno,a[j].price);
}
```

```
OUTPUT

Enter  Codeno,      Price
         002         541
         003         125

  Codeno     Price
     2       541
     3       125
```

2.9 DRAWBACKS OF LINEAR ARRAYS

1. The number of elements, which is to be stored in an array, must be known first.
2. When an array is declared, memory is allocated to it. If array is not filled completely, the vacant place occupies memory.
3. Once the array is declared, its dimension can be changed.

2.10 SPARSE MATRICES AND DENSE MATRICES

A sparse matrix is a two-dimensional array in which most of the elements are null. Figs. 2.15 (a) and 2.15 (b) indicate sparse and dense matrices. The matrix, which is not a sparse matrix, is called dense matrix. One cannot exactly determine the boundary between sparse and dense matrix. The sparse matrices are very useful in various applications. In sparse matrices, memory is wasted because the NULL values are stored and hence to overcome wastage of memory a mechanism must be followed. One of the mechanism is linked list, which will be discussed in detail in Chapter 6.

3	0	78	0	12
1	6	7	8	11
0	5	0	1	0
1	0	1	0	5

a. Dense matrix

3	0	0	0	1
2	0	0	0	0
0	0	0	1	0
1	0	1	0	0

b. Sparse matrix

Figure 2.15 Sparse matrices and Dense matrices

The classification of sparse matrices is shown below in the Fig. 2.16.

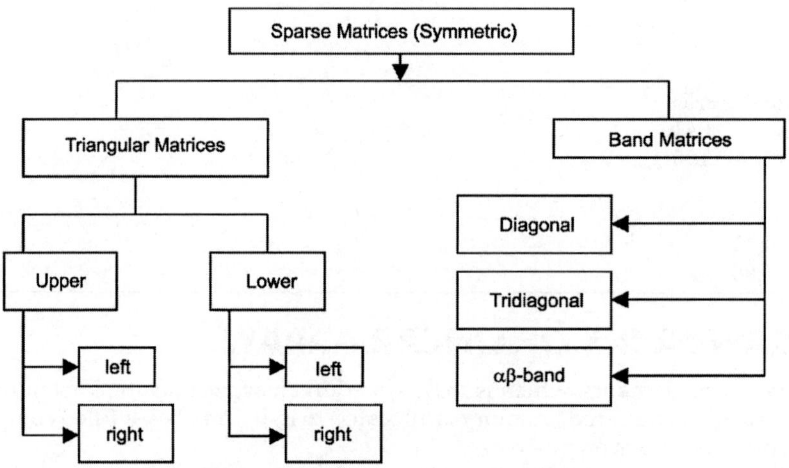

Figure 2.16 Types of sparse matrices

2.10.1 Upper Triangular Matrices

The upper matrix is a type of triangular matrix, which is also a type of sparse matrix. A sparse matrix is a matrix in which maximum of the elements are zero. The upper matrix is also of two kinds: upper left and upper-right as shown in Fig. 2.18 and Fig. 2.17 respectively.

0				
0	0			
0	0	0		
0	0	0	0	
0	0	0	0	0

Figure 2.17 Upper right triangular

In Fig. 2.17, a triangle of null elements and non-element is present. The triangle of NULL elements is present the left side and the triangle of non-element is present on the right side.

Example 2.22

Write a program to initialize and display upper right triangular matrix.

Solution

```
# include <stdio.h>
# include <conio.h>

main()
{
   int j,k,urt[5][5]={ 0,4,3,2,1,
                       0,0,3,2,1,
                       0,0,0,2,1,
                       0,0,0,0,1,
                       0,0,0,0,0,
                                 };
   clrscr();
   printf ("\n UPPER RIGHT TRIANGULAR\n");
   for (j=0;j<5;j++)
   {
   for (k=0;k<5;k++)
   printf (" %d ",urt[j][k]);
   printf ("\n");
   }
}
OUTPUT

UPPER RIGHT TRIANGULAR
0 4 3 2 1
0 0 3 2 1
0 0 0 2 1
0 0 0 0 1
0 0 0 0 0
```

Explanation In this program an array is initialized and the NULL elements form an upper right triangular matrix and it is displayed. Fig. 2.18 shows the upper left triangular matrix.

				0
			0	0
		0	0	0
	0	0	0	0
0	0	0	0	0

Figure 2.18 Upper left triangular

Example 2.23

Write a program to initialize and display upper left triangular.

Solution

```
# include <stdio.h>
# include <conio.h>

main ()
{
   int j,k,ult[5][5]={ 1,2,3,4,0,
                       1,2,3,0,0,
                       1,2,0,0,0,
                       1,0,0,0,0,
                       0,0,0,0,0,
                                    };
   clrscr();
   printf ("\n UPPER LEFT TRIANGULAR\n");
   for (j=0;j<5;j++)
   {
      for (k=0;k<5;k++)
      printf (" %d ",ult[j][k]);
      printf ("\n");
   }
}
```

```
OUTPUT

 UPPER LEFT TRIANGULAR
 1 2 3 4 0
 1 2 3 0 0
 1 2 0 0 0
 1 0 0 0 0
 0 0 0 0 0
```

2.10.2 Lower Triangular Matrices

0	0	0	0	0
	0	0	0	0
		0	0	0
			0	0
				0

Figure 2.19 Lower-left triangular

Example 2.24

Write a program to display lower left triangular matrix.

Solutions

```
# include <stdio.h>
# include <conio.h>

main ()
{
   int j,k,llt[5][5]={ 0,0,0,0,0,
                       1,0,0,0,0,
                       1,2,0,0,0,
                       1,2,3,0,0,
                       1,2,3,4,0,
                                  };
   clrscr();
   printf ("\n LOWER LEFT TRIANGULAR\n");
   for (j=0;j<5;j++)
   {
      for (k=0;k<5;k++)
      printf (" %d ",llt[j][k]);
      printf ("\n");
   }
}
```

Explanation In this program an array *llt [][]* is initialized. The *array* is initialized in such a way that maximum elements are NULL and hence, it is sparse matrix. The NULL elements form a triangular at lower left side. Hence, this matrix is called lower left triangular matrix. The Fig. 2.19 shows the lower left triangular matrix.

```
OUTPUT

LOWER LEFT TRIANGULAR

0 0 0 0 0
1 0 0 0 0
1 2 0 0 0
1 2 3 0 0
1 2 3 4 0
```

0	0	0	0	0
0	0	0	0	
0	0	0		
0	0			

Figure 2.20 Lower right triangular

Example 2.25

Write a program to initialize and display lower right triangular matrix.

Solution

```
# include <stdio.h>
# include <conio.h>

main ()
{
   int j,k,lrt[5][5]={ 0,0,0,0,0,
                       0,0,0,0,1,
                       0,0,0,2,1,
                       0,0,3,2,1,
                       0,4,3,2,1,
                                 };
   clrscr();
   printf ("\n LOWER RIGHT TRIANGULAR\n");
   for (j=0;j<5;j++)
   {
      for (k=0;k<5;k++)
      printf (" %d ",lrt[j][k]);
      printf ("\n");
   }
}
```

Explanation This program is the same as the last one and displays lower right triangular matrix. Fig. 2.20 is an example of lower right triangular matrix.

OUTPUT

```
LOWER RIGHT TRIANGULAR
0 0 0 0 0
0 0 0 0 1
0 0 0 2 1
0 0 3 2 1
0 4 3 2 1
```

Example 2.26

Write a program to find whether the given matrix is lower right triangular matrix or not.

Solution

```
# include <stdio.h>
# include <conio.h>
int matrix[3][3];
```

```
main ()
{
    clrscr();
    input();
    display();
    lowe_r();
}

input ()
{
int n,j,k;
printf("\n Enter elements for matrix ");
for (j=0;j<3;j++)
{
for (k=0;k<3;k++)
scanf ("%d",&matrix[j][k]);
}
return 0;}display ()
{
int n,j,k;
printf("\n Elements of matrix\n");
for (j=0;j<3;j++)
{
for (k=0;k<3;k++)
printf ("%4d",matrix[j][k]);
printf("\n"); }
return 0;}
lowe_r ()
{
int n,j,k,u=3; char b=' ';
printf("\n Elements of matrix\n");
for (j=0;j<3;j++)
{
for (k=0;k<u;k++)
{
printf ("%4d",matrix[j][k]);
if (matrix[j][k]==0)
b='Y'; else b='N';
}
u—;
printf("\n");

}
if (b=='Y')
puts ("\n The given matrix is lower right triangular matrix");
else
puts ("\n Not a sparse matrix");
```

Explanation In this program *matrix [3][3]* is declared. Through *input ()* function, elements are entered. The *display ()* function displays the elements of the matrices. Through use of *lowe_r ()* function, elements of rows 1st, 2nd and 3rd are checked. The numbers of elements are 3,2 and 1, respectively. If these elements are NULL, the matrix is lower right triangular matrix.

```
return 0;
}
```

```
OUTPUT

Enter elements for matrix 0 0 0 0 0 0 0 1 5

Elements of matrix
0 0 0
0 0 0
0 1 5

Elements of matrix
0 0 0
0 0
0

The given matrix is lower right triangular matrix.
```

In some of the earlier programs, arrays, i.e. matrix, are initialized and displayed. This can be implemented easily. However, in the above program, elements are entered during program execution. Hence, few additional statements are required.

1	0	0	0	0
0	**2**	0	0	0
0	0	**3**	0	0
0	0	0	**4**	0
0	0	0	0	**5**

0	0	0	0	**5**
0	0	0	**4**	0
0	0	**3**	0	0
0	**2**	0	0	0
1	0	0	0	0

Figure 2.21 Diagonal matrices

In case of diagonal matrices, only diagonal elements are non-zero and other values are NULL as shown in the Fig. 2.21.

Example 2.27

Write a program to initialize and display diagonal matrix.

Solution

```
# include <stdio.h>
# include <conio.h>

main ()
{
```

```
    int j,k,dgl[5][5]={    1,0,0,0,0,
                           0,2,0,0,0,
                           0,0,3,0,0,
                           0,0,0,4,0,
                           0,0,0,0,5,
                                      };
    clrscr();
    printf ("\n DIAGONAL MATRIX\n");
    for (j=0;j<5;j++)
    {
        for (k=0;k<5;k++)
        printf (" %d ",dgl[j][k]);
        printf ("\n");
    }
}
```

Explanation In this program an array is initialized in which diagonal elements are non-zero.

```
OUTPUT

DIAGONAL MATRIX
1 0 0 0 0
0 2 0 0 0
0 0 3 0 0
0 0 0 4 0
0 0 0 0 5
```

1	1	0	0	0
1	2	8	0	0
0	4	3	3	0
0	0	5	4	5
0	0	0	8	5

0	0	0	2	5
0	0	4	4	1
0	7	3	9	0
8	2	7	0	0
1	4	0	0	0

Figure 2.22 Tri-diagonal matrices

Example 2.28

Write a program to initialize and display tri-diagonal matrix.

Solution

```
# include <stdio.h>
# include <conio.h>

main ()
{
```

```
   int j,k,dgl[5][5]={   5,1,0,0,0,
                         1,6,2,0,0,
                         0,2,7,3,0,
                         0,0,3,8,4,
                         0,0,0,4,9,
                                   };
   clrscr();
   printf ("\n DIAGONAL MATRIX\n");
   for (j=0;j<5;j++)
   {
      for (k=0;k<5;k++)
      printf (" %d ",dgl[j][k]);
      printf ("\n");
   }
}
```

Explanation In this program, tri-diagonal matrix is initialized and displayed as shown in Fig. 2.22.

```
OUTPUT

DIAGONAL MATRIX
5 1 0 0 0
1 6 2 0 0
0 2 7 3 0
0 0 3 8 4
0 0 0 4 9
```

2.11 ROW-MAJOR ARRAYS

Row-major implementation is a liberalization technique in which elements in an array are arranged row-wise. Elements are stored row by row as shown in Fig. 2.23.

Consider an array

int *X[3][3]*;

COLUMN-0	COLUMN-1	COLUMN-2	
X[0][0]	X[0][1]	X[0][2]	Row-0
X[1][0]	X[1][1]	X[1][2]	Row-1
X[2][0]	X[2][1]	X[2][2]	Row-2

<table>
<tr><td>X[0][0]</td><td>X[0][1]</td><td>X[0][2]</td><td>X[1][0]</td><td>X[1][1]</td><td>X[1][2]</td><td>X[2][0]</td><td>X[2][1]</td><td>X[2][2]</td></tr>
<tr><td colspan="3">ROW-0</td><td colspan="3">ROW-1</td><td colspan="3">ROW-2</td></tr>
</table>

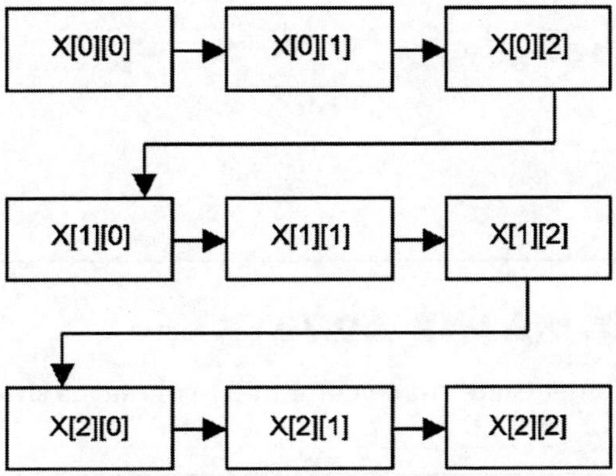

Figure 2.23 Row-major array

Consider the following program.

Example 2.29

Write a program to implement an array by row-major method.

Solution

```
# include <stdio.h>
# include <conio.h>

main ()
{
   int j,k,x[3][3];
   clrscr();
   printf ("\n Enter nine elements: ");
   for (j=0;j<=2;j++)
   for (k=0;k<=2;k++)
   scanf ("%d",&x[j][k]);

   printf ("\n Row major array\n");
   for (j=0;j<=2;j++)
   {
      for (k=0;k<=2;k++)
      printf (" %d ",x[j][k]);
   printf ("row- [ %d ]\n",j+1);
   }
}
```

Explanation In this program two for loops are used. The elements are entered through the keyboard. The outer loop indicates row and inner loop indicates column. After finishing the execution of inner loop, outer loop is executed once. Thus, when one complete row is filled with elements, the outer loop is executed and it indicates next row, which is to be filled. Again, the inner loop is used to fill the elements. Thus, elements are stored row-by-row.

OUTPUT

```
Enter nine elements: 7 8 9 4 5 2 1 5 9

Row major array
7 8 9 row- [ 1 ]
4 5 2 row- [ 2 ]
1 5 9 row- [ 3 ]
```

2.12 COLUMN-MAJOR ARRAYS

In column major array elements are stored column-by-column as shown in Fig. 2.24.

COLUMN-0	COLUMN-1	COLUMN-2	
X[0][0]	X[0][1]	X[0][2]	Row-0
X[1][0]	X[1][1]	X[1][2]	Row-1
X[2][0]	X[2][1]	X[2][2]	Row-2

X[0][0]	X[1][0]	X[2][0]	X[0][1]	X[1][1]	X[2][1]	X[0][2]	X[1][2]	X[2][2]
COLUMN-0			COLUMN-1			COLUMN-2		

Figure 2.24 Column major array

Example 2.30

Write a program to implement an array by column major method.

Solution

```
# include <stdio.h>
# include <conio.h>

main ()
{
   int j,k,x[3][3];
   clrscr();
   printf ("\n Enter nine elements: ");
   for (j=0;j<=2;j++)
   for (k=0;k<=2;k++)
   scanf ("%d",&x[k][j]);
   printf ("\n Column major array\n");
```

Explanation In column major method the elements entered are stored column by column. The outer loop indicates column number and inner loop indicates row. When one complete column is filled, next column is considered for filling.

```
   for (j=0;j<=2;j++)
   {
      for (k=0;k<=2;k++)
      printf (" %d ",x[j][k]);
      printf("\n");
   }
}
OUTPUT

Enter nine elements: 1 2 3 4 5 6 7 8 9

Column major array
1 4 7
2 5 8
3 6 9
```

2.13 POINTERS AND ARRAYS

Array name by itself is an address or pointer. It points to the address of the first element (0th element of an array). The elements of the array together with their addresses can be displayed by using array name itself. Array elements are always stored in contiguous memory locations.

Programs in this regard are explained below.

Example 2.31

Write a program to display elements of an array. Start element counting from 1 instead of 0.

Solution

```
# include <stdio.h>
# include <conio.h>

main()
{

   int x[]={2,4,6,8,10},k=1;

   clrscr();

   while (k<=5)
   {
         printf ("%3d",k[x-1]);
         k++;
   }

}
```

Explanation Array element counting always starts from *'0'*. The element number is added in the base address and each element of an array is accessed. If one is subtracted from base address of an array, it points to the prior address of 0th element. By adding one to its reduced base address it is possible to start element counting from '1'.

OUTPUT:

2 4 6 8 10

Example 2.32

Write a program to display array element with their addresses using array name as a pointer.

Solution

```
# include <stdio.h>
# include <conio.h>

main()
{
   int x[5]={2,4,6,8,10},k=0;
   clrscr();
   printf ("\nElement No. Element Address");

   while (k<5)
   {
      printf ("\nx[%d] = \t%8d %9u",k,*(x+k),x+k);
      k++;
   }

}
```

Explanation In this program variable *'k'* acts as element number and its value varies from 0 to 4. When it is added with array name *'x'*, i.e. with address of the first element, it points to the consecutive memory location. Thus, element no., element, and their addresses are displayed.

OUTPUT:

```
Element No.  Element  Address
   x[0]         2      4056
   x[1]         4      4058
   x[2]         6      4060
   x[3]         8      4062
   x[4]        10      4064
```

OR

Example 2.33

Write a program to display array elements with their addresses using array name as a pointer.

Solution

```
# include <stdio.h>
# include <conio.h>

main()
```

```
{
  int num[4]={10,25,35,45},i;
  clrscr();

  printf ("Element Address\n");

  for (i=0;i<4;i++)
  {
     printf("num[%d]=%d",i,*(num+i));
     printf ("%8u\n",num+i);
  }

}
```

Explanation Here, the array name *'num'* itself acts as a pointer to the array *num [ ]*. The pointer *'num'* provides address of first element and *'*num'* gives value stored at that address. When *'i'* is added with *'num'*, the equations **(num+i)* and *num+i* show *'i'* the element and its location, respectively.

```
OUTPUT:

     Element        Address
   num[0] = 10       4062
   num[1] = 25       4064
   num[2] = 35       4066
   num[3] = 45       4068
```

Example 2.34

Write a program to access elements of array through different ways using pointer.

Solution

```
# include <stdio.h>
# include <conio.h>

main()
  {
     int arr[5]={10,20,30,40,50},p=0;
     clrscr();

  for (p=0;p<5;p++)
  {
     printf ("Value of arr[%d]=",p);
     printf ("%d | ",arr[p]);
     printf ("%d | ",*(arr+p));
     printf ("%d | ",*(p+arr));
     printf ("%d |",p[arr]);
     printf (" address of arr[%d]=%u\n",p,&arr[p] );
  }
}
```

Explanation In this program elements are displayed using different syntax, a. *arr[p]* b. **(arr+p))* c) **(p+arr))* d) *p[arr])*. The results of all of them would be the same.

a. *arr[p]*: This statement displays various array elements. Here, *'arr'* refers to the address and *'p'* refers to the element number.
b. **(arr+p)*: The *arr+p* is addition of constant with base address of the array. It shows address of pth element. The **(arr+p)* points to the pth element of the array.
c. **(p+arr)*: This statement is same as (b).

```
OUTPUT:
Value of arr[0]=10 | 10 | 10 | 10 | address of arr[0]=4056
Value of arr[1]=20 | 20 | 20 | 20 | address of arr[1]=4058
Value of arr[2]=30 | 30 | 30 | 30 | address of arr[2]=4060
Value of arr[3]=40 | 40 | 40 | 40 | address of arr[3]=4062
Value of arr[4]=50 | 50 | 50 | 50 | address of arr[4]=4064

OUTPUT:
Value of arr[0]=10 | 10 | 10 | 10 | address of arr[0]=4056
Value of arr[1]=20 | 20 | 20 | 20 | address of arr[1]=4058
Value of arr[2]=30 | 30 | 30 | 30 | address of arr[2]=4060
Value of arr[3]=40 | 40 | 40 | 40 | address of arr[3]=4062
Value of arr[4]=50 | 50 | 50 | 50 | address of arr[4]=4064
```

d. *p[arr]*: This statement is same as (a). Here, *'p'* refers to the element number and *'arr'* refers to the base address. By varying *'p'* and *'arr'* the various elements of the array are displayed.

Example 2.35

Write a program to find sum of all the elements of an array. Use array name itself as a pointer.

Solution

```
# include <stdio.h>
# include <conio.h>

main()
   {
      int sum=0,i=0,a[]={1,2,3,4,5};
      clrscr();
      printf ("Elements Values Address\n\n");
      while (i<5)
      {
         printf ("a[%d]\t%5d\t%8u\n",i,*(a+i),(a+i));
         sum=sum+*(a+i++);
      }

      printf ("\nSum of Array Elements = %d",sum);
   }
```

Explanation In this program array name *'a'* acts as pointer and variable *'i'* is used for referring element numbers. Using the *for* loop and expressions **(a+i)* and *(a+i)* various elements and their addresses are displayed respectively. In the *'sum'* variable sum of all elements is obtained.

```
OUTPUT:

  Elements    Values    Address
    a[0]        1        4056
    a[1]        2        4058
    a[2]        3        4060
    a[3]        4        4062
    a[4]        5        4064

Sum of Array Elements = 15
```

Example 2.36

Write a program to display the sum of squares and cubes of array elements using pointer.

Solution

```
# include <stdio.h>
# include <conio.h>
# include <math.h>

main()
  {

     int b[]={1,2,3,4,5},j,sumsq=0,sumc=0;

     clrscr();

     for (j=0;j<5;j++)
     {
        sumsq=sumsq+pow(*(j+b),2);
        sumc=sumc+pow(b[j],3);
     }
     printf ("\nSum of Squares of array elements: %d", sumsq);
     printf ("\nSum of Cubes of array elements: %d",sumc);
  }

OUTPUT:

Sum of Squares of array elements: 55
Sum of Cubes of array elements: 225
```

Explanation In this program using *pow()* function square and cube of array elements are computed and added to variable *'sumsq'* and *'sumc'* respectively. Using *printf()* statement sum of square and cube of array elements are displayed.

Example 2.37

Write a program to copy elements of one array to another array using pointers.

Solution

```
# include <stdio.h>
# include <conio.h>
main()
  {
     int so[]={10,20,30,40,50},*pb,ds[5],i;
     pb=so;
     clrscr();
     for (i=0;i<5;i++)
     {
        ds[i]=*pb;
        pb++;
     }
```

Explanation In this program pointer *'pb'* contains base address of array *so []*. In the for loop pointer *'pb'* is assigned to corresponding element of array *ds []* and then incremented. After increment it points to the address of next element of the array. Thus, all the elements are copied to *ds []* array.

```
    printf ("Orignal Array Duplicated Array");

    for (i=0;i<5;i++)
    printf ("\n\t%d\t\t %d", so[i],ds[i]);
}
```

OUTPUT:

```
    Original Array    Duplicated Array
         10                10
         20                20
         30                30
         40                40
         50                50
```

Example 2.38

Write a program to copy one array into another array. Order of elements of second array should be opposite to first array.

Solution

```
# include <stdio.h>
# include <conio.h>

main()
{

    int arr1[]={15,25,35,45,55},arr2[5],i;
    clrscr();

    printf ("\nOrigonal Array Duplicate Array");

    for (i=0;i<5;i++)
    {
       arr2[i]=*(arr1+4-i);
       printf ("\n\t%d \t\t%d",arr1[i],arr2[i]);
    }

}
```

Explanation The logic of the program is the same as the previous one. Here, instead of starting from base address of the array, address of last element of the array is selected first. Using *for loop,* the addresses are read in the reverse order and their contents are copied to destination *array arr2 [].*

OUTPUT:

```
   Original Array    Duplicate Array
        15                55
        25                45
        35                35
        45                25
        55                15
```

2.14 POINTERS AND TWO-DIMENSIONAL ARRAYS

A matrix can represent two-dimensional elements of an array. Here, the first argument is *row number* and second is *column number*. To display the elements of two-dimensional array using pointer it is essential to have *'&'* operator as pre-fix with array name followed by element numbers, otherwise compiler shows an error.

Example 2.39

Write a program to display array elements and their address using pointers.

Solution

```
# include <stdio.h>
# include <conio.h>

main()
{

    int i,j=1,*p;
    int a[3][3]={{1,2,3},{4,5,6},{7,8,9}};
    clrscr();
    printf ("\tElements of An Array with their addresses\n\n");

    p=&a[0][0];

    for (i=0;i<9;i++,j++)
    {
        printf ("%5d [%5u ]",*(p),p);
        p++;


        if (j==3)
        {
            printf ("\n");
            j=0;
        }
    }

}
```

Explanation In this program two-dimensional array is declared and initialized. The base address of array is assigned to integer pointer *'p'*. While assigning base address of two-dimensional array, *'&'* operator is to be prefixed with array name followed by element numbers are necessary otherwise compiler shows an error. The statement *p=&a[0][0] is* used in this context. The pointer *'p'* is printed and incremented in *for loop* till it prints entire array elements. The *if* statement splits a line when three elements in each row are printed.

```
OUTPUT:
Elements of an Array with their addresses.
 1 [4052] 2 [4054] 3 [4056]
 4 [4058] 5 [4060] 6 [4062]
 7 [4064] 8 [4066] 9 [4068]
```

OR

Example 2.40

Write a program to display array elements and their address. Use array name itself as a pointer.

Solution

```
# include <stdio.h>
# include <conio.h>

main()
{

      int i;
      int a[][3]={{1,2,3},{4,5,6},{7,8,9}};
      clrscr();
      printf ("\tElements of An Array with their addresses.\n\n");


      for (i=0;i<9;i++)
      {
         printf ("%8u",&a[0][0]+i);
         printf (" [%d]",*(&a[0][0]+i));

         if (i==2 || i==5)
         printf ("\n");

      }
}

OUTPUT:
Elements of an Array with their addresses.
1 [4052] 2 [4054] 3 [4056]
4 [4058] 5 [4060] 6 [4062]
7 [4064] 8 [4066] 9 [4068]
```

Explanation The logic of the program is the same as the previous one. The only difference is that the array name itself is used as pointer. The *if* statement inserts a line after displaying every three elements.

2.15 ARRAY OF POINTERS

So far, we have studied array of different standard data types such as array of *int, float, characters,* etc. In the same way the 'C' language also supports array of pointers. It is nothing but a collection of addresses. Here, we store address of variables for which we have to declare array as pointer.

Example 2.41

Write a program to store addresses of different elements of an array—using array of pointers.

Solution

```
# include <stdio.h>
# include <conio.h>

main()
{

    int *arrp[3];
    int arr[3]={5,10,15},k;

    for (k=0;k<3;k++)
    arrp[k]=arr+k;

    clrscr();
    printf ("\n\tAddress Element\n");

    for (k=0;k<3;k++)
    {
       printf ("\t%u",arrp[k]);
       printf ("\t%7d \n",*(arrp[k]));
    }

  }
```

```
OUTPUT:
Address Element
4060        5
4062       10
4064       15
```

Explanation In this program **arrp[3]* is declared as array of pointer. Using first *for loop* addresses of various elements of array *'arr [ ]'* are assigned to *'*arrp[]'*. The second for loop picks up addresses from *'*arrp[]'* and displays the value present at those locations. Here, each element of *'*arrp[]'* points to respective element of array *'arr[]'*.

Table 2.1 Array of pointers in memory

Element no.	Array of values	Element no.	Array of addresses
arr[0]	5	arrp[0]	4060
arr[1]	10	arrp[1]	4062
arr[2]	15	arrp[2]	4064

Example 2.42

Write a program to display address of elements and pointers.

Solution

```
# include <stdio.h>
# include <conio.h>
```

```
main()
{

      int a[5]={0,1,2,3,4};
      int *p[5],i;

      for (i=0;i<5;i++)
      p[i]=a+i;

      clrscr();

      for (i=0;i<5;i++)
      {
         printf ("\n\t%d at location",*(*p+i));
         printf ("\t%u at location ",*(p+i));
         printf ("%u",p+i);
      }

      printf ("\n\n Integer requires 2 bytes, address require 4 bytes");

}
```

Explanation In this program the first *for loop* assigns addresses of elements of integer array to pointer array. The first *printf()* statement prints element, the second displays address of element and the third displays address of the address, i.e. address of the pointer. Thus, it is clear from the above example that integer requires *two bytes* and pointer requires *four bytes*.

```
OUTPUT:
0 at location 4036 at location 4046
1 at location 4038 at location 4050
2 at location 4040 at location 4054
3 at location 4042 at location 4058
4 at location 4044 at location 4062

Integer requires 2 bytes, address requires 4 bytes
```

2.16 POINTERS AND STRINGS

Example 2.43

Write a program to read string from keyboard and display it using character pointer.

Solution

```
#include <stdio.h>
#include <conio.h>

main()
{
      char name[15],*ch;
      printf ("Enter Your Name:");
```

```
    gets(name);
    ch=name;
    /* store base address of string name */

    while (*ch!='\0')

    {
        printf ("%c",*ch);
        ch++;
    }
}
```

OUTPUT:
Enter Your Name: KUMAR

KUMAR

Explanation Here, the address of *0th* element is assigned to character pointer *'ch'*. In other words, base address of string is assigned to *'ch'*. The pointer *'*ch'* points to the value stored at that memory location and it is printed through *printf()* statement. After every increment of *'ch'* the pointer goes to the next character of the string. When it encounters *NULL* character the *while* loop terminates the program.

Example 2.44

Write a program to find length of a given string including and excluding spaces using pointers.

Solution

```
# include <stdio.h>
# include <conio.h>
main()
{
    char str[20],*s;
    int p=0,q=0;
    clrscr();
    printf ("Enter String:");
    gets(str);
    s=str;
    while (*s!='\0')
    {
        printf ("%c",*s);
        p++;
        s++;
        if (*s==32) /* ASCII equivalnet of ' ' (space)is 32*/
        q++;
    }
    printf ("\nLength of String including spaces: %d",p);
    printf ("\nLength of String excluding spaces: %d",p-q);
}
```

OUTPUT:
Enter String: POINTERS ARE EASY

Explanation Here, the address of *0th* element is assigned to character pointer *'ch'*. In other words, base address of string is assigned to *'ch'*. The pointer *'*ch'* points to the value stored at that memory location and it is printed through *printf()* statement. After every increment of *'ch'* the pointer goes to the next character of the string. When it encounters *NULL* character the *while loop* terminates the program.

```
POINTERS ARE EASY
Length of String including spaces: 17
Length of String excluding spaces: 15
```

Example 2.45

Write a program to find length of a given string including and excluding spaces using pointers.

Solution

```
# include <stdio.h>
# include <conio.h>
main()
{
      char str[20],*s;
      int p=0,q=0;
      clrscr();
      printf("Enter String:");
      gets(str);
      s=str;
      while (*s!='\0')
      {
         printf("%c",*s);
         p++;
         s++;
         if (*s==32) /* ASCII equivalent of ' ' (space)is 32*/
         q++;
      }
      printf("\nLength of String including spaces: %d",p);
      printf("\nLength of String excluding spaces: %d",p-q);
}
```

Explanation This program is the same as the previous one. Here, the counter variables *'p'* and *'q'* are incremented to count number of characters and spaces found in the string. The *ASCII* value of space is *32*. Thus, at the end of the program both the variables are printed.

```
OUTPUT:
Enter String: POINTERS ARE EASY

POINTERS ARE EASY

Length of String including spaces: 17
Length of String excluding spaces: 15
```

Example 2.46

Write a program to interchange elements of character array using pointer.

Solution

```
# include <stdio.h>
```

```
# include <conio.h>
main()
{
  char *names[]={
  "kapil",
  "manoj",
  "amit",
  "amol",
  "pavan",
  "mahesh"
  };
  char *tmp;
  clrscr();
  printf ("Original: %s %s",names[3],names[4]);
  tmp=names[3];
  names[3]=names[4];
  names[4]=tmp;
  printf ("\nNew: %s %s",names[3],names[4]);
  }
```

Explanation In this program character array **names []* is declared and initialized. Another character pointer **tmp* is declared. The destination name that is to be replaced is assigned to variable '**tmp*'. The destination name is replaced with source name and the source name is replaced with **tmp* variable. Thus, using simple assignment statements two names are interchanged.

```
OUTPUT:
Original: amol pavan
New: pavan amol
```

Example 2.47

Write a program to read two strings through the keyboard. Compare these two strings character by character. Display the similar characters found in both the strings and count the number of dissimilar characters.

Solution

```
# include <stdio.h>
# include <conio.h>
# include <string.h>
main()
{
    char str1[20],str2[20],l,*a,*b;
    int c=0;
    clrscr();
        printf ("\n Enter First String:");
        gets(str1);
        printf ("\n Enter Second String:");
        gets(str2);
    a=str1;
    b=str2;
    printf ("\n Similar Characters Found in Both String.");
```

Explanation In this program two strings are entered in the character array *str1 []* and *str2 []*. Their base addresses are assigned to pointer '**a*' and '**b*'. In the *while* loop two pointers are compared using *stricmp ()* function. If the characters of two strings are same the counter variable '*l*' is incremented and characters are printed. Otherwise, the counter '*c*' is incremented. This job is done in the *if* statement. The character pointers '*a*' and '*b*' are incremented throughout the

```
        while (*a!='\0')
        {
            if(stricmp(*a,*b)==0)
        {
    printf("\n\t%c \t%c",*a,*b);
        l++;
    }
    else
        c++;

        a++;
        b++;
        }
        if(c==0)
        printf("\n The Strings are Identical.");
        else
        printf("\nThe Strings are different at %d places.",c);
        printf("\n The String Characters are similar at %d places.",l);
}
```

while loop to obtain the successive characters from both the strings. The last *if* statement displays a message stating that the given string is different or identical depending on the value of *'c'*.

```
OUTPUT:
Enter First String: SUNDAY
Enter Second String: MONDAY
Similar Characters Found in Both Strings.
    N   N
    D   D
    A   A
    Y   Y
The Strings are different at 2 places.
The String Characters are similar at 4 places.
```

Example 2.48

Write a program to enter three characters, using pointers. Use the *memcmp ()* function for comparing the three characters. In case the entered characters are same, display the message "the characters are same"; otherwise, indicate their appearance before or after one another or display the status of characters in alphabetical order. *(The memcmp () function compares a specified number of characters from two buffers.)*

Solution

```
#include <stdio.h>
#include <conio.h>
#include <string.h>
#include <process.h>
main()
{
```

Explanation In this program three characters are entered in the character variable *'x'*,*'y'* and *'z'* and their base addresses are stored in the pointers *'xp'*, *'yp'* and *'zp'*, respectively. The function

```
char x,y,z,*xp,*yp,*zp;
int stat=0;
clrscr();
printf ("Enter Three Characters");
scanf ("%c %c %c",&x,&y,&z);
xp=&x,yp =&y, zp =&z;
stat = memcmp(yp, xp, strlen(yp));
if (*xp==*yp)
{
   printf ("\n1st and 2nd Character are same.\n");
   goto next;
}
   if (stat > 0)
   printf("2nd Character appears after the 1st Character in Alphabetic.\n");
   else
   printf("2nd Character appears before the first Character in Alphabetic \n");
next:
   stat = memcmp(yp,zp, strlen(yp));
      if (*yp==*zp)
      {
      printf ("\n2nd and 3rd Character are same.");
      exit(1);
      }
      if (stat > 0)
      printf("2nd Character appears after the 3rd Character in Alphabetic. \n");
      else
      printf("2nd Character appears before 3rd Character in Alphabetic.\n");
}
```

memcmp () is used to compare two pointers for specified length. If first two characters are same, a message is displayed and control goes to *next* label. In the *next* label, second and third characters are compared. Using the value of variable *'stat'* locations of characters are decided.

```
OUTPUT:
Enter Three Character C C A
1st and 2nd Character are same.
2nd Character appears after the 3rd Character in Alphabetic.
```

Example 2.49

Write a program to compare two strings irrespective of case. Compare the characters at the specific position. If they are same display ' The characters are same at that position".

Solution

```
#include <stdio.h>
#include <string.h>
# include <conio.h>
main()
{
   char *buf1 = "computer";
```

Explanation The *memicmp ()* function compares two strings for specified number of characters. It returns zero if both the strings are same up to specified length of characters. Otherwise, non-zero

```
    char *buf2 = "comp ter";
    int stat;
    stat = memicmp(buf1, buf2, 4);
    clrscr();
    printf("The Characters up to 4th position are ");
    if (stat) */ if stat is non zero then prints 'not' otherwise 'same'.t */
    printf("not ");
    printf("same\n");
}
```

value will be returned. Depending upon the value it returns, the *if* statement displays respective message.

OUTPUT:
The Characters up to 4th position are same.

Summary

1. Array is a very popular and useful data structure used to store data elements in successive manner. Array is a linear and homogenous data structure. Homogenous means same types of elements are stored in it. It may be non-homogenous if structure is associated with it.
2. One-dimensional arrays having only one row of elements and elements are stored in successive memory locations.
3. The various operations carried out with arrays are insertion, deletion, searching, sorting, etc.
4. Two-dimensional arrays can be thought of as rectangular display of elements with rows and columns.
5. A three-dimensional arrays can be thought of as array of arrays.
6. The collection of characters, digits, and symbols enclosed within quotation marks are called strings. Strings are always declared as character array. Like other type of arrays, elements of character array are also stored in continuous memory location. Each character array occupies one byte in memory. One different thing about strings is that, the compiler automatically adds NULL ('\0') character at the end of string.

Exercises

A. Answer the following questions:
   1. What are arrays?
   2. How are elements of array stored?
   3. What are one-dimensional arrays?
   4. What are two-dimensional arrays?
   5. Explain multi-dimensional array.
   6. What are strings? How are they declared?
   7. What is NULL character?
   8. Explain various operations with arrays.
   9. What are sparse matrices?
   10. Distinguish between character and integers arrays.
   11. Can we store values and addresses in the same array?

12. Explain the difference between row major and column major array.

B. Attempt following programs:

1. Write a program to declare one-dimensional float type array. Display elements with memory addresses.
2. Write a program to read ten integers in an array and find the number of even and odd numbers in it.
3. Write a program to input a number containing five digits. Obtain cube of each digit and display the cubes of all digits on the screen.
4. Read the marks in physics, chemistry and mathematics obtained by ten students. Display the top three students with their total marks.
5. Write a program to enter a four-digit number using array and arrange it in the reverse order.
6. Write a program to demonstrate use of two-dimensional array.
7. Write a program to access elements of an array using another pointer.
8. Write a program to declare a character array. Initialize with the string and display the contents.
9. Write a program to demonstrate the use of multi-dimensional array.
10. Write a program to create array of structure objects. Read and display the data.
11. Write a program to delete and insert an element in an array.
12. Write a program to find whether the given matrix is lower-left matrix or not.
13. Write a program to enter and store elements in an array. Display only diagonal elements.
14. Write a program to find whether the given matrix is sparse matrix or dense matrix.

C. Select the appropriate option for each of the following questions:

1. Array elements are stored in
   a. successive memory locations c. both (a) and (b)
   b. random memory locations d. none of the above.
2. Accessing all elements of the array is known as
   a. transverse c. deletion
   b. insertion d. listing.
3. Merging of array elements means
   a. combining two or more arrays c. interchanging elements of two arrays
   b. addition of elements of two arrays d. none of the above.
4. Following one operation cannot be performed on arrays
   a. merging c. deletion
   b. insertion d. memory re-allocation.
5. Base address means
   a. address of 0th element c. address of last element
   b. address of array name d. none of the above.
6. Array elements are stored in
   a. random memory locations c. both of the above.
   b. sequential memory locations

7. A character array always ends with
   a. comma(,)
   b. question mark (?)
   c. null character (\0)
   d. Full stop (.).
8. Arrays can not be initialized if they are
   a. automatic
   b. static
   c. external
   d. none of the above.
9. All the elements in the array must be
   a. initialized
   b. defined
   c. none of the above.

D. What will be the output of the following programs?

1.

```
#include <stdio.h>
#include <conio.h>
main()
{
char nam[10],*h;
printf ("Enter Your Name:");
scanf("%s",&nam);
h=nam;
   while (*h!='\0')
   {
   printf ("%c",*h);
   h++;
   }
}
```

2.

```
# include <stdio.h>
# include <conio.h>

main()
{
int x[5]={12,42,26,18,80},a=0;
clrscr();
while (a<5)
{
printf ("\n%d",x[a]);
a++;
}
}
```

3.

```
# include <stdio.h>
# include <conio.h>
main ()
{
   int i;
   char name[10];
   clrscr();
   scanf("%s",name);
   for (i=0;i<10;i++)
   {
   if(name[i]=='\0')
   exit(1);
   printf("%c",name[i]+3);
}
}
```

4.

```
# include <stdio.h>
# include <conio.h>

main ()
{
   char name[6]="DATA";
   clrscr();
   printf("%c",name);
   printf ("%s",name);
}
```

5.

```
# include <stdio.h>
# include <conio.h>
int main ()
{
int *p,n[5]={4,5,6,7,8},j;
clrscr();
p=n;
for (j=0;j<5;j++)
printf ("\n%d", *(p+j));
}
```

6.

```
# include <stdio.h>
# include <conio.h>

main()
{
    int m[5]={0},j;
    for (j=0;j<5;j++)
    printf ("\n%d",m[j]);
}
```

7.

```
# include <stdio.h>
# include <conio.h>

main()
{
int x[5]={2,27,6,86,60},a;
clrscr();
for(a=5;a>=0;a—)
printf ("\n%d",x[a]);
}
```

8.

```
# include <stdio.h>
# include <conio.h>
main (){
char a[5]={'1','2','3','4','5'};
int i;
clrscr();
for(i=0;i<5;i++)
printf ("%c",a[i]);
}
```

9.

```
# include <stdio.h>
# include <conio.h>
main (){
char a[5]={65,66,67,68,69};
int i;
clrscr();
for(i=0;i<5;i++)
printf ("%c",a[i]);
}
```

Chapter 3

Recursion

Chapter Outline

3.1 INTRODUCTION TO FUNCTION

A function is a block of statements that can be used to perform a specific task. Fig. 3.1 describes the various parts of the function. A function has the following parts:

a. Function prototype declaration
b. Definition of a function (function declarator)
c. Actual and formal arguments
d. Return statement
e. Invoking function.

3.1.1 Function Prototypes

We use many built-in functions. The prototypes of these functions are given in the respective header files. We include them using # *include* directive. In C++, while defining user-defined functions, it is unavoidable to declare its prototype. A prototype statement helps the compiler to check the return and argument types of the function.

A function prototype declaration consists of function's return type, name, and arguments list. It tells the compiler:

a. Name of the function
b. Type of value returned
c. The type and number of arguments.

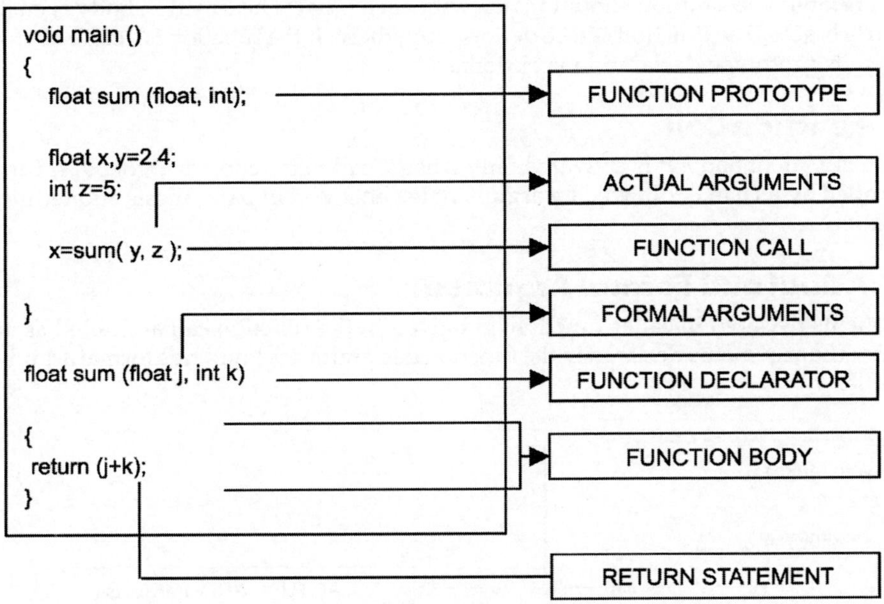

Figure 3.1 Parts of function

When the programmer defines the function, the definition of function must be similar to its prototype declaration. If the programmer makes a mistake, the compiler flags an error message. The function prototype declaration statement is always terminated with a semi-colon. The statements given below are examples of function prototypes.

A. *void show (void);*
B. *float sum (float, int);*
C. *float sum (float x, int y);*

In example (A) the return type is *void,* i.e. the function will not return any value. The *void* functions are always without return statement. The argument *void* indicates the function will not require any argument. By default, every function returns an integer value. To return a non-integer value, the data type should be mentioned in function prototype and definition. While writing definition of function, the return type must be preceded by the function name and it is optional if return type is default (int).

In example (B) the prototype of function *sum ()* is declared. Its return type is *float* and arguments are *float* and *integer* type, respectively. It is shown in the Fig. 3.1.

In example (C) with argument type, argument names are also declared. It is optional and not compulsory to use the same variable name in the program.

3.1.2 Function Definition

The first line is called as function declarator and then function body follows it. The block of statements followed by function declarator is called as function definition. The declarator and function prototype declaration should match with each other. The function body is enclosed within curly braces. The function can be defined anywhere. If the function is defined before its caller, then its prototype declaration is optional.

3.1.3 Function Call

A function is a latent body. It is activated only when a call to function is invoked. A function must be called by its name followed by argument list enclosed in parenthesis and terminated by semi-colon.

3.1.4 Actual and Formal Argument

The arguments declared in caller function and given in the function call are called as actual arguments. The arguments declared in the function declarator are known as formal arguments. For example,

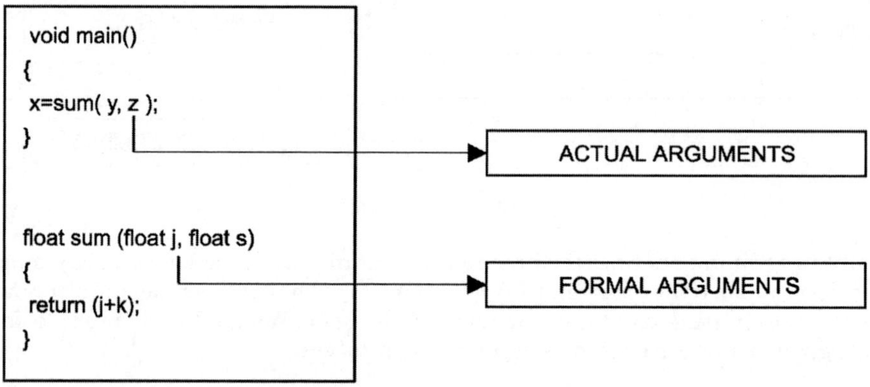

Figure 3.2 Actual and formal arguments

As shown in Fig. 3.2, variable *y* and *z* are actual arguments and *j* and *k* are formal arguments. The values of *y* and *z* are stored in *j* and *k*, respectively. The values of actual arguments are assigned to formal arguments. The function uses formal arguments for computing.

3.1.5 The Return Statement

The return statement is used to return value to the caller function. The return statement returns only one value at a time. When a return statement is encountered, the compiler transfers the control of the program to caller function. The syntax of return statement is as follows:

return (variable name); or return variable name;

The parenthesis is optional.

3.2 TYPES OF RECURSIONS

Recursion a little bit tough, but if we keep track of the program, in which sequence it is executing, it is easy to understand. Recursion is one of the most dominant tools used in the programming technique. There are various situations when we need to execute a block of statements for a number of times depending on condition at that time recursion is useful. Recursion is used to solve a problem, which has iterations in reverse order. Data structures also support recursion, for example, tree supports recursion. Various programs are solved with the use of recursion. The major application of recursion is game programming where series of steps can be solved with recursion.

When a function calls itself recursively it is known as recursion. Recursion is of two types:

1. Direct recursion
2. Indirect recursion.

The recursion in which the function calls itself is called direct recursion. In this type, only one function is involved. In indirect recursion two functions call each other. Fig. 3.3 describes direct and indirect recursion.

```
int num ()
{
---
int num ();
}
```

a. Direct recursion

```
int num ()
{
---
int sum ();
}

int sum ()
{
---
num();
}
```

b. Indirect recursion

Figure 3.3 Types of recursions

Recursion is one of the applications of stack. Stacks are explained in the next chapter. There are several problems in which without recursion their solution is lengthy.

The programming languages like C, C++ allow us to define user defined functions. Functions in the programming languages are very useful, because by using function a separate block of statements can be defined. This block can be invoked a number of times anywhere in the program. A function which can call itself or another function and which eventually calls another function is known as recursive function.

Two essential conditions should be satisfied by a recursive function. First, every time a function should call itself directly or indirectly. Second, the function should have a condition to stop the recursion. Otherwise, an infinite loop is generated that will halt the system.

Some people think that recursion is a very needless luxury in the programming language. Using iteration one can solve the problems. However, in programming in some situation there is no substitute for recursion.

There are some kinds of problems associated with recursive function which are not present in the non-recursive function. The recursive function can be invoked by itself or any other function. To make sure execution it is very essential for the function to save the return address in order to return to proper location. Also, the function has to save the formal and local variables.

Example 3.1

Write a program to calculate factorial of given number using recursion using C statements

Solution

```
# include <stdio.h>
# include <conio.h>

int fact (int);

main ()
{
   int num,f;
   clrscr();
   printf ("\n Enter a number: ");
   scanf ("%d",&num);
   f=fact(num);
      printf ("\n Factorial of %d is %d",num,f);
}

   int fact(int f)
   {
      if (f==1) return f;
   else return f*fact(f-1);
   }

OUTPUT
 Enter a number: 4
 Factorial of 4 is 24
```

Explanation In this program *fact ()* is a recursive function. The entered number is passed to function *fact ()*. When function *fact ()* is executed, it is repeatedly invoked by itself. Every time a function is invoked, the value of *f* is reduced by one and multiplication is carried. The recursive function produces the numbers 4,3,2 and 1. The multiplication value of these numbers is taken and returned to *main ()* function.

3.3 RULES FOR RECURSIVE FUNCTION

1. In recursion, it is essential for a function to call itself, otherwise recursion will not take place, as shown in Fig. 3.3.
2. Only user defined function can be involved in the recursion. Library function cannot be involved in recursion because their source code cannot be viewed.
3. A recursive function can be invoked by itself or by other function. It saves return address in order with the intention that to return at proper location when return to a calling

statement is made. The last-in-first-out nature of recursion indicates that stack data structure can be used to implement it.

4. Recursion is turning out to be increasingly important in non-numeric applications and symbolic manipulations.
5. To stop the recursive function it is necessary to base the recursion on test condition and proper terminating statement such as *exit ()* or return must be written using if () statement as shown in the Fig. 3.4.

```
int num()
{
---
 if (condition)
---
 num();
}
```

Figure 3.4 Terminating statement in recursion

6. The user defined function main () can be invoked recursively. To implement such recursion it is necessary to mention prototype of function main (). An example in this regard is explained as follows:

Example 3.2

Write a program to call main () recursively.

Solution

```
# include <stdio.h>
# include <conio.h>
# include <process.h>

char str[]="Have a Good Day";
int x=0;

main();

void main ()
 {
   switch(str[x])
   {
```

Explanation In this program *main ()* function is invoked recursively. A prototype of function *main ()* is given before function definition. However, in normal practice it is not necessary to give prototype. A recursive function must know its return type and number and type of the arguments passed.

```
    case 'H':
    clrscr();
    default:
    printf("%c",str[x]);
    break;
    case '\0':
    exit(0);
    break;
    }
 x++;
 main();
}
```

```
OUTPUT
Have a Good Day
```

7. Any function can be called recursively. An example is illustrated as above.
8. When a recursive function is executed, the recursion calls are not implemented instantly. All the recursive calls are pushed onto the stack until the terminating condition is not detected. As soon as the terminating condition is detected, the recursive calls stored in the stack are popped and executed. The last call is executed first then second, then third and so on.
9. During recursion, at each recursive call new memory is allocated to all the local variables of the recursive functions with the same name.
10. At each call the new memory is allocated to all the local variables, their previous values are pushed onto the stack and with its call. All these values can be available to corresponding function call when it is popped from the stack.

3.4 DIRECT RECURSION

In this type, only one function is involved which calls itself until the given condition is true. Consider the following program:

Example 3.3

Write a program call function main () and perform sum of first five numbers.

Solution

```
# include <stdio.h>
# include <process.h>
void main (int);
int x,s;
void main (x)
{
   s=s+x;
```

Explanation In this program variable *x* and *y* are declared outside *main ()*. Initially their values are zero. The prototype if function *main ()* is declared. This is essential because while calling, the compiler checks the function with its

```
    printf ("\n x=%d s=%d",x,s);

    if (x==5) exit(0);
    main (++x);
}

OUTPUT
x=1 s=1
x=2 s=3
x=3 s=6
x=4 s=10
x=5 s=15
```

prototype. It is advance information regarding the function. The variable *x* is passed to the function *main ()*. The variable *x* is added to variable *s* until the value of *x* reaches to five. When *x* reaches to five, the program terminates.

Table 3.1 Steps of recursive function

Function Call	*Value of x*	*Value of s (sum)*
main(1)	x=1	s=1 (0+1)
main(2)	x=2	s=3 (2+1+0)
main(3)	x=3	s=6 (3+2+1+0)
main(4)	x=4	s=10 (4+3+2+1+0)
main(5)	x=5	s=15 (5+4+3+2+1+0)

Example 3.4

Write a program to calculate triangular number using recursion.

Solution

```
# include <stdio.h>
# include <conio.h>
# include <process.h>

main ()
{
    int trinum(int );
    int t,x;
    clrscr();
    printf ("\n Enter a Number: ");
    scanf ("%d",&x);
    t=trinum(x);
    printf ("\n Triangular Number of %d is %d",x,t);
}

int trinum(int x)
```

Explanation In this program a function *trinum ()* is defined which calls itself. An integer is entered through the keyboard and it is stored in the variable *x*. The function *trinum ()* calls itself and the argument passed to this called function is one less than the value of *x*. The return values are added to variable *f*. When value of *x* becomes zero, the recursion ends and the total is returned to variable *t* in function *main ()*. The value of *t* is triangular number of the entered number, which is nothing but the sum of all the integers between 1 to the entered number. The recursive function is called repetitively by itself without completing the execution of previous call. When

```
{
    int f=0;
    if (x==0) return f;
    else f=f+x+trinum(x-1);
    return f;
}

OUTPUT
Enter a Number: 4
Triangular Number of 4 is 10
```

program ends and the control is about to return to caller function the number of times the return statement executed is equal to the number of times the function is called recursively. The compiler keeps track of how many times a function is executed. To see, these points execute the program in single step by pressing F7 key.

When a function returns three actions are done. The return address is placed in the safe location. The data stored in local variables of function are freed. The previously saved address is retrieved. The return value of function is returned and put in the safe location and calling program receives it. Normally, the location is a hardware register, which is placed in CPU for the same purpose.

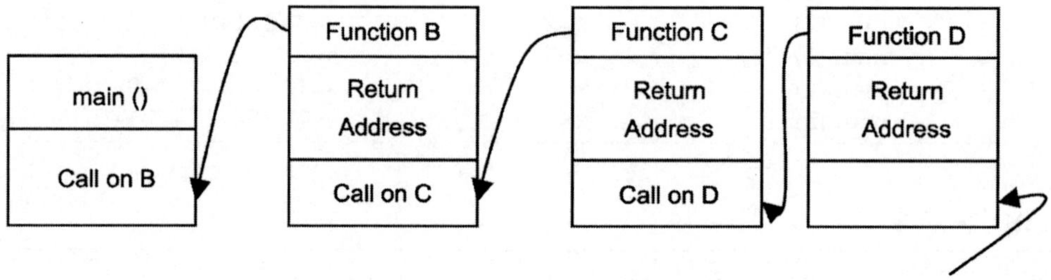

Figure 3.5 Functions calling one another

As shown in the above Fig. 3.5 the main function call invokes the function B. The function B invokes the *function* C and again *C invokes D*. The figure shows the control is present in the function D. In every function, a location is reserved for storage of return address. The return address location of function D contains the address of statement in C immediately after the function invocation statement.

Whenever a recursive function invokes itself, new data variables are created and memory is allocated for data. The data area contains all local variables and return address. In the recursion function, the data area is not connected only with the function but closely associated with the particular function call. In every call new data area is allocated and the particular function's data area contains information about recent call. Every time control returns, the data area is de-allocated or freed and the former data area turn into current.

The recursion in C and C++ language is more expensive as compared to non-recursive function. It takes not only more space but it is also time consuming. In some system program such as compiler or operating system, if program contains recursive function it will be executed many a time. In such a case, an alternate non-recursive function may be defined.

Example 3.5

Write a program to define to a recursive function to calculate factorial of a number.

Solution

```
# include <stdio.h>
# include <conio.h>

main()
{
   int fact(int);
   int f,n;
   clrscr();
   printf ("\n Enter a Number: ");
   scanf ("%d",&n);
   f=fact(n);
   printf ("Factorial of Number %d: %d",n,f);
}

int fact (int j)
{
   int f=1;

   if (j==1)
   return 1;
   else
   f=j*fact(j-1);
   return f;
}

OUTPUT
Enter a Number: 5
Factorial of Number 5: 120
```

Explanation In this program function *fact ()* is defined and the number entered by the user is passed to the function *fact ()*. In the function *fact ()* the if statement checks the value of variable *j* (formal argument of *n*). If the value is 1 the return statement returns 1 otherwise the *fact ()* function is called. At this point, the recursion actually begins. When the function *fact ()* is recursively invoked the value of *j* is decreased by one and then passed.

3.5 INDIRECT RECURSION

In this type of recursion two or more functions are involved in the recursion. The indirect recursion does not make any overhead as direct recursion. When control exits from one function and enters into another function, the local variables of former function are destroyed. Hence, memory is not engaged. The following program explains the indirect recursion.

Example 3.6

Write a program to demonstrate recursion between two functions.

Solution

```
# include <stdio.h>
# include <conio.h>
#include <process.h>

int s;
void show(void);

main()
{
   if (s==5) exit(0);
   show ();
}

void show ()
{
   printf ("%d",s);
   s++;
   main();
}

OUTPUT
0 1 2 3 4
```

Explanation In this program two user defined functions are defined *main ()* and *show ()*. The *s* is global variable. The *main ()* function invokes *show ()* function and the *show ()* function invokes *main ()* function. The value of *s* is increased and displayed. When value of *s* reaches to 5 the program is terminated.

Example 3.7

Write a program to display numbers in several rows.

Solution

```
# include <stdio.h>
# include <conio.h>
# include <process.h>

int s;
void show(void);

main()
{
   if (s==0)
   clrscr();
   if (s==10)
   exit(0);
   show ();
}

void show ()
```

Explanation This program is same as the last one. Here, depending on the value of variable *s*, the iteration of *for loop* is performed.

```
{
   int j;
   for (j=0;j<=s;j++)
   printf("%d",j);
   printf("\n");
   s++;
   main();
}
```

```
OUTPUT
0
0 1
0 1 2
0 1 2 3
0 1 2 3 4
0 1 2 3 4 5
0 1 2 3 4 5 6
0 1 2 3 4 5 6 7
0 1 2 3 4 5 6 7 8
0 1 2 3 4 5 6 7 8 9
```

3.6 RECURSION VS. ITERATIONS

We have studied both recursion and iteration. They can be applied to a program depending upon the situation. Table 3.2 explains the differences between recursion and iteration.

Table 3.2 Recursion Vs. Iteration

Recursion	*Iteration*
Recursion is the term given to the mechanism of defining a set or procedure in terms of itself.	The block of statement executed repeatedly using loops.
A conditional statement is required in the body of the function for stopping the function execution.	The iteration control statement itself contains statement for stopping the iteration. At every execution, the condition is checked.
At some places, use of recursion generates extra overhead. Hence, better to skip when easy solution is available with iteration.	All problems can be solved with iteration.
Recursion is expensive in terms of speed and memory.	Iteration does not create any overhead. All the programming languages support iteration.

Figure 3.6 illustrates the iterative process.

Initialization The variables involved in the iteration process are initialized. These variables are used to decide when to end the loop.

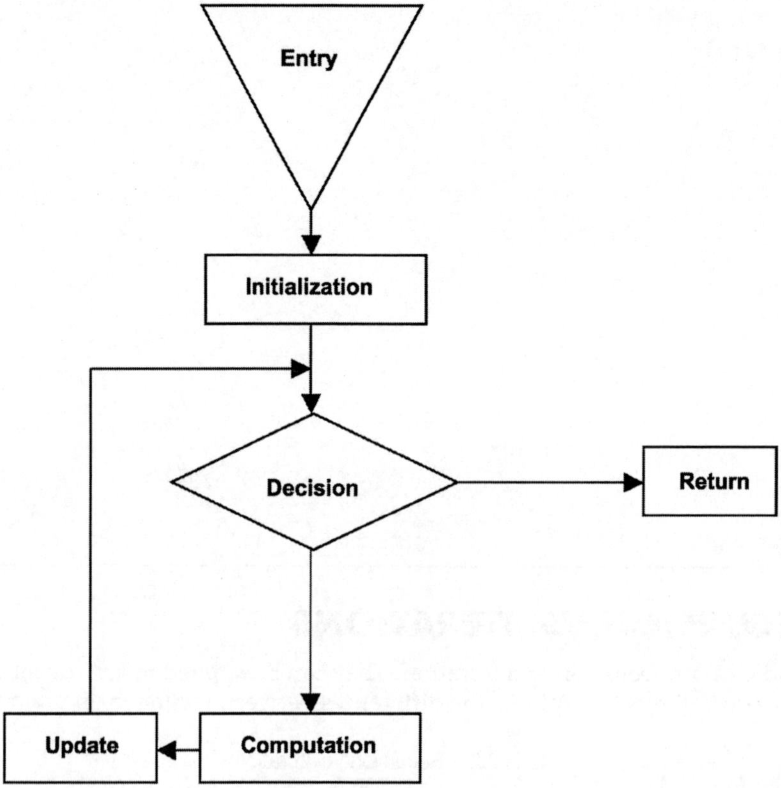

Figure 3.6 Iterative processes

Decision The decision variable is used to decide whether to continue or discontinue the loop. When the condition is satisfied, control goes to return, or else it goes to computation block.

Computation The required processing or computation is carried out in this block.

Update The decision argument is changed and shifted to next iteration.

The common algorithm for any kind of recursive function is shown in Fig. 3.7.

Preliminary part The use of this block is to store the local variables, formal arguments and return address. The end-part will restore these data. Only recently saved arguments, local variables and return address are restored. The variables last saved are restored first.

Body If the test condition is satisfied, it performs the complete processing and control passes to end-block. If not, partial processing is performed and a recursive call is made. The body also contains call to itself and one or more calls can be made. Every time a recursive call is made,

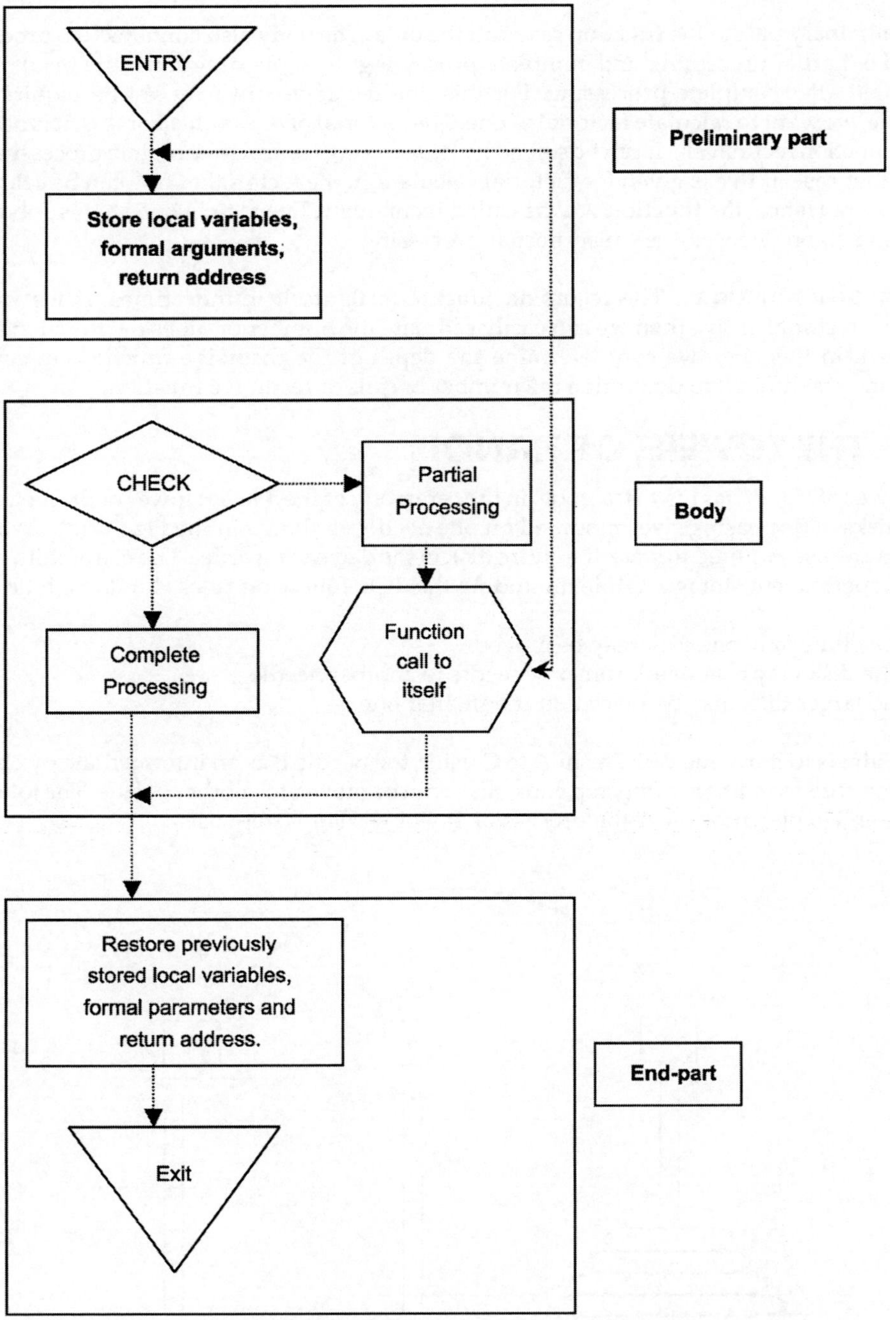

Figure 3.7 Recursive process

the preliminary part of the function saves all the data. The body also contains two processing boxes i.e. partial processing and complete processing. In some programs, the result can be calculated after complete processing. For this, the recursive call may not be required. For example, we want to calculate factorial of one. The factorial of one is one. For this, it is needless to call function recursively. It can be solved by transferring control to complete processing box.

In other case, if five is given for factorial calculation, the factorial of five can be calculated in one step. Hence, the function will be called recursively. Every time one step is solved, i.e. 5*4*3 and so on. Hence, it is called partial processing.

Depth of Recursion The recursion function calls itself infinite times. If we want to calculate factorial of five then we can easily estimate the number of times the function would be called. In this case, we can determine the depth of the recursive function. In complex program, it is difficult to determine the number of calls of recursive function.

3.7 THE TOWERS OF HANOI

The Tower of Hanoi has historical roots in the ceremony of the ancient tower of Brahma. There are *n* disks of decreasing sizes mounted on one needle as shown in the Fig. 3.8(a). Two more needles are also required to stack the entire disk in the decreasing order. The use of third needle is for impermanent storage. While mounding the disk, following rules should be followed.

1. At a time only one disk may be moved.
2. The disk may be moved from any needle to another needle.
3. No larger disk may be placed on the smaller one.

Our aim is to move the disks from A to C using the needle B as an intermediate by obeying the above three conditions. Only top-most disks can be moved to another needle. The following figures and explanation clear the process of Tower of Hanoi stepwise.

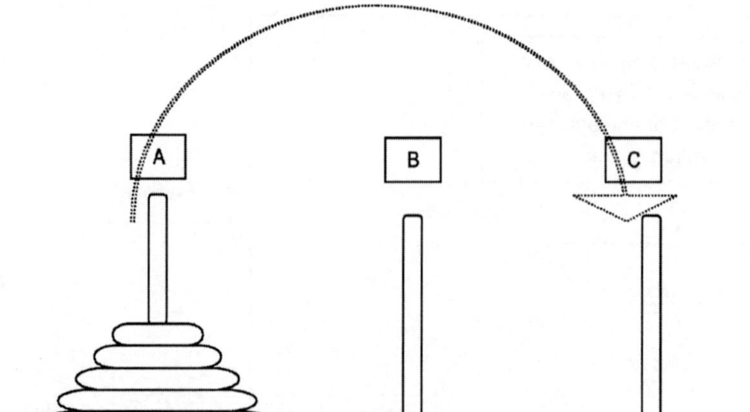

Figure 3.8 (a) Recursive Towers of Hanoi

In Fig. 3.8 (a), the three needles are displayed in their initial states. The needle A contains five disks and there are no disk on needle B and C. The arrow indicates the next operation to be performed, i.e. move first four disk from A to C.

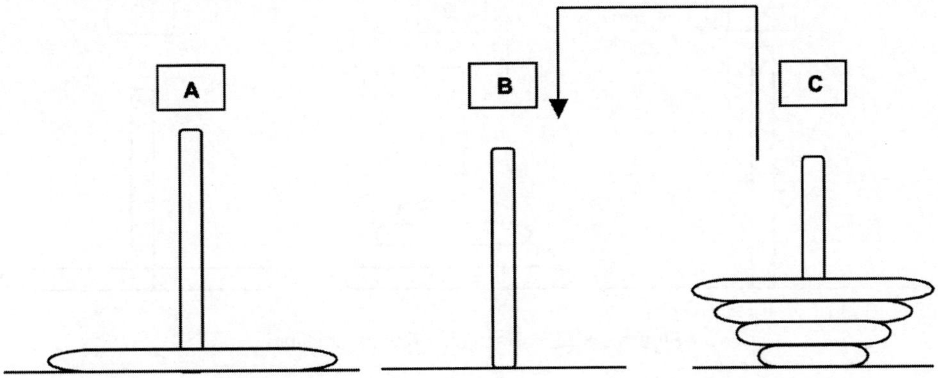

Figure 3.8 (b) Recursive Towers of Hanoi

In Fig. 3.8(b) the needle, A has only one disk. The needle C contains four disks. The arrow indicates the next operation, i.e. move four disks from C to B.

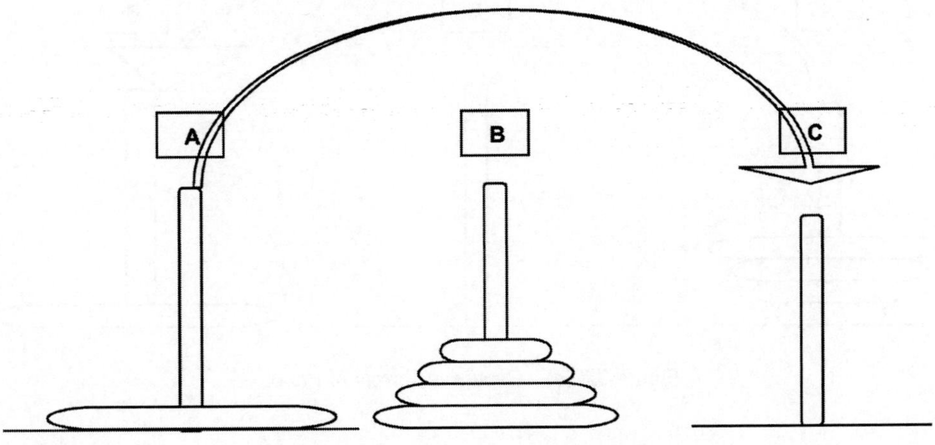

Figure 3.8 (c) Recursive Towers of Hanoi

In Fig. 3.8(c), the needle B has four disks. The needle A has only one disk, which will be moved to needle C.

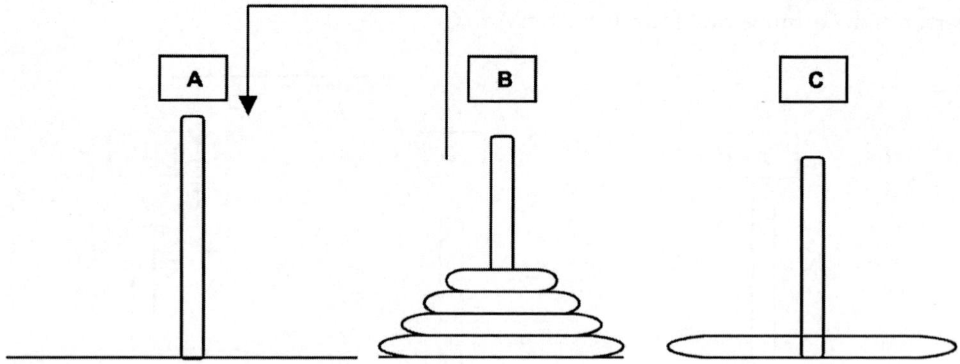

Figure 3.8 (d) Recursive Towers of Hanoi

In Fig. 3.8(d), the needle A has no disk. The needle B contains four disks and C contains one disk. The four disks move from B to A.

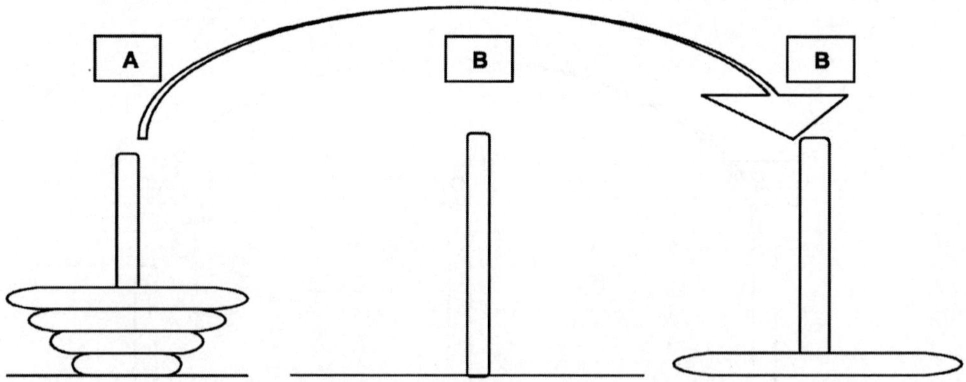

Figure 3.8 (e) Recursive Towers of Hanoi

In Fig. 3.8(e), the four disks from needle A are moved to needle C. Finally, the final position of needles A, B and C will be as shown in Fig. 3.8(f). Here, solution of Tower of Hanoi is complete.

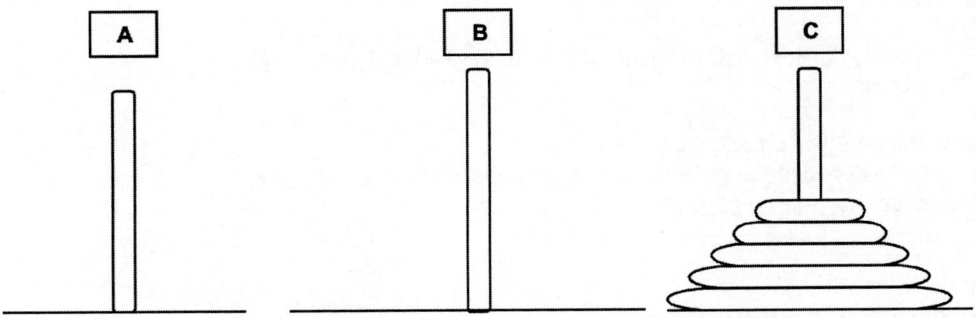

Figure 3.8 (f) Recursive Towers of Hanoi

The above process can be summarized as:

1. Move first four disks from needle A to C
2. Move four disks from C to B
3. Move the disk one from A to C
4. Move four disks from B to A
5. Move four disks from A to C.

Example 3.8

Write a program to illustrate Towers of Hanoi.

Solution

```
# include <conio.h>
# include <stdio.h>

void hanoi (int,char,char,char);

main ()
{
   int num;
   clrscr();
   printf ("\n Enter a Number: ");
   scanf ("%d",&num);
   clrscr();
   hanoi(num,'A','C','B');
}

void hanoi( int num, char f_peg,char t_peg, char a_peg)
{
```

Explanation In the above program numbers of disks are entered. The function *Hanoi ()* is invoked from *main ()*. The *A, B* and *C* are needles. If value of *num* is one, the disk is transferred from *A* to *C* and program ends. If the value of *num* is greater than one, then the *Hanoi ()* function invokes itself recursively, every time value of *num* is decreased by one. The output of the program is shown as above.

```
    if(num==1)
    {
        printf ("\nMove disk 1 from Needle %c to Needle %c",f_peg,t_peg);
        return;
    }
    hanoi(num-1,f_peg,a_peg,t_peg);
    printf ("\nMove disk %d from Needle %c to Needle %c",num,f_peg,t_peg);
    hanoi(num-1,a_peg,t_peg,f_peg);
}
```

```
OUTPUT
Move disk 1 from Needle A to Needle C
Move disk 2 from Needle A to Needle B
Move disk 1 from Needle C to Needle B
Move disk 3 from Needle A to Needle C
Move disk 1 from Needle B to Needle A
Move disk 2 from Needle B to Needle C
Move disk 1 from Needle A to Needle C
```

3.8 ADVANTAGES & DISADVANTAGES OF RECURSION

Advantages of recursion,

1. Sometimes, in programming a problem can be solved without recursion, but at some situations in programming it is must to use recursion. For example, a program to display the list of all files of the system cannot be solved without recursion.
2. The recursion is very flexible in data structure like stacks, queues, linked list and quick sort.
3. Using recursion, the length of the program can be reduced.

Disadvantages of recursion,

1. It requires extra storage space. The recursive calls and automatic variables are stored on the stack. For every recursive call separate memory is allocated to automatic variables with the same name.
2. If the programmer forgot to specify the exit condition in the recursive function, the program will execute out of memory. In such a situation user has to press *ctrl+ break* to pause or stop the function.
3. The recursion function is not efficient in execution speed and time.
4. If possible, try to solve problem with iteration instead of recursion.

3.9 TAIL RECURSION

In this chapter we have studied the recursion and we can say that recursion is a method in which set of process is given in terms of itself. Recursive function is invoked by itself and this function call is given in the same function body. If the function call statement is the last statement in the function body, this recursion is called tail recursion. In tail recursion, we can use return value as a parameter for the function. All the functions are maintained using stack, however, in this type, it will not push new function call to stack but it will replace the value of previous call with new call. This approach provides decreased stack implementation time and gives faster execution. The program 3.7 is an example of tail recursion.

3.10 EFFICIENCY OF RECURSION

We have studied both advantages and disadvantages of recursion. We have also studied the iteration which is an alternative to recursion. The major overhead of recursion is the memory it occupies and execution time. A non-recursive function will require minimum memory and less time for execution as compared with recursive function. The recursive function uses stack to push and pop the local variables. In non-recursive function the above push and pop operations with stack can be skipped. However, at some situation in programming use of recursion is must. If the part of program is to be invoked frequently, in such a case it is better to develop non-recursive function.

Summary

1. A function is a block of statements that can be used to define to perform a special task.
2. A function prototype declaration consists of function's return type, name, and arguments list. It tells the compiler, a) name of the function, b) type of value returned, c) the type and number of arguments.
3. When a function calls itself is called direct recursion.
4. When a function calls another function it is called indirect recursion
5. The user defined function main () can be invoked recursively. The library functions cannot be invoked recursively.
6. Constructor is a special member function used to initialize the data members. The constructor can also be invoked recursively.
7. Whenever a recursive function invokes itself, every time new data variables are created and data area and memory is allocated. The data area contains all local variables and return address. In the recursion of function, the data area is not connected only with the function but closely associated with the particular function call.

Exercises

A. Answer the following questions:
   1. Explain recursion process in detail.
   2. Differentiate between direct and indirect recursions.
   3. Differentiate between recursion and iteration.
   4. Mention the advantages and disadvantages of recursions.
   5. List the three rules of tower of Hanoi problem.
   6. What is depth of recursion?
   7. Explain tail recursion.

B. Attempt following program with recursion:
   1. Write a program to compute the nth number of fibonacci series.
   2. Write a program to reverse a number.

3. Write a program to display list of prime numbers up to 15.
4. Write a program to display a message "Hello" for 10 times.
5. Write a program to call function main () recursively.
6. Write a program to demonstrate tail recursion.
7. Consider the following list
   58,69,59,12,34,78,25,98,20
   a. Find elements 34,25 and 20 using recursion
   b. Calculate product of all elements of array
   c. Sum of all the elements.

C. Select the appropriate option for each of the following questions:

1. When a function calls itself is called
   a. Recursion
   b. iteration
   c. function
   d. none of the above.
2. In indirect recursion a function calls
   a. another function
   b. itself
   c. only main () function
   d. none of the above.
3. In tower of Hanoi the following one condition is not applicable:
   a. at a time only one disk may be moved
   b. the disc may be moved from any needle to another needle
   c. No larger disk may be placed on the smaller one
   d. The disks can be placed in any order.
4. The function declarator is used to
   a. declare formal arguments
   b. declare function prototype
   c. function call
   d. all of the above.

D. What will be the output of the following programs:

1.

```
# include <stdio.h>
# include <conio.h>

main ()
{
   int main (void);
   printf ("\n Hello");

   return (main ());
}
```

2.

```
# include <stdio.h>
# include <conio.h>
int x;
int main ()
{
   clrscr();
   int num(void);
   printf (" %d ",num());

   return 0;
}
int num()
{
   x++;
   if (x>8) return x;
   else
   return main();
}
```

3.

```
# include <stdio.h>
# include <conio.h>

int main ()
{
int num (void);
clrscr();
int n[]={num()};

for (int i=0;i<3;i++)
printf (" %d ",n[i]);
return 0;
}

int num ()
{
    int x;
    printf ("\n Enter a number: ");
    scanf ("%d",&x);
    if (x==0)
    return x;
    num();
    return x;
}
```

4.

```
# include <stdio.h>
# include <conio.h>

void show(void);

main()
{
    clrscr();
    show ();
}

void show ()
{
int i,j;
for (i=0;i<=5;i++)
for (j=0;j<=i;j++)
printf ("%d",j);
printf ("\n");
}
```

5.

```
# include <stdio.h>
# include <conio.h>

void dis();
int k=9
main()
{
    clrscr();
    dis();
    k=100;
    printf("%d",k);
}

void dis()
{
printf ("%d",k);
}
```

6.

```
# include <stdio.h>
# include <conio.h>
void fun(int);
void fun1(int);
void fun2(int);
main()
{
    int a=109;
    clrscr();
    fun(a);
    fun1(a);
    fun2(a);
}

void fun (int a)
{   printf ("%d",a++); }

void fun (int a)
{   printf ("%d",a—); }

void fun (int a)
{   printf ("%d",a++); }
```

Chapter 4

Stacks

Chapter Outline

4.1 INTRODUCTION

In this chapter, we will study one of the most important simple data structures 'stack'. *Stack* is an important tool in programming languages. Stack is one of the most essential linear data structures. Implementation of most of the system programs is based on stack data structure. We can insert or delete an element from a list, which takes place from one end. The insertion of element onto the stack is called as *"push"* and deletion operation is called *"pop"*, i.e. when an item is added to the stack the operation is called *"push"* and when it is removed the operation is called *"pop"*. Due to the push operation from one end, elements are added to the stack, the stack is also known as *pushdown list.* The most and least reachable elements in the stack are respectively known as the *"top"* and *"bottom"* of the stack. A stack is an arranged collection of elements into which new elements can be inserted or from which existing new elements can be deleted at one end. Stack is a set of elements in a *last-in-first-out* technique. As per Fig. 4.1 the last item pushed onto the stack is always the first to be removed from the stack. The end of the stack from where the insertion or deletion operation is carried out is called *top*. In Fig. 4.1(a) a stack of numbers is shown.

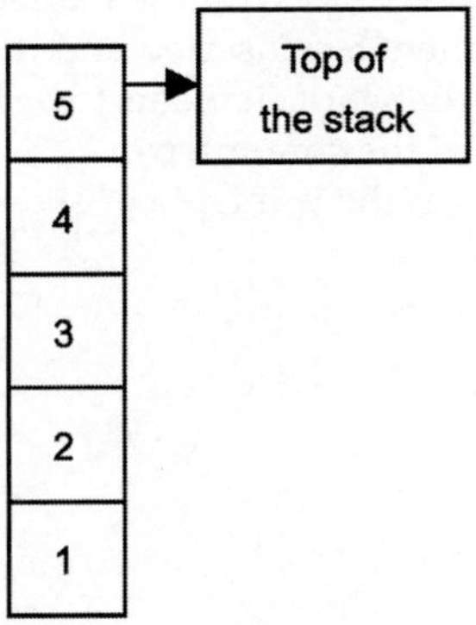

Figure 4.1 (a) Stack

Figure 4.1 (b) A pot with plates

As shown in Fig. 4.1(a) the stack is based on the rule *last-in-first-out*. The element appended lastly is deleted first. If we want to delete element 3 it is necessary to delete the top elements 5 and 4 first.

In Fig. 4.1(b), you can see a pot containing plates kept one above the other. Plates can be inserted or removed from the top. The top plate can be removed first in case *pop* operation is carried out, otherwise plates are to be added on the top. In other words, the removal operation has to be carried out from the top. Thus, placing or removing takes place from top, i.e. from the same end.

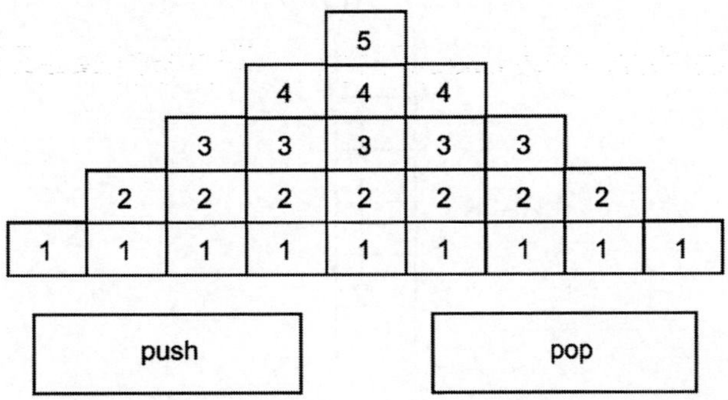

Figure 4.2 Working of stack

As shown in the first half portion of Fig. 4.2, first integer 1 is inserted and then 2,3,4 and 5 are pushed on to the stack. In the second half portion of the same figure, the elements are deleted (*pop*) one by one from the top. The elements are deleted in the order from 5 to 1. The insertion and deletion operation is carried out at one end (*top*). Hence, the recently inserted element is deleted first. If we want to delete a particular element of the stack, it is necessary to delete all the elements present above that element. It is not possible to delete element 2 without deleting elements 5,4 and 3. The stack expands or shrinks with the passage of time. In the above example, the stack initially expands until element 5 is inserted and then shrinks after removal of elements. There is no higher limit on the number of elements to be inserted in the stack. The total capacity of stack depends on memory of the computer.

In practical life, we come across many examples based on the principle of stack.

Figure 4.3 Stack of books

Fig. 4.3 illustrates the stack of books that we keep in the order. Whenever we want to remove a book the removal operation is made from the top or new books can be added at the top.

Another example of stack that can be cited is a railway system for shunting the trains. Figure 4.4 shows a picture of a railway system. The incoming trains arrive in a sequence in the stack. The last entered train in the stack leaves first and it will be placed at first on the outgoing track.

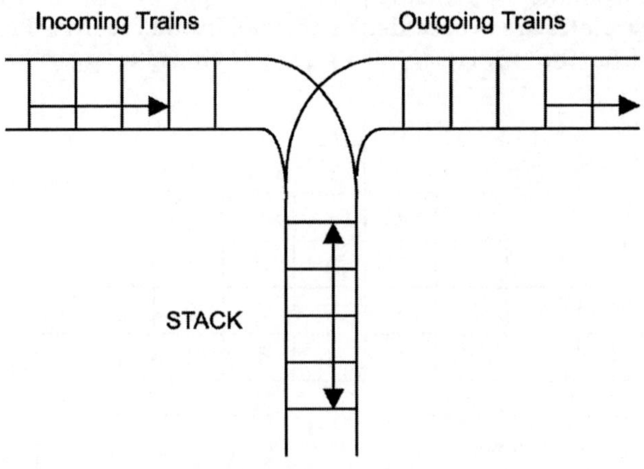

Figure 4.4 A Railway Track

4.2 STACK-RELATED TERMS

Stack Stack is a memory portion, which is used for storing the elements. The elements are stored based on the principle of last-in-first-out. In the stack the elements are kept one above the other and its size is based on the memory.

Top The top of the pointer points to the top element in the stack. The top of the stack indicates its door from where elements are entered or deleted. The stack top is used to verify stack's current position, i.e. underflow, overflow, etc. The top has value 0 when the stack is empty. Some programmers assign –1 to the top as initial value. This is because when the element is added, the top is incremented and it would become zero. The stack is generally implemented with the help of an array. In an array, counting of elements begins from 0 onwards. Hence, on the similar grounds stack top also begins from 0 and it is convenient to assign –1 to top as initial value.

Stack Underflow When there is no element in the stack or stack holds elements less than its capacity, the status of stack is known as *stack underflow*. In this situation, the top is present at the bottom of the stack. When an element is pushed, it will be the first element of the stack and top will be moved one step up.

Stack Overflow When the stack contains equal number of elements as per its capacity and no more elements can be added, the status of stack is known as *stack overflow*. In such a position, the top rests at the highest position.

Storage A function containing local variables and constants are stored in stack. Only global variables are stored in a stack frame.

Stack Frames This data structure holds all formal arguments; return address and local variables on the stack at the time when function is invoked.

4.2.1 Representation of Stack

The stack is represented in various ways. The stack can be shown as completely empty or fully filled or filled with few elements. When stack has no element, it is called *empty stack* which is shown in Fig. 4.5(a). The stack with completely filled elements is shown in the Fig. 4.5 (b) and no further elements can be inserted.

A top pointer maintains track of the top elements as shown in Fig. 4.5(c). For empty stack, the top value is zero. When stack has one element the value of top is one. Whenever an element is inserted (*push* operation) in the stack the value of pointer top is incremented by one. In the same manner, the value of pointer is reduced when an element is deleted from the stack (*pop* operation). The push operation can be applied to any stack, but before applying pop operation on the stack, it is necessary to make sure that the stack is not empty. If a *pop* operation is performed on empty stack, it results in *underflow*.

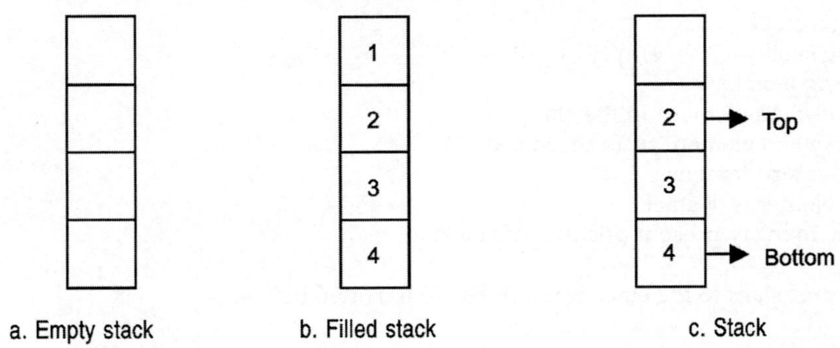

Figure 4.5 Representation of stack

Stack is very helpful in every ordered and chronological processing of functions. The most useful application of stack is in recursion (explained in previous chapter). It saves memory space. The mechanism of stack last-in-first-out (LIFO) is commonly useful in applications such as manufacturing and accounting calculations. It is a well-known accounting concept.

4.3 STACK IMPLEMENTATION

The stack implementation can be done in the following two ways:

4.3.1 Static Implementation

Static implementation can be achieved using arrays. Though, it is a very simple method, it has few limitations. Once a size of an array is declared, its size cannot be modified during program execution. It is also inefficient for utilization of memory. While declaration of an array, memory is allocated which is equal to array size. The vacant space of stack (array) also occupies memory space. In both cases, if we store less argument than declared, memory is wasted and if we want to store more elements than declared, array cannot be expanded. It is suitable only when we exactly know the number of elements to be stored.

4.3.2 Dynamic Implementation

Pointers can also be used for implementation of stack. The linked list is an example of this implementation. The limitations noticed in static implementation can be removed using dynamic implementation. The dynamic implementation is achieved using pointers. Using pointer implementation at run time there is no restriction on the number of elements. The stack may be expandable. The memory is efficiently utilized with pointers. Memory is allocated only after element is pushed to the stack. Both the above implementations are illustrated with suitable examples in the next section.

4.4 OPERATION ON STACK

The following fundamental operations on stack can be carried out through static implementation called array implementation. Operation on stack is also possible with the pointers, which is called dynamic implementation. We will perform the following operations on the stack:

1. Creating a stack
2. Checking stack—either empty or full
3. Initializing a stack
4. Insert (*push*) an element in the stack
5. Delete (*pop*) an element from the stack
6. Access the top element
7. Display elements of stack
8. Status: to identify present position of stack.

Some terms relevant to the stack operations are narrated below.

Push The procedure of inserting a new element to the top of the stack is known as push operation. After every push operation, the top is incremented by one. When the array is full (if static implementation is applied) the status of stack is full and this condition is called as stack overflow. In such a case, no further element can be inserted. After every *push* operation, the new element rests at the top. Fig. 4.6(a) shows the push operation.

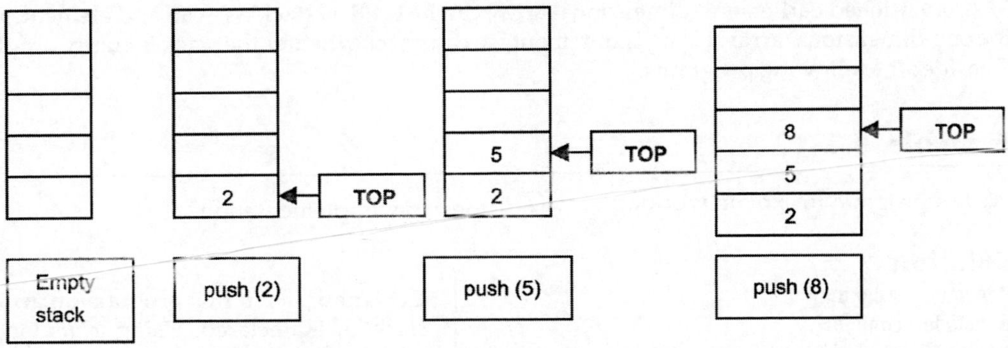

Figure 4.6 (a) Push operation with stack

Pop The procedure of removing element from the top of the stack is called as *pop* operation. After every *pop* operation, the top is decremented by one. If there is no element in the stack, it is called as empty stack or stack underflow. In such a case, *pop* operation cannot be applied. Fig. 4.6(b) illustrates the pop operation.

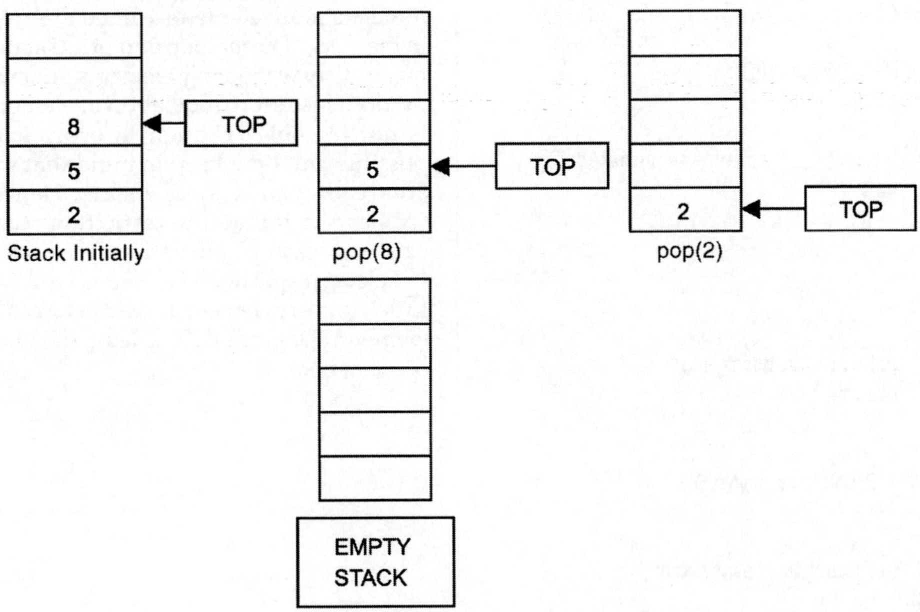

Figure 4.6 (b) Pop operation with stack

The stack can be supposed as a one-dimensional array. The various operations listed above can be carried out with one-dimensional array. The following programs explain the operations listed above.

As mentioned earlier, one-dimensional array can be used as stack. We can add elements in the one-dimensional array. Using if statement we can check whether the stack is empty or full. Consider the following programs.

Example 4.1

Write a program to explain working of stack using array implementation.

Solution

```
# include <stdio.h>
# include <conio.h>
# include <process.h>

main ()
{
   int j,stack[5]={0};
   int p=0;
   clrscr();
   printf ("Enter Elements, put zero to exit: \n");

      while (1)
      {
      scanf ("%d",&stack[p]);
      if (stack[p]==0)
      {
            printf ("\n By choice terminated: ");
            exit(0);
      }
      p++;

      if (p>4)
      {
            printf ("Stack is full \n");
            break;
      }
      else
      printf ("Stack is empty\n");
}

   printf ("\n Elements of stack are: ");
   for (j=0;j<5;j++)
   printf (" %d ",stack[j]);
}
```

Explanation In this program an array *stack [5]* is declared. Using *while* loop, elements are read through the keyboard and placed in an array. The value of variable *p* is initially zero. The variable *p* increases in every iteration. The variable *p* acts as a top of stack. The if statement checks the value of *p*. If the value of *p* is greater than four it means that, the stack is full and no more elements can be added. When value of *p* is less than four it means more elements can be inserted in the stack. The *for* loop and printf statements display the array elements. In stack random insertion or deletion of element is not possible (Though in array it is possible, but here keep in mind that we are treating an array as a stack. Hence, we have to follow the restrictions that exist in stack implementation). If we want to delete any particular element, we have to delete every element present before that element. Program 4.2 explains deletion of elements.

```
OUTPUT
Enter Elements, put zero to exit:
4
Stack is empty
2
Stack is empty
6
Stack is empty
8
Stack is empty
3
Stack is full
Elements of stack are: 4 2 6 8 3
```

Example 4.2

Write a program to store elements in the stack. Delete the specified element.

Solution

```
# include <stdio.h>
# include <conio.h>
main ()
{
   int j,stack[5];
   int p=0;
   clrscr();
   printf ("Enter Elements put zero to exit: \n");

      while (1)
      {
      scanf ("%d",&stack[p]);
      if (stack[p]==0)
      break;
      p++;

         if (p>4)
         {
         printf ("Stack is full \n"); break;
      }
   }

   printf ("\nStack elements are: ");

      for (j=0;j<5;j++)
      printf (" %d ",stack[j]);
      printf ("\n Enter element position to delete: ");
```

Explanation In this program, as usual, elements are entered and stored in the stack. The element number that is to be deleted from the stack will be entered from the keyboard. Recall that in a stack, before deleting any element, it is compulsory to delete all elements before that element. In this program, the elements before a target element are replaced with value NULL (0). The elements after target element are kept as it is. Recall that when an element is inserted in the stack the operation is called *"push."* When an element is deleted from the stack the operation is *"pop"*. Program 4.3 explains the *push* and *pop* operations.

```
        scanf ("%d",&p);
        p--;
        for (j=4;j>=p;j--)
        stack[j]=NULL;
        printf ("Stack elements are: ");

        for (j=0;j<5;j++)
        printf (" %d ",stack[j]);
        getch();
}
```

```
OUTPUT
Enter Elements put zero to exit:
8
9
4
5
3
Stack is full
Stack elements are: 8 9 4 5 3
Enter element position to delete: 3
Stack elements are: 8 9 0 0 0
```

Example 4.3

Write a simple program to demonstrate push () and pop () operations

Solution

```
# include <stdio.h>
# include <conio.h>

static int stack[10], top=-1;

main ()
{
   void push(int);
   void pop(void);
   void show(void);
   clrscr();
   printf ("\n\n push operation: ");

   push(5);
   show();
   push(8);
   show();
   push(9);
```

Explanation In this program *stack []* and *top* variables are declared as static. The variable *top* is initialized with –1. It is not necessary to declare *top* as static. The *push ()* operation inserts an element into the stack. The next element pushed is displayed after the first element and so on. The *pop ()* operation removes the element from the stack. The last element inserted is firstly deleted. In the output the element 9 is deleted first as it is entered at last. Then, element 8 is removed. At last, the stack holds only one element having number 5.

```
    show();
    printf ("\n\n pop operation: ");
    show();
    pop();
    show();
    pop();
    show();
}

void push (int j)
{
    top++;
    stack[top]=j;
}

void pop ()
{
    stack[top]=0;
    top--;
}

void show ()
{
    int j;
    printf ("\n stack elements are: ");
    for (j=0;j<10;j++)
        stack[j]!=0 ? printf (" %d ",stack[j]): printf("");
}
```

```
OUTPUT
push operation:
stack elements are: 5
stack elements are: 5 8
stack elements are: 5 8 9

pop operation:
stack elements are: 5 8 9
stack elements are: 5 8
Stack elements are: 5
```

Example 4.4

Write a program to perform *pop* and *push* operation on the stack.

Solution

```
# include <stdio.h>
```

```
# include <conio.h>
# include <process.h>

int ch,p,z=6,top=0,stack[7],c;

main()
{
   void make ();
   void push();
   void pop();
   void show();
   clrscr();
   while(ch<5)
   {
      printf("\n1] Stack creation");
      printf("\n2] Insert element");
      printf("\n3] Delete Element");
      printf("\n4] Display Element");
      printf("\n5] Exit\n");
      printf("Enter the choice:- ");
      scanf("%d",&ch);

      switch(ch)

      {
         case 1: make();
         continue;
         case 2: push();
         continue;
         case 3: pop();
         continue;
         case 4: show ();
         continue;
         default: exit(0);
      }
   }
}

void make ()
{
      printf("\n Enter number of elements in the stack (<7): ");
      scanf("%d",&c);
      for (top=0;top<c;++top)
      {
         printf("Enter Element[%d]:- ",top);
         scanf("%d",&stack[top]);
      }
```

Explanation In this program few variables and array *stack []* are declared globally so that every program can access them. Functions *make (), push (), void pop ()* and *void show ()* are defined. When the user selects first option, the user is prompted to enter the number of elements. Immediately followed by this, the user has to enter choice by entering the integer number. These integers are stored in the array *stack []*. The user can see the stack elements by selecting fourth choice on the screen. When delete operation is performed, the top element of the stack is deleted. The user can confirm this operation by selecting display element operation. When insert operation is selected, the entered element is inserted at the top of the stack. The global variable top keeps track of the total number of elements present in the stack.

```
}

void push ()
{
   if (top>=z)
   {
         printf("\n Stack is full ");
         getch();
   }
   else
   {
         printf("\n Enter number to be pushed:- ");
         scanf("%d",&stack[top]);
         top++;
   }
}

void pop ()
{
      if (top<=0)
      {
         printf("\nThe stack is empty ");
         getch();
      }
   else
   top--;
}

void show ()
{
      for (p=top-1;p>=0;--p)
      printf(" %d ",stack[p]);
}
```

OUTPUT

```
1] Stack creation
2] Insert element
3] Delete Element
4] Display Element
5] Exit
1

 Enter number of elements in the stack (<7): 4
 Enter Elements: 1 2 3 4
1] Stack creation
2] Insert element
```

```
3] Delete Element
4] Display Element
5] Exit
4
0 4 3 2 1

1] Stack creation
2] Insert element
3] Delete Element
4] Display Element
5] Exit
```

Example 4.5

Write a program to create a class stack and define member function push () and pop ().

Solution

```
# include <stdio.h>
# include <conio.h>

int stacks[10];
int top;

main ()
{
    void show(void);
    void push (int j);
    void pop ();
    int n,j;
    top=-1;
    stacks[10]=NULL;
    clrscr();
    printf("\nInsert four element in stack");
    printf("\npush operation: ");
    push(2);
    push(5);
    push(8);
    push(3);
    show();
    printf("\n\nDeleting two elements from the stack");
    printf("\npop operation: ");
    pop();
    pop();
    show();
}
```

Explanation In this program an array *stack* is declared. Both two *array* variables, *stacks [10]* and *top*, are static and they are initialized. Three-functions *push (), pop ()* and *show ()* are defined. Invoking *push ()* function elements are pushed. The *pop ()* operation removes the elements. The *show ()* function displays the elements of stack.

```
   void push (int j)
   {
      top++;
      stacks[top]=j;

      }

void pop ()
{

   stacks[top]=0;
   top--;
}

void show ()
{
   int j;
   for ( j=0;j<=top;j++)
   printf(" %d",stacks[j]);
 }
```

```
OUTPUT
Insert four element in stack
push operation: 2 5 8 3
Deleting two elements from the stack
pop operation: 2 5
```

4.5 POINTERS AND STACK

We are already aware that array name itself is a pointer. Pointer implementation of a stack carried out is similar to array implementation. Stack is particularly straightforward version of linked lists. The implementation of array-like elements can be done using pointer. Like array, elements can be stored in successive memory location using pointer. First, we learn a simple program to create stack using pointer instead of array.

Example 4.6

Write a program to create an array-like list of integers using pointer.

Solution

```
# include <stdio.h>
# include <conio.h>

main()
{
```

```
    int *p,j,e;
    clrscr();
    printf ("\n Enter five Integers: ");
    for (e=4;e>=0;e--)
    scanf ("%d",(p+e));
    for (e=0;e<5;e++)
    printf ("%d ",*(p+e));

}

OUTPUT
Enter five Integers: 4 5 8 7 5
5 7 8 5 4
```

Explanation In this program a pointer **p* is declared. The first for loop is used to read numbers in association with *scanf()* statement. The value of variable *e* is added to the address of pointer *p*, so that successive locations are accessed and the number is placed in the location. For displaying elements, same logic is applied.

Example 4.7

Write a program to implement stack operation push and pop with pointer.

Solution

```
# include <stdio.h>
# include <conio.h>
# include <stdlib.h>

    struct stack
    {
    int num;
    struct stack *next;
       } *T=0;

       typedef struct stack it;

       void push ();
       int pop();
       void show ();

       main ()
       {
       char chr;
       int opt,no;

          do
          {
          clrscr();
          printf ("\n 1: push ");
          printf ("\n 2: pop ");
          printf ("\n 3: show ");
```

Explanation In this program the structure stack is defined with variables *num* and a pointer variable **next* of stack (itself) type. Later **T* a pointer is declared. The prototype declaration of *pop (), push ()* and *show ()* is done. The user is asked to entered option and the entered option number is passed to *switch ()* case structure to execute the anticipated option. The user has to press *'y'* to continue the program, else if other alphabet is entered, the program will terminate.

```
        printf ("\n >3: exit");
        printf ("\n Enter your option: ");
        scanf ("%d",&opt);

            switch(opt)
    {
        case 1: push (); break;
        case 2: no = pop ();
        printf ("\n The delete number was %d ", no);
        break;
        case 3: show (); break;
        default: printf ("\n Good Bye ");
        exit(0);
    }

        printf ("\n Continue (y/n )" );
        fflush(stdin);
        chr=getche();

    }  while (chr=='Y' || chr=='y');
}

void push()
{
    it *node;
    node=(it*) malloc(sizeof(it));
    printf ("\n Enter the number ");
    scanf ("%d",&node->num);
    node->next=T;
    T=node;
}

int pop ()
{
    it *temp;
    temp=T;

        if (T==NULL)
        {
        puts ("\n Stack underflow ");
        getch();
        exit(0);
    }

    else
    {
```

```
        T=T->next;
        free(temp);
    }
    return (temp->num);
}


void show ()
{
    it *tmp;
    tmp=T;

    while (tmp->next !=NULL)
    {
        printf (" %d ", tmp->num);
        tmp=tmp->next;
    }
    printf (" %d ", tmp->num);
}
```

```
OUTPUT
1: push
2: pop
3: show
>3: exit
Enter your option: 3
7 2
Continue (y/n)
```

In the *push ()* function, it is a custom data type created with typedef statement. The variable **node* is variable of type structure stack. The *malloc ()* function is used to allocate memory to **node* pointer equal to the size of structure variable. The element entered immediately by the user is stored in allocated memory. The number is stored in the num variable and the *T* is assigned to *node->next*.

In *pop ()* function, another variable tmp is declared. If the *T* is NULL, i.e. the stack is still underflow and we can continue the push operation. Otherwise, the free function de-allocates the memory of last element pointed by next. When the memory is de-allocated the element also is destroyed. The *show ()* function is used to print the elements. This is achieved using while loop.

4.6 REPRESENTATION OF ARITHMETIC EXPRESSIONS

An arithmetic expression contains operators and operands. Variables and constants are operands. The operators are of various kinds such as arithmetic binary, unary for example, + (addition), – (subtraction), *(multiplication), / (division) and % (modular division). The following Table 4.1 describes types of operators and the Fig. 4.7 shows the numbers of operators.

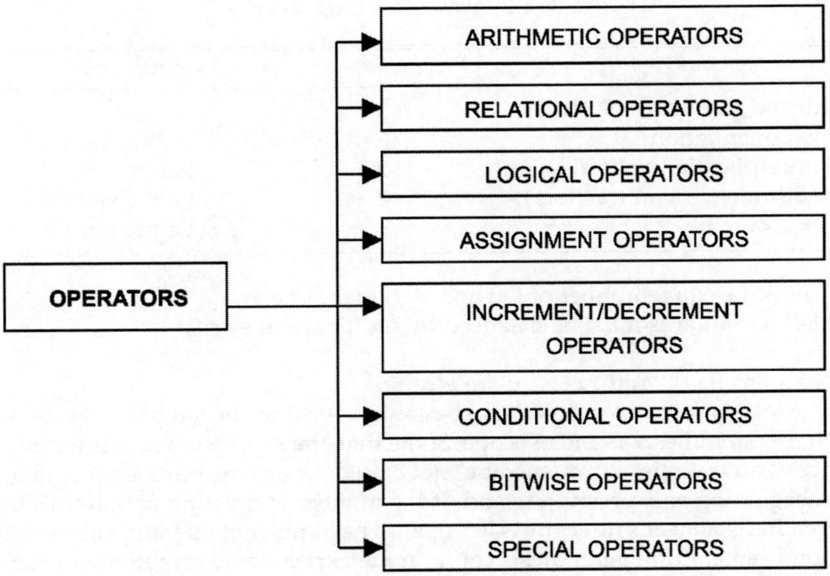

Figure 4.7 Types of operators

Table 4.1 Operators and its symbolic representation

<table>
<tr><th>Types of operators</th><th>Symbolic representation</th></tr>
<tr><td>Arithmetic operators</td><td>+,-, *, / and %</td></tr>
<tr><td>Relational operators</td><td>>, <, =, ==, >=, <= and !=</td></tr>
<tr><td>Logical operators</td><td>&&, | |, !</td></tr>
<tr><td>Increment/decrement operators</td><td>++, —</td></tr>
<tr><td>Assignment operators</td><td>=</td></tr>
<tr><td>Bitwise operators</td><td>&, |, ^, >>, <<, ~</td></tr>
<tr><td>Special operators</td><td>, (comma)</td></tr>
<tr><td>Conditional operators</td><td>?:</td></tr>
</table>

The precedence of operator also plays an important role in expression solving. The precedence of operators is given in Table 4.2.

We have already studied the different stack operations. Now, we will study how stack can be useful in problem solving. Consider a mathematical expression.

5 - ((*A* * ((*B* + *K*)/ (*U*-4))+*K*) / 8 (8-4.3))

The common mistake, which can be made frequently by the programmer, is unbalance of parenthesis. For correct representation of mathematical expression, the following precautions must be taken:

Table 4.2 Precedence of operators

Operators	Precedence	Associativity
+ (unary), - (unary), NOT	6	—
^ (Exponentiation)	6	Right to left
* (multiplication), / (division)	5	Left to right
+ (addition), - (subtraction)	4	Left to right
<,<=,+,<,>,>=	3	Left to right

1. There must be equal number of left and right parenthesis.
2. Each left parenthesis must be balanced by right parenthesis.

The expressions ((*x*+*y*) and) *x*+*y* (-u are wrong.

Thus, by using stack such a problem can be solved. Assume the left parenthesis as opening scope and right parenthesis as end of scope. Some time the expression contains nested parenthesis, hence various scopes are opened but not closed. Count the number of opening parenthesis from beginning of expression to end. If the number of opening parenthesis is equal to closing parenthesis it means no scope is left open. The number of opening and closing parenthesis is found same. If the parenthesis count in the expression is negative, it means a right parenthesis is found, but no left parenthesis of its pair is defined.

```
( ( x + y )
1 2 1
```

In the above example, when opening parenthesis is encountered, counter is incremented and when closing parenthesis is encountered, counter is decremented.

```
) x + y ( - z
-1 0
```

In the above example, when the first closing parenthesis is encountered, the counter is decremented.

```
5 - ( ( A * ( ( B + K ) / ( U-4 ) ) + K ) / 8 ( 8-4.3 ) )
0 1 2 3 4 3 4 3 2 1 2 1 0
```

In the above example the opening and closing parenthesis are balanced.

Example 4.8

Write a program to count opening and closing parenthesis and test the expression having balanced parenthesis or not.

Solution

```
# include <stdio.h>
# include <conio.h>
```

```
int stack[10];
int top=9;

main()
{
     int c=0,p=0;
     char exp[]="(p+(q-(m+n))*j-((x+y)))/(j-(k-(-k(l-n))))";

     clrscr();
     printf("\n%s\n",exp);

     while (exp[c]!='\0')
     {
     switch(exp[c])
     {
        case '{':
        case '(':
        case '[':
        p++;
        printf("%d",p);
        break;

        case '}':
        case ')':
        case ']':
        p--;
        printf("%d",p);
        break;
        default:
        printf("%d",p);
     }

     c++;
  }

}
```

Explanation In this program whatever we discussed in last paragraph are applied practically. When an opening parenthesis is found counter *p* is incremented and when closing parenthesis is found counter is decremented. The counter value is displayed in the output. In the above program if expressions *")p+(p+q)"* are entered the output will be *-1-1-10000-1*. So far, we used only one type of parenthesis, i.e. (). In expression other type of parenthesis like {}, [] can be used. In such case, it is necessary to keep record of not only number of opening and closing braces but also their type. The stack can be used in such application.

```
OUTPUT
(p+(q-(m+n))*j-((x+y)))/(j-(k-(-k(l-n))))
11122233332111123333210000111222333444443210
```

When an opening parenthesis is found it is pushed into the stack. When a closing parenthesis is found the pop operation is carried and it is tested, the deleted parenthesis corresponds to the opening parenthesis. If the opening and closing parentheses match, the program will continue otherwise the entered string is invalid. When the end of string is found, the stack must be empty. If the stack contains elements, it means there is opening parenthesis that had not been closed.

Consider the following expression.

{p+(q-[m+n])*j-[(x+y)]}/ (j-(k-(k-[l-n])))

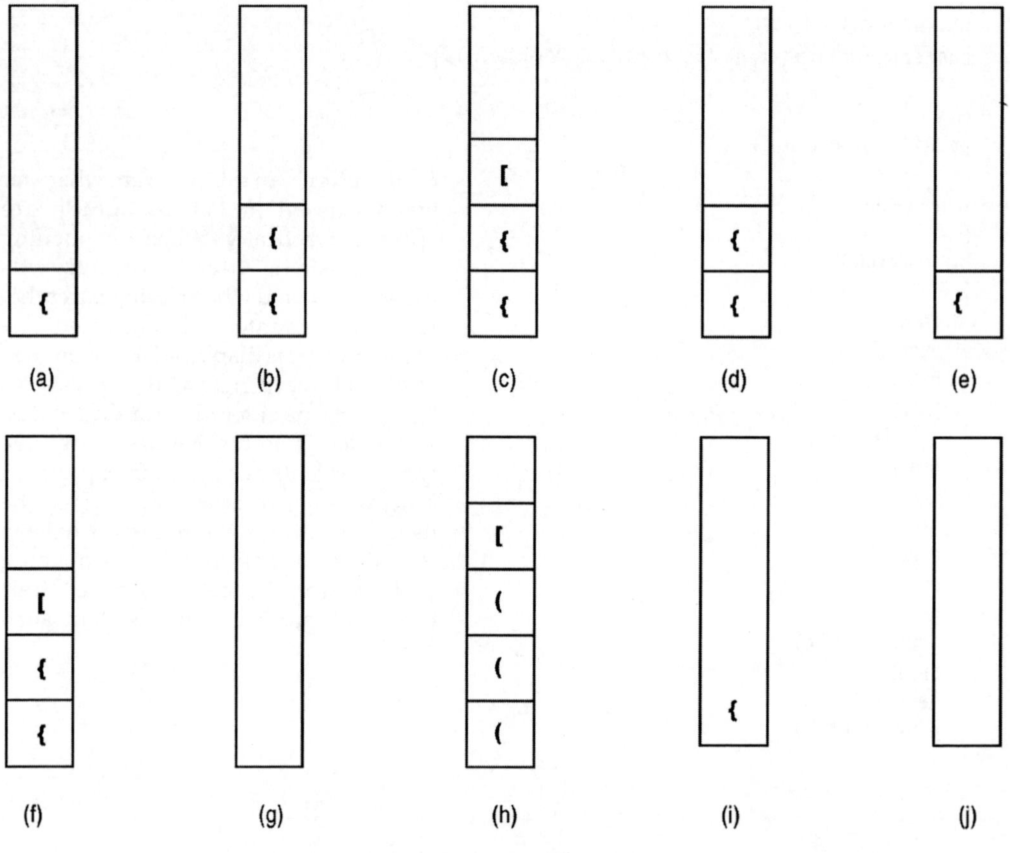

Figure 4.8 Different views of stack

As soon as the opening parenthesis of types (, {or [is encountered it is pushed on to the stack. We can see this in the figure 4.8 (a), (b) and (c). When a closing parenthesis is found the top element of the stack is popped. Only when the encountered closing bracket and the top element of the stack matching, i.e. {}, () and []. We can observe this in figure 4.8 (d) and (e). In Fig. 4.8(g) the stack is empty because there expression up to {*p*+(*q*-[*m*+*n*])*j-[(*x*+*y*)]} is read. The number of opening and closing brackets are same. Hence, the expression is correct. When an element remains in the stack, it means the expression is wrong and parentheses are not properly closed. Again, the expression is read and same push and pop procedure is applied. The remaining expression (*j*- (*k*-(*k*-[*l*-*n*]))) is read.

Example 4.9

Write a program to compare opening and closing brackets.

Solution

```
# include <stdio.h>
# include <conio.h>

char stack[15];
int t=14;

main()
{
   void pop(void);
   void show (void);
   void push (char);

   char exp[20];
   int j=0,b=0;
   clrscr();

   printf ("\n Enter an Expression: ");
   scanf ("%s",exp);

   while (exp[j]!='\0')
   {
      switch(exp[j])
      {
         case '{':
         case '(':
         case '[':
         push (exp[j]);
         show();
         b++;
         break;

      case '}':

      if (stack[t+1]=='{')
      {
         pop();
         b--;
         }
      else
      printf ("\n Error in expression");
      break;
```

Explanation An entered expression by the user is stored in the array *exp []*. Using *while loop* the entire string (expression) is scanned. The *switch ()* case structure within while loop is used to check different conditions. If any opening bracket comes across, it is pushed on to the stack by invoking *push ()* function, i.e. the meet opening bracket is stored in the array stack using *push ()* function.

```
    case ')':

    if(stack[t+1]=='(')
    {
          pop();
          b--;
    }
    else
    printf ("\n No matching opening and closing brackets");
    break;

    case ']':

    if(stack[t+1]=='[')
    {
          pop();
          b--;
    }
    else
        printf ("\n No matching opening and closing brackets");
    break;
   }

j++;
}

if (b==0)
       printf ("\n Expression is correct");
       else
       printf ("\n %d closing brackets are not closed",b);
 show();
}

void push ( char c)
{
   stack[t]=c;
   t--;
}

void pop ( )
{
   t++;
   stack[t]=NULL;
}

void show ()
```

```
{
    int k;
    printf("\n");
    for (k=0;k<=14;k++)
    printf("%c",stack[k]);
}
```

OUTPUT

1)

```
Enter an Expression: {(a+b)}

  {
  ({
Expression is correct
```

2)

```
Enter an Expression: {(a+b}

  {
  ({
Error in expression
2 closing brackets are not closed
  ({
```

We know that in any valid expression, the first opened parenthesis is closed lastly and the lastly opened parenthesis is closed first, i.e. the parenthesis arrangement is like stack mechanism first-in-last-out. The encountered opening parenthesis are pushed onto the stack. When closing parenthesis of same type is found the item is popped from the stack. Thus, matching pairs of parenthesis are checked. If no match is found, the error will be displayed. In case an opening parenthesis does not have closing parenthesis, the message displayed will be "Error in expression".

4.7 INFIX, PREFIX AND POSTFIX NOTATIONS

This topic illustrates an important application of different kinds of stacks, various operations defined upon them and compilation of infix expressions. Stack has various real life applications. Stack is very useful to keep sequence of processing. In solving arithmetic expressions, stacks are used. Stacks are used to convert bases of numbers. In a large program, various functions are invoked by the *main ()* function; all these functions are stacked in the memory. Most of the calculators work on stack mechanism.

Arithmetic expressions can be defined in three kinds of notation: infix, prefix and postfix. The prefixes in, pre and post indicate the relative location of the operator with two operands.

Infix Notation Expressions are generally expressed in infix notation with binary operator between the operands. The binary operator means the operator requires two operands such as +, *, / and %. In this type, the operator precedes the operands. Following are examples of infix notation:

1. *x+y*
2. *x+y*z*
3. *(x+y)*z*
4. *(x+y)*(p+q)*

Every single letter (*A-Z*) and an unsigned integer is a legal infix expression. If *X* and *Y* are two valid expressions then (*X+Y*), then (*X–Y*) and (*X/Y*) are legal infix expressions.

Prefix Notation The prefix notation is also called polish notation. The polish mathematician Lukasiewicx invented it. In this type also the operator precedes the operands. Following are the examples of prefix notation:

1. *+xy*
2. *+x*yz*
3. **+xyz*
4. **+xy+pq*

Postfix Notation The postfix notation is also called as reverse polish notation. The operator trails the operand. Following are the examples of postfix notation:

1. *xy+*
2. *xyz*+*
3. *xy+z**
4. *xy+pq*+*

Consider the following example:

X+Y*Z

In the above expression, we know that the multiplication has higher precedence than addition. The expression X+(Y*Z) is same as the expression X+Y*Z. By applying rules of priority, we can convert the above expression to postfix notation.

*X+(Y*Z)*

Here, parentheses are not necessary.

X+(YZ)*

Here, multiplication is converted to postfix.

X(YZ)+*

Here, addition is converted to postfix.

XYZ+*

The above equation is postfix form. While doing the conversion operations, following points are important.

1. When we convert an expression from prefix to postfix form, it is essential that properties like, precedence, commutability and well-formed expressions of operators must be preserved.

2. The operations with high priority are converted first and after the remaining part of the expression are converted to postfix form. Table 4.3 shows infix to postfix of an expression. The remaining part is considered as a single operand.

Table 4.3 Infix to postfix

Infix	*Postfix*
X+Y	XY+

Here, *XY* is considered as single operand.

3. In suffix and prefix equivalent of an infix expressions, the variables must be in the relative place. The expressions in prefix or suffix are without parenthesis. The operators are set according to precedence rule of operators.
4. A fully parenthesized infix expression converted directly to postfix form, starting the conversion from innermost parenthesis to outer most parenthesis. For example

$(X + Y + (P + Q + (T+Y)))$

The innermost parenthesis ($T+Y$) is solved first.

The precedence can be changed on purpose by insertion of parenthesis. Consider the following example:

$(X+Y)*Z$

In the above example, if parenthesis is not inserted the multiplication operation gets first priority. Due to parenthesis the addition operation gets first priority.

$(XY+)*Z$

Here, the addition is converted in the postfix form.

$(XY+)Z*$

Here, the multiplication is converted to postfix form.

There are five binary operations such as addition (+), subtraction (–), multiplication (*), division (/) and exponentiation. In C/C++, there is no exponentiation operator. Here, ^ is used to denote exponent operation.

The equation X^Y means X raised to Y. 2^ 3 means 8. When any expression is without parenthesis the order of operation is left to right. Only in exponent the order is from right to left.

X+Y+Z means (X+Y)+Z, on the other hand X^Y^Z means X^(Y^Z). The operation inside the parenthesis gets first priority. Consider the following Table 4.4 which converts infix to postfix to make your understanding perfect.

Table 4.4 Infix to postfix.

Infix	*Postfix*
X+Y	XY+
X+Y–Z	XY+Z–
(X+Y)*(P–Q)	XY+PQ–*
L^M*N–O+P/Q/(R+S)	LM^N*O–PQ/RS+/+
((L+M)*N–(O–P)^(Q+R)	LM+N*OP—QR+^
L-M/(N*O^P)	LMNOP^*/–

For converting an expression from infix to prefix the rules are same as like conversion from infix to postfix. In the prefix conversion the operator is placed before the operand. The Table 4.5 converts the infix expression to the prefix.

Table 4.5 Infix to prefix

Infix	*Prefix*
X+Y	+XY
X+Y–Z	–+XYZ
(X+Y)*(P–Q)	*+XY–PQ
L^M*N–O+P/Q/(R+S)	+–*^LMNO//PQ+RS
((L+M)*N–(O–P)^(Q+R)	^–*+LMN–OP+QR
L–M/(N*O^P)	–L/M*N^OP

The postfix form doesn't require parenthesis. Consider the following expressions:

X+(*Y** *Z*) and (*X*+*Y*)* *Z*

Table 4.6 Postfix

Infix	*Postfix*
X+(Y*Z)	XYZ*+
(X+Y)*Z	XY+Z*

You can see the above Table 4.6 that the postfix expressions have no parenthesis. In the postfix expressions, sequence or precedence of operators decides sequence of operation.

While converting infix expression to postfix, it is difficult to know the operation associated with operand.

To write a valid expression whole parenthesization should be applied. However, the parenthesis must not be large. The expression (*X*+*Y*)*Z is valid expression and need not be written like ((*X*+*Y*)*Z). Here, the outer parenthesis can be omitted and has no purpose. Consider the following expression. The above expression can be written as (*P*+(*Q***R*))+(*S***T*). To evaluate the expression it must be scanned from left to right. Fig. 4.9 illustrates the expression.

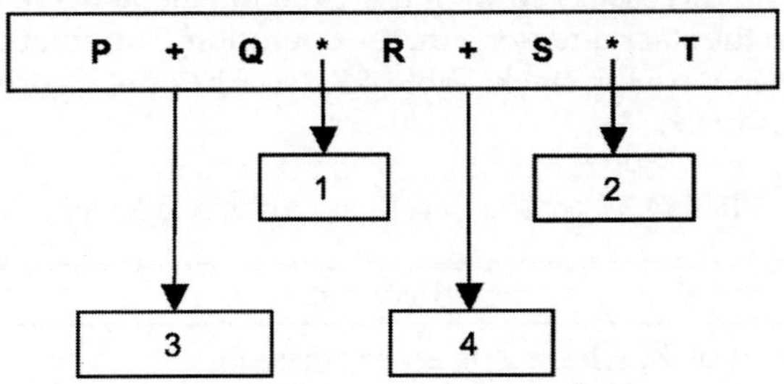

Figure 4.9 Expression and operation precedence rank

If parentheses are present in the expression, then the precedence will be changed. For example, in expression (*P*+*Q*)**R*, first *P*+*Q* is solved and then multiplication takes place. Actually, it is possible to declare an expression that makes the sequence of evaluation of expression independent of the priority of the operators. This can be done by putting sub-expressions in the parentheses. The operators and operands are enclosed in the parentheses. Thus, we have several parenthetical levels as shown in the Fig. 4.10. Such expressions are called *fully parenthesized expressions*. Consider the following example,

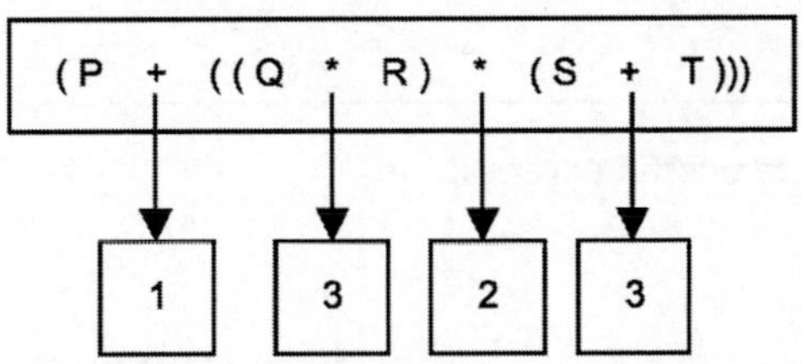

Figure 4.10 Fully parenthesized expressions

The numbers indicate parenthetical level of operators. When such an expression is solved, the sub-expression having the operator with top parenthetical level is solved first. When two parentheses have equal parenthetical levels, the left-sided parentheses are evaluated first. Followed by parenthesis 2 and 1.

In case the expression is partially parenthesized, a repetitive scanning from left to right is essential to evaluate the expressions. This is because the operators present in conjunction with the operands within the expression. The scanning is shunned in case the infix expression is converted to postfix or prefix expression.

4.8 EVALUATION OF POSTFIX EXPRESSION

The postfix expressions are very simple. On the other hand, programming of evaluation of expression is complicated. This is because the numbers and characters are mixed in one string. The programmer needs to separate digits and symbols and perform arithmetic operation.

Each operator in the postfix expression is associated with the previous two operands. When we read an operand from a given expression it is pushed onto the stack. When an operator symbol is read, the operands associated with it are the top elements of the stack. We can pop these two elements from the stack and perform the operation. The obtained result from the last operation is again pushed onto the stack. Table 4.7 describes the algorithm for conversion of the infix expression to postfix.

Table 4.7 Algorithm for conversion of infix to postfix

Algorithm
1. Insert *a* ')' at the end of X, where X is an expression
2. Check X from left to right and go back over the next 3 and 4 steps for every element of X until ')' is found.
3. In case operands are found, push it on the stack.
4. a. If any operator is found, pop the top-most two elements from stack. b. Evaluate the expression formed by top two elements. c. Push the result obtained onto the stack.
5. Allocate value equal to top stack element.
6 Quit.

Example 4.10

Write a program to evaluate postfix expressions.

Solution

```
# include <stdio.h>
# include <conio.h>
# include <ctype.h>
# include <math.h>

   float stack[10];
   int top=-1;
   void push(char);
   float pop();
   float exp_eval(char[],float[]);

main ()
{
```

Explanation In this program before *main ()* function, the float type array *stack [10]* and integer variable *top* are defined. They are initialized with –1. The prototype of functions *push (), pop ()* and *exp_val ()* are declared. User has to enter expression and the *gets ()* function activates the input stream and the entered expression is stored in the *s_fix[]* character array.

```
    int j=0;
    char s_fix[20];
    float number[20],res;
    clrscr();
    printf ("\n Enter a postfix expression: ");
    gets(s_fix);

        while (s_fix[j]!='\0')
        {
        if(isalpha(s_fix[j]))
        {
            fflush(stdin);
            printf ("\n Enter number for %c: ",s_fix[j]);
            scanf ("%f",&number[j]);
        }
        j++;
    }

    res=exp_eval(s_fix, number);
    printf("The res of %s =%f", s_fix,res);
    getch();
}

float exp_eval( char s_fix[], float data[])
{
    int j=0;
    float opA,opB,fs;
    char ch;

    while (s_fix[j]!='\0')
    {
        ch=s_fix[j];
        if (isalpha(s_fix[j]))
        {
            push(data[j]);
        }
        else
        {
            opB=pop();
            opA=pop();

                switch(ch)
                {
                case '+': push(opA+opB); break;
                case '-': push(opA-opB); break;
                case '*': push(opA*opB); break;
                case '/': push(opA/opB); break;
```

```
            case '^': push(pow(opA,opB)); break;
        }
        }
        j++;
    }
  fs=pop();
  return(fs);
}


void push (char c)
{
  top=++top;
  stack[top]=c;
}

 float pop()
{
  float n;
  n=stack[top];
  top=--top;
  return(n);
}

OUTPUT
Enter a postfix expression: jk*
Enter number for j: 4
Enter number for k: 5
The res of jk* =20.000000
```

The expression is checked and for every alphabet user has to enter a number. Immediately after this, the function *exp_eval ()* is invoked with two arguments, i.e. *s_fix* and *number*. Both the arguments are array *name* and holds base address. This function returns result and is stored in variable res.

In the *exp_eval ()* function the variable *ch* holds the arithmetic operation. The *switch ()* case structure determines the operation to be carried out. The *pop ()* function is invoked and the two popped values are stored in variables *popB* and *popA*. These variables are passed to *push ()* function in *switch ()* case structure.

4.9 CONVERSION OF EXPRESSION FROM INFIX TO POSTFIX

In any expression, there are two types of components clubbed together. They are operand and operators. The operator indicates the operation to be carried out and the operand indicates the values. The operands are the variables on which the operator operates. Operators have their priority of execution. When one or more operations are clubbed together in a single expression the priority decides which operation is to be performed first. Suppose, an expression contain two operations with high and low priority. We can force the low priority operation to evaluate first by putting that particular operation in parenthesis. When nested parenthesis are present in the expression the inner-most parenthesis is solved first. In any expression the parenthesis are solved first. The operations are generally solved from left to right. Table 4.8 shows the operator precedence.

Table 4.8 For operator precedence

Operator	*Precedence*
Exponent	High
Multiplication (*), Division (/)	Next
Addition (+), Subtraction (–)	Low

Consider the following example:

*x-y/(p^q)+(u*v)*

The operators are -,/,^,+,* and *x,y,p,q,u* and *v* are variables. The parenthesis are used to provide higher priority to the operation (*p^q*) and (*u*v*).

Consider the example

Expression: *X+Y*Z*

Table 4.9 Conversion of X+Y*Z into postfix

Character	*Postfix string*	*Stack*
X	X	
+	X	+
Y	XY	+
*	XY	+*
Z	XYZ	+*
	XYZ*	+
	XYZ*+	

The expression is scanned and when operators are found, they are pushed on the stack. The operators are pushed according to priority of execution of the stack. When operator + is found it is pushed onto the stack. The precedence of * is higher than +. The symbol * is pushed onto the stack. At last, when string reaches to end the stack is popped and its content is appended to the postfix string. These operations are illustrated in Table 4.9.

Expression: $(P+Q)*C$

Table 4.10 Conversion of (P+Q)*C into postfix

Character	*Postfix string*	*Stack*
(		(
P	P	(
+	P	(+
Q	PQ	(+
)	PQ+	
*	PQ+	*
R	PQ+R	*
	PQ+R*	

In the above example, opening parenthesis is found. Until the left parenthesis is not found the entire stack is popped. Here, the parentheses provide first priority to addition. Table 4.10 explains the conversion. Table 4.11 describes the algorithm for infix to postfix.

Table 4.11 Algorithm for conversion infix expression into postfix

Algorithm for Conversion of Infix Expression to Postfix
1. Push to the end of X, where X is an arithmetic expression. 2. Check expression from left to right and follow the steps 3 to 6 for every element of X until the stack is vacant. 3. In case an operand is found, add it to R, where R is the equivalent postfix expression. 4. In case left '(' parenthesis is found push it onto stack. 5. In case an operator is found, then follow the following steps: a. Continually pop from the stack and add each operator to R at the top of stack. The pushed item should have same or upper precedence than the former operator encountered. b. Append operator (recently encountered) onto stack. 6. In case ')' right parenthesis is found, then follow the following steps: a. Continually pop from the stack and append to every operator to R until left parenthesis is found. b. Eliminate the left parenthesis.

Example 4.11

Write a program to convert infix expression to postfix form.

Solution

```
# include <stdio.h>
# include <conio.h>
# include <string.h>
# include <process.h>
```

```
char stack[20];
int T=-1;

void topost(char in_fix[]);
void push(char);
char pop();

main()
{
  char in_fix[25];
  clrscr();
  puts (" Enter an infix expressions: ");
  gets(in_fix);
   puts ("\n Postfix Expression: ");
  topost(in_fix);
}

void push (char s)
{
  if (T>=19)
  {
  puts (" Stack overflow ");
  exit(0);
  }
 else
 {
  T=T+1;
  stack[T]=s;
  }
}

char pop ()
{
  char num;


if (T==-1)
{
  puts (" Stack is Empty ");
  getch();
  return (0);
}
else
{
  num=stack[T];
  T--;
}
```

Explanation In this program an infix expression is converted to postfix form. The prototype of function *topost (), push ()* and *pop ()* are declared. The array *stack [20]* is declared. In addition, the integer variable *T* is declared and initialized with –1. In function *main (),* a character array *in_fix[]* is declared. The infix expression is entered by the user. The function *topost ()* is invoked and *in_fix* is sent as an argument.

```
return (num);
}

int prefix (char ch)
{
   if(ch=='/') return (5);
   else if (ch=='*') return (4);
   else if (ch=='+') return (3);
   else return (2);
}

void topost (char in_fix[])
{
   int len;
   static int index=0,pos=0;
   char s,t;
   char postfix[40];
   len=strlen(in_fix);
   push('#');

while(index<len)
{
   s=in_fix[index];

   switch(s)
{
   case '(': push(s); break;
    case ')': t=pop();

    while (t!='(')
    {
       postfix[pos]=t;
       pos++;
       t=pop();
    }

    break;
    case '+':
    case '-':
    case '*':
    case '/':
    case '^':

   while (prefix(stack[T])>prefix(s))
   {
      t=pop();
      postfix[pos]=t;
```

```
        pos++;
    }

    push (s); break;
    default: postfix[pos++]=s; break;
    }
    index++;
    }

    while (T>0)
    {
    t=pop();
    postfix[pos++]=t;
    }
    postfix[pos++]='\0';
    puts(postfix);
    return;
}
```

```
OUTPUT
Enter an infix expressions: m+s+p
Postfix Expression: msp++
```

In the function *topost ()*, length of *in_fix* array is counted. Using *push ()* function '#' is pushed. The integer variable index is initialized to zero. The *while* loop executes until the value of index is less than len. The variable *s* contains the value of *in_fix[index]* character. If the value of *s* is '(', it is pushed and if it contains ')' and *pop ()* function is executed. The variable *s* is passed to *switch ()* case statement. Accordingly, case statements are executed.

4.10 APPLICATIONS OF STACKS

Few applications of stack are narrated together with examples.

4.10.1 Reverse String

We know the stack is based on last-in-first-out rule. It can be achieved simply by pushing each character of the string onto the stack. The same can be popped in reverse fashion. Thus, reverse string can be done. Consider the following program.

Example 4.12

Write a program to reverse the string using stack.

Solution

```
# include <stdio.h>
# include <conio.h>
```

```
char text[40];
void main ()
{
 char ch;
 void push (char,int);
 char pop(int);
 int j=39,k;
 clrscr();
 puts ("\n Enter a string (* to end): ");

while (ch!='*' && j>=0)
{
 ch=getche();
 push (ch,j);
  j--;
}
k=j;
j=0;

printf ("\n Reverse string is: ");

while (k!=40)
{
 ch=pop(k);
 printf ("%c",ch);
  k++;
}
}
void push ( char c, int j)
{
 if (c!='*')
 text[j]=c;
}

char pop (int j)
{
 char c;
 c=text[j];
 text[j]=text[j+1];
 return c;
}
```

```
OUTPUT
Enter a string (* to end):
HELLO*
Reverse string is: OLLEH
```

Explanation In this program the array *text [40]* is declared as global. So, other two functions *push ()* and *pop ()* have access to it. The character entered is pushed on the stack. When user enters '*' the character reading loop is interrupted and immediately pop operation is carried out. During pop operation the *pop ()* function returns one character its per execution. The string is displayed as reverse because the pop operation is reverse of push. The Fig. 4.11 represents the process.

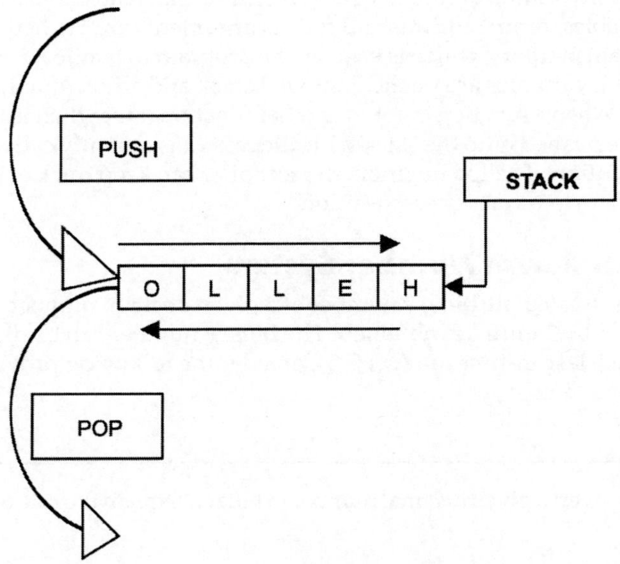

Figure 4.11 Reverse string

4.10.2 Stack Frames

All the programs compiled using high-level language compilers uses stack frame for function invocation. Operational memory uses stack frames to store the variables declared in the program. During the function, execution number of data is pushed onto the stack. When the function execution terminates, the stack content is popped. When a function is invoked, local variables, formal arguments and return address are pushed onto the stack. Thus, every function executes in a particular or a separate circumstance and hence recursion of function is also possible. Consider the following program code:

```
fun (int p, int q)
{
   int h;
   if (condition) return (value);
   h=10;
   return joy(int h);
}
joy ( int l)
{
   int m,u;
   m=1, u=2;
   return fun(m,u);
}
```

The above is an example of indirect function in which two functions fun () and joy () invokes each other. For every invocation of function new stack frame is created and as mentioned earlier new copy local variables, return address and formal arguments are pushed. Conceptually, the stack is a piece of main memory, which is used by the program to temporarily store data. When a function is invoked, variables are pushed onto the stack and when function execution ends, the stack is popped. When a function invokes another function (other than itself) the parameters of caller function are pushed onto the stack with address subsequently called instruction. This is because after execution of called function, the compiler can keep track of previous path and it can determine where to return after execution.

4.10.3 Conversion of Number System

Suppose, one wants to calculate binary number of a given decimal number, the given number is repeatedly divided by 2 until 0 is obtained. The binary number can be displayed in reverse order using stack rule last-in-first-out (LIFO). Consider the following program:

Example 4.13

Write a program to convert a given decimal number to binary. Explain the role of stack mechanism.

Solution

```
# include <stdio.h>
# include <conio.h>

int num[7];

main ()
{
   int n,k,T=7;
   void show();
   void push(int,int );
   clrscr();
   printf ("\n Enter a number: ");
   scanf ("%d",&n);
   printf ("\n The binary number is: ");
   while (n)
   {
   k=n%2;
   push(--T,k);
   n=n/2;
   }

show();
}

void push (int j, int b)
{
```

Explanation In this program the binary equivalent is obtained by repeatedly dividing by two. Here, the first binary digit obtained is pushed on the stack. This process is continued. The *show ()* function displays the binary digits stored in the stack, i.e. an array.

```
 num[j]=b;
}
void show ()
{
 int j;
 for (j=0;j<7;j++)
 printf (" %d ",num[j]);
}
```

```
OUTPUT
Enter a number: 9
The binary number is: 0 0 0 1 0 0 1
```

4.10.4 Recursion

The recursion is the fundamental concept of the mathematical logic. Recursion is one of the important facilities provided in many languages. C also supports recursion. There are many problems, which can be solved recursively. The loop which performs repeated actions on a set of instructions can be classified as either iterative or recursive. The recursive loop is different from the iterative loop. In the recursion, the procedure can call itself directly or indirectly. In the directly called recursion the procedure calls itself repeatedly. On the other hand, if the procedure calls another procedure then it is an indirect recursion. In recursion, some statements, which are specified in the function, are executed repeatedly. Every time a new value is passed to the recursive function till the condition is satisfied. A simple programming example is given below.

Example 4.14

Write a program and find the greatest common divisor of the given two numbers.

Solution

```
# include <stdio.h>
# include <conio.h>
int stack[40],top=-1;
main ()
{
 void gcd(int,int );
 int n1,n2;
 clrscr();
 printf("\nEnter number:- ");
 scanf("%d",&n1);
 printf("\nEnter number:- ");
 scanf("%d",&n2);
 gcd(n1,n2);
 printf("\nThe gcd of %d & %d is:- %d",n1,n2,stack[top]);
}
```

Explanation In this program the *stack[]* and the *top* are the global variables. By using the *n1* and *n2* variables the two numbers are input by the user. The *gcd()* function is the recursive function which is recursively called till the greatest common divisor of the two given numbers is obtained. The program stores the difference of the two numbers, which are passed by the function into *stack []*. The value present at *top* is the greatest common divisor of the two numbers.

```
void gcd(int a,int b)
{
 if(a!=b)
   {
   if(a>b)
   {
   top++;
   stack[top]=a-b;
   printf("\nTop value is:- %d",stack[top]);
   gcd(a-b,b);
   }
 else
   {
   top++;
   stack[top]=b-a;
   printf("\nTop value is:- %d",stack[top]);
   gcd(a,b-a);
   }
 }
}
```

```
OUTPUT:
Enter number:- 5
Enter number:- 25
Top value is:- 20
Top value is:- 15
Top value is:- 10
Top value is:- 5
The gcd of 5 & 25 is:- 5
```

Example 4.15

Write a program to convert decimal to binary by using the concept of recursion.

Solution

```
# include <stdio.h>
# include <conio.h>
int stack[40],top=-1;
main ()
{
   void binary(int);
   int no;
   clrscr();
   printf("\nEnter number:- ");
   scanf("%d",&no);
   binary(no);
```

```
printf("\nThe binary of the given number is:-");

while(top>=0)
{
printf(" %d ",stack[top]);
 top--;
 }

}

void binary(int b)
{
   if(b>0)
   { top++;
   stack[top]=b%2;
   binary(b/2);
 }
}

OUTPUT:
Enter number:- 255
The binary of the given number is:- 1 1 1 1 1 1 1 1
```

Explanation This program includes the function *binary ()* which is called recursively for calculating the binary of a given decimal number. The number is prompted by the user in variable no. On modulus operation, the reminders are stored in the stack. At first, the least significant bit is obtained and it is stored on the top of the stack. Subsequently, the other reminders are obtained and pushed into the stack and the pop operation is carried out for displaying them.

4.11 ACTIVATION RECORD ORGANIZATION

The group of fields such as: a) memory for local variables, b) declaration of function, c) return addresses, and d) pointer to location are pushed, when a function is invoked and popped, when a function execution is completed. This particular record of function is known as an activation record.

The details of the fields are described in the following topics. In the block structure programming languages, the programmer can define variable with same name but with different scopes. Two variables with the same name cannot be declared in a single block. The scope can be categorized in two types: a) *Local* b) *Global*. The local scope of a variable is limited to a specific block in which a variable is declared. The global scope covers entire program. The variables declared in a global scope can be accessed by any sub-program. If, in a program, a variable with same name is declared in local and global variable then the local variable gets first priority. Consider the following program:

Example 4.16

Write a program to declare same variable within different blocks and display their values and addresses.

Solution

```
# include <stdio.h>
# include <conio.h>
```

```
main ()
{
   int j=10;
   clrscr();
   printf ("\n Value of j is %2d & it's address is = %u",j,&j);
   {
   int j=5;
   printf ("\n Value of j is %2d & it's address is = %u",j,&j);
   }
   printf ("\n Value of j is %2d & it's address is = %u",j,&j);
}
```

```
OUTPUT:
Value of j is 10 & it's address is = 65496
Value of j is 5 & it's address is = 65494
Value of j is 10 & it's address is = 65496
```

Explanation In this program you can observe that a variable *int j* is declared twice, first, immediately in *main ()* function and second, declaration is done in a separate block inside the *main ()* function. The values and their addresses displayed of both variables are different. The first and last *printf ()* statement displays the same value and address because they are in *main ()* block. The second statement is in the sub block.

4.12 SCOPE RULES

The above program is based on scope rule of the variable. The scope rules are of two kinds:

1. Static scope
2. Dynamic scope.

Static Scope The static scope declares the variable in circumstances of syntactic program structure. In such a program structure, one can easily conclude the declaration of variable by only reading the program. This is why the rule is known as static. The static rule can be defined as follows:

a. The scope of a variable is limited to the current block in which it is declared, other blocks have no access to the variable.
b. If a variable is not declared in a particular block, in such a case, the variable declaration of previous block is considered. If declaration, not found, it searches the nested blocks until the declaration is found. This rule is called *"most closely nested rule"*.

For example, consider the following program code from the previous program:

```
{
   int j;
   printf ("\n Address of j =%u",&j);
}
```

If we remove the statement *int j*, the output of the program would be:

```
Address of j =65524
Address of j =65524
Address of j =65524
```

This is because, when declaration is not found in the above block, the nearest closely declaration is considered and this is why the address of variable *j* declared in *main ()* is printed.

Dynamic Scope The dynamic scope is different from static scope. In the dynamic scope, address of variable is determined at the time of program execution. The same variable name can be defined several times in the same program. The variable is activated in the memory when a sub-block is under execution. However, the variables have same name but their addresses are different. Hence, no ambiguous situation occurs for compiler.

The declaration of variables is considered from the nearly occurring and currently active definition of the variable during execution of the program.

Consider the following program:

Example 4.17

Write a program to demonstrate dynamic scope of variable.

Solution

```
# include <stdio.h>
# include <conio.h>

main ()
{
   int j;
   void A(void);
   void B(void);
   clrscr();
   A();
   printf ("\n Address of j in main() %u",&j);
   B();
}
 void A ()
 {
   int j;
   printf ("\n Address of j in A() is %u",&j);
 }

 void B ()
 {
   int j;
   printf ("\n Address of j in B() is %u",&j);
 }

OUTPUT
 Address of j in A() is 65518
 Address of j in main() 65524
 Address of j in B() is 65518
```

Explanation In this program, the variable *int j* is declared in functions *main ()*, *A ()* and *B ()*. Only declaration does not allocates memory, when a program execution starts, only at that time memory is allocated to the variable. If execution of *main ()* is started, the memory is not allocated to the variables of other functions. Memory is allocated to variables only when a function is invoked. From the output, we can observe that though variable names are same, their memory locations are different.

4.13 SCOPE RULES THROUGH STACK

So far, we have studied the scope rules of variable. Now, we will learn its implementation through stack. While following scope rules with stack, the system programmer needs to take care of memory allocation of variables declared in different blocks. There are two types of storage allocation:

a. Static storage allocation
b. Dynamic storage allocation.

Static Storage Allocation The static storage allocation is simple to define. It is a compile time binding. The space required for variables including all sub-programs are reserved. All sub-programs are compiled. The total memory required can be calculated by adding the total amount of memory required by each individual program. The amount of memory calculated cannot further increase or decrease during the program execution. Thus, it is very safe for program execution. Thus, the program is only executed when the system is able to provide required resources to the program. Otherwise, compile time error or warning message will be displayed.

Dynamic Storage Allocation In dynamic storage allocation, memory is allocated during program execution as per the requirement of the program. When a sub-function is invoked, memory is allocated and de-allocated when control returns. The space requirement is not constant. At different calls of a function, the amount of memory required may be different. For example, if a function is invoked recursively, one cannot determine how deep the recursion will proceed and it is not possible to calculate the accurate amount of memory required by the function. The program related to dynamic storage allocation is required to take necessary precautions to shun accidental failure of system due to insufficient memory. Thus, it is as well necessary to check whether the memory allocation is successfully carried or not. If memory allocation fails, the sub-routine should transfer the control to next statement. The explanation of such routines is out of the scope of the book.

Now, we are going to discuss scope rules implementation with dynamic memory allocation. The handy implementation tool is stack. Such implementation is known as run-time stack. When a sub-function is invoked, memory is allocated and as soon as execution ends the memory is de-allocated. That specific block of memory is called an *activation record*. Such record consists of following structure:

- Storage space for all variables including sub functions
- Definition of functions and pointers
- Return address
- A pointer to activation record.

The Fig. 4.12 shows *activation record*.

Activation records are stored in the stack. The stack is controlled during program execution. When a new function is invoked, control passes to it. Its activation record is pushed onto the stack. The return address is stored in return address field. When function execution completes, the control returns to the caller function. It obtains the return address from the return address field of the activation record. Immediately after that the activation record is popped. The Fig. 4.12 shows the activation records.

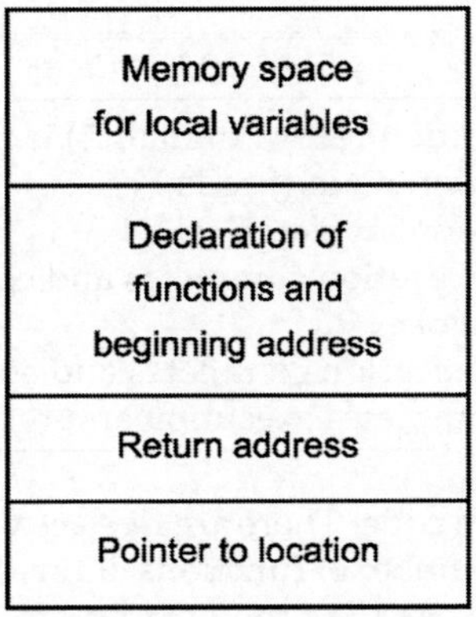

Figure 4.12 Activation record

Consider the following program code and Fig. 4.13.

```
void main ()
{
 P()
}


P()
{
 Q();
 R();
}
```

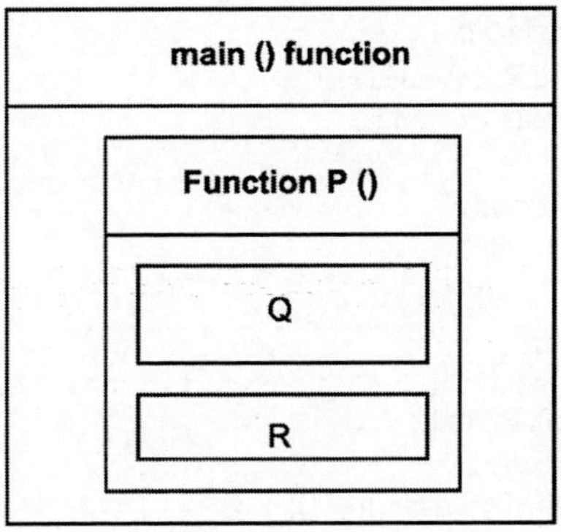

Figure 4.13 Functions

The function *main ()* invokes function *P ()*. The function *P ()* invokes function *Q ()* and *R ()*. When a new function is invoked, the activation record is pushed and when function execution completes the record is popped. Thus, the stack is updated when new function is invoked and a function completes its execution. Thus, by maintaining the stack the next function, which is to be executed, is decided. Table 4.12 shows the stack operation.

Table 4.12 Stack operation of a program

Stack Status	*Operation*
MAIN()	Activation record of main () is pushed onto the stack
MAIN() P	Function main () calls P()
MAIN() P Q	Function invokes Q()
MAIN() P	Q () execution completes and control returns to P
MAIN() P R	P() invokes R()
MAIN() P	R () execution completes and control returns to P
MAIN()	P() completes execution and return to main ().

Consider the following program code. There are five activation records. The total numbers of activation records are equal to number of functions defined. The filed pointer to the location is defined only in dynamic scope. At the time of program execution, activation records of functions are pushed and popped to and from the stack.

Example 4.18

Write a program to demonstrate the above theory with an example.

Solution

```
# include <stdio.h>
# include <conio.h>

void Q(void);
void R(void);

main ()
{
   void P(void);
   clrscr();
   printf ("\n main ()");
   P();
   printf ("\n Again in main () ");
}
void P ()
{
   printf ("\n In P() ");
   Q();
   printf ("Execution of Q complete");
   R();
   printf ("Execution of R complete");
}
void Q () { printf ("\n In Q() "); }
void R () { printf ("\n In R() "); }
```

Explanation In this program *P ()*, *Q ()* and *R ()* are three functions defined. The *main ()* function invokes *P ()*. The function *P ()* invokes *Q ()* and *R ()* one by one. Messages are displayed when a function is invoked which help the user to understand the flow of the program. From the following Fig. 4.14 we can observe that the program execution sequence is *main ()-P ()- Q ()-P ()-R ()-main ()*. Here, function *P ()* is not invoked twice. After complete execution of *Q ()*, control returns in function *P ()*.

```
OUTPUT
 main ()
 In P()
 In Q() Execution of Q complete
 In R() Execution of R complete
 Again in main ()
```

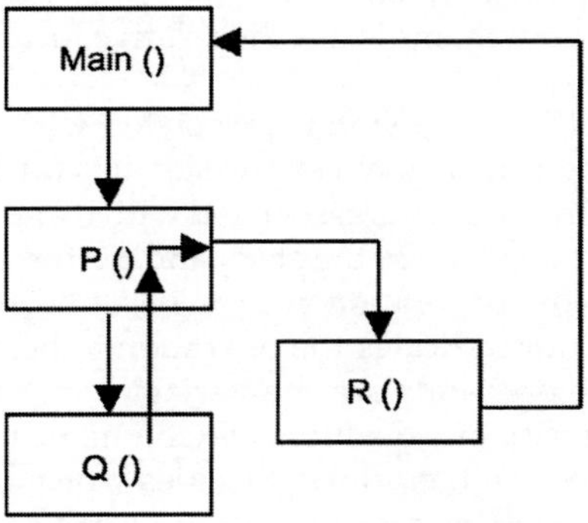

Figure 4.14 Flow of program execution

Summary

1. Stack is an important tool in programming languages. Most of the programming languages support stack operations. The main operations are *push* and *pop*. The insertion of element onto the stack is called *"push"* and deletion operation is called *"pop"*. Due to the push operation that adds elements in the stack, the stack is also known as *pushdown list*. The most and least reachable elements in the stack are known as the *"top"* and *"bottom"* of the stack. Stack is a set of elements in a *last-in-first-out* technique.
2. The insertion and deletion operations are carried out at one end. Hence, the recent element inserted is deleted first. If we want to delete the particular element of the stack, it is necessary to delete all the elements appearing before that element.
3. A top pointer maintains track of the top elements.
4. When stack has no element, it is called *empty stack.*
5. Whenever an element is inserted (push operation) in the stack the value of pointer top is increased by one. In the same manner, the value of pointer is decremented when an element is deleted from the stack (pop operation).
6. If a pop operation is performed on an empty stack it is called as *underflow stack.* An operation to insert an element more than the capacity of stack is known as *overflow stack.*
7. Static implementation can be implemented using arrays. However, it is a very simple method but it has few limitations.
8. Pointers can also be used for implementation of stack. The linked list is an example of this type of implementation. The limitations noticed in static implementation can be removed by using dynamic implementation.

9. Recall that array name itself is a pointer. Pointer implementation of a stack is carried out similar to array implementation.
10. An arithmetic expression contains operators and operands. Variable and constant are operands. The operators are of various kinds such as arithmetic binary, unary, for example, + (Addition), – (subtraction), *(multiplication), / (division) and % (modular division).
11. Arithmetic expressions can be defined in three kinds of notation: infix, prefix and postfix. The prefixes 'pre', 'post' and 'in' indicates the relative location of the operator with two operands.
12. Each operator in the postfix expression is associated with the previous two operands. When we read an operand from a given expression it is pushed onto the stack. When an operator symbol is read, the operands associated with it are the top elements of the stack. We can pop these two elements from the stack and perform the operation.
13. In any expression, two types of components can be clubbed together. They are operand and operators. The operator indicates the operation to be carried out and the operand indicates the values. The operands are the variables on which the operator operates. Operators have their priority of execution. When one or more operations are clubbed together in a single expression the priority decides which operation is performed first.
14. The group of field such as a) memory for local variables, b) declaration of function, c) return addresses and d) pointer to location are pushed when a function is invoked and popped when a function execution completed. This particular record of function is known as an activation record.
15. The static scope declares the variable in circumstances of syntactic program structure.
16. The dynamic scope is different from static scope. In the dynamic scope, address of a variable is determined at the time of program execution.
17. The static storage allocation is simple to define. It is a compile time binding.
18. In dynamic storage allocation, memory is allocated during program execution as per the requirement of the program. When a sub-function is invoked, memory is allocated and de-allocated when control returns.

Exercises

A. Answer the following question:
   1. What do you mean by stack?
   2. Define various terms related to stack.
   3. Explain implementation procedure of stack.
   4. What is the top of the stack?
   5. What do you mean by stack *overflow* and *stack underflow?*
   6. Explain the terms infix expression, postfix expression, and polish notation.
   7. Distinguish between prefix and postfix expressions.
   8. What are the applications of stacks?
   9. Explain the *push* and *pop* operations.
   10. Explain scope rules.
   11. Explain activation record.
   12. Explain stack mechanism.
   13. Distinguish between static and dynamic implementation of stack.

14. Explain the stack technique last-in-first-out with two real life examples.
15. Translate following infix expressions to its equivalent prefix expressions:
    a. (x+y–z)/(h+k)–z
    b. (j+k)*(c/d)
16. Explain solution for following expressions:
    a. From infix to postfix j–k /(g^h)+(n+m)
    b. From infix to prefix j–k /(g^h)+(n+m)
    c. From infix to postfix x*(c+d)+(j/k)*n+m*p
    d. From infix to postfix A^B^C
    e. From infix to postfix A&&B | | ! (A>B)
17. Evaluate the expression 123+*78 3/–. Show the contents of stack after every step in tabular form

B. Attempt following programs:
1. Write a program to demonstrate push () and pop () operation using class and member function.
2. Write a program to enter an integer. Reverse the digits of the integer. Use stack mechanism.
3. Write a program to implement stack operation push and pop with pointer.
4. Write a program to perform following operations:
    a. push
    b. pop
    c. stack underflow
    d. stack overflow
    e. display all elements.
5. Write a program to implement stack with two-dimensional array. Perform push () and pop () operation.
6. Write a program to perform following stack operations:
    a. Create a stack with item code and quantity

Item code	*Quantity*
001	450
002	0
003	487
004	101
005	500
006	0
007	359
008	0
009	458

    b. Delete the items having quantity zero and update the stack.

C. Select the appropriate option for each of the following questions:
1. The stack is based on the rule
    a. first-in-last-out
    b. last-in-first-out
    c. both (a) and (b)
    d. first-in-first-out

2. The push () operation is used
   a. to insert an element
   b. to remove an element
   c. to move an element
   d. all of the above.
3. The pop operation removes
   a. the element lastly inserted
   b. first element of the stack
   c. any element randomly
   d. none of the above.
4. The top pointer is increased
   a. when push () operation is done
   b. when pop () operation is done
   c. both (a) and (b)
   d. none of the above.
5. A stack holding elements equal to its capacity and if push is performed then such situation is called
   a. stack overflow
   b. stack underflow
   c. illegal operation
   d. none of the above.
6. The prefix notation is also called as
   a. polish notation
   b. postfix notation
   c. infix notation
   d. none of the above.
7. From the given options one is not a stack application
   a. template
   b. recursion
   c. reverse string
   d. conversion of number.
8. An expression containing more than one operation are solved according to
   a. priority of operators
   b. priority of operands
   c. from left to right
   d. right to left.
9. The following brackets changes the priority
   a. ()
   b. [ ]
   c. { }
   d. &
10. The postfix notation is also called as
   a. reverse polish notation
   b. polish notation
   c. prefix notation
   d. postfix notation.

D. Find the output.

1.

```
# include <stdio.h>
# include <conio.h>
main ()
{
static int stack[6],j;
clrscr();
   printf ("Enter Elements, put zero to exit: \n");
   for(j=0;j<6;j++)
   {
   printf ("\n Elements of stack are: ");
   scanf ("%d",&stack[j]);
   if (stack[j]==0)
   {
     printf ("\nBy choice terminated:- ");
     break;
     }
     }
     if (j>5)
     printf ("Stack is full \n");
   printf("\nStack elements are:-");
   for (j=0;j<6;j++)
   printf (" %d ",stack[j]);

   }
```

2.

```
# include <stdio.h>
# include <conio.h>
main ()
{
char stack[5];
int j,p=0;
clrscr();
printf ("Enter less than seven Characters: \n");
scanf ("%s",&stack);
printf("\nStack characters are:-");
for(j=0;j<6;j++)
{
p=j;
    if(stack[j]=='\0')
    break;
}

if (j>5)
{
    for (j=0;j<6;j++)
    printf (" %c ",stack[j]);
    printf ("\nStack is full \n");
    }
else
{
    for (j=0;j<p;j++)
    printf (" %c ",stack[j]);
}
}
```

3.

```
# include <stdio.h>
# include <conio.h>
int p,top=0,stack[3],c;
main()
{
void push();
void show();
clrscr();
push();
show();
push();
show();
}

void push ()
{
    printf("\n Enter number to be pushed:- ");
    scanf("%d",&stack[top]);
    top++;
}

void show ()
{
printf("\nContents of stack are:-");
for (p=top-1;p>=0;--p)
printf("\n%d ",stack[p]);
}
```

4.

```
# include <stdio.h>
# include <conio.h>
# include <process.h>
int p,z=6,top=0,stack[7],c;
main()
{
void push();
void pop();
void show();
clrscr();
push();
show();
push();
show();
pop();
printf("\n\t After pop operation:");
show();
}

void push ()
{
printf("\nEnter number to be pushed:- ");
scanf("%d",&stack[top]);
top++;
}

void pop ()
{
top--;
}
void show ()
{
printf("\nStack elements are:");
```

```
for (p=top-1;p>=0;—p)
printf(" \n%d ",stack[p]);
}
```

5.

```
# include <stdio.h>
# include <conio.h>
main ()
{

char text[40];
int k=0,j;
clrscr();
puts ("\n Enter a string:- ");
scanf("%s",&text);
while (text[k]!='\0')
   k++;
printf("\nValue of top is:- %d",k);
printf ("\nReverse string is: ");
for(j=k;j>=0;j—)
   {
   printf ("%c",text[k]);
   k--;
}

}
```

6.

```
# include <stdio.h>
# include <conio.h>
main ()
{

static int arra[40];
int k=0,j;
clrscr();
puts ("\nEnter numbers (insert 0 to end):- ");
while(1)
{
scanf("%d",&arra[k]);
if(arra[k]==0)
break;
k++;
}

printf("\nValue of top is:- %d",k);
printf ("\nReverse array of numbers is: ");
while(k>0)
{
   k--;
   printf (" %d ",arra[k]);
}

}
```

7.

```
# include <stdio.h>
# include <conio.h>
int sum=0,stack[40],top=-1;
main ()
{
void sum_num(int);
int n,i;
clrscr();
printf("\nEnter the number:- ");
scanf("%d",&n);
sum_num(n);
printf("\nThe sum of 1 ");
for(i=2;i<=n;i++)
   printf("+ %d ",i);
printf(" is:- %d",stack[top]);
}

void sum_num(int d)
{
if(d>0)
{
top++;
sum=sum+d;
stack[top]=sum;
sum_num(d-1);
}
}
```

8.

```
# include <stdio.h>
# include <conio.h>
int fact=1,stack[40],top=-1;
main ()
{
   void fact_num(int);
   int n,i;
   clrscr();
   printf("\nEnter the number:- ");
```

```
    scanf("%d",&n);
    fact_num(n);
    printf("\nThe multiplication of 1 ");
    for(i=2;i<=n;i++)
    printf("* %d ",i);
    printf(" is:- %d",stack[top]);
}

void fact_num(int d)
{
if(d>0)
{
    top++;
    fact=fact*d;
    stack[top]=fact;
    fact_num(d-1);
}
if(d==0)
    {
    fact=fact*1;
    top++;
    stack[top]=fact;
    }
}
```

9.

```
# include <stdio.h>
# include <conio.h>

main ()
{
    int j;
    clrscr();
    printf ("\n Address of j =%u",&j);

    {
    int j;
    printf ("\n Address of j =%u",&j);
}

printf ("\n Address of j =%u",&j);

}
```

10.

```
# include<stdio.h>
# include <conio.h>
main ()
{

int a=5;
void fun1(void);
void fun2(void);
clrscr();
fun1();
printf ("\n Value of j is %2d & it's address in
main() is %u ",a,&a);
fun2();
}

void fun1 ()
{
int a=10;
printf ("\n Value of j is %2d & it's address in
fun1() is %u",a,&a);
}

void fun2()
{
int a=20;
printf ("\n Value of j is %2d & it's address in
fun2() is %u",a,&a);
    }
```

Chapter 5

Queues

Chapter Outline

5.1 INTRODUCTION

A queue is one of the simplest data structures and can be implemented with different methods on a computer. Queue of tasks to be executed in a computer is analogous to the queue that we see in our daily life at various places. The theory of a queue is common to all. Queue of people in a bank, students queue in school, a travellers' queue for tickets at railway station are few examples of queue. It is necessary to wait in a queue for obtaining the service. In the same fashion, in a computer there may be a queue of tasks waiting for execution, few others for printing, and some are for inputting the data and instructions through the keyboard. Unless the task turns and comes on front, it will not be executed. This data structure is very useful in solving various real life problems. One can simulate the real life situations with this data structure. This chapter describes the queue and its types.

A queue is a non-primitive, linear data structure, and a sub-class of list data structure. It is an ordered, homogenous collection of elements in which elements are appended at one end called *rear end* and elements are deleted at other end called *front end*. The meaning of front is face side and rear means back side. The first entry in a queue to which the service is offered is to the element that is on front. After servicing, it is removed from the queue. The information is manipulated in the same sequence as it was collected. Queue follows the rule first-in-first-out (FIFO). Fig. 5.1 illustrates a queue.

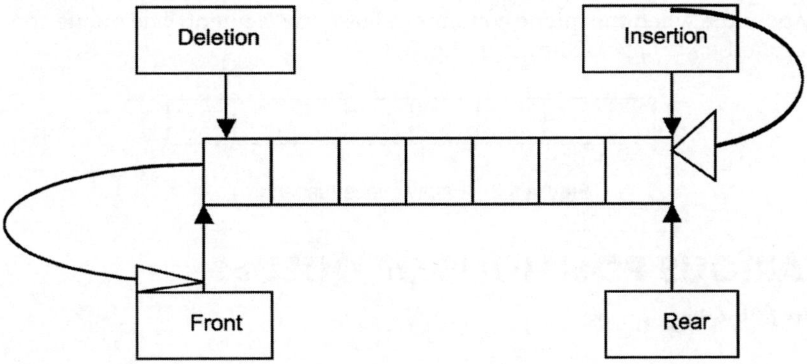

Figure 5.1 Queue

Figure 5.1 shows that insertion of elements is done at the rear end and deletion at the front end.

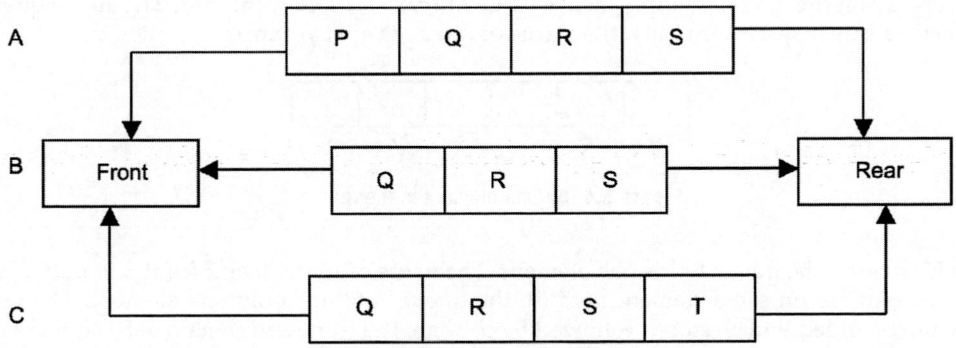

Figure 5.2 Queues

The Fig. 5.2 illustrates the queue containing elements. The queue (Fig. 5.2(a)) contains four elements P, Q, R and S. The element P is at the front end and element S is at the rear end. In the Fig. (b), an element P has been deleted from the queue. Now, the element Q is the first element and it is on the front. In Fig. (c), element T is inserted from the rear end. Thus, the elements are inserted from the rear end of queue. The element T is inserted after S. As far as removal operation is concerned, the S is to be removed before T.

In other words, the service is provided to the element, which is at front and this element is to be removed first. We call this entry front of the queue. The entry of element that is recently added is done from rear of the queue or it can be called as tail end of the queue.

Two operations are frequently carried on queue. They are insertion and deletion of elements. These two operations depend upon the status of the queue. The insertion operation is possible, only when the queue contains elements less than the capacity it can hold. The deletion operation is only possible when the queue contains at least one element. The queue containing no elements is called *underflow* as shown in Fig. 5.3.

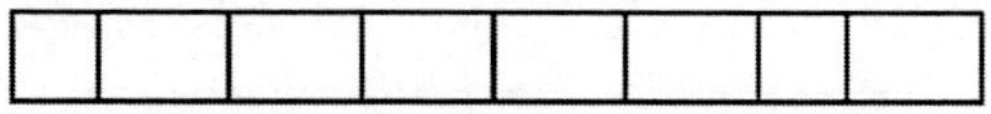

Figure 5.3 Empty queue (underflow)

5.2 VARIOUS POSITIONS OF QUEUES

Consider the following figures:

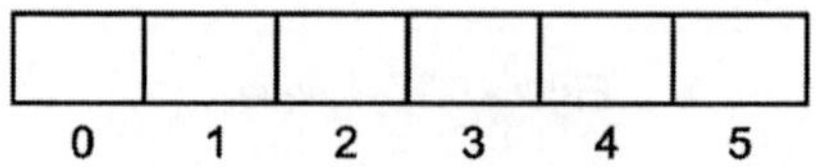

Figure 5.4(a) Empty queue

In Fig. 5.4(a) the queue is empty, hence value of rear = –1 and front = –1. The above queue is called as empty queue. Initially, the status of queue is always empty.

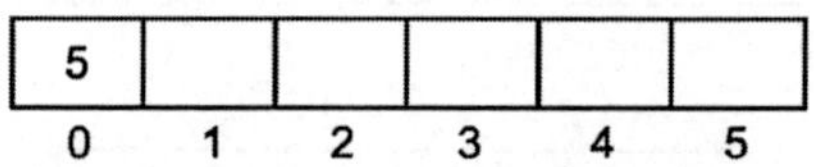

Figure 5.4 (b) One element in the queue

In Fig. 5.4(b), the queue holds one element. The value of rear = 0 and front = 0. Both front and rear end are on same element because the queue contains only one element. The next element appended will be stored followed by 5. Then, the front will remain at 5 but rear will be shifted on to the new element. The value of front is changed only once when the first element is inserted in the queue. Later, for every insertion of element, the front remains same but the value of rear changes.

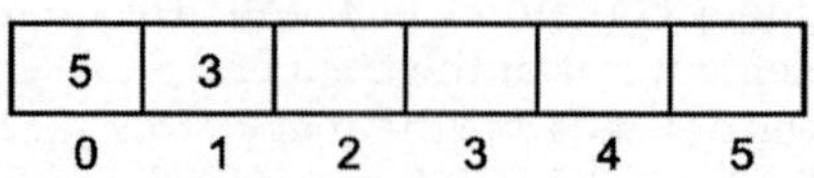

Figure 5.4(c) Two elements in the queue

In Fig. 5.4(c), another element is inserted from the rear side and it is stored behind 5. Whenever we insert an element in the queue the value of rear is incremented, i.e. the rear end is shifted towards the right. At this step the value of front = 0 and rear = 1.

5	3	2			
0	1	2	3	4	5

Figure 5.4(d) Three elements in the queue

In Fig. 5.4(d), the value of rear is 2.

	3	2			
0	1	2	3	4	5

Figure 5.4(e)

In Fig. 5.4 (e), one element is deleted from the queue. Now, the front is shifted towards bottom. Thus, the front will be on element 3 now. The value of the front will be increased when an element is removed. The value of front = 1 and rear = 2. The programs on above discussion are explained in queue implementation.

5.3 QUEUE IMPLEMENTATION

Queue can be put into operation in two ways:

a. Static implementation (array)
b. Dynamic implementation (pointers).

5.3.1 Static Implementation

The static implementation is done with an array. In this implementation, we should know the exact number of elements to be stored in the queue. The size of array is decided before execution at compile time. Once the array is declared, its size cannot be altered during the run time of the program. The beginning of the array, i.e. 0th element is the front and the last memory location will be rear of the queue. A queue can be created by declaring an array that hold the entries. Here, we should keep the track of both front as well as rear of the queue. Assume an array of integer data types as declared below.

```
int queue[8];
```

In the above statement, an array *queue []* of integer type is declared.

From the Fig. 5.5 we can say that first six locations of a queue are filled and the remaining two are vacant. The element 5 is at front and 8 is at rear.

1. If the value of front element is zero, then queue is empty.
2. If the value of *queue [8]* is non-zero then the queue is full.
3. When an element is inserted, the position of rear increases.
4. When an element is deleted from the queue the value of front increases by one.

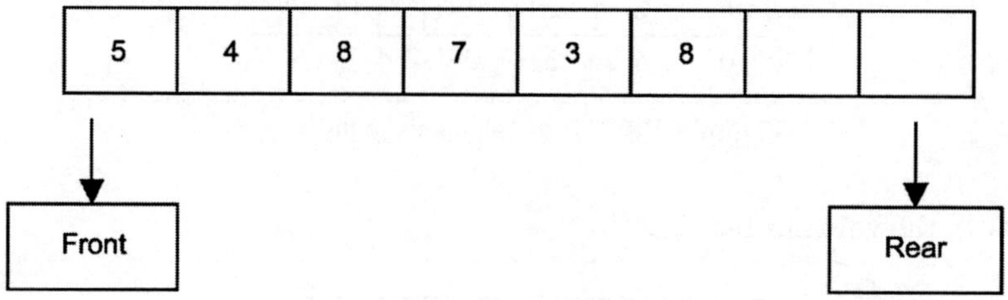

Figure 5.5 Queues

The above operation can be shown with few programs as described below. Consider the following program,

Example 5.1

Write a program to implement a queue using an array

Solution

```
# include <stdio.h>
# include <conio.h>
# include <process.h>

main ()
{

   int queue[8];
    int rear=0;
   clrscr();
   while(1)
 {
   printf ("Enter element: ");
   scanf ("%d",&queue[rear]);
   rear++;
    if (rear==7)
    {
    printf ("\n Queue is full ");
    break;
    }
 }
 printf ("\n Elements of Queue are: ");
 rear=0;

 while (1)
 {
```

Explanation This a simple example of queue. All the elements are entered and stored in the queue. Of course, the queue is implemented by declaring an array. The *while loop* and *scanf ()* statement read elements through the keyboard. The variable *rear* is incremented to get successive position in the queue. In the same way, the second *while loop* displays the elements.

```
    printf (" %d ", queue[rear]);
    rear++;
    if (rear==7) break;
  }
}
```

```
OUTPUT
Enter element: 1
Enter element: 2
Enter element: 3
Enter element: 4
Enter element: 5
Enter element: 6
Enter element: 7
Queue is full
Elements of Queue are: 1 2 3 4 5 6 7
```

5.4 OPERATIONS ON QUEUES

Two operations can be carried out on queue.

5.4.1 Insertion of Element

Table 5.1 Algorithm for insertion in queue

Algorithm for Insertion of Element in a Queue		
1.	Initialize front = 0 rear = -1, queue[SIZE]	Initialization of queue
2.	If rear ≥ size (Display queue overflow message and exit) Else <enter element>	Test for overflow condition
3.	Queue[rear] = element Rear++	Element is stored in an array Rear is incremented
4.	Go to step 2	Loop rotated to beginning

A program based on algorithm, which is shown in Table 5.1, is described below.

Example 5.2

Write a program to insert elements in a queue.

Solution

```
# include <stdio.h>
# include <conio.h>
```

```
# include <process.h>
# define S 5

main ()
{
 int queue[S];
 int r=0,n;

 clrscr();

 while (1)
 {
 if (r>=S)
 {
 printf ("\n Queue overflow");
 break;
 }
 else
 printf ("Enter a number: ");
 scanf ("%d",&n);
 queue[r]=n;
 r++;
 }

printf ("\n Queue elements are: ");
for (n=0;n<S;n++)
printf (" %d ",queue[n]);

}
```

Explanation This a simple example of queue that contains maximum 5 elements. All the elements are entered and stored in the queue. The queue is implemented by declaring *array[s]*. The while loop and *scanf ()* statement read elements through the keyboard. The variable *rear* is incremented to get successive position in the queue. The *for* loop displays the elements.

```
OUTPUT
Enter a number: 3
Enter a number: 4
Enter a number: 5
Enter a number: 6
Enter a number: 7
Queue overflow
Queue elements are: 3 4 5 6 7
```

Example 5.3

Write a program to perform insertion operation and show value of front and rear.

Solution

```
# include<stdio.h>
# include <conio.h>
```

```
main ()
{
   int queue[7];
   int r=-1,f=-1,j;
   clrscr();


   while (r<6)
   {
   r++;
   printf ("rear=%d front=%d Enter element:",r,f);
   scanf ("%d",&queue[r]);

   if (r==0 ) f=0;

 }

 printf ("\n Queue elements are: ");
 for ( j=0;j<7;j++)
 printf (" %d ",queue[j]);

 }
```

```
OUTPUT
rear=-1 front=-1 Enter element:8
rear=0 front=0 Enter element:9
rear=1 front=0 Enter element:4
rear=2 front=0 Enter element:5
rear=3 front=0 Enter element:1
rear=4 front=0 Enter element:2
rear=5 front=0 Enter element:3
Queue elements are: 8 9 4 5 1 2 3
```

Explanation In this program our aim is to concentrate only at element insertion operation and the values of front and rear ends displayed after insertion of every element. Initially, rear and front are initialized to –1. Conceptually, it is not necessary to initialize these variables to –1. The user can also initialize them to zero. The values of rear start from –1 to 6. Here, –1 is the value before insertion operation. When one element is added the value of rear is increased to 1 and later the value reaches up to 6. On the other hand the value of front changes only once from –1 to 0 and then its value remains same.

5.4.2 Deletion of Element

The following program explains insertion and deletion operations.

Example 5.4

Write a program to perform deletion operation on queue and show value of front and rear.

Solution

```
# include<stdio.h>
# include <conio.h>

main ()
```

```
{
 int queue[7]={11,12,13,14,15,16,17};
 int i,r=6,f=0,n;
 clrscr();

 printf("\nThe Elements of queue are as follows:-\n");
 for(i=0;i<7;i++)
 printf("%2d ",queue[i]);

 printf ("\nInitial values rear=%d front=%d",r,f);
 printf ("\n\nHow many elements u want to delete: ");
 scanf ("%d",&n);

 while (f<n)
 {
  queue[f]=NULL;
  f++;
 printf ("\nrear=%d front=%d",r,f);
 }
 printf ("\n Queue elements are: ");
 for ( n=0;n<7;n++)
 printf (" %d ",queue[n]);
}
```

Explanation This program is the second part of the first program. We have started exactly from where we ended the last program. The output of the last program is starting of this program. The array is initialized with entered values and rear and front are initialized to six and zero, respectively.

```
OUTPUT
The Elements of queue are as follows:-
11 12 13 14 15 16 17
Initial values rear=6 front=0
How many elements u want to delete: 3
rear=6 front=1
rear=6 front=2
rear=6 front=3
Queue elements are: 0 0 0 14 15 16 17
```

The user is asked to enter number of elements to be deleted. The loop is executed for n times and zero to n elements of the array are nullified. At every deletion operation the front is shifted to inside. It is shifted from 0 to 3 when three elements are deleted. The output of the program is easy to understand.

5.5 DISADVANTAGES OF SIMPLE QUEUES

In the previous sections we have studied implementation of queues using arrays and pointers. There are some disadvantages in simple queue implementation using arrays. In the following example, it is considered that the elements after deletion are not shifted to beginning of an array. Consider the following example:

Queue [5] is a simple queue declared. The queue is initially empty. In the following figures insertion and deletion operations will be performed.

0	1	2	3	4

The above figure is an empty queue. Initially the queue is always empty. Here, rear = –1 and front = –1. The user can also assign 0 instead of –1. However, the –1 is suitable because we are implementing this problem with arrays and an array element counting begins always with zero. Thus, it is suitable for problem logic.

5				
0	1	2	3	4

In the above figure, one element is inserted. So, the new values of front and rear are increased and reaches to 0 (zero). This is the only stage where front and rear have same values.

5	7	9		
0	1	2	3	4

In the above figure, two elements are appended in the queue. At this moment, the value of *rear* = 2 and *front* = 0.

	7	9		
0	1	2	3	4

In the above figure one element is deleted and the value of rear = 2 and f = 1. The value of front is increased due deletion of one element.

	7	9	8	1
0	1	2	3	4

In the above figure, two more elements are appended to queue. The value of rear = 4 and front = 1.

If more elements are deleted, the value of front will be increased and as a result, the beginning portion of queue will be empty. In such a situation if we try to insert new elements to queue, no elements can be inserted in the queue. This is because, new elements are always inserted from the rear and if the last location of queue (rear) holds an element, even though the space is available at the beginning of queue, no elements will be inserted. The queue will be treated as overflow.

To overcome this problem, we have to update the queue. Let us take an example, suppose we have allocated n number of bytes to pointer *p using either *malloc ()* (c) or *new* (c++) function. After successful allocation of memory (though the program is not utilizing the memory), memory will be part of the program and cannot be used by other program or cannot be allocated to other program. To utilize this memory, memory must be released using free or delete functions. Thus, whatever the portion of memory is not in use, can be used. In our example of queue the beginning portion of queue which is empty due to delete operations, can be filled by shifting following element to beginning of the array. Thus, the space will be available at the rear end and new elements can be inserted at the end. Thus, entire queue can be used to store the element. This approach also has a problem when the queue contains more elements. The solution to this problem is circular queue, which is discussed separately in this chapter.

Here, a program is provided with menu driven with different choices such as insertion, deletion, display, etc.

Example 5.5

Write a program to perform different operations with queue such as insert, delete and display of elements.

Solution

```
# include <stdio.h>
# include <conio.h>
int queue[8];
int r;
void insert(void);
void del ();
void show (void);
main ()
{
int c;
clrscr();
printf ("\n 1] Insert Element ");
printf ("\n 2] Delete Element ");
printf ("\n 3] Display element/s");
printf ("\n 4] Exit");
printf ("\n Enter your choice:- ");
scanf ("%d",&c);
switch (c)
{
case 1: insert(); break;
case 2: del(); show();break;
case 3: show(); break;
default: exit(0);
}
main ();
}

void insert ()
{
char ans='Y';
```

Explanation In this program, the different tasks such as insert, delete and display of elements are performed using individual functions. A menu appears on the screen and user is required to enter choice. When user enters 1, the *insert ()* function is executed. The integers entered by the user are stored in the queue one after another.

```
if (r>=7)
{
printf ("\n Queue is full \n\n\n");
main();
}

while (ans=='Y'|| ans=='y')
{
printf ("\n Enter element:- ");
scanf ("%d",&queue[r]);
if (r==7)
{
clrscr();
printf ("\n Queue is Full");
getch();
break;
}
else
r++;
printf ("\nContinue [Y/N]:-");
ans=getche();

}
}
void show()
{
int j;
for (j=0;j<r;j++)
printf (" %d ",queue[j]);
getch();
}
void del ()
{
int j;
if (r==0)
{
clrscr();
printf ("\n Queue is empty \n\n\n");
main();
}

for (j=0;j<r;j++)
queue[j]= queue[j+1];
queue[r]=0;
r--;
}
```

```
OUTPUT
1] Insert element
2] Delete element
3] Display element/s
4] Exit
Enter your choice:- 1
Enter element:- 23
Continue [Y/N]:-y
Enter element:- 45
Continue [Y/N]:-
```

When the choice is 2, the element at the front is deleted. In queue, the elements are inserted from the rear side and deleted from the front side. The display option displays the elements presently stored in the queue. When *del ()* function is executed, the element present at front is deleted. Here, the elements are shifted to front side. This is accomplished by the statement *queue [j] = queue [j+1];* the next element is shifted to the previous location and the last element is replaced with zero.

In the above program, necessary care is taken to prevent overflow and underflow. When queue is full with the elements, a message will be displayed *"Queue is Full"* and further no elements can be added. When queue is empty user cannot delete any element. The function *show ()* is used to display elements, this is achieved by using for loop and *printf ()* statement.

1	2	3	4	5	6	7

Figure 5.6 Queues with elements

2	3	4	5	6	7

Figure 5.7 Queue (After delete operation)

2	3	4	5	6	7	8

Figure 5.8 Queue (After insert operation)

As shown in the Fig. 5.6, element 1 is at front side and seven is at rear side. When delete operation is performed one is deleted first and the element two is shifted at front as shown in the Fig. 5.7. When an element is inserted, it is inserted after seven as shown in the Fig. 5.8. When eight is inserted, it is inserted after seven. Consider another program that explains the operation insertion and deletion.

Example 5.6

Write a program to perform different operations with queue such as insert, delete and display of elements.

Solution

```
# include <stdio.h>
# include <process.h>
# include <conio.h>

create ();
void insert ();
void del();
void show ();

int m,n=10,fr=0, queue[11],re=0,num,cur;

main ()
{
   int choice;
   clrscr();
   puts("1] Create");
   puts("2] Insert");
   puts("3] Delete");
   puts("4] Show");
   puts("5] End");
   puts("\nEnter Your choice: ");
   scanf("%d",&choice);

 switch(choice)
 {
   case 1: create (); break;
   case 2: insert (); break;
   case 3: del (); break;
   case 4: show(); break;
   case 5: puts("Bye"); exit(0);
 }
 main();
}


 create ()
 {
   puts ("Insert number of elements <11 in the queue: ");
   scanf ("%d",&cur);
   puts ("Enter elements: ");
```

Explanation We are already familiar with the operation create, insert and delete in the previous program. In this program, separate functions are defined for different tasks such as create, insert, and delete operation. Now, we will discuss one by one.

```
   if ( fr==0)
   {
       fr++;
       scanf ("%d",&num);

       if (num==0) return 0;
       queue[fr]=num;
       re=fr;
}
   do
   {
    ++re;

    if (re>cur) break;
    scanf ("%d",&num);

    if (num==0) break;
    queue[re]=num;
   }while(re<cur);
   return 0;
}

   void insert ()
   {

    if (re<cur)
    {
    puts ("Queue is full");
    exit (0);
    }

puts ("Enter a number to be inserted ");
    scanf ("%d",&num);
    queue[re]=num;
}

    void del ()
    {

    if (fr==re)
    {
    puts("The queue is empty"); exit(0); }
    fr++;
    num=queue[fr];

    if (fr==n)
    {
```

```
      fr=1;
      re=1;
    }
  }
  void show ()
  {
  for (m=fr;m<=re;++m)
  printf (" %d ",queue[m]);
  getch();
  }
```

```
OUTPUT
1] Create
2] Insert
3] Delete
4] Show
5] End
Enter Your choice:
4
2 3 0
```

In the create function, user has to enter number of elements to be entered in the queue. User also needs to enter elements. If zero is inserted the control exits from the function. The zero will not be considered as an element, it is entered to exit from the function. If elements entered are less than the capacity entered, the remaining portion remains vacant.

The *insert ()* function is used to insert elements if the space is available. If the queue is already filled, this function will not work. The *del ()* function is used to delete element. To display the element *show ()* function is used. You might have noticed that the function *main ()* is invoked recursively by itself. This is to enable the user to enter choice of operation.

5.6 DYNAMIC IMPLEMENTATION (POINTERS)

Dynamic implementation is carried out using pointers. By applying increment operation on pointer successive locations of memory can be accessed and an element can be stored in that location. Thus, the series of elements can be contiguously stored up to any number of elements. The programmer has to keep the starting address of the pointer in which first element is stored. Thus, in the same way the numbers can be viewed or altered. Here is the simple example.

Example 5.7

Write a program to implement queue using pointers.

Solution

```
# include <stdio.h>
# include <conio.h>
# include <process.h>
```

```
main ()
{
   int *q;
   int rear=0;
   clrscr();

while(1)
{
   printf ("Enter element: ");
   scanf ("%d",q);
   q++;
   rear++;
if (rear==7)
{
   printf ("\n Queue is full ");
   break;
}
}

q=q-rear;
printf ("\n Elements of Queue are: ");
rear=0;

while (rear<7)
{
   printf ("\n Element: %d rear=%d", *(q+rear),rear);
   rear++;
}
}
```

Explanation In this program, pointer **q* and integer rear are declared. The variable *rear* is initialized with zero. Using *scanf ()*, statement elements are entered. In the *while loop pointer q* and *rear* are increased. If the rear reaches to seven, the break statement terminates the loop. After the execution of *while loop*, the pointer *q* points to last memory location of the queue. The starting address of the queue is again set by the statement *q = q–rear*. Finally, using second *while loop* and continuous increment operation with rear, successive memory locations are accessed and elements are displayed.

```
OUTPUT
Enter element: 4
Enter element: 2
Enter element: 3
Enter element: 4
Enter element: 7
Enter element: 8
Enter element: 9
Queue is full
Elements of Queue are:
Element: 4 rear=0
Element: 2 rear=1
Element: 3 rear=2
Element: 4 rear=3
Element: 7 rear=4
Element: 8 rear=5
Element: 9 rear=6
```

5.7 INSERTION AND DELETION OPERATION

The insertion and deletion operations can also be performed with the queue. The following program explains both the insertion and deletion operation with the queue. Queue implementation is done with an array.

Example 5.8

Write a program to perform insert and delete operation with queue.

Solution

```
# include <stdio.h>
# include <conio.h>

  void create ();
  insert ();
  erase ();
  void show ();
  int k,j=10,f=0, queue[11],r=0, e_ment, crn,s;

main ()
{
  int option;
  clrscr();
  do
  {
  puts ("\n\n QUEUE OPERATIONS\n");
  puts ("1: Create");
  puts ("2: Insertion");
  puts ("3: Erase");
  puts ("4: Show");
  puts ("5: Exit");
  puts ("Enter your option: ");
  scanf ("%d",&option);
  switch(option)
  {
     case 1: create (); continue;
     case 2: s=insert (); continue;
     case 3: erase(); continue;
     case 4: show (); continue;
     case 5:
     printf ("\n s=%d",s);
     return 0;
}
getche();
clrscr();
```

Explanation In this program, required variables and function prototypes are declared before *main ()*. The user can perform different operations and they are displayed. Program will ask the user to enter a choice. The option entered by user is passed to *switch ()* case statement where appropriate case statement is executed. Actually, the case statement body invokes function and operation gets started.

```
} while (option!=5);
}

void create ()
{
   puts ("Insert number of elements<11 in the queue: ");
   scanf ("%d",&crn);
   puts("Enter elements: ");

   if (f==0)
   {
      f++;
      scanf ("%d",&e_ment);
      queue[f]=e_ment;
      r=f;
}

do
{
   ++r;
   if(r>crn) break;
   scanf ("%d",&e_ment);
   queue[r]=e_ment;
   }while(r<crn);
   }

   insert ()
   {
   r++;
   if (r>j)
   {
   puts("Queue is full "); return (1); }
   puts("Enter number to be inserted: ");
   scanf ("%d",&e_ment);
   queue[r]=e_ment;
   return 0;
   }

   erase()
   {
   if ( f==r)
   {
   puts("The queue is empty "); return (0); }
   f++;
   e_ment=queue[f];

   if (f==j)
```

```
{
f=1;
r=1;
}
return 0;
}

void show ()
{
for (k=f;k<=r;++k)
printf (" %d ",queue[k]);
}
```

```
OUTPUT
1 2 2 4 5
QUEUE OPERATIONS
1: Create
2: Insertion
3: Erase
4: Show
5: Exit
Enter your option:
4
1 2 2 4 5
```

The *create function* is used to insert numbers into the queue. In this function user has to enter number of elements to be inserted and followed by this user has to enter numbers. The *if block* is executed if the value of *f* (front) is zero. The element entered is stored in the *queue*. Using while loop repeatedly elements are entered and stored in the queue. The variable r is incremented in every loop. The *insert ()* function is used to insert an element at the given position in the queue. The variable *j* has value 10 and it shows maximum number which the queue can hold. If the value of *r* (rear) is greater than *j* its simple meaning is that queue is full and the return statement suspends the function execution. If the queue is empty and in the next available location, the entered element is stored.

In the *erase ()* function, first value of *r* (rear) and *f* (front) are compared and if they are same its meaning is that queue is empty. Because value of front and rear are same means the queue has no element. If *f* and *j* (maximum number) are same, both these variables are set to one.

The *show()* function is used to display the element as output. The loop is executed from value of front variable to rear. In the *erase ()* function, the elements are not actually erased, just position of front is increased. The same value of front is used to display the elements. Before the fth position, the elements exist physically. We can also erase them physically, but then we have to move the elements to the beginning of the array.

5.8 TYPES OF QUEUES

In the last few topics, we have studied simple queue and already seen the disadvantages. When rear pointer reaches to the end of the queue (array), no more elements can be added in the queue, even if beginning memory locations of array are empty. To overcome the above disadvantage, different types of queues can be applied. Different types of queues are:

5.8.1 Circular Queue

The simple or in a straight line queue there are several limitations we know, even if memory locations at the beginning of queue are available, elements cannot be inserted as shown in the Fig. 5.9. We can efficiently utilize the space available of straight-line queue by using circular queue.

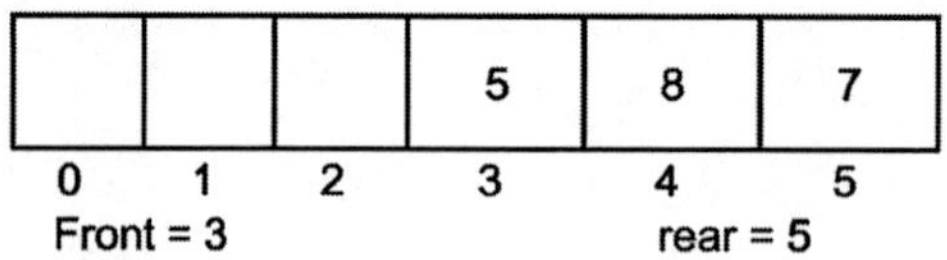

Figure 5.9 Simple queues with empty spaces

In the above discussion, it is supposed that front is not shifted to the beginning of the queue. As shown in the Fig. 5.10 a circular queue is like a wheel or a perfect ring. Suppose, *c [4]* is an array declared for implementation of circular queue. However, logically elements appear in circular fashion but physically in computer memory, they are stored in successive memory locations.

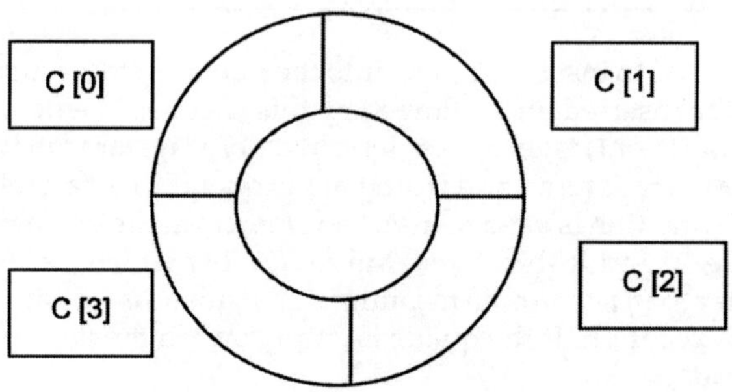

Figure 5.10 Circular queue

In the circular queue, the first element is stored immediately after last element. If last location of the queue is occupied, the new element is inserted at the first memory location of queue implementing an array (queue). For example, *C[n]*, C is queue of n elements. After inserting, storing an element in the last memory location [(n–1th) element], the next element will be stored at the first location, if space is available. It is like a chain of where starting and ending points are joined and a circle is formed. When an element is stored in the last location wrapping takes place and element inserting routine of the program pointed to beginning of the queue.

Recall that a pointer (stack and queue pointer) plays an important role to know the position of the elements in the stack and queue. Here, as soon as last element is filled, the pointer is wrapped to the beginning of the queue by shifting the pointer value to one.

A circular queue overcomes the limitation of the simple queue by utilizing the entire space of the queue. Like a simple queue, the circular queue also have front and rear ends. The rear and front ends help us to know the status of the queue after the insertion and deletion operations. In the circular queue implementation, the element shifting operation of queue that we apply in the simple queue is not required. The pointer itself takes care to move at vacant location of the queue and element is placed at that location. In order to simulate the circular queue a programmer should follow the following points:

1. The front end of the queue always points to the first element of the queue.
2. If the values of front and queue are equal, the queue is empty. The values of front and rear pointers are only increased/decreased after insertion/deletion operation.
3. Like simple queue, rear pointer is incremented by one when a new element is inserted and front pointer is incremented by one when an element is deleted.

Insertion

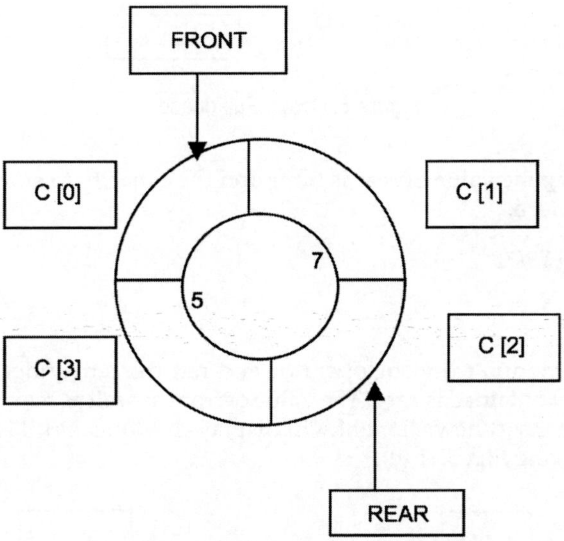

Figure 5.11(a) Insertion in a queue

As per Fig. 5.11(a), the insertion of an element in a queue will be same as in a linear queue. The programmer must have to trace the values of front and rear variables.

In Fig. 5.11 (a), only two elements are there in the queue. If we continue to add elements, the queue would be as shown in Fig. 5.11 (b). The new element is always inserted from the rear end. The position where the next element is to be placed can be calculated by the following formula.

REAR = (1+*REAR*) % *MAXSIZE*
C[REAR] = *NUMBER*

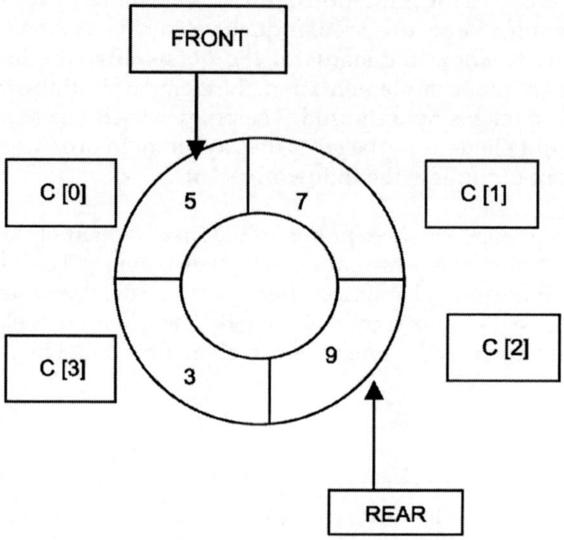

Figure 5.11(b) Full queue

From the Fig. 5.11(b), the value of rear is three and the capacity to store maximum element of queue is four. Therefore,

REAR = (1+*REAR*) % *MAXSIZE*
REAR = (1+3)%4
REAR = 4%4 = 0.

The operator % is modular divisor operator and returns remainder. Thus, in the above equation the remainder obtained is zero. The value of front as well as rear is zero, it means stack is full. Any attempt to insert new element will display the "queue full" message.

Consider, the following Fig. 5.11 (c),

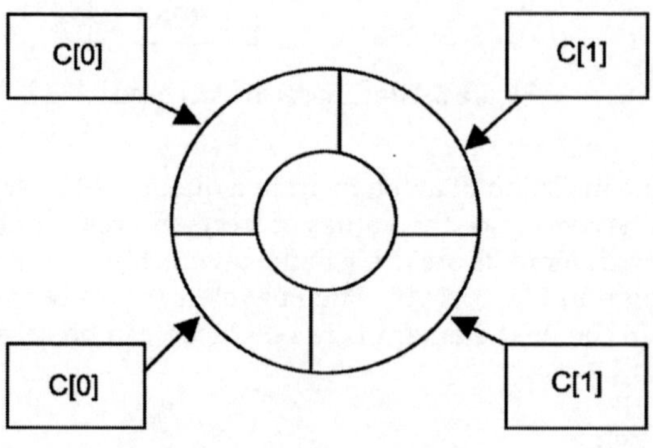

Figure 5.11(c) Circular queue

Example 5.9

Write a program to perform insert, delete operations with circular queue and display elements.

Solution

```
# include <stdio.h>
# include <conio.h>
# include <process.h>

int queue[8];int r,f=0,x=0;
void insert(void);
void del ();
void show (void);

main ()
{
 int c;
 clrscr();
 printf ("\n 1] Insert Element ");
 printf ("\n 2] Delete Element ");
 printf ("\n 3] Display element");
 printf ("\n 4] Exit");
 printf ("\n Enter your choice: ");
 scanf ("%d",&c);

switch (c)
{
 case 1: insert(); break;
 case 2: del(); show();break;
 case 3: show(); break;
 default: exit(0);
}
 main ();
 }

 void insert ()
 {
 int n;
 char ch,ans='Y';
 if (r>=7)
 {
    while (queue[x]==0)
    {
     printf ("\n Enter a Number: ");
     scanf ("%d",&n);
      queue[x]=n;
```

Explanation In this program, various operations such as insert, delete and display are performed. When an insert operation is performed and elements are inserted, elements appear one after another in sequence. If we remove element, the beginning location remains empty. If the last location holds an element and if insertion request is made by the user, the new element inserted is stored at the starting location. If we go on continuously performing remove operation, the elements at the beginning are not removed first (see Fig. 5.12).

```
x++;
puts("\n Continue Y/N: ");
ch=getch();

if (ch!='Y') break;

}
printf ("\n Queue is full \n\n\n");

main();
}

printf ("\n Enter elements: ");
while (ans=='Y')
{
scanf ("%d",&queue[r]);
if (r==7)
{
clrscr();
printf ("\n Queue is Full");
getch();
break;
}
else
r++;
printf ("\n Continue Y/N: ");
ans=getche();
}
}

void show()
{
int j;
for (j=0;j<8;j++)
printf (" %d ",queue[j]);
getch();
}

void del ()
{
int j;
if (r==0)
{
clrscr();
printf ("\n Queue is empty \n\n\n");
main();
}
```

```
if (f==8) f=0;

queue[f]=0;
f++;
}
```

```
OUTPUT
1] Insert Element
2] Delete Element
3] Display element
4] Exit
Enter your choice: 2
0 2 0 0 0 0 0 0
```

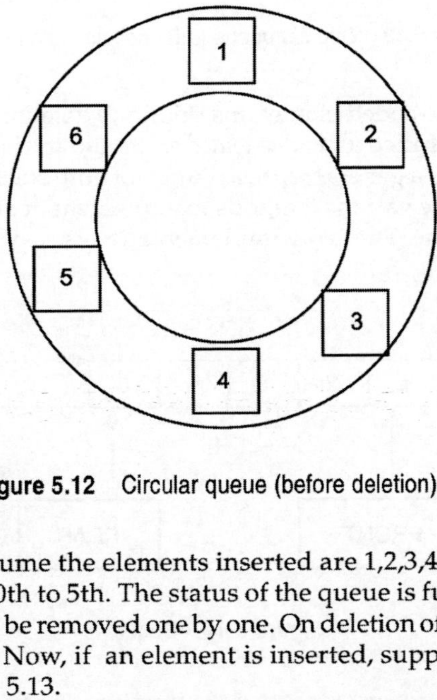

Figure 5.12 Circular queue (before deletion)

In the above program, assume the elements inserted are 1,2,3,4,5 and 6 and consider their position in the array is from 0th to 5th. The status of the queue is full. If we keep on removing elements, the elements would be removed one by one. On deletion of element of the 0th location, this location remains empty. Now, if an element is inserted, suppose seven, it will be stored in the 0th location as in Fig. 5.13.

Due to circular queue mechanism, if last location is occupied and the beginning locations are empty, the element is inserted at the empty location. If we keep on removing elements, the elements will be removed in the order from 2,3,4,5,6 and 7. However, the seven is stored at 0th location of the array but it was the last element inserted.

5.8.2 Double Ended Queues

Till now, we have studied stack and queue. The stack has only one end and can be used alternately to insert and delete elements. On the other hand, the double-ended queue has two ends, front and rear. The front end is used to remove element and rear end is used to insert

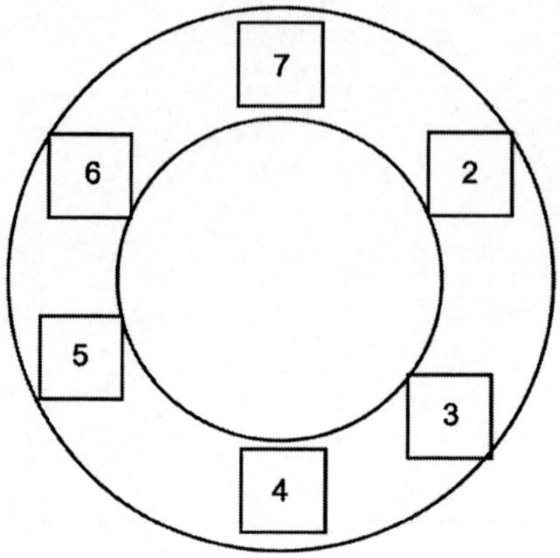

Figure 5.13 Circular queue (after deletion and insertion)

elements. Here, in the double-ended queues, insertion and deletion can be performed from both the ends and therefore, it is called as *double-ended queue* and in short *deque*. It is a homogenous list of elements. The deque is a general representation of both stack and queue and can be used as stack and queue. There are various methods to implement deque. Linked list and array can be used to perform the deque. The array implementation is easy and straightforward.

Consider the following Fig. 5.14:

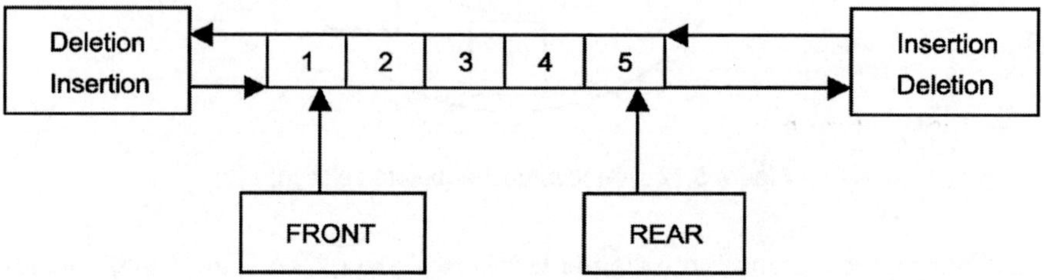

Figure 5.14 Deque

In deque, it is necessary to fix the type of operation to be performed on front and rear ends. The deque can be classified into two types:

Input Restricted Deque In the input restricted deque, insertion and deletion operation are performed at rear end whereas only deletion operation is performed at front end. The Fig. 5.15 represents the input restricted deque.

The following operations are possible in the input restricted deque:

1. Insertion of an element at the rear end.
2. Deletion of element at both front and rear ends.

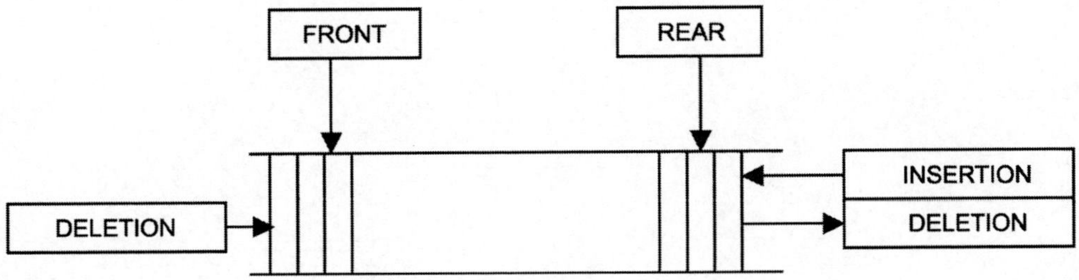

Figure 5.15 Input restricted deque

Thus, input restricted deque allows insertion at one and deletion at both ends.

Example 5.10

Write a program to demonstrate input restricted deque.

Solution

```
# include <stdio.h>
# include <conio.h>
int ird[5];
main()
{
 int r=0,c=1,op,f=-1;
 int insert(int);
 void deleter(int,int);
 void deletef(int,int);
 void show(void);

 while (1)
 {
 clrscr();
 printf ("\n (1) Insert ");
 printf ("\n (2) Delete from rear");
 printf ("\n (3) Delete from front");
 printf ("\n (4) Display ");
 printf ("\n (0) Exit");
 printf ("\n Enter Your choice:- ");
 scanf ("%d",&op);
 switch(op)
 {
 case 1:     while (c && r<5)
 {
 c=insert(r);
```

Explanation The output of the program is not fully displayed here. User can see it by executing it. Recall that in input restricted queue, insertion can be done only from rear end and it is carried out by the function *insert ()*. The while loop is executed for continuous execution of the *insert ()* function. User can enter element and when zero is entered, the loop is terminated. Thus, insertion of elements is carried out. The variable *r (rear)* is incremented and its value should not exceed the maximum capacity of the array, i.e. 5 and the same is done in the *while loop* condition.

```
r++;
}
if (c==0 )
{
c=1;
r—;
}
else
if (f<0)
printf ("\n Deque is full ");
getch();
break;
case 2: deleter(—r,f);break;
case 3: deletef(r,++f); break;
case 4: show (); break;
default: exit(0);
}
}
}

void show ()
{
int j;
printf ("\n Elements of deque are: ");
for (j=0;j<5;j++)
printf (" %d ",ird[j]);
getche();
}

int insert (int h)
{
int k;
printf ("\n Enter an element (enter 0 to exit): ");
scanf ("%d",&k);
ird[h]=k;
return (k);
}

void deleter(int m,int n)

{
if(m<=n)
printf("Deque is empty");
else
{
printf ("\n %d The element deleted: %d",m,ird[m]);
ird[m]=0;
```

```
}
getch();

}

void deletef(int f,int j)
{
if(f<j)
printf("Deque is empty");
else
{
printf("\n %d The element deleted:- %d",j,ird[j]);
ird[f]=NULL;
}
getch();
}
```

```
OUTPUT:
(1) Insert
(2) Delete from rear
(3) Delete from front
(4) Display
(0) Exit
Enter Your choice:- 1
Enter an element (enter 0 to exit): 2
Enter an element (enter 0 to exit): 3
Enter an element (enter 0 to exit): 5
Enter an element (enter 0 to exit): 8
Enter an element (enter 0 to exit): 6
Deque is full
(1) Insert
(2) Delete from rear
(3) Delete from front
(4) Display
(0) Exit
Enter Your choice:- 4
Elements of deque are: 2 3 5 8 6
```

We have a choice to remove the elements. We can remove elements from both the ends. If we go for second choice, elements from rear side are removed. The variable *r (rear)* is decremented and the *r*th element of the deque is erased. This option has a side effect. The empty locations generated by the deletion operation can be filled using insertion operation. However, if we go for option 3 the case is different. In this case, the elements are deleted from front and vacant space is created at the beginning of the deque. If we want to insert the element in that place, the insert option will fail here. This is because it is programmed in circular fashion. This is the drawback of input restricted deque.

Output Restricted Deque In the output restricted deque insertion of an element can be done at both front and rear end and deletion operation can be done only at front end. The output restricted deque is shown in Fig. 5.16.

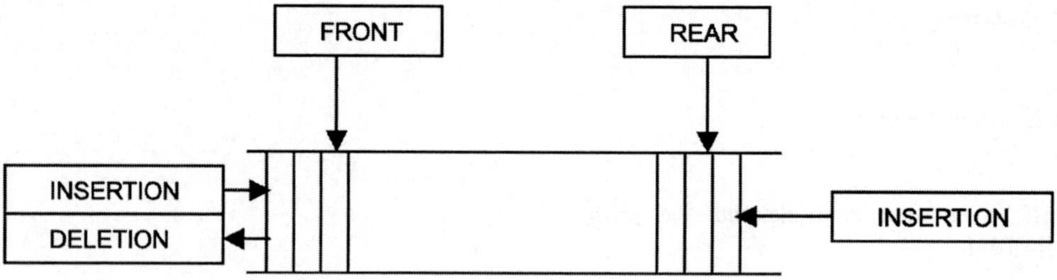

Figure 5.16 Output restricted deque

The following operations are possible in the output restricted deque:

1. Insertion at both front and rear end.
2. Deletion at only front end.

An example to demonstrate output restricted deque is illustrated below.

Example 5.11

Write a program to demonstrate output restricted deque

Solution

```
# include <stdio.h>
# include <conio.h>
# include <process.h>

int ird[5];
main ()
{

   int r=0,c=1,op,f=-1;
   int insertr(int);
   int insertf(int);
   void deletef(int);
   void show(void);
   clrscr();

   while (1)
   {
```

```
    printf ("\n 1 Insert from rear: ");
    printf ("\n 2 Insert from front");
    printf ("\n 3 Delete from front");
    printf ("\n 4 Display ");
    printf ("\n 0 Exit");
    printf ("\n Enter Your choice: ");
    scanf ("%d",&op);

    switch(op)
    {
     case 1:
        while (c && r<5)
        {
        c=insertr(r);
        r++;
        }

        if (c==0 )
        {
        c=1;
        r—;
        }
        else if (f<0)
        printf ("\n Deque is full ");
        getch();
        break;

     case 2: f=insertf(f); break;
     case 3: deletef(++f); break;
     case 4: show (); break;
     default: exit(0);
    }
    }
}

void show ()
{
   int j;
   printf ("\n Elements of deque are: ");
   for (j=0;j<5;j++)
   printf (" %d ",ird[j]);
   getche();
}

int insertr (int h)
{
int k;
```

Explanation In the output restricted queue, insertion can be done at both the ends and deletion can be done only at front end. The deletion procedure is same as the last program. In addition, insertion from rear end follows the same instruction as described in the previous program. The newly introduced function is *insertf ()*, which performs insertion of elements from front of the deque. First, the space availability is checked. If space is available and request is made, the user has to insert the element and the same is stored in the empty location. The variable *f* is decremented. This is because while performing deletion operation the front is shifted forward and to reverse it, the value of *f* is decremented.

```
printf ("\n Enter a Element (enter 0 to exit): ");
scanf ("%d",&k);
ird[h]=k;
return (k);

}

int insertf(int m)
{
int h;
if (ird[m]==0 && m>=0)
{
   printf ("\n Enter a element: ");
   scanf ("%d",&h);
   ird[m]=h;
}
else
printf ("\n no space available ");
return —m;
}

void deletef(int f) { ird[f]=NULL; }
```

```
OUTPUT
1 Insert from rear:
2 insert from front
3 Delete from front
4 Display
0 Exit
Enter Your choice: 1
Enter a Element (enter 0 to exit): 1
Enter a Element (enter 0 to exit): 2
Enter a Element (enter 0 to exit): 3
Enter a Element (enter 0 to exit): 0
1 Insert from rear:
2 insert from front
3 Delete from front
4 Display
0 Exit
Enter Your choice: 4
Elements of deque are: 1 2 3 0 0
```

5.8.3 Priority Queues

We know that queue is based on the technique first come first out (FIFO). The element inserted first will be deleted first. A priority queue is another type of queue. Here, the priority is determined according to the position of the queue, which is to be entered. Various real life problems are based on priority queues. For example, in the buses few seats are reserved for ladies and handicapped; if a company is providing any scheme, the employees of the same company are given second priority.

Priority queue is a data structure in which prioritized insertion and deletion operations on elements can be performed according to their priority values.

There are two types of priority queues:

Ascending Priority Queue In this queue elements can be inserted randomly. The smallest element of the queue is deleted first.

Example 5.12

Write a program to create ascending priority queue. Insert and remove the element.

Solution

```
# include <stdio.h>
# include <conio.h>


int prq[5]={0};
int insert();
void remove1();
void show();

main()
{
int j,c=1;
while (c!=0)
{
clrscr();
printf ("\n 1. Insert");
printf ("\n 2. Remove");
printf ("\n 3. Display");
printf ("\n 0. Exit");
printf ("\n Enter Your choice: ");
scanf ("%d",&c);
switch(c)
{
case 1: insert(); break;
case 2: remove1(); break;
case 3: show(); break;
default: exit(0);
}
}
}
int insert()
```

Explanation In this program an array *prq []* is defined. The array *prq[]* is used to implement priority queue. The *insert ()* function is used to insert an element in the queue. The position and element number are to be provided by the user. According to user entered values, the process is executed. User can randomly insert position numbers from 1 to 5. If the user repeats the same location number in which the element is already stored, the insertion will be terminated. The replacement of element is not allowed here. If the location is empty then only insertion of element is possible.

```
{
int n,j;
printf ("\n Enter the position: ");
scanf ("%d",&n);
n—;
if (n>4 || prq[n]!=0 )
{
printf ("\n Location is not available");
return 0;
}
printf ("\n Enter Element: ");
scanf ("%d",&j);
prq[n]=j;
return 0;
}

void remove1()
{
int j,k,min=0,s=0;
for (j=0;j<=4;j++)
s=s+prq[j];
for (j=s;j>0;j—)
{
for (k=0;k<5;k++)
{
if (j==prq[k])
min=prq[k];
}
}
for (j=0;j<5;j++)
{
if (prq[j]==min)
{
prq[j]=0;
break;
}
}
}
void show()
{ int h;
for (h=0;h<5;h++)
printf (" %d ",prq[h]);
getch();
}
```

```
OUTPUT
1. Insert
2. Remove
3. Display
0. Exit
Enter Your choice: 1
Enter the position: 1
Enter Element: 3
```

The show () function is used to display elements only. The remove1() function is used to remove the element. Before the removal of an element, it must be sorted first (in ascending or descending order). We know that in ascending order queue, the smallest element is deleted first. Hence, instead of arranging all the elements of the queue in ascending order, here the smallest element of the queue is searched and it is removed. In the priority queue, we can insert an element anywhere in the queue. Hence, it may not be compulsory to arrange the numbers in ascending order. If we arrange the elements in ascending order and then begin the removal operation, it will also change the exact position of the element. The user can also implement this program by sorting the queue elements, storing elements temporarily and then the smallest element can be erased. The program for descending priority queue can be done in the same fashion.

Descending Priority Queue In this queue also, elements can be inserted randomly but the largest element is deleted first.

Example 5.13

Write a program to create descending priority queue. Insert and remove the element.

Solution

```
# include <stdio.h>
# include <conio.h>

int prq[5]={0};
   int insert (void);
   void remove1(void);
   void show (void);

main ()
{
   int j,c=1;
   clrscr();

   while (c!=0)
   {
   printf ("\n 1. Insert");
   printf ("\n 2. Remove");
   printf ("\n 3. Display");
```

Explanation This program is same as previous one. Here, only the largest element is deleted first. It is an example of descending order queue.

```
    printf ("\n 0. Exit");
    printf ("\n Enter Your choice: ");
    scanf ("%d",&c);

 switch(c)
 {
  case 1: insert(); break;
  case 2: remove1 (); break;
  case 3: show (); break;
    }
 }
 }

int insert ()
{
    int n,j;
    printf ("\n Enter the position: ");
    scanf ("%d",&n);
    n—;

 if (n>4 || prq[n]!=0 )
 {
    printf ("\n Location is not avaliable");
    return 0;
 }

    printf ("\n Enter Element: ");
    scanf ("%d",&j);
    prq[n]=j;
    return 0;
}

void remove1 ()
{
    int j,k,max=0,s=0;
    for (j=0;j<=4;j++)
    s=s+prq[j];

    for (j=0;j<s;j++)
    {
 for (k=0;k<5;k++)
 {
  if (j==prq[k]) max=prq[k];
 }
 }
    for (j=0;j<5;j++)
 {
```

```
    if (prq[j]==max)
    {
        prq[j]=0;
        break;
    }
  }
}
void show ()
{
    int h;
    for (h=0;h<5;h++)
    printf (" %d ",prq[h]);
}
```

```
OUTPUT
1. Insert
2. Remove
3. Display
0. Exit
Enter Your choice: 3
8 3 1 10 9
1. Insert
2. Remove
3. Display
0. Exit
Enter Your choice: 2
1. Insert
2. Remove
3. Display
0. Exit
Enter Your choice: 3
8 3 1 0 9
```

In both the above types, if elements with equal priority are present, the *FIFO* technique is applied. In case the queue elements are sorted, the deletion of an element will be quick and easy because elements will appear either in ascending or descending order. However, the insertion operation will be easier said than done because empty locations will have to be searched and only then elements can be placed at that location.

In case the queue elements are not in order, i.e. not sorted, insertion operation will be quick and easy. However, the deletion operation will take place after the priority value set.

Therefore, we can say that in both the above types insertion operation can be carried out easily. However, the deletion operation, which is, based on certain priority, i.e. the smallest or largest is first searched out and later it is removed from the queue. The locations of that element do not matter. In stack and queues deletion operation is performed at the ends. Conceptually, there is no provision for deleting an element, which is neither first nor last element of the list.

In the above program, we have not arranged the elements in an ascending or descending order. Just smallest or largest element is searched and erased.

In deletion operation the element may not be physically removed from the queue and it can be kept inaccessible in the program. Alternatively, special character called *empty indicator* such as #, $ can be placed at that place. Both the insertion and deletion operation perform scanning of the queue elements. While performing deletion operation the element must be deleted physically. It is possible to make its access denied. However, for other computation operation, the element logically deleted but physically existing will be taken into account and will change the result. So, for sure result, the element must be removed.

The elements of the queue can be number, character or any complex object which is a composition of one or more basic data types.

In priority queue every element has been assigned with a priority value called priority. The elements can be inserted or deleted randomly anywhere in the queue. Consider the following points of queue:

1. An element of upper priority is processed prior to an element of lower priority.
2. If two elements have the same priority, they are processed depending on the order they are inserted in the queue, i.e. FIFO.

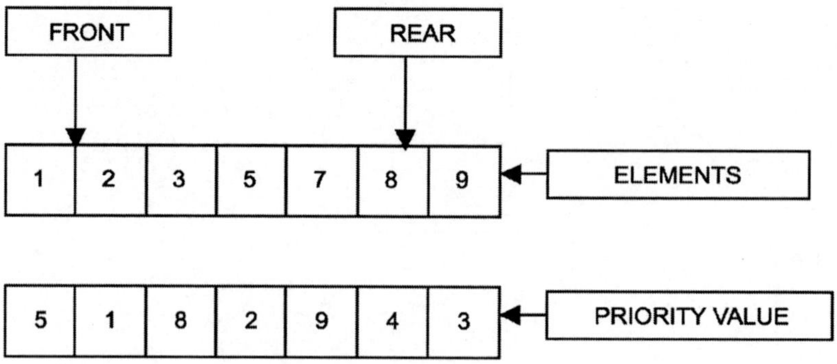

Figure 5.17 Priority queue

As shown in Fig. 5.17, the element 7 is deleted first. However, the element 1 is nearer to the front as compared to 7, but 7's priority value is nine, which is higher, and hence it is deleted first. Though the queue is based on FIFO technique, the priority queue is not based on FIFO operation firmly. A program on priority queue is provided below for detailed understanding.

Example 5.14

Write a program to demonstrate priority queue. Enter number and priority value. Perform insert and deletion operation.

Solution

```
#include<stdio.h>
#include <conio.h>
```

```
int pq[2][5]={0};

main ()
{
    int c=1;
    int insert (void);
    void show(void);
    void remove1(void);
    clrscr();
    do
    {
    printf ("\n1 Insert ");
    printf ("\n2 Remove ");
    printf ("\n3 Display");
    printf ("\n0 Exit");
    printf ("\n Enter Your Choice: ");
    scanf ("%d",&c);
    switch(c)
    {
    case 1: insert (); break;
    case 2: remove1(); break;
    case 3: show(); break;
    case 0: c=0;
    }
 }
 while (c!=0);
}

int insert ()
{
    int p,e,r;
    printf ("\n Position: ");
    scanf ("%d",&p);
    if (p>5 || p<0)
    {
    printf ("\n Invalid Argument ");
    return 0;
    }
    p—;
    printf ("\n Element: ");
    scanf ("%d",&e);
    if (pq[0][p]==0)
    pq[0][p]=e;
    printf ("\n Priority: ");
    scanf ("%d",&r);
    pq[1][p]=r;
    return 0;
```

Explanation This program is the same as the last few programs. Here, in this program two-dimensional array is defined. Using *insert function,* elements position number, element and its priority value are entered. Replacement of element is not allowed. When remove function is executed, the element with higher priority is detected and removed. The *show ()* function is used to display the elements and priority value.

```
}

void show ()
{
    int j,k;
    for (j=0;j<2;j++)
   {
 if (j==0)
 printf ("\n Elements: ");
 else
 printf ("\n Priority: ");
 for (k=0;k<5;k++)
    printf (" %d ",pq[j][k]);
    printf ("\n");
    }
}

void remove1 ()
{
    int j,maxp=0;
    for (j=0;j<5;j++)
    {
    if (pq[1][j]>maxp)
    maxp=pq[1][j];
 }
 for (j=0;j<5;j++)
 {
    if (pq[1][j]==maxp)
    {
    pq[0][j]=pq[1][j]=0;
    break;
    }
    }
 }
```

```
OUTPUT
Elements: 1 2 8 9 4
Priority: 1 3 9 8 3
1 Insert
2 Remove
3 Display
0 Exit
Enter Your Choice: 2
1 Insert
2 Remove
3 Display
0 Exit
```

```
Enter Your Choice: 3
Elements: 1 2 0 9 4
Priority: 1 3 0 8 3
```

5.9 APPLICATIONS OF QUEUES

There are various applications of computer science, which are performed using data structure queue. This data structure is usually used in simulation, various features of operating system, multiprogramming platform systems and different type of scheduling algorithm are implemented using queues. Round robin technique is implemented using queues. Printer server routines, various applications software are also based on queue data structure.

5.9.1 Round Robin Algorithm

Round Robin (RR) algorithm is an important scheduling algorithm. It is used especially for the time-sharing system. The circular queue is used to implement such algorithms.

For example, there are *N* procedures or tasks such as *P1, P2, P3* ... P_N. All these tasks are to be executed by the central processing unit (CPU) of the computer system. The execution times of the tasks or processes are different. The tasks are executed in sequence *P1*, P_2, P_3 and P_N.

In time, sharing mode the tasks are executed one by one. The algorithm forms a small unit of time, say, from 10 to 100 milliseconds for each task. This time is called *time slice* or *time quantum* of a task. The CPU executes tasks from P_1 to P_N allocating fixed amount of time for each process. On allocating time to all tasks, CPU resumes the first task. That is, when all tasks are completed, it returns to P_1. In the time-sharing system, if any task is completed before the estimated time, the next task is taken up for execution immediately. Consider the following table:

Tasks	*Expiry Time (Units)*
P1	10
P2	19
P3	8
P4	5

There are total four tasks and the total time to complete all the tasks would be (10+19+8+5) 42 units. Suppose, the time slice is of 7 minutes. The RR scheduling for the above case would be

In the first pass each task takes seven units of time-task *P4* is executed in the first pass whereas task *P1, P2, P3* requires more than 7 units of time. Hence, in the second round task *P1* and *P3* are executed. At last, *P2* is executed.

5.9.2 Simulation

It is an extremely powerful tool used for experimentation purpose. Without performing real experiments simulation permits to take the results and if necessary modification can be done as per expected results. One of the standard applications of queue can be implemented with simulation. Simulation is a method of managing a theoretical illustration of a real life problem with the purpose of understanding the effect of modification, concern factors and implementing some approaches to get reliable solution. The main goal of simulation is to help the user or to guess for obtaining the output of the program after implementing some approaches. It permits the user to make several trials for getting the actual results and planned situations without disturbing the real situation.

There are few disadvantages in the simulation. Lengthy simulation creates execution overhead on computer. For solving a real life problem, various assumptions are made to find out the key solution. If the assumption is straightforward, the outcome will be less reliable. In contrast, if the assumption is having more particulars, the outcome will be reliable and better. If the primary assumptions are wrong, even though, the program source code is given in detail, the guess obtained will be incorrect. In this situation, the program developed becomes futile.

5.10 TYPES OF SYSTEMS

A system may be *isolated* or *continuous*. The continuous system has some arguments, which can receive any real value in some gaps. Simulation of this system runs on these continuous arguments. In the *discrete system*, the method is different, it takes only selected set of values. The moving of a fan at home is a discrete system and its speed can be controlled. The motion of earth or sun is an example of continuous system and its motion is out of our control. The input and output parameters also defines system. The system can be either *deterministic* or *stochastic*. The input and output parameters also have a relationship. The various systems are descried in Fig. 5.18.

Deterministic System In this case if input values and initial state are available the result can be determined.

Stochastic System This system necessitates efforts for simulation. There is no standard clarification for this system.

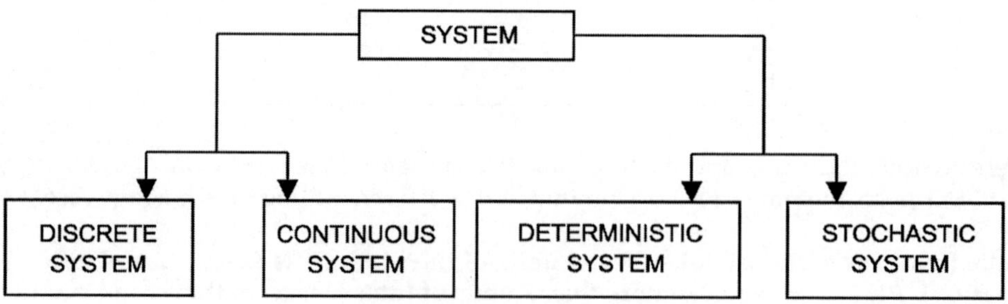

Figure 5.18 Types of systems

To simulate a system a model is formed. It is a body of detailed particulars and applied to represent the system in various forms. There are various models as *event-driven, simulation* and *time-simulation model* and selection of model depends upon particulars of information available. The first step in solving the problem is selecting structure of model because the model indicates the system and it is easier than the problem. The model should be restricted and should not provide information out of the system. To facilitate the formation of model for a state, the characteristics, entities, activities and operations of the system must be determined. Activity refers to change of system state. The entities indicate the mechanism of the system and serves as an object in the simulation. The objects have characteristics. The characteristics of objects denote the state of the system and association between various entities at that particular movement. The program must execute given steps and activities (change of state) must occur in sequence.

Summary

1. A queue is a non-primitive, linear data structure and a sub-class of list data structure. It is an ordered, homogenous collection of elements in which elements are appended at one end called rear end and elements are deleted at other end called front end.
2. The static implementation means the array implementation. In this implementation, we should be assured about the number of elements we want to have in the queue.
3. Two operations can be carried out on queue:
   a. insertion of element
   b. deletion of element.
4. Dynamic implementation is carried out using pointers. By applying increment, operation on pointer successive locations of memory can be accessed and an element can be stored in that location.
5. There are three types of queue, i.e. circular queue, deque and priority queue.
6. In the circular queue, the first element is stored immediately after last element. If last location of the queue is occupied then the new element is inserted at the first memory location of queue implementing array (queue).
7. In the double-ended queue, insertion and deletion can be performed from both the ends and therefore, it is called double-ended queues and in short called deque. It is a homogenous list of elements.
8. In the input restricted deque, insertion and deletion operation are performed at rear end whereas only deletion operation is performed at front end.
9. In the output restricted deque, insertion of an element can be done at both front and rear end and deletion operation can be done at only front end.
10. Priority queue is a data structure in which prioritized insertion and deletion operations on elements can be performed according to their priority value.
11. *Ascending priority queue*: In this, queue elements can be inserted randomly. The smallest element of the queue is deleted first.
12. *Descending priority queue*: In this queue also, elements can be inserted randomly and the largest element is deleted first.
13. Simulation is a method of organizing a theoretical representation of a real life problem with the purpose of understanding the effect of alteration, concern factors and implementing some approaches to get reliable solution.

Exercises

A. Answer the following questions:
   1. What is queue? Explain it with real life examples.

2. Explain the terms front and rear with relevance to queue. Which operations are to be performed at these ends?
3. Explain different types of queues.
4. How is implementation of queue done?
5. What are the limitations of simple queue?
6. Explain the insertion and deletion operations of queue.
7. Differentiate between simple and circular queues.
8. Differentiate between stack and queue.
9. Distinguish between FIFO and LIFO.
10. Give the definition of priority queue. Explain its types.
11. Explain types of deque.
12. Explain types of priority queues.
13. Explain system and types of systems.

B. Attempt the following programs:

1. Write a program to insert and display the eight alphabetic characters in a queue.
2. Write a program to declare a priority queue using two-dimensional array, store elements and priority. Display the elements according to priority from higher to lower.
3. Write a program to implement circular queue with the pointers.
4. Write a program to insert and display the elements of deque, with the array and pointers.
5. Write a program to insert five elements in the ascending priority queue. Sort the elements in ascending order. Perform the deletion operation and shift the empty location at the end of array.
6. Write a program to create a priority queue. Store element and priority value. Assume square root of entered number as its priority value. Insert and delete the elements.
7. Write a program to implement a circular queue containing eight elements and perform the insertion and deletion operation.

C. Select the appropriate option for each of the following questions:

1. Queue follows the rule
   a. FIFO c. LILO
   b. LIFO d. FILO.
2. The rear end of the queue is used
   a. to insert an element c. both (a) and (b)
   b. to remove an element d. none of the above.
3. The front end of the queue is used
   a. to insert an element c. both (a) and (b)
   b. to remove an element d. none of the above.
4. When an element is inserted in queue, the position of rear
   a. increases c. remains constant
   b. decreased d. none of the above.
5. When an element is inserted in queue, the position of front
   a. increments c. unchanged
   b. decrements d. none of the above.
6. Which one of the following is not a type of queue?
   a. output restricted deque c. deque
   b. circular queue d. priority queue.

7. In this queue elements can be inserted randomly
   a. priority queue c. circular queue
   b. simple queue d. none of the above.
8. In the input restricted queue
   a. deletion of element at both front and rear ends is done c. deletion at only front end
   b. insertion of element at both front and rear ends is done d. all of the above.
9. In this queue, smallest element of the queue is deleted first.
   a. ascending priority queue c. circular queue
   b. descending priority queue d. simple queue.
10. When the circular queue is full, and if one element is removed the next inserted element is stored at
   a. first location c. intermediate location
   b. last location d. none of the above.

D. Find the output

1.

```
# include <stdio.h>
# include <conio.h>
main ()
{
   int que[8];
   int r=0;
   clrscr();
   while(r<7)
   {
   printf ("Enter element: ");
   scanf ("%d",&que[r]);
   r++;
}
printf ("\n Elements of Queue are: ");
r=0;
while (r<7)
{
printf (" %d ", que[r]);
r++;
   }
}
```

2.

```
# include<stdio.h>
# include <conio.h>
main ()
{
int q[7];
int r=0,f=0,j;
clrscr();
while (r<6)
{
printf ("rear=%d front=%d Enter element:",r,f);
scanf ("%d",&q[r]);
r++;
}
printf ("\n Queue elements are: ");
for (j=0;j<6;j++)
printf (" %d ",q[j]);
}
```

3.

```
# include<stdio.h>
# include <conio.h>
main ()
{
int q[7];
int r=0,f=0,j;
char ch;
clrscr();
while (r<6)
{
printf ("rear=%d front=%d Enter element:",r,f);
scanf ("%d",&q[r]);
r++;
}
printf ("\nQueue elements are: ");
```

```
for (j=0;j<6;j++)
      printf (" %d ",q[j]);
      printf("\nWould you like to delete one element
      from queue?[Y/N]:-");
      scanf("%s",&ch);
      if(ch=='y'||ch=='Y')
      {
      q[f]=0;
      f++;
      printf ("\nAfter deletion of one element
      rear=%d front=%d\n ",r,f);
      printf("\nQueue elements are:- ");
      for (j=f;j<6;j++)
      printf (" %d ",q[j]);
         }
      }
```

4.

```
# include<stdio.h>
# include <conio.h>
main ()
{
int q[6];
int i,r=6,f=0,n;
clrscr();
printf("Enter the seven elements of a queue:- ");
for(i=0;i<7;i++)
scanf("%d",&q[i]);

printf("\nThe queue element are as:-\n");
for(i=0;i<7;i++)
printf("%2d ",q[i]);
printf ("\nValues of at start rear=%d
front=%d",r,f);
printf ("\n\nHow many elements you want to
delete: ");
scanf ("%d",&n);
while (f<n)
{
q[f]=NULL;
f++;
printf ("\nrear=%d front=%d",r,f);
}
printf ("\n Queue elements are: ");
for ( n=0;n<7;n++)
printf (" %d ",q[n]);
}
```

5.

```
# include <stdio.h>
# include <conio.h>
# include <process.h>
int qe[8];
int r=0,j;
char ans='Y';
void insert();
void del ();
void show ();
main ()
{
int c;
while(1)
{
clrscr();
printf ("\n 1] Insert Element ");
printf ("\n 2] Delete Element ");
printf ("\n 3] Display element");
printf ("\n 4] Exit");
printf ("\n Enter your choice: ");
scanf ("%d",&c);
switch (c)
{
case 1: insert(); break;
case 2: del(); show();break;
case 3: show(); break;
default: exit(0);
}
}
}
void insert ()
{
if (r>=7)
printf ("\n Queue is full \n\n\n");
else
{
ans='y';
while (ans=='Y'||ans=='y')
{
printf ("\n Enter element:- ");
scanf ("%d",&qe[r]);
if (r==7)
{
clrscr();
printf ("\n Queue is Full");
getch();
break;
```

```
}
else
r++;
printf ("\n Continue Y/N: ");
ans=getch();
    }
    }
    }

void show()
{
int j;
for (j=0;j<r;j++)
printf (" %d ",qe[j]);
getch();
}
void del ()
{
if (r<=0)
{
clrscr();
printf ("\n Queue is empty \n\n\n");
}
for (j=0;j<r;j++)
qe[j]=  qe[j+1];
qe[r]=0;
r--;
}
```

6.

```
# include <stdio.h>
# include <conio.h>
void insert ();
void del();
void show ();
int m,n=10,fr=0, queue[11],re=0,num,cur;
main ()
{
int ch;
do
{
clrscr();
printf("\n[1] Insert");
printf("\n[2] Delete");
printf("\n[3] Show");
printf("\n[4] Exit");
printf("\nEnter Your choice: ");
scanf("%d",&ch);
switch(ch)
{
case 1: insert (); break;
case 2: del (); break;
case 3: show(); break;
default: exit(0);
}
}
while(1);
}
void insert ()
{
if (re<cur)
{
printf("\nQueue is full");
exit (0);
}
printf("\nEnter a number to be inserted ");
scanf ("%d",&queue[re]);
re++;

}
void del ()
{
if (fr==re)
{
printf("\nThe queue is empty");
exit(0);
}
fr++;
if (fr==n)
{
fr=1;
re=1;
}
}
void show ()
{
for (m=fr;m<re;++m)
printf (" %d ",queue[m]);
getch();
}
```

7.

```
# include <stdio.h>
# include <conio.h>
```

```
main ()
{
int *q;
int re=0,r;
clrscr();
printf("\nEnter zero for exit\n");
while(1)
{
printf ("Enter element: ");
scanf ("%d",q);
if(*q==0)
{ break; }
q++;
re++;
if (re==7)
{
printf ("\n Queue is full ");
break;
}
}
q=q-re;
printf ("\n Elements of Queue are: ");
r=0;
while (r<re)
{
printf ("\n Element: %d rear=%d", *(q+r),r);
r++;
}
return 0;
}
```

8.

```
# include <stdio.h>
# include <conio.h>
int qu[8],r,f=0,x=0;
void insert();
void del ();
void show ();
void main ()
{
int c;
clrscr();
printf ("\n [1] Insert Element ");
printf ("\n [2] Delete Element ");
printf ("\n [3] Display element");
printf ("\n [4] Exit");
printf ("\n Enter your choice:- ");
scanf ("%d",&c);
switch (c)
{
case 1: insert(); break;
case 2: del(); show();break;
case 3: show(); break;
default: exit(0);
}
main ();
}
void insert ()
{
int n;
char ch,ans='Y';
if (r>=7)
{
while (qu[x]==0)
{
printf ("\n Enter a Number: ");
scanf ("%d",&n);
qu[x]=n;
x++;
puts("\n Continue Y/N: ");
ch=getch();
if (ch!='Y'||ch!='y')
break;
}
printf ("\n Queue is full \n\n\n");
main();
}
printf ("\n Enter elements: ");
while (ans=='Y')
{
scanf ("%d",&qu[r]);
if (r==7)
{
clrscr();
printf ("\n Queue is Full");
getch();
break;
}
else
r++;
printf ("\n Continue Y/N: ");
ans=getche();
}
}
```

```
void show()
{
int j;
for (j=0;j<8;j++)
printf (" %d ",qu[j]);
getch();
}
void del ()
{
int j;
if (r==0)
{
clrscr();
printf ("\n Queue is empty \n\n\n");
main();
}
if (f==8)
f=0;
qu[f]=0;
f++;
}
```

Chapter 6

Static List and Linked List

Chapter Outline

6.1 INTRODUCTION

A list is a series of linearly arranged finite elements (numbers) of same type. The data elements are called nodes. The list can be of two types, i.e. basic data type or custom data type. The elements are positioned one after the other and their position numbers appear in sequence. The first element of the list is known as head and the last element is known as tail.

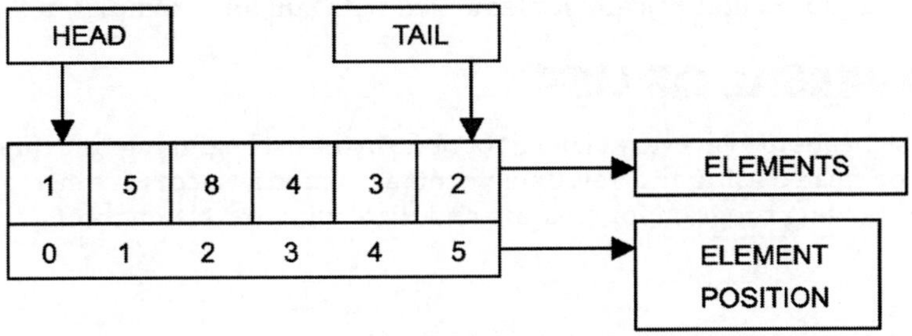

Figure 6.1 Static list

As shown in the above Fig. 6.1, the element 1 is at head position (0th) and element 2 is at tail position (5th). The element 5 is *predecessor* of element 8 and 4 is *successor*. Every element can act as *predecessor* excluding the first element because it does not have predecessor in the list. The list has following properties:

a. The list can be enlarged or reduced from both the ends.
b. The tail (ending) position of the list depends on how long the list is extended by the user.
c. Various operations such as transverse, insertion and deletion can be performed on the list.
d. The list can be implemented by applying static (array) or dynamic (pointer) implementation.

6.2 IMPLEMENTATION OF LIST

There are two methods of implementation of the list: they are static and dynamic.

6.2.1 Static Implementation

Static implementation can be implemented using arrays. It is a very simple method but it has few limitations. Once a size is declared, it cannot be changed during the program. It is also not efficient for memory. When array is declared, memory allocated is equal to the size of the array. The vacant space of array also occupies the memory space. In both the cases, if we store less arguments than declared, the memory is wasted and if more elements are stored than declared, array cannot be expanded. It is suitable only when exact number of elements are to be stored.

6.2.2 Dynamic Implementation

The linked list is a major application of the dynamic implementation and the pointers are used for the implementation. The limitations noticed in static implementation can be removed by using dynamic implementation. The memory is utilized efficiently in this method. Hence, it is superior than the static implementation. With pointers, link does not have any restriction on number of elements at run time. The list can be stretched like elastic. Memory is allocated only after node is added or element is accepted in the list. Memory is de-allocated whenever node or element is removed. Dynamic memory management policy is used in the implementation of linked list and because of this memory is used resourcefully. In addition to that insertion and deletion of a node can be done easily.

Both the above representations are implemented with suitable examples in this chapter.

6.3 TRAVERSAL OF LIST

Traversing a list means to visit every element or node in the list beginning from first to last. The simple list can be created using an array. Its elements are stored in successive memory locations. Consider the following program for creating and displaying the elements of a list:

Example 6.1

Write a program to create a simple list of elements. Display the contents of list and reverse it.

Solution

```
# include <stdio.h>
# include <conio.h>

main ()
{
   int sim[5],j;
   clrscr();
   printf ("\nEnter five elements: ");
   for (j=0;j<5;j++)
   scanf ("%d",&sim[j]);

   printf ("\n List: ");
   for (j=0;j<5;j++)
   printf (" %d ",sim[j]);

   printf ("\n Reverse List: ");
   for (j=4;j>=0;j--)
   printf (" %d ",sim[j]);
   getchar();
}
```

Explanation This program is simple. Using simple declaration of an array a list can be implemented. Using *for loop* and *scanf ()* statements, five integers are entered. The list can be displayed using *printf ()* statement. Once a list is created, various operations such as sorting, searching can be applied. These operations are already explained in Chapters 4 and 5. The reader is advised to refer to Chapter 2 for more information on arrays.

```
OUTPUT
Enter five elements: 1 5 9 7 3
List: 1 5 9 7 3
Reverse List: 3 7 9 5 1
```

6.4 SEARCHING AND RETRIEVING AN ELEMENT

Once a list is created, one can access and perform operations with the elements. In the last program, all the elements are displayed. One can also specify some conditions such as to display numbers after a number 10 or remove the duplicate numbers from the list, finding a specific number or concatenate two lists. If the list contains large elements, it may be difficult to find a particular element and its position. It consumes more time for locating that element. Consider the following program for searching a number in a list:

Example 6.2

Write a program to create a list of integer elements and search the entered number from the list.

Solution

```
# include <stdio.h>
# include <conio.h>
main ()
{

int sim[7],j,n,flg;
clrscr();

printf ("\nEnter Seven Integers: ");
for (j=0;j<7;j++)
scanf ("%d",&sim[j]);

printf ("\n Enter Integer to Search: ");
scanf ("%d",&n);

for (j=0;j<7;j++)
{
if (sim[j]==n)
{
flg=1;
printf ("\n Found ! Position of integer %d is %d ", n,j+1 );
break;
}

}
if(flg!=1)
printf ("\n Element not found !");

}
```

Explanation In this program an array *sim [7]* seven integers are entered. Followed by this, an element is entered to search in the list. This is done by the *for loop* and embedded in the *if statement*. The *if* statement checks the entered element with the list elements. When match is found the number and its positions are displayed.

```
OUTPUT
Enter Seven Integers: 12 12 23 45 56 76 67
Enter Integer to Search: 67
Found ! Position of integer 67 is 7
Or
Enter Integers: 12 45 56 34 233 2345 56
Enter Integer to Search: 555
Element not found !
```

6.5 PREDECESSOR AND SUCCESSOR

In the list of elements, for any location *n*, *(n–1)* is predecessor and *(n+1)* is *successor*. In other words, for any location n in the list, the left element is *predecessor* and the right element is *successor*. The first element does not have *predecessor* and last element does not have *successor*. The Fig. 6.2 shows it.

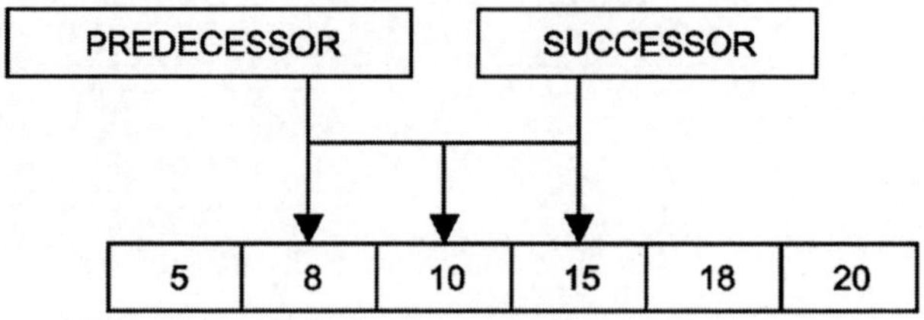

Figure 6.2 Predecessor and successor

The following program displays the predecessor and successor of the entered element from the list.

Example 6.3

Write a program to find predecessor and successor of the entered number in the list.

Solution

```
# include <stdio.h>
# include <conio.h>

main ()
{
   int num[8],j,n,k=0;
   clrscr();
   printf ("\n Enter eight elements: ");
   for (j=0;j<8;j++)
   scanf ("%d",&num[j]);

 printf ("\n Enter any element from the above: ");
 scanf ("%d",&n);

 for (j=0;j<8;j++)
 {
 if (n==num[j])
 {
 (j>0) ? printf ("\n The Predecessor of %d is %d ",num[j],num[j-1]):
 printf (" No Predecessor");
```

Explanation In this program eight elements are entered. The user has to enter an element whose predecessor and successor elements are to be displayed. All the elements of the array are checked with the entered number. When the match is found, the next element is displayed as successor and the previous element is displayed as predecessor. If the element entered is the first element of the list then only successor is displayed. If the entered element is the last then only predecessor is displayed. The above conditions are checked using *conditional operator (?:)*.

```
(j==7) ? printf ("\n No Successor"):
   printf ("\n The Successor of %d is %d", num[j],num[j+1]);
   break;
 }
 k++;
 }
}
```

```
OUTPUT
Enter eight elements: 1 2 5 8 7 4 4 6
Enter any element from the above: 5
The Predecessor of 5 is 2
The Successor of 5 is 8
```

6.6 INSERTION

Appending is a process in which new element is added at the end of the list. However, insertion of an element can also be done in the list. Insertion means an element is added in between two elements in the list. The insertion can be done at the beginning or at the end or anywhere in the list. Thus, the insertion of an element can be done at various positions in the list.

For successful insertion of an element, the array-implementing list should have at least one empty location. If the array is full, insertion is not possible. The target location where element is to be inserted is made empty by shifting elements downwards by one position and the newly entered element is placed at that location. Consider the following Fig. 6.3(a).

5	7	9	10	12		
0	1	2	3	4	5	6

Figure 6.3 (a)

As shown in Fig. 6.3(a), two empty spaces are available. Suppose, we want to insert 3 in between 7 and 9. All the elements after 7 must be shifted towards the end of the array. The resulting array would be as shown in Fig. 6.3(b).

5	7		9	10	12	
0	1	2	3	4	5	6

Figure 6.3 (b)

The entered number 3 can be assigned to that memory location and the array can be as shown in Fig. 6.3(c).

5	7	3	9	10	12	
0	1	2	3	4	5	6

Figure 6.3 (c)

A program for insertion of an element in a list is illustrated below.

Example 6.4

Write a program to create a list. Insert an element at the specific location.

Solution

```
# include <stdio.h>
# include <conio.h>
main ()
{
   int num[9]={0},j,p,n;
   clrscr();
   printf ("\n Enter eight elements: ");
   for (j=0;j<8;j++)
   scanf ("%d",&num[j]);
   printf ("\n Enter Position and element for insertion:-");
   scanf ("%d %d",&p,&n);
   --p;
   for (j=8;j>=p;j--)
   num[j]=num[j-1];
 num[p]=n;
 printf("\nList after insertion of element\n");
 for (j=0;j<=8;j++)
   printf (" %d ", num[j]);
 getch();
}
```

Explanation In this program an array *num [8]* is declared. The user has to enter eight elements continuously. Thus, the list contains one empty memory location, which is enough to carry insertion operation.

```
OUTPUT
Enter eight elements: 1 2 3 4 5 6 7 8
Enter Position and element for insertion:-6 12
List after insertion of element
1 2 3 4 5 12 6 7 8
```

The element and the position number where element is to be inserted, are to be entered. The user provides the values. Using *for loop* the position of vacant location is obtained. As the user specifies the position number, next all elements are shifted one memory location towards the end of the array. Due to shifting, space is generated and the entered element is placed at that location.

6.7 DELETION

Like insertion, deletion of an element can be done from the list. In deletion, the elements are moved upwards by one position.

5	7	3	9	10	12	
0	1	2	3	4	5	6

Figure 6.4 (a) Before deletion

The deletion of any element is very simple. Suppose, we want to remove element 3, then 3 is replaced with 9, 9 is replaced with 10, 10 is replaced with 12 and finally 12 is replaced with null. Thus, shifting of element is done. The Fig. 6.4 (a) and (b) shows status of static list before and after deletion of an element.

5	7	9	10	12		
0	1	2	3	4	5	6

Figure 6.4 (b) After deletion

Example 6.5

Write a program to create a list of integer elements. Delete the specific element from the list.

Solution

```
# include <stdio.h>
# include <conio.h>
# include <process.h>
main ()
{
 int num[8]={0},j,k=0,p,n,count;
 clrscr();
 printf ("\n Enter elements ( 0 to exit ): " );
 for (j=0;j<8;j++)
 {
 scanf ("%d",&num[j]);
 if ( num[j]==0)
   {
   count=j;
   break;
   }
 }
```

Explanation In this program, elements are entered by the user. User can enter maximum eight elements. The element, which is to be removed, is also entered. The *while loop* calculates the position of the element in the list. The second *for loop* shifts all the elements next to the specified element one position up towards the beginning of array. The element, which is to be deleted, is replaced with successor element. The last element is replaced with zero. Thus, the empty spaces are generated at the end of the array.

```
printf ("\n Enter an element to remove: ");
scanf ("%d",&n);
while (num[k]!=n)
k++;
for (j=k;j<count;j++)
num[j]=num[j+1];
num[j]=0;
for (j=0;j<count-1;j++)
printf (" %d ", num[j]);
}
```

```
OUTPUT
Enter elements ( 0 to exit ): 5 8 9 4 2 3 4 7
Enter an element to remove: 9
5 8 4 2 3 4 7
```

6.8 SORTING

Sorting and searching are two oft-used operations in data structures. In every walk of life one comes across these processes. Various methods would be applied for sorting and searching of records or elements. The following program explains sorting by exchange method. The reader can refer to chapters 10 and 11 where comprehensive information is provided about sorting and searching.

Example 6.6

Write a program to sort entered numbers by exchange method.

Solution

```
# include <stdio.h>
# include <conio.h>

main ()
{
   int num[8]={0};
   int k=0,h,a,n,tmp;
   clrscr();
   printf ("\n Enter Eight Numbers: ");
   for (a=0;a<8;++a)
   scanf ("%d",&num[a]);

   while (k<7)
   {
   for (h=k+1;h<8;++h)

   if (num[k]>num[h])
```

Explanation In this program eight numbers are entered. The *while loop* and *for loop* are used to access, compare and exchange the elements. Every element of an array is compared with all successive elements. When small element is found it is stored at the beginning location in the array using *tmp* variable.

```
   {
   tmp=num[k];
   num[k]=num[h];
   num[h]=tmp;
}
k++;
}
printf ("\n Sorted array: ");

for (k=0;k<8;++k)
printf (" %d ",num[k]);
}
```

```
OUTPUT
Enter Eight Numbers: 4 5 8 7 9 3 2 1
Sorted array: 1 2 3 4 5 7 8 9
```

6.9 MERGING LIST

Merging is a process in which two or more lists are merged to form a new list. The procedure involved in merging is very straightforward. Consider the following program for merging of two lists:

Example 6.7

Write a program to create two-array list of integers. Sort and store elements of both the list in the third list.

Solution

```
# include <stdio.h>
# include <conio.h>
# include <math.h>

main ()
{
 int m,n,p,sum=0;
 int listA[5],listB[5],listC[10]={0};
 clrscr();

 printf ("\n Enter five elements of first list: ");

 for (m=0;m<5;m++)
 {
    scanf ("%d",&listA[m]);
    if (listA[m]==0) m--;
    sum=sum+abs(listA[m]);
```

Explanation In this program three arrays *listA [], listB []* and *listC []* are declared. Using *for loops* elements in *listA []* and *listB []* are declared. The sum of all ten elements entered in both the lists are taken in variable *sum*. The *while* and nested *for loop* checks corresponding elements of both the lists.

```
    }

    printf ("\n Enter five elements of second list: ");


    for (n=0;n<5;n++)
    {
    scanf ("%d",&listB[n]);
    if (listA[n]==0) n--;
    sum=sum+abs(listB[n]);
 }
 p=n=m=0;
 m=m-sum;

 while (m<sum)
 {
    for (n=0;n<5;n++)
 {
    if (m==listA[n] || m==listB[n])
    listC[p++]=m;

    if (m==listA[n] && m==listB[n])
    listC[p++]=m;
 }
 m++;
 }

 puts (" Merged sorted list: ");
 for (n=0;n<10;++n)
 printf (" %d ",listC[n]);
 }
```

```
OUTPUT
Enter five elements of first list: 1 5 4 -3 2
Enter five elements of second list: 9 5 1 2 10
Merged sorted list:
-3 1 1 2 2 4 5 5 9 10
```

a. If one of the corresponding elements is same, that element is stored in the *listC []* array.
b. If both the corresponding elements are same, they are stored in successive locations in the *listC []*.

The value of m is initially zero. The sum obtained is again subtracted from m. This is because if negative numbers are entered, they are to be considered in the sorting. For example, the value of *sum=20*. In real execution, the sum may be different depending on integers entered.

Value of m would be = –20 (as per $m=m-20$ when $m=0$).

Thus, in the *while loop* value of m varies from –20 to 20. In this range all the entered elements are covered. The value of *m* changes from –20 to 20, i.e. –20,–19 up to +20 in ascending order. Thus, the same order is applied while saving elements in the *arrayC[]*.

6.10 LINKED LIST

A linked list is a dynamic data structure. It is an ideal technique to store data when the user is not aware of the number of elements to be stored. The dynamic implementation of list using pointers is also known as *linked list.* Each element of the list is called as *node*. Each element points to the next element. In the linked list a node can be inserted or deleted at any position. Each node of linked list has two components. The first component contains the information or any data field and second part the address of the next node. In other words, the second part holds address of the next element. This pointer points to the next data item. The pointer variable member of the last record of the list is generally assigned a NULL value to indicate the end of the list. Fig. 6.5 indicates the linked list.

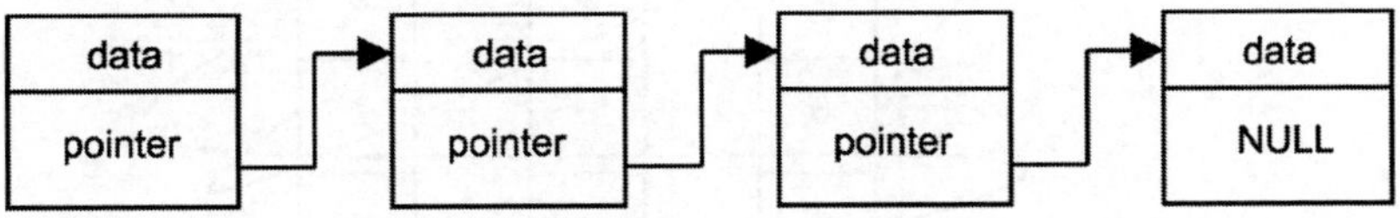

Figure 6.5 Linked list

The basic data type in the linked list can be *int, float* and user defined data types can be created by struct *cla*. The link structure as well as a pointer of structure type to the next object in the link is observed in it.

A simple example describing the operation of linked list is illustrated in the following section.

6.10.1 Illustration of Linked List for Storing a String

In this example, a linked list containing a string of characters to be stored in the memory, is described. The linked list has two field data, i.e. actual data stored and links, i.e. pointing to the next node of the linked list. These two fields are shown with two arrays such as data[j] and link[j] where 'j' is the position of an element. A variable begin is initiated which contains the beginning location of the list. The field '*No.*' is taken for numbering the nodes of the linked list. It is not the part of the linked list. It is given simply for understanding. In the link[j] '0' (zero) indicate the NULL pointer which is end of the string. In this type of lists the nodes or elements are not stored in the successive memory locations. Many links have been shown between data and link.

The nodes of the linked list are not ordered sequentially. The characters are stored dynamically with their link fields. The link field shows the link to the next node of the linked list. The information obtained from the above linked list is 'computer'. Its explanation is as follows:

a. Begin =5, data[5] is 'c' and link[5]= '3'.
b. Link[3]=6 and data[3]= 'o'.

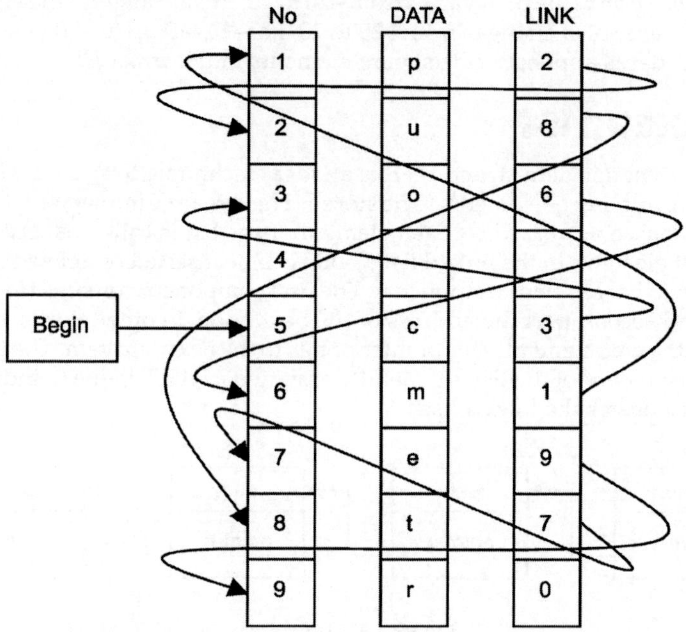

c. Link[6]=1 and data[6]= 'm'.
d. Link[2]=8 and data[1]= 'p'.
e. Link[2]=8 and data[2]= 'u'.
f. Link[8]=7 and data[8]= 't'.
g. Link[7]=9 and data[7]= 'e'.
h. Link[9]=NULL (0) and data[9]= 'r'.

The string stored in the memory as per above listing is 'computer'.

6.11 IMPORTANT TERMS

We have already discussed in previous sections that a linked list is a non-sequential collection of elements called nodes. These nodes are nothing but objects. These nodes are declared using structure or classes. Every node has two fields and they are:

1. Data field: In this field, the data or values are stored and processed.
2. Link field: This field holds address of the next data element of the list. This address is used to access the successive elements of the list.

In the linked list the ordering of elements is not done by their physical location in the memory but by logical links, which are stored in the link field.

Node The components or objects which form the list are called nodes.

Null Pointer The link field of the last record is assigned a NULL value instead of any address. It means NULL pointer not pointing to any element.

External Pointer It is a pointer to the starting node. The external pointer contains the base, i.e. address of first node. Once a base address is available, its next successive nodes can be accessed.

Empty List When there is no node in the list, it is called as empty list. If the external pointer were assigned a value NULL, the list would be empty.

6.11.1 Static List vs. Linked List

1. The static list is implemented using arrays. The linked list uses pointer in which memory can be allocated or de-allocated during program execution. The linked list is more efficient in memory management. The linked list can be expanded or shrunk as per requirement whereas in static list once an array is defined its size remains the same throughout the program.
2. Once an array is declared, its size remains the same. The memory allocated for array may be extra or insufficient. The user cannot determine the exact amount of memory required. Due to this, the program execution may not be safe. The pointer has intrinsic flexibility to enlarge or reduce the capacity of storage. We are acquainted with pointer arithmetic operations increment/decrement, which enables pointer to access any memory location. The use of pointer to point the next node in the linked list data structure indicates that elements which are logically contiguous due to linear organization need not be physically contiguous in the memory. This type of memory allocation is called linked allocation.
3. The elements are stored in order logically as well as physically. Array elements are stored in successive memory locations. This is not the case in the linked list. Insertion and deletion with static list are time consuming and shifting of elements is done to rearrange the numbers in order. In the linked list the insertion and deletion operations are done very easily. The element can be deleted by de-allocating the memory of that particular element. The insertion can be done by allocating space at the specified position.
4. A list has been created to hold an ordered set of elements without knowing the number of nodes. The simple method to create link is to enlarge each node and it should contain reference of the next node. This is called *singly linked linear list* or *one-way chain* as shown in Fig. 6.6. The arrow (first) indicates the address of the first node.

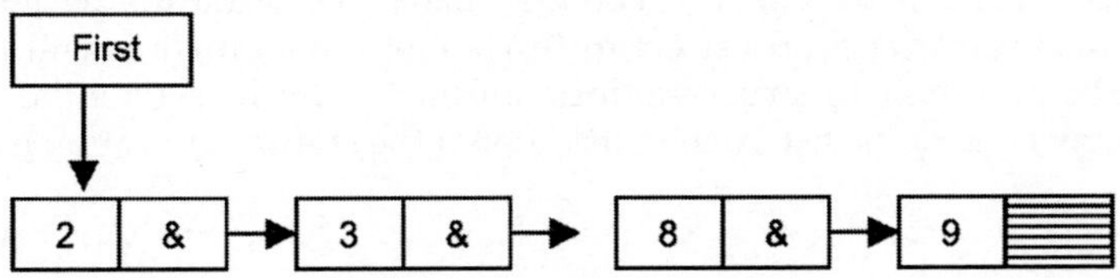

Figure 6.6 Singly linked linear list

5. By using linked list more complex data structures such as circular linked list, doubly linked list, stack and queues can be formed.
6. A pointer plays an important role in the dynamic implementation of linked list. The interpretation of pointer is an address, which is in-built, and the programmer need not take care of how the addresses are assigned in the memory. Mostly, all computer systems use addresses to know the instruction to be executed. Pointers of any data type always

are of same length and occupy equal space in the memory, i.e. 2 bytes only. The pointer is always of unsigned integer type. Consider the following program:

Example 6.8

Write a program to demonstrate the size of pointers of different data types.

Solution

```
# include <stdio.h>
# include <conio.h>

struct node { long int a; }*s;

main ()
{
   int *p;
   float *f;
   clrscr();

   printf ("\n Integer Pointer Size=%d",sizeof(p));
   printf ("\n Float Pointer Size=%d",sizeof(f));
   printf ("\n Structure pointer Size=%d",sizeof(s));
}

OUTPUT
Integer Pointer Size=2
Float Pointer Size=2
Structure pointer Size=2
```

Explanation In this program pointers of *integer, float* and *structure* type are declared. The *sizeof ()* operator returns the size of pointers. The size of any pointer is always two bytes. The address is always of unsigned integer having range 0 to 65535.

7. In the above program we have demonstrated that pointers occupy only two bytes irrespective of the type of data. This property of pointers makes it possible for the pointer to operate in carrying out the referencing of structure in a homogeneous manner with easy allocation methods. The prototype of structure does not matter. In the sequential allocation, the address of any node in the list can be calculated if the storage allocation must be in same pattern.

Example 6.9

Write a program to create a simple linked list.

Solution

```
# include <stdio.h>
# include <conio.h>
struct list
{
```

```
int n;
int *p;
};
main ()
{
struct list item0,item1, item2;
item2.n=3;
item2.p=NULL;
item1.n=5;
item1.p=&item2.n;
item0.n=7;
item0.p=&item1.n;
clrscr();
printf ("\n Linked list elements are: ");
printf (" %d ",item0.n);
printf (" %d ",*item0.p);
printf (" %d ",*item1.p);
printf (" %d ",*item2.p);
}
```

Explanation In this program the structure list is declared with two elements *int n* and **p*. The pointer **p* recursively points to the same structure. The struct *item0*, *item1* and *item2* are three variables of type *list*. Consider the initialization.

```
OUTPUT
Linked list elements are: 7 5 3 0
```

```
item2.n=3;
item2.p=NULL;
```

The item2 is the third (last) node of the list. The pointer p is initialized with null because next to this no node is present and thus no need to point any address.

```
item1.n=5;
item1.p=&item2.n;
```

In this node, n is assigned with five. The pointer points to the data field of the next node i.e. item2.n (7).

```
item0.n=7;
item0.p=&item1.n;
```

This is the first node. The n is assigned 7 and pointer points to data field of *item1*, i.e. 5. Fig. 6.7 simulates the operation more clearly.

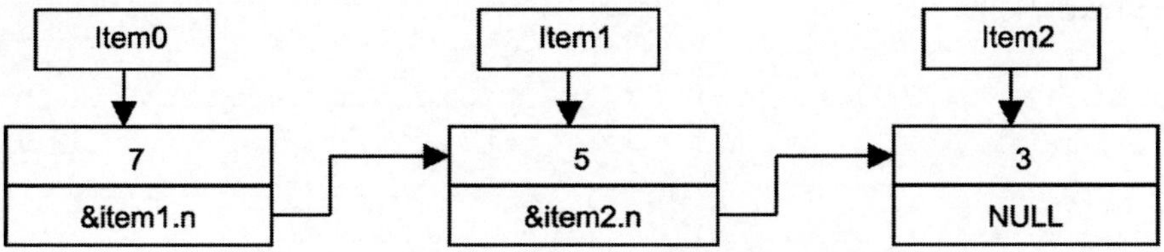

Figure 6.7 Linked list

Example 6.10

Write a program to display string using linked list.

Solution

```
# include <stdio.h>
# include <conio.h>
# include <malloc.h>
struct link
{
char str[30];
struct link *next;
};

typedef struct link linked;
main ()
{
linked *begin, node1,node2,node3, node4;
int j;
clrscr();
printf("\nEnter four words in four lines:-\n ");
begin=(struct link*) malloc(sizeof(linked));
begin=&node1;
gets(node1.str);
node1.next=&node2;
gets(node2.str);
node2.next=&node3;
gets(node3.str);
node3.next=&node4;
gets(node4.str);
node4.next='\0';
printf ("Output: ");

printf ("%s ",begin->str);

do
{
begin=begin->next;
printf ("%s ",begin->str);
}
while (begin->next!='\0');
}

OUTPUT
Data
Structure
with
C
Output: Data Structure with C
```

Explanation In this program, structure link is declared. The *str [] char* array is used to store string. The pointer **begin* and objects *node1, node2, node3* and *node4* are declared. In the address field of object address of other object is stored. For example, in address field of *node1* address of *node2* is stored. In address field of *node2*, address of *node3* is stored and so on. Similarly, using *gets ()* in *str []* array string (entered by user) is stored. Using *while loop* successive addresses are accessed and complete string is displayed.

6.11.2 Types of Linked List

The linked lists are classified in the following types:

Singly Linked List In this type of linked list two successive nodes of the linked list are linked with each other in sequential linear manner. An example of a singly linked list can be cited as train in which two successive compartments are connected as shown in Fig. 6.8.

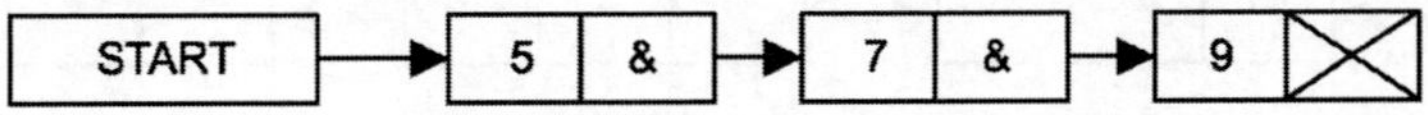

Figure 6.8 Singly linked list

Doubly Linked List In this type of linked list each node holds two-pointer field. In the singly linked list, address of only next element is pointed. Unlike that, in doubly linked list addresses of next as well as preceding elements are linked with current node. An example of doubly linked list is shown in Fig. 6.9.

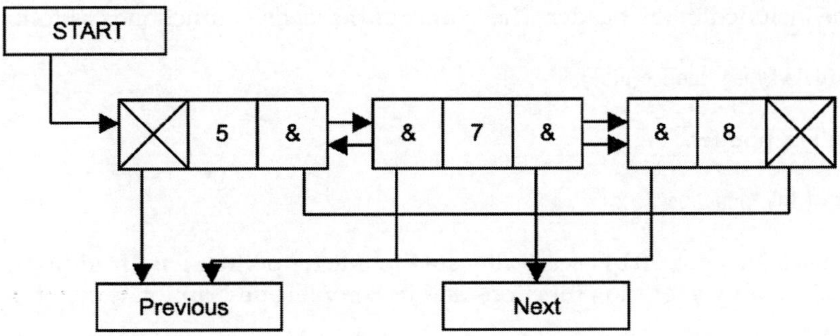

Figure 6.9 Doubly linked list

A Circular Linked List Recall that in circular list the first and last elements are adjacent. This type of list has neither end node *nor starting node*. A linear single linked list can be circled by storing the address of first node in the link field of last node as shown in Fig. 6.10.

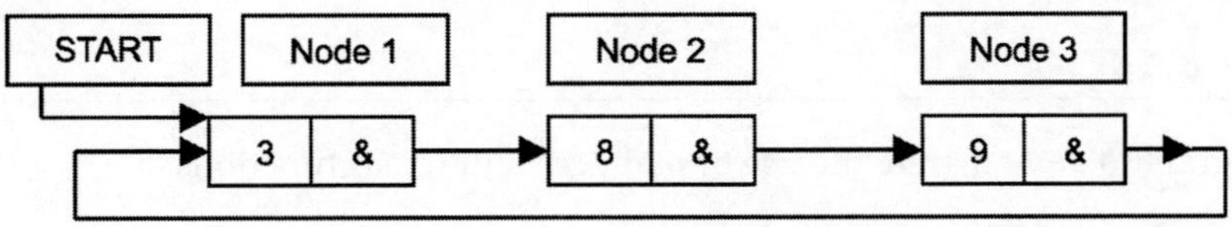

Figure 6.10 A circular linked list

A Circular Doubly Linked List In this type of linked list each node contains three fields: two link fields and one data field. The link field holds address of previous and next elements. The address of end node is linked to first node and vice-verse. The Fig. 6.11 shows the circular double link list.

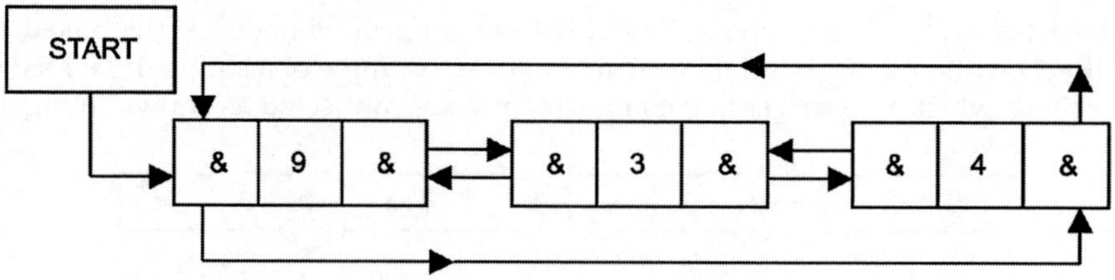

Figure 6.11 A circular doubly linked list

6.12 MEMORY ALLOCATION AND DE-ALLOCATION

Malloc (): This library function is used to allocate memory space in bytes to the variable. The function reserves bytes of requested size and returns the base address to pointer variable. The prototype of this function is declared in the header file *alloc.h* and *stdlib.h*. One of the header files must be included in the header. The syntax of the *malloc()* function is as follows:

Syntax: pnt=(data type*) malloc(size);

Here, pnt is a pointer.

Example: pnt =(int *) malloc(20);

In the above statement, 20 bytes are allocated to integer pointer *pnt*. In addition, there are other various memory allocation functions and its complete description is out of the scope of this book.

free(): This function is used to release the memory allocated by the *malloc ()* function.

Syntax: free(pointer variable)
Example: free(pnt)

The above statement releases the memory allocated to pointer *pnt*. Consider the following program based on this concept:

Example 6.11

Write a program to demonstrate the use of malloc () and free () functions.

Solution

```
# include <stdio.h>
# include <conio.h>
# include <alloc.h>
main ()
```

```
{
char *str;
str=(char *) malloc(6);
clrscr();
printf("Enter string:-");
scanf("%s",str);
printf ("\n str=%s",str);
free(str);
}
```

Explanation In this program a character pointer variable *str* is declared. The *malloc ()* function allocates seven bytes to character pointer **str*. The string *"India"* is assigned to pointer *str* and it is displayed. The *free ()* function releases the memory from pointer *str*.

```
OUTPUT
Enter string:-India
str=India
```

6.13 OPERATIONS ON LINKED LISTS

The following primitive operations can be performed with linked list:

1. Creation
2. Display
   a. Ascending
   b. Descending
3. Traversing
4. Insertion
   a. At beginning
   b. Before or after specified position
5. Searching
6. Concatenation
7. Merging

Creation The linked list creation operation involves allocation of structure size memory to pointer of the same structure. The structure must have a member which points recursively to the same structure. In this operation, constituent node is created and it is linked to the link field of preceding node.

Traversing It is the procedure of passing through (visiting) all the nodes of the linked list from starting to end. When any given record is to be searched in the linked list, traversing is applied. When the given element is found, the operation can be terminated or continued for next search. The traversing is a common procedure and it is necessary because operations like insertion, deletion, listing cannot be carried out without traversing linked list.

Display The operation in which data field of every node is accessed and displayed on the screen. In the display operation from beginning to end, link field of every node is accessed which contains address of next node. The data of that field is displayed. When NULL is detected the operation ends. Each node points to the next node and this recursion fashion enables the pointer to reach the successive elements.

The above three operations are common and every program involves these operations. Hence, separate program is not given.

Searching The searching is a process, in which a given element is compared with all the linked list elements. The *if* statement is placed and it checks entire list elements with the given element. When an element is found it is displayed.

Besides the above operations additional operations such as concatenation and merging of list can be done.

6.14 SINGLY LINKED LIST

Recall that linked list is a dynamic data structure with ability to expand and shrink as per the program requirement. The singly linked list is easy and straightforward data structure as compared to other structures. By changing the link position other type of linked list such as circular, doubly linked list can be formed. For creating linked list the structure is defined as follows,

```
struct node
{
 int number;
 struct node *p;
};
```

The above structure is used to implement the linked list. In the *number,* variable entered numbers are stored. The second member is pointer to the same structure. The pointer **p* points to the same structure. Here, though the declaration of struct node has not been completed, the pointer declaration of the same structure type is permitted by the compiler. However, the variable declaration is not allowed. This is because, the pointers are dynamic in nature whereas variables are formed by early binding. The declaration of objects inside the struct leads to preparation of very complex data structure. This concept is called object composition and its detailed discussion is out of the scope of this book.

We are familiar with the array and we know the importance of base address. Once a base address is obtained, successive elements can also be accessed. In the linked list, list can be created with or without *header node.* The *head* holds the starting address.

6.15 LINKED LIST WITH HEADER

The following steps are used to create linked list with header:

1. Three pointers, i.e. header, first and rear are declared. The header pointer is initialized with *NULL*. For example, header=*NULL* where, header is a pointer to structure. If it remains *NULL*, it implies that the list has no element. Such list is known as *NULL* list or empty list, which is shown in Fig. 6.12(a).

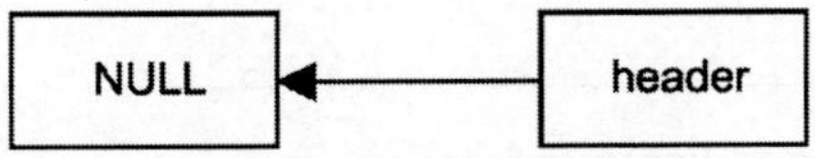

Figure 6.12(a) Empty list

2. In the second step, memory is allocated for the first node of the linked list. For example, the address of first node is 1888. An integer, say 3, is stored in the variable num and value of header is assigned to pointer *next*.

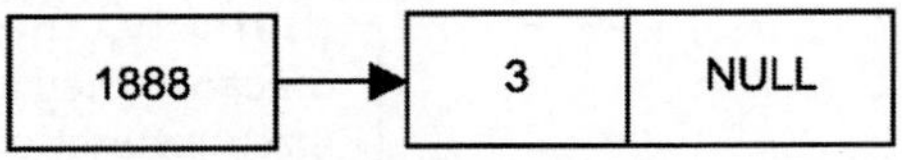

Figure 6.12(b) Link list

The address of first node is initialized by both the header and rear.
The statement would be,

```
header=first;
rear=first;
```

3. The address of pointer *first* is assigned to pointers *header* and *rear*. The *rear* pointer is used to identify the end of the list and to detect the NULL pointer.
4. Again, create a memory location suppose 1890 for the successive node.

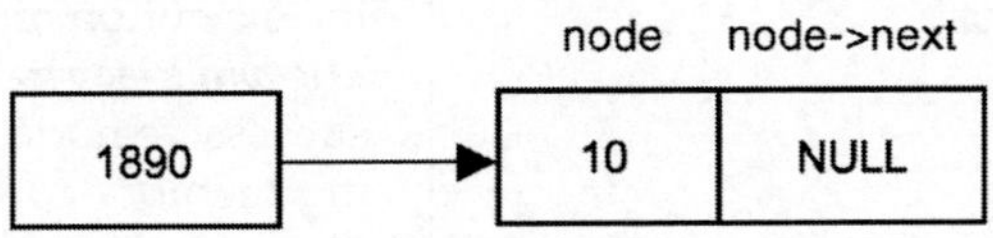

Figure 6.12(c)

5. Link the element of 1890 by assigning the value of node *rear->next*. Move the *rear* pointer to the last node.

Figure 6.12(d)

The following program explains the above concept.

Example 6.12

Write a program to create linked list with header.

Solution

```
# include <stdio.h>
# include <conio.h>
# include <malloc.h>

struct num
{
   int num;
   struct num *next;
} *header,*first,*rear;

main ()
{
   void create ( void);
   clrscr();

   create ();

   printf ("\n Linked list elements are: ");

   while (header!=NULL)
 {
   printf (" %d ",header->num);
   header=header->next;
 }

}

void create ( void )
{
   struct num *node;
   printf ("\n Enter number ( 0 exit ): ");

 if (header==NULL)
 {
   first=(struct num*)malloc(sizeof(struct num));
   scanf ("%d",&first->num);
   first->next=header;
   header=first;
   rear=first;
 }

while (1)
```

Explanation This program is an example of linked list with header. Three structure pointers **header, *first,* and **rear* are declared after structure declaration. Initially, these pointers are NULL because they are declared as global. The create function is used to create linked list nodes. Inside the function *create ()* another structure pointer **node* is defined and its scope is local to the same function. The procedure for creating first and later successive nodes is different. The *if* statement checks the value of header. The value of header is NULL. The *malloc ()* function allocates memory to pointer first and the entered number is stored in variable num of the node. In the same *if* block, both the pointers header and rear are assigned the value of first. Once, the first node is created, next time the execution of *if* block is not required. The *while loop* iterated continuously and successive nodes are created by allocating memory to pointer node. Consider the following statements:

```
{
   node=(struct num*) malloc(sizeof(struct num));
   scanf ("%d",&node->num);
   if (node->num==0) break;

   node->next=NULL;
   rear->next=node;
   rear=node;
 }
}
```

```
OUTPUT
Enter number ( 0 exit ): 1 3 4 8 7 9 0
Linked list elements are: 1 3 4 8 7 9
```

1. node->next=NULL;

The above statement, assigns NULL to the pointer next of current node. The user can initiate this step if no further elements are desired in the linked list.

2. rear->next=node;

The rear pointer keeps track of last node; the address of current node (node) is assigned to link field of previous node.

3. rear=node;

Before creating next node, the address of last created node is assigned to pointer rear, which is used for statement (2). In function main (), using while loop the elements of linked list are displayed.

The pointer header is very useful in the formation of linked list. The address of *first* node (*1888*) is stored in pointer header. The value of header remains unchanged until it turns out to be NULL. The starting location of the list only can be determined by pointer header only.

```
while (header!=NULL)
{
printf (" %d ",header->num);
header=header->next;
}
```

6.15.1 Traverse a List with Header

We are familiar with traverse operation, which involves visiting all the elements of the queue. The above *while () loop* and associated statement are used to traverse and display the elements of the list.

6.16 LINKED LIST WITHOUT HEADER

In the previous topic, we discussed how linked list is created using header. The implementation of linked list without header is similar to the linked list with header. The only difference in manipulation is that in the header list pointer header contains address of first node. In the list without header list, pointer first itself is starting of the linked list. Consider the following program:

Example 6.13

Write a program to create a linked list without header.

Solution

```
# include <stdio.h>
# include <conio.h>
# include <malloc.h>

struct num
{
   int num;
   struct num *next;
} *first,*rear;

main ()
{
   void create ( void);
   clrscr();

   create ();
   printf ("Double linked list elements: ");

   while (first!=NULL)
 {
printf (" %d",first->num);
first=first->next;
 }
}

void create ( void )
{
   struct num *node;
   printf ("\n Enter number (0 to exit): ");

if (first==NULL)
 {
   first=(struct num*)malloc(sizeof(struct num));
```

Explanation In this program only two pointers, *first* and *rear*, are declared. They are global pointers; hence, their contents are NULL. The function *create ()* is invoked and the rest of the execution of the program is the same as the previous program.

```
scanf("%d",&first->num);
first->next=first;
rear=first;
}

while (1)
{
   node=(struct num*) malloc(sizeof(struct num));
   scanf("%d",&node->num);
   if (node->num==0) break;
   node->next=NULL;
   rear->next=node;
   rear=node;
}
}
```

```
OUTPUT
Enter number (0 to exit): 1 5 9 8 7 4 2 0
Double linked list elements: 1 5 9 8 7 4 2
```

6.16.1 Traverse a List Without Header

In the list without header, the lists are traversed with the first node as shown in the above code.

Example 6.14

Write a program to create a single linked list and display the elements.

Solution

```
# include <stdio.h>
# include <conio.h>

struct node
{
   int number;
   struct node *p;
} *h,*f,*t;

main()
{
   char c;
   clrscr();
   f=NULL;
 do
 {
```

Explanation In this program, the structure node is declared. The *structure node* contains integer variable number and pointer to the same structure **p*. The structure pointer variables **h*, **f* and **t* are also declared. In function *main ()*, variable of character type c is defined. The pointer f is initialized to NULL.

```
h=(struct node *)malloc(sizeof(struct node));
printf ("Enter a number: ");
scanf ("%d",&h->number);

if (f!=NULL)
{
t->p=h;
t=h;
}
else f=t=h;
fflush(stdin);
printf ("Continue (y/n): ");
scanf ("%c",&c);

} while (c=='y');

t->p=NULL;
t=f;
printf ("\nThe list elements are: ");
while (t!=NULL)
{
printf (" %d ",t->number);
t=t->p;
}
}
```

```
OUTPUT
Enter a number: 5
Continue (y/n): y
Enter a number: 3
Continue (y/n): y
Enter a number: 8
Continue (y/n): y
Enter a number: 9
Continue (y/n): n
The list elements are: 5 3 8 9
```

In the *do–while loop*, using *malloc ()* function memory equal to size of structure node *(4 byte)* is allocated to pointer *h*. The entered number is stored in the number variable. The *if* statement checks the pointer *f*. If it is NULL, the *h* is assigned to other two pointers, i.e. *f* and *t*. Here, *f* is first node. *h* is header and *t* is used for temporary storage. The user has to enter *'y'* to enter next elements. First time, the value of *f* is NULL and hence, else block is executed. The purpose of assignment of *h* to *f* and *t* is as follows:

1. In *if ()* block *t* is used to assign address of newly created next node to the current, i.e. *h*.
2. Only for the first time else block is executed and in which address of *h* (when first node is created) is assigned to *f*. *f* contains address of first node.

When the user finishes entering number, *t->p=NULL;* this statement assigns NULL to pointer *p* and link ends here. The address of the first *node (f)* is assigned to *t*. Using *while loop*, the pointer *p* is accessed and elements are accessed. When NULL pointer is encountered, the *while loop* terminates.

In the following Fig. 6.13 the number contains the actual data of the node. The structure node pointer is used to point to the next node in the linked list hence it is called as the linked field. The link field refers to itself in recursive form.

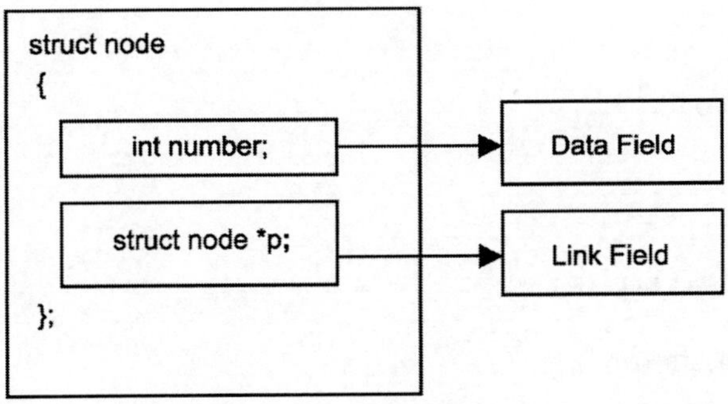

Figure 6.13 Structure for linked list creation

Example 6.15

Write a program to create a list. Display the list up to specified element.

Solution

```
# include <stdio.h>
# include <conio.h>

struct node
{
   int number;
   struct node *p;
} *h,*f,*t;

main ()
```

Explanation This program is based on searching operation. This is same as program 6.14. In this program, the specific element is compared with every element of the linked list. When the given element is found in the list, the *while loop* terminates.

```
{
    char c,n;
    clrscr();
    f=NULL;
    do
    {
    h=(struct node *)malloc(sizeof(struct node));
    printf ("Enter a number: ");
    scanf ("%d",&h->number);
    if (f!=NULL)
    {
    t->p=h;
    t=h;
 }
    else f=t=h;
    fflush(stdin);
    printf ("Continue (y/n): ");
    scanf ("%c",&c);
 } while (c=='y');
 t->p=NULL;
 t=f;
 printf ("\n Enter a element to search: ");
 scanf ("%d",&n);
 printf ("\nThe list elements are: ");

 while (t!=NULL)
 {
 printf (" %d ",t->number);
 if (t->number==n)
 break;
 t=t->p;
 }
 }
```

```
OUTPUT
Enter a number: 1
Continue (y/n): y
Enter a number: 3
Continue (y/n): y
Enter a number: 5
Continue (y/n): y
Enter a number: 4
Continue (y/n): y
Enter a number: 9
Continue (y/n): n
Enter a element to search: 4
The list elements are: 1 3 5 4
```

6.17 INSERTION IN THE LINKED LIST

Insertion of an element in the linked list leads to several operations. The following steps are involved in inserting an element:

a. Creation of node: Before insertion, the node is created. Using *malloc()* function memory space for node is booked.
b. Assignment of data: Once the node is created, data values are assigned to members.
c. Adjusting pointers: The insertion operation changes the sequence. Hence, according to the sequence, the address of next element is assigned to inserted node. The address of current node (inserted) is assigned to previous node.

The insertion of node can be done in different positions in the list by the following ways:

a. Insertion of the node at the starting: The created node is inserted before the first element. After insertion, the newly inserted element will be the first element of the linked list. In this insertion only the contents of successive node's pointer are changed.
b. Insertion at the end of the list: A new element is appended at the end of the list. This operation is easy as compared to other two (a) and (c) operations. In this insertion only the contents of previous node's pointer is changed.
c. Insertion at the given position in the list: In this operation, the user has to enter the position number. The given position is counted and the element is inserted. In this insertion contents of both previous and next node's pointer are altered.

6.18 INSERTION OF NODE AT START

Inserting an element at the beginning involves updating links between link fields of two pointers. After insertion of new node, the previously existing nodes are moved to the front. Fig. 6.14 (a) and (b) and program 6.16 illustrates the insertion at the starting.

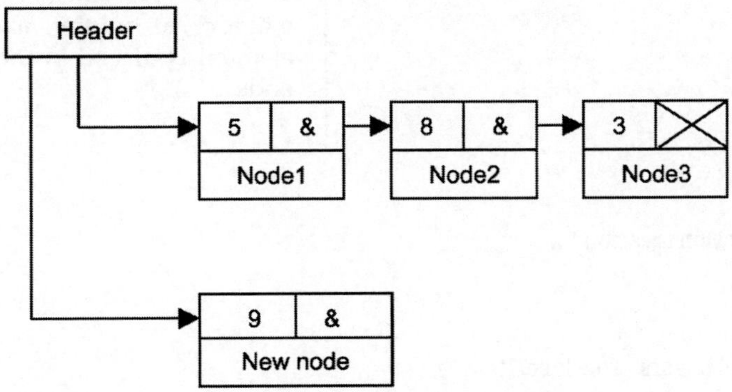

Figure 6.14 (a) Before insertion

The arrow indicates the location of insertion of new node.

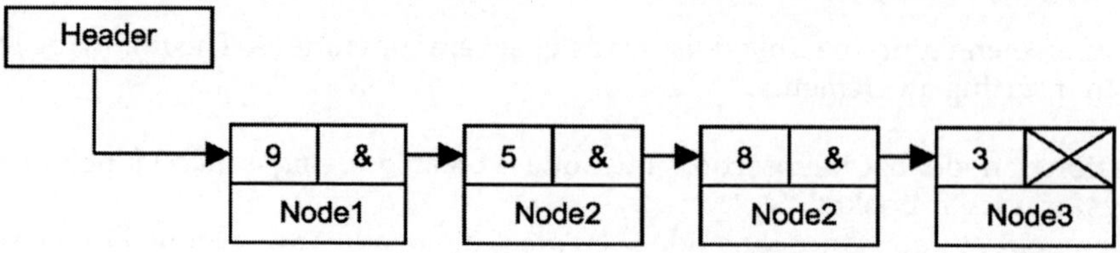

Figure 6.14 (b) After insertion

After insertion, the new node will be first node and its link field points to the second element, which was ex-first element.

The program given below explains the insertion of an element in the list.

Example 6.16

Write a program to insert an element at the beginning.

Solution

```
# include <stdio.h>
# include <conio.h>
# include <malloc.h>

struct num
{
   int num;
   struct num *next;
} *header,*first,*rear;

main ()
{
   void atbeg(void);
   void create ( void);
   void show (void);
   clrscr();
   printf ("\n Operation creation:");
   create ();
   show();
   atbeg();
   printf ("\n The elements after insertion: ");
   show();
   atbeg();
   show();
   atbeg();
   show();
```

Explanation The creation of linked list is same as explained in program 6.15. Here, an element is inserted at the beginning. The function void *atbeg ()* performs this task. In this function two pointers **node* (local to this function) and **t* are declared. The *malloc()* function allocates memory to pointer *node*. The entered element is placed in the newly created node.

```
}

void create ( void )
{
   struct num *node;
   printf ("\n Enter numbers( 0 to exit): ");

 if (header==NULL)
 {
   first=(struct num*)malloc(sizeof(struct num));
   scanf ("%d",&first->num);
   first->next=header;
   header=first;
   rear=first;
 }

 while (1)
 {
   node=(struct num*) malloc(sizeof(struct num));
   scanf ("%d",&node->num);
   if (node->num==0) break;
   node->next=NULL;
   rear->next=node;
   rear=node;
 }
}

void atbeg()
{
   struct num *node,*t;
   node=(struct num*) malloc(sizeof(struct num));
   printf ("\n Insert an element at starting: ");
   scanf ("%d",&node->num);
   t=first;
   header=node;
   header->next=t;
   first=header;
 }

 void show()
 {
   printf ("\n Linked list elements are: ");

   while (header!=NULL)
 {
   printf (" %d ",header->num);
   header=header->next;
```

```
 }
}
```

```
OUTPUT
Operation creation:
Enter numbers( 0 to exit): 1 2 3 4 0
Linked list elements are: 1 2 3 4
Insert an element at starting: 5
The elements after insertion:
Linked list elements are: 5 1 2 3 4
Insert an element at starting: 9
Linked list elements are: 9 5 1 2 3 4
Insert an element at starting: 3
Linked list elements are: 3 9 5 1 2 3 4
```

Consider the following statements:

```
t=first;
header=node;
header->next=t;
first=header;
```

The above four statements adjust the pointer links:

t=first This statement assigns contents of *first* to pointer *t*. This is essential because the newly created node will become first. Hence, before changing pointer *first*, it is assigned to pointer *t*.

Header=node We know that header always points to the first node. The newly created node, that is to be inserted at starting is assigned to pointer header.

header->next=t The pointer *t* holds address of first element (before insertion). After insertion, it will be second. The address of second node is assigned to first. The pointer header holds address of first node and pointer *t* holds address of second element. Thus, these two successive elements are linked by this statement.

first=header Before execution of this statement the first points to second node. If we remove this statement, only one element can be inserted. If we try to insert second element, it will be replaced by the first element. After assignment of address of header to first, the insertion can be carried out successfully.

6.19 INSERTION OF NODE AT END

A new element is inserted or appended at the end of existing linked list. The address of newly created node is linked to previous node that is NULL. The new node link field is assigned a NULL value. The Fig. 6.15 shows the insertion operation at the end.

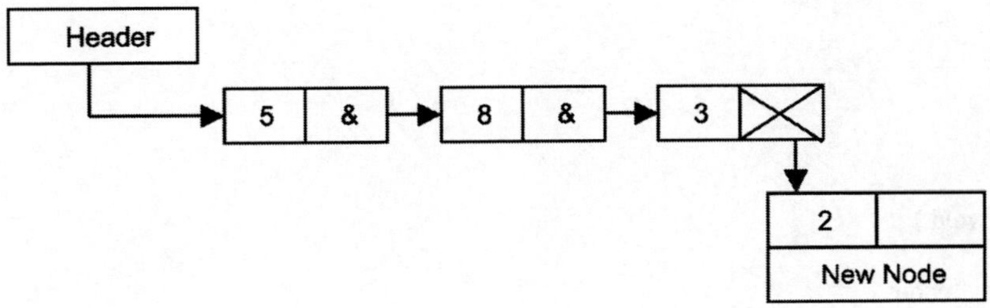

(a) Before insertion

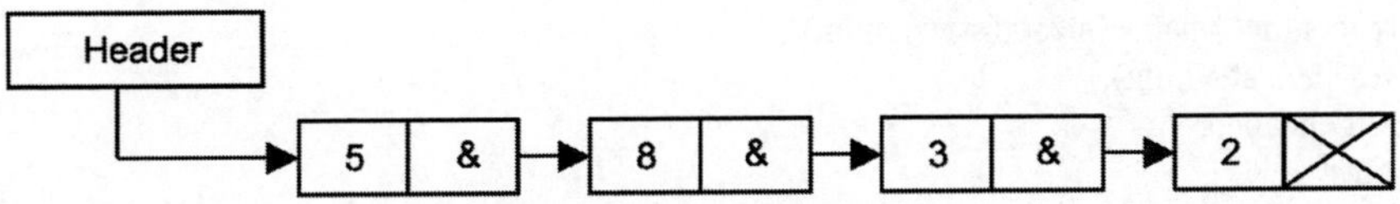

(b) After insertion

Figure 6.15 Insertion of element at the end

Example 6.17

Write a program to insert an element at the end of the linked list.

Solution

```
# include <stdio.h>
# include <conio.h>
# include <malloc.h>

struct num
{
    int num;
    struct num *next;
} *header,*first,*rear;

main ()
{
    void atend(void);
    void create ( void);
    void show (void);
    clrscr();
    printf ("\n Operation creation:");
    create ();
```

Explanation In this program the function *atend ()* is used to insert element at the end of the list.

```
    show();
    atend();
    show();
    atend();
    show();
}
void create ( void )
{
    struct num *node;
    printf ("\n Enter numbers( 0 to exit): ");

 if (header==NULL)
 {
    first=(struct num*)malloc(sizeof(struct num));
    scanf ("%d",&first->num);
    first->next=header;
    header=first;
    rear=first;
 }

 while (1)
 {
    node=(struct num*) malloc(sizeof(struct num));
    scanf ("%d",&node->num);
    if (node->num==0) break;
    node->next=NULL;
    rear->next=node;
    rear=node;
 }
}

void atend()
{
    struct num *node,*t;
    t=rear;
    rear=(struct num*) malloc(sizeof(struct num));
    printf ("\n Insert an element at end: ");
    scanf ("%d",&rear->num);
    t->next=rear;
    rear->next=NULL;
 }
void show()
 {
    printf ("\n Linked list elements are: ");

    while (header!=NULL)
 {
```

```
    printf (" %d ",header->num);
    header=header->next;
  }

 header=first;
 }
```

```
OUTPUT
Operation creation:
Enter numbers( 0 to exit): 1 2 3 0
Linked list elements are: 1 2 3
Insert an element at end: 4
Linked list elements are: 1 2 3 4
Insert an element at end: 5
Linked list elements are: 1 2 3 4 5
```

Consider the following statements:

t=rear This statement assigns address of last node to pointer *t*.

rear=(struct num*) malloc(sizeof(struct num)) After assigning address of *rear* pointer to *t*, new memory location is allocated to pointer *rear*. The new element entered is stored in the data field of pointer *rear*.

t->next=rear Now, the pointer *t* holds the last but one node of the linked list. The address of new inserted end node is assigned to link field of node through pointer *t*.

rear->next=NULL The rear pointer holds address of last node and its link field is assigned a NULL value.

6.20 INSERTION OF NODE AT A GIVEN POSITION

Insertion of node can be done at a specific position in the linked list. Fig. 6.16 and the program explain insertion of a node at the specific position in the linked list. If we want to insert a node at third position, then observe Figs 6.16(a) and 6.16(b).

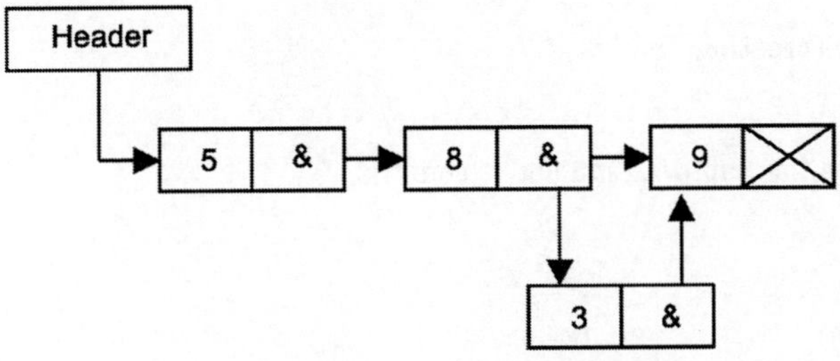

Figure 6.16a. Formed linked list

Node is inserted at third position and after insertion, the linked list would be

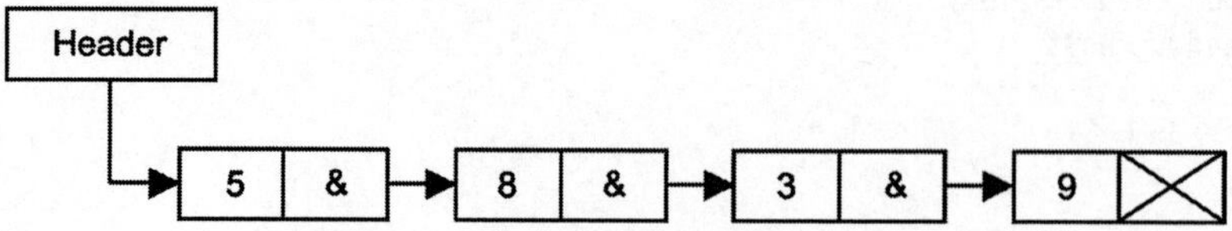

Fig. 16.16b. Linked list after insertion

Figure 6.16 Linked list after and before insertion

Example 6.18

Write a program to insert an element at a specific position.

Solution

```
# include <stdio.h>
# include <conio.h>
# include <malloc.h>

struct num
{
   int num;
   struct num *next;
} *header,*first,*rear;

int count;
main ()
{
   void atpo(int);
   void create ( void);
   void show (void);
   int p;
   clrscr();

   printf ("\n Operation creation:");
   create ();
   show();
   printf ("\n Enter position (upto %d )number:",count );
   scanf ("%d",&p);
   atpo(--p);
   show();
}

void create ( void )
{
```

Explanation In this program the operation creation and display of linked nodes is similar as explained in the last programs. Here, we are going to discuss insertion at a specified position carried out by a function *atpo()*.

```
   struct num *node;
   printf ("\n Enter numbers( 0 to exit): ");
   if (header==NULL)
 {
   first=(struct num*)malloc(sizeof(struct num));
   scanf ("%d",&first->num);
   first->next=header;
   header=first;
   rear=first;
 }
 while (1)
 {
   node=(struct num*) malloc(sizeof(struct num));
   scanf ("%d",&node->num);
   if (node->num==0) break;
   node->next=NULL;
   rear->next=node;
   rear=node;
 }
}

void atpo(int k)
{
   struct num *nw,*su,*pr;
   int c=1;

 while (header!=NULL)
 {
   c++;
   header=header->next;

   if (k==1) pr=first;
   if (c==k) pr=header;
   if (c==(k+1)) su=header;
 }

nw=(struct num*) malloc(sizeof(struct num));
printf ("\n Enter an element: ");
scanf ("%d", &nw->num);

pr->next=nw;
nw->next=su;
header=first;
}

void show()
{
```

```
    printf ("\n Linked list elements are: ");

    while (header!=NULL)
  {
    printf (" %d ",header->num);
    count++;
    header=header->next;
  }
  header=first;
}
```

```
OUTPUT
Operation creation:
Enter numbers( 0 to exit): 1 2 3 4 5 0
Linked list elements are: 1 2 3 4 5
Enter position (upto 5 )number:3
Enter an element: 8
Linked list elements are: 1 2 8 3 4 5
```

The position number specified by the user after reducing value by one is passed to function *atpo ()*. The variable *k*, formal argument of *p*, gets this value. Another variable *c* is declared in the body of *atop ()*. The variable *c* is incremented and successive nodes of the linked list are accessed by the statement *header=header->next;*

Consider the statements

a. *if (k==1) pr=first;*
b. *if (c==k) pr=header;*
c. *if (c==(k+1)) su=header;*

The insertion of node can be done in between two nodes and hence the preceding and succeeding nodes must be stored in separate pointer variables. When the user specifies two, the entered value is reduced by one and becomes one and stored in variable *k*.

When value of *k* is one, i.e. the address of *first* node is stored in the pointer *pr*. When *k* is one the statement (b) has no reason to consider. The address of succeeding node is obtained in the statement (c). The address obtained is stored in the pointer variable *su*. Thus, by using following statements proper links are connected:

a. *pr->next=nw;*
b. *nw->next=su;*
c. *header=first;*

Before execution of the above statements, the new node is created using *nw* pointer. The *nw* is a node to be inserted.

The address of data field of node *nw* is linked to the previous node (*pr*) by the statement *pr->next=nw.*

The address of succeeding node is stored in the linked field of new node *nw* by the statement *nw->next=su.*

6.20.1 Counting Nodes

Sometimes, it may be essential to know how many nodes exist in the linked list. The linked list elements can be counted and displayed. The solution is very easy. In the last few programs, the procedure applied for displaying elements can be applied here. A counter variable can be inserted there to count the nodes. One can get the number of nodes simply by incrementing the counter variable. Consider the following program for counting the total number of nodes in the list.

Example 6.19

Write a program to count the total nodes of the linked list.

Solution

```
# include <stdio.h>
# include <conio.h>
# include <malloc.h>
struct num
{
   int num;
   struct num *next;
} *header,*first,*rear;

main()
{
   void create ( void);
   int count=0;
   clrscr();

   create ();
   printf ("\n Linked list elements are: ");

   while (header!=NULL)
   {
   printf (" %d ",header->num);
   header=header->next;
   count++;
   }
   printf ("\n Total Nodes are: %d ",count);
}
void create ( void )
{
   struct num *node;
   printf ("\n Enter number: ");
   if (header==NULL)
   {
      first=(struct num*)malloc(sizeof(struct num));
      scanf ("%d",&first->num);
```

Explanation This program is same as the last few programs. The *count* variable is placed in the *while loop* and incremented. The *count* variable displays the number of nodes.

```
        first->next=header;
        header=first;
        rear=first;
    }
    while (1)
    {
        node=(struct num*) malloc(sizeof(struct num));
        scanf ("%d",&node->num);
        if (node->num==0) break;
        node->next=NULL;
        rear->next=node;
        rear=node;
    }
}
```

```
OUTPUT
Enter number: 1 2 3 4 5 6 7 8 0
Linked list elements are: 1 2 3 4 5 6 7 8
Total Nodes are: 8
```

6.20.2 Deletion

An element that is to be deleted from the linked list is to be searched first. For this, the traversing operation must be carried out thoroughly on the list. Deleting a node from the linked list means

1. Deleting the first node
2. Deleting the last node
3. Deleting a specified node.

If first node is to be deleted, then the second node is assigned to header.

If the last node is to be deleted, NULL value is assigned to link field of the last but one node.

If the node which is to be deleted is in between the linked list then access the predecessor and successor node of the specified node and link them. Fig. 6.17 shows the deletion of first node.

1. Deleting the first node

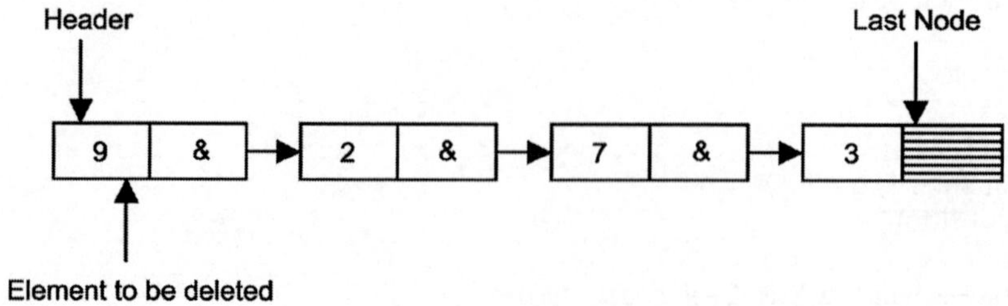

(a) Before deletion

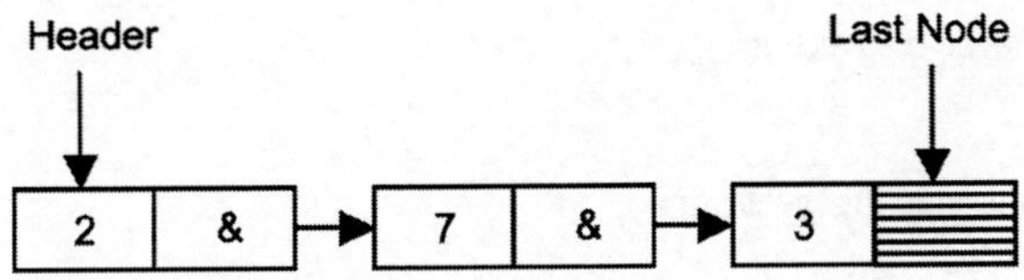

(b) After deletion

Figure 6.17 Deletion operation with linked list

Example 6.20

Write a program to remove elements from the beginning of the linked list.

Solution

```
# include <stdio.h>
# include <conio.h>
# include <malloc.h>

struct num
    { int num;
struct num *next;
} *header,*first,*rear,*k;

main ()
{
    void erase(void);
    void create ( void);
    void show (void);
    clrscr();

 printf ("\n Operation creation:");
 create ();
 show();
 printf ("\n After deletion: ");
 erase();
 show();
 erase();
 show();
 erase();
 show();
}

void create ( void )
{
```

Explanation In this program *erase ()* function is used to remove the beginning node of the linked list. The creation of linked list is similar as discussed in the last few program. In the *erase ()* function another object **s* is declared. The pointer header is assigned to pointer **s*. The pointer **s* occupies same amount of memory like header. The *free ()* function is used to release the memory. The memory allocated with pointer **s* is released. The address of second node is assigned to header and first node. Thus, whenever the function *erase ()* is invoked, the beginning element is removed and the updated list is displayed by the function *show ()*.

```
struct num *node;
printf ("\n Enter numbers( 0 to exit): ");
if (header==NULL)
{
first=(struct num*)malloc(sizeof(struct num));
scanf ("%d",&first->num);
first->next=header;
header=first;
rear=first;
}
while (1)
{
node=(struct num*) malloc(sizeof(struct num));
scanf ("%d",&node->num);
if (node->num==0) break;
node->next=NULL;
rear->next=node;
rear=node;
}
}
void erase()
{
   struct num *s;
   s=header;
   free(s);
   header=first->next;
   first=first->next;
}
void show()
{
printf ("\n Linked list elements are: ");
while (header!=NULL)
{
printf (" %d ",header->num);
header=header->next;
}

}
```

```
OUTPUT
Operation creation:
Enter numbers( 0 to exit): 1 2 3 4 5 0
Linked list elements are: 1 2 3 4 5
After deletion:
Linked list elements are: 2 3 4 5
Linked list elements are: 3 4 5
Linked list elements are: 4 5
```

2. Deleting the last node
This operation is shown in Fig. 6. 18.

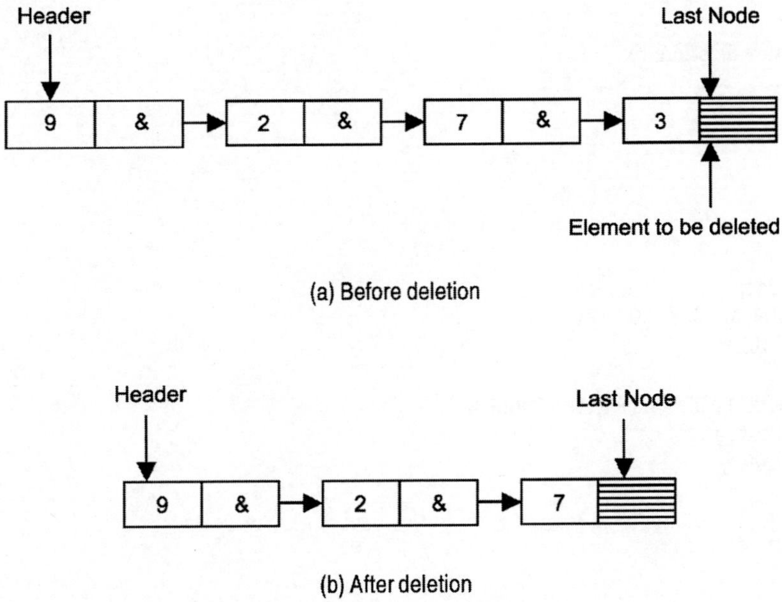

Figure 6.18 Deletion operation with linked list

Example 6.21

Write a program to remove last elements of the linked list.

Solution

```
# include <stdio.h>
# include <conio.h>
# include <malloc.h>

int c;
struct num
{
   int num;
   struct num *next;
} *header,*first,*rear,*k;

main ()
{
 void create ( void);
```

Explanation This program demonstrates the deletion from the end of the list. Here, the *show ()* function performs the deletion function and after the function is executed, the rear pointer of the list is freed and an address of previous node is assigned to it. The *show ()* function also displays the elements.

```
void show (void);
clrscr();
printf ("\n Operation creation:");
create ();
show();
printf ("\n After deletion: ");
show();
show();
show();
}

void create ( void )
{
struct num *node;
printf ("\n Enter numbers( 0 to exit): ");
if (header==NULL)
{
first=(struct num*)malloc(sizeof(struct num));
scanf ("%d",&first->num);
first->next=header;
header=first;
rear=first;
c++;
}
while (1)
{
node=(struct num*) malloc(sizeof(struct num));
scanf ("%d",&node->num);
if (node->num==0) break;
c++;
node->next=NULL;
rear->next=node;
rear=node;
}
}
void show()
{
struct num *pr;
int k=c;
printf ("\n Linked list elements are: ");
while (header!=NULL)
{
printf (" %d ",header->num);
header=header->next;
k--;
if (k==1)
{
```

```
free(rear);
 rear=header;
header=first;
 break;
 }
 }
c--;
}
```

```
OUTPUT
Operation creation:
Enter numbers( 0 to exit): 1 5 9 7 5 3 2 0
Linked list elements are: 1 5 9 7 5 3
After deletion:
Linked list elements are: 1 5 9 7 5
Linked list elements are: 1 5 9 7
Linked list elements are: 1 5 9
```

3. Deleting the specific node

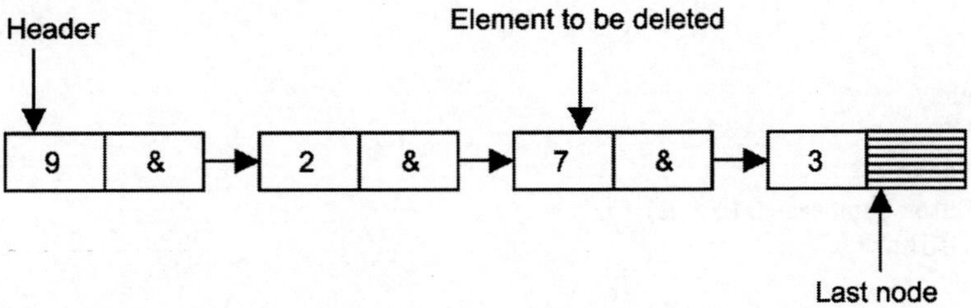

Figure 6.19 Deleting a specific node

So far, we have studied how to remove the first and last node of the list. Now, we want to remove the node randomly from the list. This case is different from the last two cases. In this deletion operation, when a specific node is removed, the previous and next nodes are linked. The memory of the given node is released. The removal of node is shown in the Fig. 6.19.

Example 6.22

Write a program to remove a specific element from the list.

Solution

```
# include <stdio.h>
# include <conio.h>
# include <malloc.h>
```

```
# include <process.h>
struct num
{
   int num;
   struct num *next;
} *header,*first,*rear,*k;
int count;

main ()
{
   void remove1(int);
   void create ( void);
   void show (void);
   int n;
   clrscr();
   printf ("\n Operation creation:");
   create ();
   show();
   printf ("\n Enter position of number for removal < %d ",count);
   scanf ("%d",&n);
   remove1(n);
   getch();
}
void create ( void )
{
   struct num *node;
   printf ("\n Enter numbers( 0 to exit): ");
   if (header==NULL)
   {
   first=(struct num*)malloc(sizeof(struct num));
   scanf ("%d",&first->num);
   first->next=header;
   header=first;
   rear=first;
   count =1;
 }
 while (1)
 {
   node=(struct num*) malloc(sizeof(struct num));
   scanf ("%d",&node->num);
   if (node->num==0) break;
   count++;
   node->next=NULL;
   rear->next=node;
   rear=node;
 }
}
```

Explanation In this program the element specified by the user is removed. After entering the number, the list of number is displayed. User has to specify only element number. Using *for loop* the specified location is searched. The address of next element is assigned to previous element by skipping the element to be deleted. Thus, the link between previous and next element is joined.

```
void remove1(int j)
{
 int p,h;
 void show(void);
 j--;

 p=j-1;
 if (j==0)
 {
 header=header->next;
 show();
 }
 for ( h=0;h<count;h++)
 {
 if (h==p)
 {
  header->next=header->next->next;
 header=first;
 show();
 }
 header=header->next;
 }
}

 void show()
 {
 printf ("\n Linked list elements are: ");
 while (header!=NULL)
 {
 printf (" %d ",header->num);
 header=header->next;
 }
 header=first;
 }
```

```
OUTPUT
Operation creation:
Enter numbers( 0 to exit): 4 8 6 5 9 7 4 0
Linked list elements are: 4 8 6 5 9 7 4
Enter position of number for removal < 7 4
Linked list elements are: 4 8 6 9 7 4
```

6.21 REVERSING THE SINGLY LINKED LIST

Conceptually, the singly linked list can be traversed in only forward direction. The structure of singly linked list contains only one pointer, pointing to the next node. The same list can be displayed in reverse fashion using the following program.

Example 6.23

Write a program to reverse the singly linked list.

Solution

```
# include <stdio.h>
# include <conio.h>
struct node
{
 int value;
 struct node *next;
 };
 void create (void);
void reverse(void);
 void show (void);
 struct node *rear;
 int nodes;
 struct node *head;

main ()
{
   clrscr();
   create();
   reverse();
   show ();
}
void create ( )
{
   struct node *item;
   printf ("Enter numbers( 0 to exit): ");
 if (head==NULL)
 {
   head=(struct node*)malloc(sizeof(struct node));
   scanf ("%d",&head->value);
   head->next=NULL;
   rear=head;
 }
 while (1)
 {
   item=(struct node *)malloc(sizeof(struct node));
   scanf ("%d",&item->value);
   if (item->value==0) break;
   item->next=NULL;
   rear->next=item;
   rear=item;
 }
}
```

Explanation In this program the pointer **first* is global and hence has an initial value NULL. The logic of the program is very simple. The three pointers **prv, *cur, *next;* are used for swapping of the addresses. The end of the list is obtained and the address of previous is assigned to first. Thus, the link list is reversed. The pointer head now points to the last node and every node contains an address of the previous node instead of next node.

```
void reverse()
{
 struct node *prv, *cur, *next;
 if (head==NULL)
 {
 printf ("List is empty");
 return;
 }
 cur=head;
 prv =NULL;
 while (cur !=NULL)
 {
 next=cur->next;
 cur->next=prv;
 prv=cur;
 cur=next;
 }
 head=prv;
 }
 void show ( )
 {
 printf ("\n Reverse list is: ");
 while (head!=NULL)
 {
 nodes++;
 printf (" %d ",head->value);
 head=head->next;
 }
 nodes=0;
 }
```

```
OUTPUT
Enter numbers( 0 to exit): 1 2 3 4 5 6 7 0
Reverse list is: 7 6 5 4 3 2 1
```

6.22 CONCATENATION OF TWO LISTS

Concatenation of two lists means adding a list at the end of another list as shown in Fig. 6.20. Consider the following program.

Example 6.24

Write a program to concatenate two linked lists and display the elements.

Solution

```
# include <stdio.h>
```

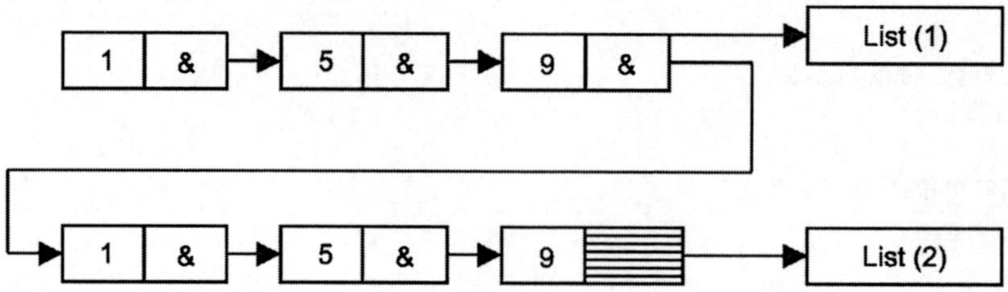

Figure 6.20 Concatenation of lists

Explanation The *creation ()* function is used to create linked lists. In this program, two lists are created. The starting address of the *list (2)* is assigned to the rear of the first list. Here, the same function is used to create both the lists. Hence, the contents of the local variables used in *create ()* function alters. In order to obtain the address of last node of the first list, *if* condition is inserted and the address of the rear node is stored in the pointer **f*. All this process is carried out by the function *concat ()*. In the function *concat (),* the starting address of the *list (2)* is assigned to rear of the *list (1)*. The pointer start is assigned the address of the *list (1)*. Using the same starting address the function *print ()* prints the element.

```
# include <conio.h>
# include <malloc.h>

struct node
{
 int value;
 struct node *next;
};
struct node *rear,*start,*f;
struct node *create (void);
void concat(void);
void print (void );
int count=1;
struct node *one,*two;
main ()
{
clrscr();
 one=create();
 two=create();
 concat();
 print();
}
struct node *create ()
 {
   struct node *item,*temp;
   temp=(struct node *)malloc(sizeof(struct node));
   printf ("\nEnter numbers of list (%d) (0) to exit: ",count);
   scanf ("%d",&temp->value);
   temp->next=NULL;
   rear=temp;
   while (1)
   {
   item=(struct node*)malloc(sizeof(struct node));
   scanf ("%d",&item->value);
   if (item->value==0)
```

```
{
break;
}
item->next=NULL;
rear->next=item;
rear=item;
if(count==1)
f=rear;
}
count++;
return(temp);
}
void concat()
{
f->next=two;
start=one;
}
void print()
{
printf("Merged list: ");
    while(start!=NULL)
{
    printf(" %d ",start->value);
    start=start->next;
}
}
```

```
OUTPUT
Enter numbers of list (1) (0) to exit: 1 5 9 0
Enter numbers of list (2) (0) to exit: 7 3 4 0
Merged list: 1 5 9 7 3 4
```

6.23 SPLITTING OF A LINKED LIST

Once a singly linked list is formed, it can split many sub-lists. The technique involved in splitting is very simple. Put the NULL value in the node where you want to finish the first sub-list in the main list. Later, the next node will act as first node of the second sub-list. Thus, two or more sub-lists can be created from a single list (see Fig. 6.21).

Example 6.25

Write a program to split a single linked list in two separate lists and display the elements.

Solution

```
# include <stdio.h>
# include <conio.h>
```

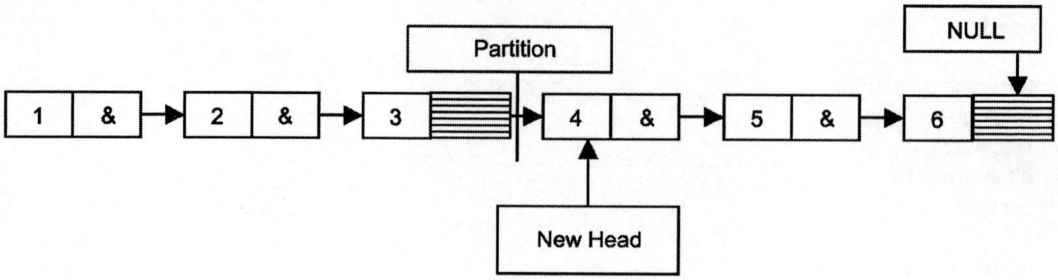

Figure 6.21 Partition of a single list

Explanation In the *create ()* function the counter variable *c* is incremented and keep an eye on the number of nodes created. In the *split ()*, function *c* is divided by two, i.e. to divide the list elements. In case, odd number of nodes are created then, the first sub-list gets more nodes. In the *split ()* function, exactly half of the nodes are traversed and the node in the middle is assigned a value NULL. Thus, the first sub-list ends here. The next node is considered as a head node for the second sub-list. The address of head node of the second sub-list is assigned to pointer two. Thus, using pointers one and two with function *print ()* two sub-lists are displayed.

```
# include <malloc.h>
struct node
{
 int value;
 struct node *next;
};
 struct node *rear,*start,*f;
 struct node *create (void);
 struct node * split(int);
 void print (struct node * );
 int count=0;
 struct node *one,*two;

main ()
{
clrscr();
one=create();
two=split(count/2);
printf("The two separated list are:-");
print(one);
print(two);
}
struct node *create ()
 {
   struct node *item,*temp;
   temp=(struct node *)malloc(sizeof(struct node));
   printf ("\nEnter numbers of list( 0 to exit): ");
   scanf ("%d",&temp->value);
   count++;
   temp->next=NULL;
   rear=temp;
   if (count==1) start=temp;
   while (1)
   {
```

```
item=(struct node*)malloc(sizeof(struct node));
scanf ("%d",&item->value);
if (item->value==0)
break;
count++;
item->next=NULL;
rear->next=item;
rear=item;
}
count++;
return (temp);
}
struct node * split (int j )
{
int c=0;
while (one!=NULL)
{
    c++;
if (c==j)
{
   two=one->next;
   one->next=NULL;
   one=start;
   break;
   }
 one=one->next;
 }
return two;
}
   void print (struct node *s )
   {
   static c;
   c++;
   printf ("\n list (%d): ",c);

   while (s!=NULL)
 {
   printf (" %d ",s->value);
   s=s->next;
 }
}
```

OUTPUT
Enter numbers of list(0 to exit): 1 2 3 4 5 6 7 8 0
The two separated list are:-
list (1): 1 2 3 4
list (2): 5 6 7 8

6.24 CIRCULAR LINKED LIST

In circular linked list the last node points to the header node. The linear link list can be converted to circular linked list by linking the last node to the first node. The last node of the linear linked list holds *NULL* pointer, which indicates the end of linked list but performance of linked list can be advanced with minor adjustment in the linear linked list. Instead of placing the NULL pointer, the address of the first node can be given to the last node, such a list is called *circular linked list* (as shown in Fig. 6.22).

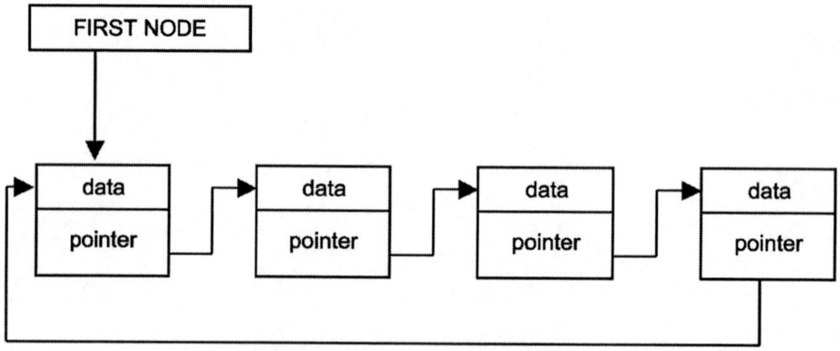

Figure 6.22 Circular linked list

The circular linked list is more helpful as compared to singly linked list. In the circular linked list, all the nodes of the list are accessible from the given node. Once a node is accessed, by traversing all the nodes can be accessed in succession.

In this type of list, the deletion operation is very easy. To delete an element from the singly linked list, it is essential to obtain the address of the first node of the list. For example, we want to delete the element, say 5, which exists in the middle of the list. To remove the element five, we need to find predecessor of five. Obviously, a particular element can be searched using searching process in which all elements are visited and compared. In the circular linked list, no such process is needed. The address of predecessor can be found from the given element itself. In addition, the operation splitting and concatenation of the list (discussed later) are easier.

Though the circular linked list has advantages over linear linked list, it also has some limitations. This list does not have first and last node. While traversing the linked list, due to lack of NULL pointer, there may be a possibility to get into an infinite *loop*. Thus, in the circular linked list it is necessary to identify the end of the list. This can be done by setting up the first and last node by convention. We detect the first node by creating the *list head*, which holds the address of the first node. The list head is also called as external pointer. We can also keep a counter, which is incremented when nodes are created and end of the node can be detected. The Fig. 6.23 gives an example of circular linked list with header.

6.25 METHOD FOR DETECTING END

There are two methods for finding or detecting the end of the circular linked list. They are:

1. Detecting end with counter
2. Detecting end with pointer.

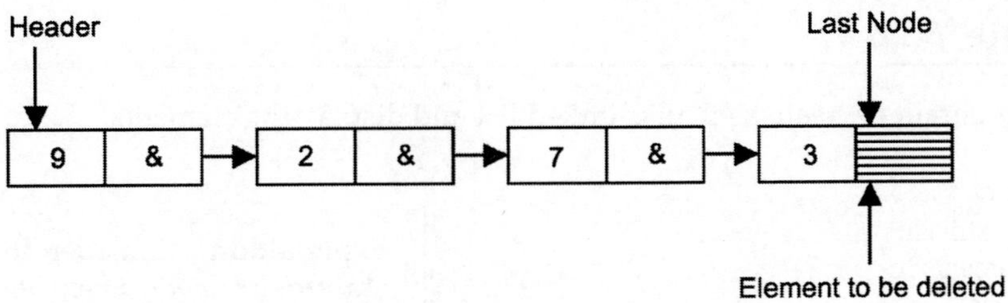

Figure 6.23 Circular linked list with header

6.25.1 Detecting End with Counter

This is the first method for detecting the end point of the circular linked list. The program 6.26 is similar to the program used for the creation of circular linked list. But only one change is done as compared to previous program, i.e. last node is pointing to the first node. Instead of assigning NULL pointer, the address of first node is assigned. Fig. 6.24 and program 6.26 explain the method for detecting end with counter.

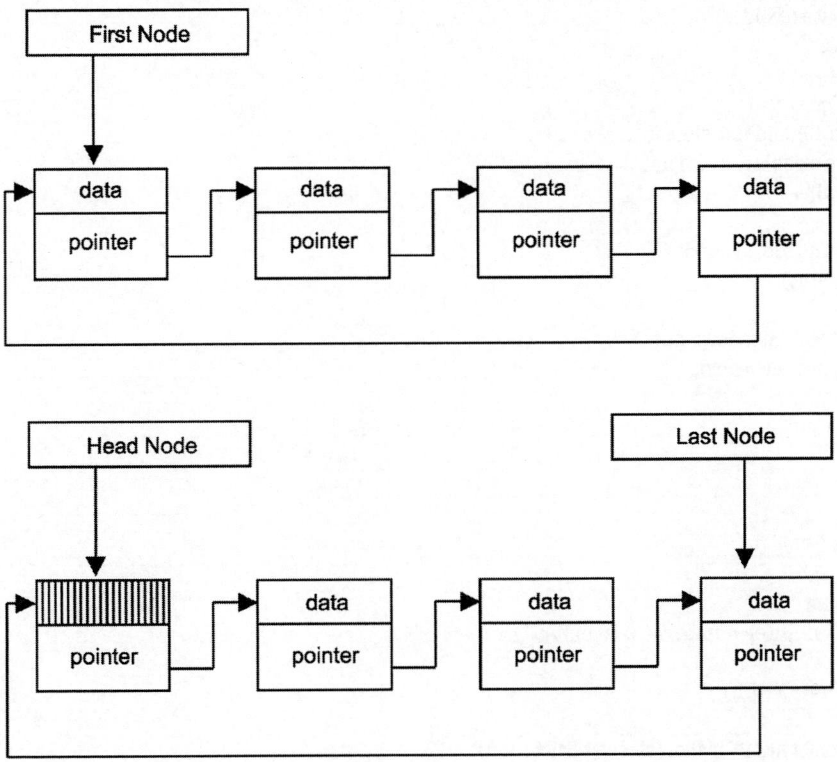

Figure 6.24 Detecting end with counter

Example 6.26

Write a program to create a circular linked list and display the elements.

Solution

Explanation Consider the following statement *node->next=header;*. The address of the first node (header node which points to the first node) is assigned to last. If you see the same statement in the creation of singly linked list, the statement is *node->next=NULL;*. Instead of NULL, header is assigned.

```
# include <stdio.h>
# include <conio.h>
# include <malloc.h>
struct num
{
   int num;
   struct num *next;
} *header,*first,*rear;
int count=0;

main ()
{

   void create ( void);
   int j,k=0;
   clrscr();
   create ();
 printf ("\n Linked list elements are: \n");
 printf("The circular linked list traversing\n");
 for (j=0;j<5;j++)
{
 printf("\n In (%d ) round: ",j+1);
 while (k<count)
{
   printf (" %d ",header->num);
   header=header->next;
   k++;
}
 k=0;
}
}
void create ( void )
{
   struct num *node;
   printf ("\n Enter numbers( 0 to exit): ");

   if (header==NULL)
   {
   first=(struct num*)malloc(sizeof(struct num));
   scanf ("%d",&first->num);
   first->next=header;
   header=first;
```

```
    rear=first;
    count++;
  }
 while (1)
 {
    node=(struct num*) malloc(sizeof(struct num));
    scanf ("%d",&node->num);
    if (node->num==0) break;
    count++;
    node->next=header;
    rear->next=node;
    rear=node;
 }
 }
```

```
OUTPUT
Enter numbers( 0 to exit): 1 5 9 8 7 0
Linked list elements are:
The circular linked list traversing
In ( 1 ) round: 1 5 9 8 7
In ( 2 ) round: 1 5 9 8 7
In ( 3 ) round: 1 5 9 8 7
In ( 4 ) round: 1 5 9 8 7
In ( 5 ) round: 1 5 9 8 7
```

With creation operation, the counter variable is incremented. The counter variable is used to count the total number of nodes in the linked list. The *for loop* iterates from zero to 5 and the linked list elements are displayed five times. The *while loop* takes loops and it contains the condition *k*<counter. The variable *k* is incremented and when it is one less than counter it means end of the circular linked lists is reached. Again, in second iteration of *for loop*, *k* is initialized to zero. The value of *k* is nothing but the position of the node in the list. The value 0 means first node, 1 means second node and so on. Thus, first and last node of the list can be obtained.

If we remove the counter and the condition statements, which terminate the loop, we get into the infinite loop. After the last node, immediately first node is accessed. After removing the statement *printf ("\nRound (%d): ", j+1);* (after *for loop*) the output of the program would be

```
OUTPUT
Enter number: 1 2 3 0
Linked list elements are:
1 2 3 1 2 3 1 2 3 1 2 3 1 2 3
```

From the output, you can observe that sequence is preserved after last element (3). First, element 1 appears and displays the remaining elements. This process would be continued.

6.25.2 Detecting End with Pointer

This is the second method to detect the end of the circular linked list. In the last few programs, a rear pointer is declared which points to the last node and useful to find the end of the singly linked list. The same pointer is used here to detect the end of the circular linked list. Recall that in the circular linked lists the last node points to the first node, i.e. the pointer field of the rear pointer points to the data field of the first node as per the Fig. 6.25.

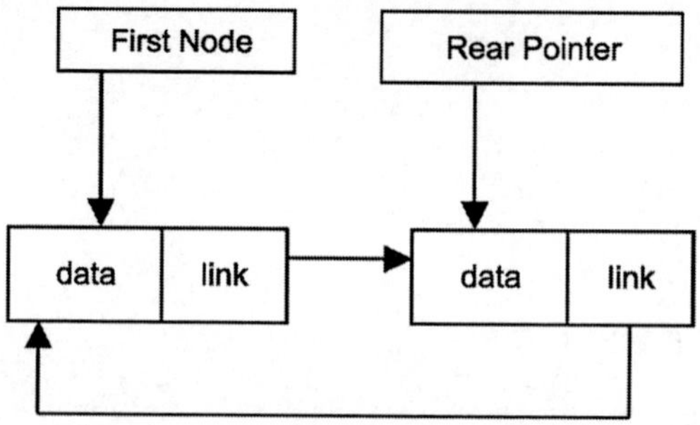

Figure 6.25 Detecting end with pointer

While scanning the circular linked list in order to get the end of the list, we have to check contents of all the pointer fields of the nodes. A link field of a node in a circular linked list pointing to the data field of the first node is the last node of the linked list. To implement this idea into a practical program we have to follow the following theory.

1. Obtain the address of the data field of the first node.
2. While traversing, compare the obtained address with the link field.
3. If the address obtained and the address pointing link field is same, i.e. that node is the last node.

Consider the following program,

Example 6.27

Write a program to detect the last node of the list using external pointer.

Solution

Explanation This program is similar to the previous program.

```
# include <stdio.h>
# include <conio.h>
# include <malloc.h>

struct num
{
   int num;
   struct num *next;
```

```
} *header,*first,*rear;
main()
{

 void create ( void);
 int j;
 clrscr();
 create ();
 printf ("\n Elements of circular linked list are:\n");
 for (j=0;j<5;j++)
{
 printf("\nRound (%d ): ",j+1);

do
{
 printf (" %d ",header->num);
  header=header->next;
 if (rear->next==(struct num *)&(header->num))
 break;
}while (1);
}
printf ("\nAddress of rear link field = %u",rear->next);
printf ("\nAddress of first data field = %u",(struct num *)&(header->num));
}
void create ( void )
{
 struct num *node;
 printf ("\n Enter numbers( 0 to exit): ");
 if (header==NULL)
 {
    first=(struct num*)malloc(sizeof(struct num));
    scanf ("%d",&first->num);
    first->next=header;
    header=first;
    rear=first;
 }
 while (1)
{
    node=(struct num*) malloc(sizeof(struct num));
    scanf ("%d",&node->num);
    if (node->num==0) break;
    node->next=header;
    rear->next=node;
    rear=node;
}
}
```

```
OUTPUT
Enter numbers( 0 to exit): 5 4 8 7 0
Elements of circular linked list are:
Round (1 ): 5 4 8 7
Round (2 ): 5 4 8 7
Round (3 ): 5 4 8 7
Round (4 ): 5 4 8 7
Round (5 ): 5 4 8 7
Address of rear link field = 1970
Address of first data field = 1970
```

Consider the statement,

```
if (rear->next==(struct num *)&(header->num))
break;
```

As soon as the last node is detected, the above statement terminates the *while loop*. The *if* statement compares the address of data field of first node with pointer field of each node. When it is found that both are same, the end of linked list is spotted. Here, the address of the data field is obtained by the typecasting statement (*struct num* *)&(*header->num*).

Here, typecasting is essential because an address of integer cannot be assigned to pointer of structure type. The syntax *(struct num *)* converts the address of integer *header->num* to pointer *rear->next*. In the output, addresses are also displayed.

6.25.3 Insertion in Circular Linked List

Insertions in the circular linked list are possible in three different ways:

1. Insertion at the beginning
2. Insertion at the end
3. Insertion at the specified position.

1. Insertion at the beginning

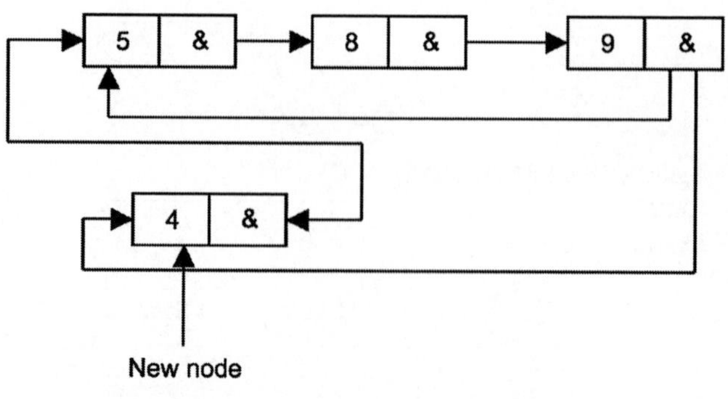

(a) A circular linked list before insertion

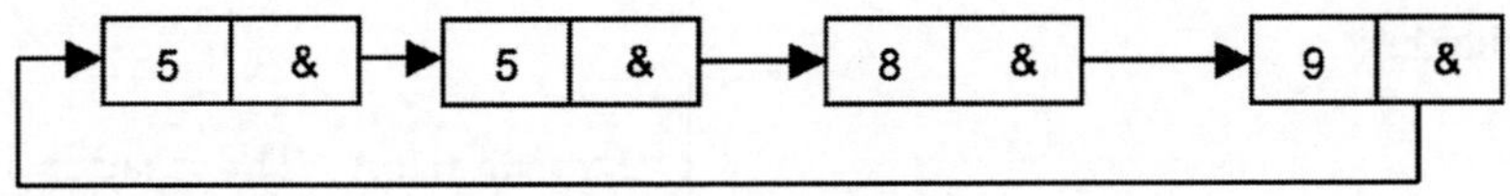

(b) After insertion

Figure 6.26 Insertion operation with circular list

Insertion of new node at the beginning involves memory allocation. Moreover, the value is assigned to the data field of the new node. When a new node is created for insertion, the address of data field of this new node is assigned to pointer of last node. Similarly, the address of data field of previously first node is assigned to new node. Thus, the new node becomes first node and the previous first node is moved to second position. Fig. 6.26 illustrates the insertion operation in circular linked list.

2. Insertion at the end

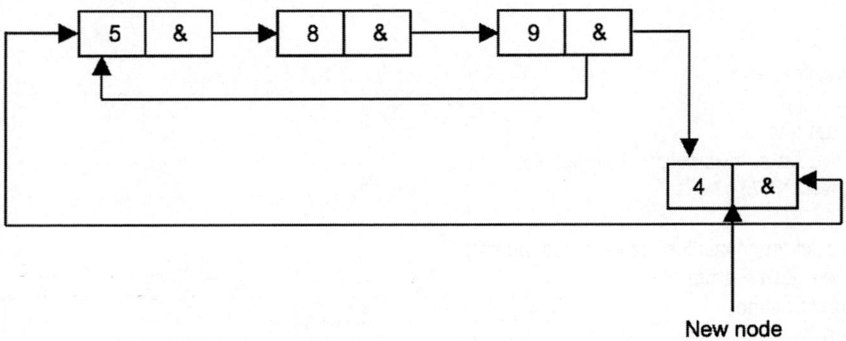

Figure 6.27 Insertion at end

When a new node is inserted at the end, the address of new node is given to the last node. The address of first node is given to the new node. Fig. 6.26 shows the insertion operation at end.

Example 6.28

Write a program to demonstrate insertion of element at the beginning and at end of the circular linked list.

Solution

```
# include <stdio.h>
# include <conio.h>
```

```
# include <malloc.h>
struct num
{
    int num;
    struct num *next;
} *header,*first,*rear;
main ()
{
    void create ( void);
    void iatend(void);
    void iatbeg(void);
    void show(void);
    clrscr();
    create (); /* creation of linked list*/
    show(); /* display of linked list*/
    iatbeg(); /* insertion at beginning*/
    show(); /* display of elements*/
    iatend(); /* insertion at the end*/
    show();
}
void create ( void )
{
    struct num *node;
    printf ("\n Enter numbers(0 to exit): ");
    if (header==NULL)
    {
    first=(struct num*)malloc(sizeof(struct num));
    scanf ("%d",&first->num);
    first->next=header;
    header=first;
    rear=first;
 }
while (1)
{
    node=(struct num*) malloc(sizeof(struct num));
    scanf ("%d",&node->num);
    if (node->num==0) break;
    node->next=header;
    rear->next=node;
    rear=node;
}
}
void iatend()
{
    struct num *node;
    node=(struct num*) malloc(sizeof(struct num));
    printf ("\nEnter a number to be inserted at end: ");
```

Explanation The reader is already aware of the creation and display of linked list. The function *iatbeg ()* inserts the element at the beginning of the list and the function *iatend ()* inserts the element at the end.

```
    scanf ("%d",&node->num);
    node->next=header;
    rear->next=node;
    rear=node;
}
void iatbeg()
{
    struct num *node;
    node=(struct num*) malloc(sizeof(struct num));
    printf ("\nEnter a number to be inserted at beginning: ");
    scanf ("%d",&node->num);
    node->next=header;
    header=node;
    rear->next=header;
}
void show ()
{
    printf ("Linked list elements are: ");
do
{ printf (" %d ",header->num);
    header=header->next;
    if (rear->next==(struct num *)&(header->num))
    break;
 } while(1);
}
```

```
OUPUT
Enter numbers( 0 to exit): 1 2 3 0
Linked list elements are: 1 2 3
Enter a number to be inserted at beginning: 4
Linked list elements are: 4 1 2 3
Enter a number to be inserted at end: 5
Linked list elements are: 4 1 2 3 5
```

We know that the statement *node=(struct num*) malloc(sizeof(struct num));* is used to create a new node. After creation of new node, only pointer adjustment is done. When we want to insert an element at the beginning the pointer adjustment is done as follows:

node->next=header;
header=node;
rear->next=header;

Remember the following points:

1. The pointer node is a new node.
2. The header points to the first node.
3. The pointer rear points to the last node.

Since we are going to insert at the beginning, the new node created will be the first node of the list. Then to accomplish this the link field of new node is assigned the address of first node, i.e. header. After this, the first node will be the second node and the new node will be the first node. The pointer header is always used to point first node. Hence, after insertion its contents must be updated. Thus, the statement *header=node;* changes the contents of the pointer header. The last pointer adjustment to be done is, to assign the address of the first node data field to last node. The statement *rear->next=header;* serves the same purpose.

The following program explains insertion at the specified position.

Example 6.29

Write a program to insert an element at a given position in the circular linked list.

Solution

```
# include <stdio.h>
# include <conio.h>
# include <malloc.h>

struct num
{
   int num;
   struct num *next;
} *header,*first,*rear;

main ()
{
   void create ( void);
   void show(void);
   void atgiven(int);
   int n;
   clrscr();
   create ();
   printf ("\n Enter position number: ");
   scanf ("%d",&n);
   n--;
   atgiven(n);
   show();
}
void create ( void )
{
   struct num *node;
   printf ("\n Enter numbers( 0 to exit): ");

   if (header==NULL)
   {
   first=(struct num*)malloc(sizeof(struct num));
```

Explanation In this program, the function *atgiven()* is used to insert the element at the specified position. The user specifies the position number where number is to be inserted. The position number is passed to the function *atgiven()*. In this function, using *while loop* the linked list is traversed and the previous and next node of the given element are stored in the pointers *prv* and *header*.

```
    scanf ("%d",&first->num);
    first->next=header;
    header=first;
    rear=first;
 }
while (1)
{
    node=(struct num*) malloc(sizeof(struct num));
    scanf ("%d",&node->num);
    if (node->num==0) break;
    node->next=header;
    rear->next=node;
    rear=node;
}
}
void show ()
{
 printf ("Linked list elements are: ");
do
{ printf (" %d ",header->num);
 header=header->next;
 if (rear->next==(struct num *)&(header->num))
 break;
 } while(1);
}
void atgiven(int j)
{
    int c=0,k=j-2;
    struct num *node,*prv;
    printf ("\nLinked list upto %d element are: ",j);
do
    { printf (" %d ",header->num);
    header=header->next;
    if (k==c) prv=header;
    c++;
 } while(c<j);
 node=(struct num*) malloc(sizeof(struct num));
 printf ("\n Enter a element: ");
 scanf ("%d",&node->num);
  node->next=header;
 prv->next=node;
 header=first;
}
```

```
OUTPUT
Enter numbers( 0 to exit): 1 2 3 5 6 7 0
Enter position number: 3
```

```
Linked list up to 3 element are: 1 2 3
Enter a element: 4
Linked list elements are: 1 2 3 4 5 6 7
```

```
node->next=header;
prv->next=node;
header=first;
```

The new node created is given the address of header. At this point *header* is not pointing to the first node. Due to traversing in the *while loop*, it is pointing to the nth element, see the statement (*header=header->next;*). The new node is assigned the address of next node. The *prv* is assigned the address of new node. Again, the header is assigned the address of first node.

Some authors describe the insertion before and after. I think there is no need to classify it differently. The above program inserts the element after the specified position. In order to insert an element before the given position, only decrease the value of variable *n* before passing to function *atgiven ()*. By changing the value of *n*, the user can accomplish the operation insertion before, after and exactly at given position.

6.25.4 Deletion in Circular Linked List

Like insertion, deletion of element in the circular linked list can be done at various positions and they are as follows:

1. Deletion at beginning
2. Deletion at the end
3. Deletion at the specified position.

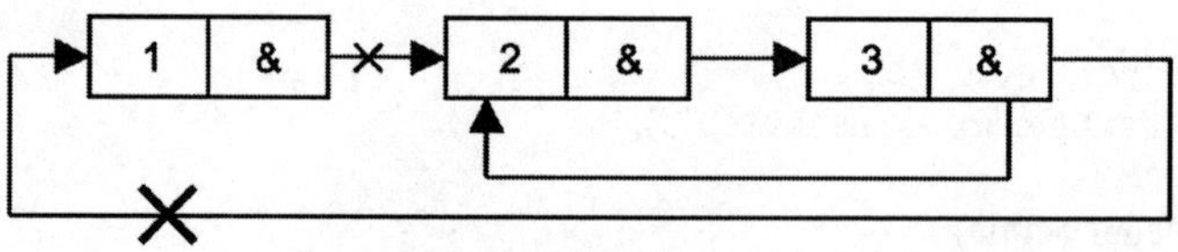

Figure 6.28 Deletion at beginning

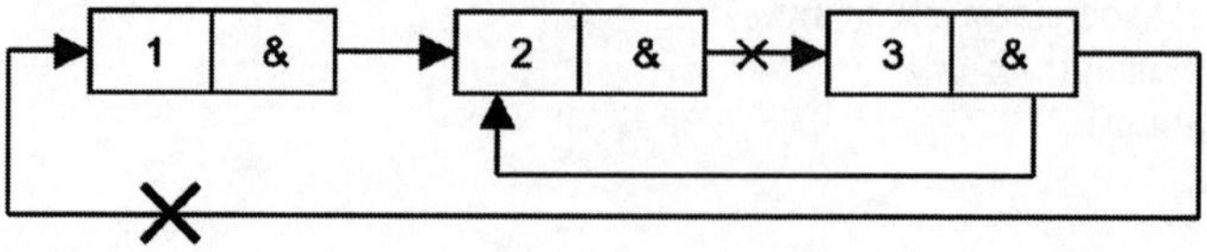

Figure 6.29 Deletion at end

The pointer adjustment is same in insertion and deletion. However, in insertion, an element is inserted and memory is allocated. In deletion, a node from the list is removed and memory is released. Consider the following program. Refer the Fig. 6.28 and 6.29.

Example 6.30

Write a program to delete an element from end and beginning of the linked list.

Solution

```
# include <stdio.h>
# include <conio.h>
# include <malloc.h>
struct num
{
int num;
struct num *next;
} *header,*first,*rear;
static int c;

main ()
{
    void create (void);
    void datend(void);
    void datbeg(void);
    void show(void);
    clrscr();
    create ();
    show();
    printf ("\nAfter deletion of beginning element");
    datbeg();
    show();
    printf ("\nAfter deletion of end element");
    datend();
    show();
    }
    void create ()
    {
    struct num *node;
    printf ("\n Enter numbers( 0 to exit): ");
    if (header==NULL)
    {
    first=(struct num*)malloc(sizeof(struct num));
    scanf ("%d",&first->num);
    first->next=header;
    header=first;
    rear=first;
    c++;
}
while (1)
{
    node=(struct num*) malloc(sizeof(struct num));
```

Explanation In this program to erase the element from beginning and end, help of counter variable is taken. The variable *c* is incremented in the function *create ()* when a new node is created. Similarly, when an element is removed the counter *c* is decremented. The counter variable is needful only in the function *datend ()*, because to erase the last element, the last but one element is obtained and it is connected to first node.

```
    scanf ("%d",&node->num);
    if (node->num==0) break;
    node->next=header;
    rear->next=node;
    rear=node;
    c++;
}
}
void datend()
{
    int k=0;
    while (k++<(c-2))
    header=header->next;
    free(rear);
    rear=header;
    rear->next=first;
    header=first;
    c--;
}
void datbeg()
{
    struct num *node;
    node=first;
    first=header=header->next;
    free(node);
    rear->next=header;
    c--;
}
void show ()
{
printf ("\nLinked list elements are: ");
do
{
printf (" %d ",header->num);
header=header->next;
if (rear->next==header) break;
} while(1);
header=first;
}
```

```
OUTPUT
Enter numbers( 0 to exit): 1 2 3 4 5 6 7 0
Linked list elements are: 1 2 3 4 5 6 7
After deletion of beginning element
Linked list elements are: 2 3 4 5 6 7
After deletion of end element
Linked list elements are: 2 3 4 5 6
```

Example 6.31

Write a program to delete the specified element from the linked list.

Solution

```
# include <stdio.h>
# include <conio.h>
# include <malloc.h>
struct num
{
   int num;
   struct num *next;
} *header,*first,*rear;
static int c;

main ()
{
   void create (void);
   void atgiven(int);
   void show(void);
   int n;
   clrscr();
   create ();
   show();
   printf ("\n Enter position number: ");
   scanf ("%d",&n);
   atgiven(n);
   show();
   getch();
}
void create ()
{
   struct num *node;
   printf ("\n Enter numbers( 0 to exit): ");
   if (header==NULL)
   {
   first=(struct num*)malloc(sizeof(struct num));
   scanf ("%d",&first->num);
   first->next=header;
   header=first;
   rear=first;
   c++;
}
 while (1)
 {
   node=(struct num*) malloc(sizeof(struct num));
```

Explanation In this program the function *atgiven ()* deletes the specified element from the circular linked list. The user enters the position number and it is passed to the function *atgiven ()*. In this function using *while loop* entire list is scanned and predecessor and successor of the given element are stored in the pointer **prv* and *header*. The node, which is to be removed, is stored in the pointer *temp*. Using *free ()* function the memory allocated is released. Then, a link between pointer *prv* and *header* is established by the following statements.

```
   scanf ("%d",&node->num);
   if (node->num==0) break;
   node->next=header;
   rear->next=node;
   rear=node;
   c++;
 }
}
   void atgiven(int g)
   {
   struct num *prv,*temp;
   int k=0,p;
   p=g-2;
   while (k++<g )
   {
   header=header->next;
   if (k==p) prv=header;
   if (k==(p+1)) temp=header;
 }
   c--;
   prv->next=header;
   header=first;
   free(temp);
}
void show ()
{
 printf ("\nLinked list elements are: ");
 do
 {
   printf (" %d ",header->num);
   header=header->next;
   if (rear->next==header) break;
 } while(1);
header=first;
}
```

OUTPUT

```
Enter numbers( 0 to exit: 5 8 7 4 5 3 2 0
Linked list elements are: 5 8 7 4 5 3 2
Enter position number: 3
Linked list elements are: 5 8 4 5 3 2
```

6.26 DOUBLY LINKED LIST

The singly linked list and circular linked list contain only one pointer field. Every node holds an address of next node. Thus, the singly linked list can traverse only in one direction, i.e. forward. This limitation can be overcome by doubly linked list. Each node of the doubly linked list has two pointer fields and holds the address of predecessor and successor elements. These pointers enable bi-directional traversing, i.e. traversing the list in backward and forward direction. In several applications, it is very essential to traverse the list in backward direction. The pointer pointing to the predecessor node is called left link and pointer pointing to successor is called right link. A list having such type of node is called doubly linked list. The pointer field of the first and last node holds NULL value, i.e. the beginning and end of the list can be identified by NULL value. The structure of the node is as shown in Fig. 6.30.

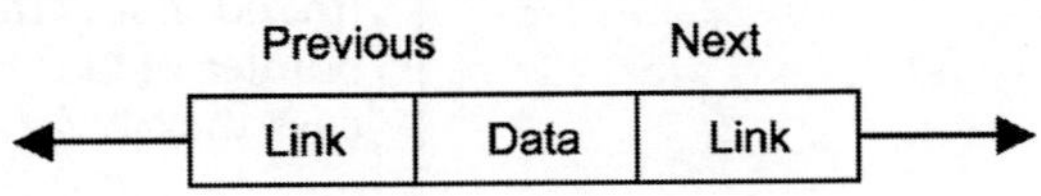

Figure 6.30 Structure of node

The structure of node would be as follows:

```
struct node
{
   int number;
   struct node *llink
   struct node *rlink;
}
```

the above structure can be represented by using the Fig. 6.31.

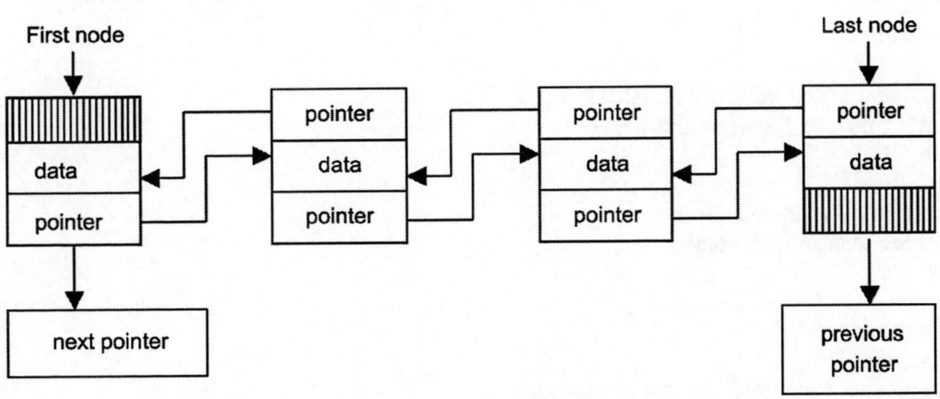

Figure 6.31 Doubly linked list

Example 6.32

Write a program to create the doubly linked list. Display the elements in original and reverse sequence.

Solution

```
# include <stdio.h>
# include <conio.h>
# include <malloc.h>

struct dlist
{
    struct dlist *prev;
    int number;
    struct dlist *next;
};
struct dlist *end,*start;
struct dlist *node=NULL;
void create (void);
void showl(void);
void showr(void);

main ()
 {

    clrscr();
    create();
    showl();
    showr();
    getch();
}
void create ()
{
    node=(struct dlist*)malloc(sizeof(struct dlist));
    printf ("\n Enter Numbers (0 to stop): ");
    while (1)
    {
    scanf ("%d",&node->number);
    if (node->number==0) break;
    else
    {
    node->prev =end;
    end=node;
    node=(struct dlist*) malloc(sizeof(struct dlist));
    }
    }
    node=end;
```

Explanation The *create ()* function is used to create the doubly linked list. The method of creation of node is same as in the previously discussed methods of the linked list. Here, an additional one pointer field is present and we will discuss that in detail in next section.

```
  start=NULL;
  while (node!=NULL)
  {
  node->next=start;
  start=node;
  node=node->prev;
  }
}
void showl( )
{
printf ("\n Original List: ");

while (start!=NULL)
{
  printf (" %d ",start->number);
  start=start->next;
}
}
void showr( )
{
printf ("\n Reverse List: ");

while (end!=NULL)
{
  printf (" %d ",end->number);
  end=end->prev;
}
}
```

```
OUTPUT
Enter Numbers (0 to stop): 1 2 4 7 5 0
Original List: 1 2 4 7 5
Reverse List: 5 7 4 2 1
```

We know the use of next pointer and how we have used it previously to access the next node. Every time a new node is inserted, the address of new node is assigned to the next pointer of previous node. This is required for details of manipulating the next pointer. The pointer **prev* (pointing to data field of previous node) is not different case. The pointer next is right hand and **prev* is the left hand of the node. Every time a new node is created, the address of data field of previous node is assigned to the previous pointer. The rest of the operations are same for accessing the elements. Go through the functions *showl()* and *showr()*.

6.26.1 Insertion and Deletion with Doubly Linked List

We are aware of insertion process in which an element can be inserted at beginning, at end and at the specified position. Fig. 6.32 shows the insertion in the doubly linked list.

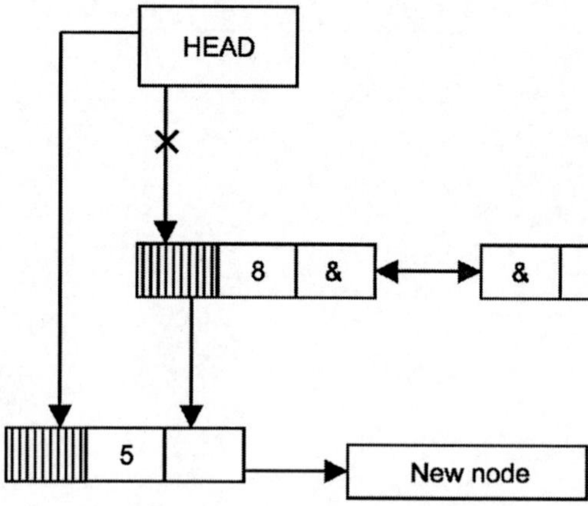

Figure 6.32 Inserting a node at the beginning

We know that the head node of the doubly linked list contains NULL value. When a new node is to be inserted at the beginning, the address of the head node is assigned to the new node. The previous pointer of the node is assigned a NULL value. The arrow ↔ indicates that the node has both previous and next pointer.

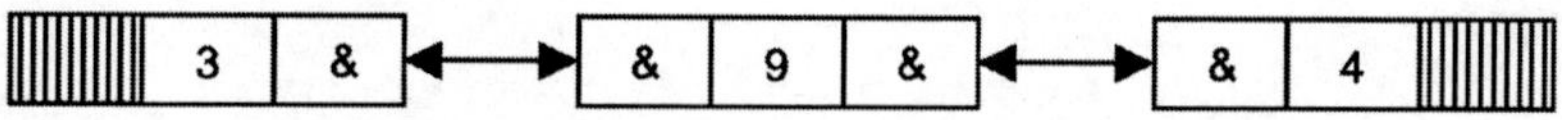

Figure 6.33 Inserting a node at the end

When a node is inserted at the end, the next pointer of the new node is assigned a NULL value and the previous pointer of the node is assigned the address of last node. The Fig. 6.33 describes the insertion at the end.

In the deletion operation as shown in the Fig. 6.34 when a node is deleted, the memory allocated to that node is released and the previous and next nodes of that node are linked.

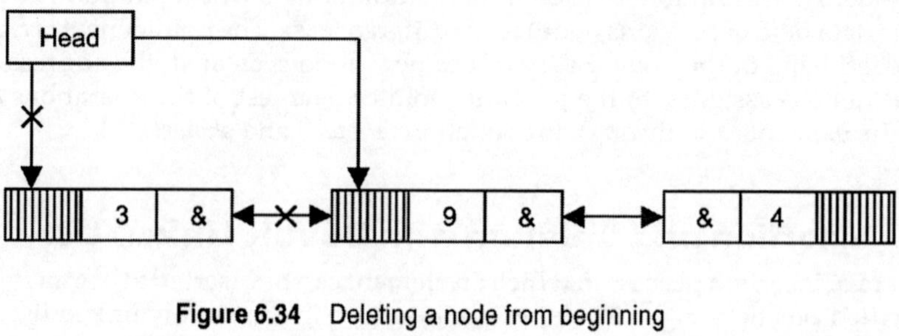

Figure 6.34 Deleting a node from beginning

When a node is to be deleted from the beginning of the node, the head pointer points to the second node. Because after deletion of first node, the second node becomes the first. The symbol × indicates the link will be destroyed. This is shown in the Fig. 6.35.

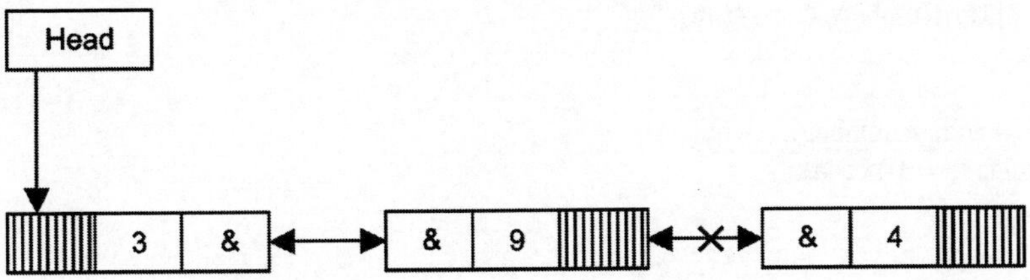

Figure 6.35 Deleting a node from the end

Example 6.33

Write a program to perform insertion and deletion operation on the doubly linked list.

Solution

```
# include <stdio.h>
# include <conio.h>
# include <malloc.h>

struct dlist
{
    struct dlist *prev;
    int number;
    struct dlist *next;
};
struct dlist *end,*start;
struct dlist *node=NULL;
void create (void);
void show(void);
void insert (void);
void re_move(void);

main ()
 {
    clrscr();
    create();
    insert();
    show();
    re_move();
    show();
    getch();
```

Explanation In this program both insertion and deletion operations are performed. The method of adjusting pointer is same as explained in the programs of singly and circular linked list operations. The user can insert or delete the element of any position including beginning and end.

```
}
void create ()
{
    node=(struct dlist*)malloc(sizeof(struct dlist));
    printf ("\n Enter Numbers (0 to stop): ");
    while (1)
 {
    scanf ("%d",&node->number);
    if (node->number==0) break;
    else
 {
    node->prev =end;
    end=node;
    node=(struct dlist*) malloc(sizeof(struct dlist));
 }
 }
 node=end;
 start=NULL;
 while (node!=NULL)
 {
 node->next=start;
 start=node;
 node=node->prev;
    }
 }
 void show( )
 {
    struct dlist *x;
 printf ("\n Origional List: ");

 x=start;

 while (start!=NULL)
 {
 printf (" %d ",start->number);
 start=start->next;
 }
 start=x;
}
void insert ()
{
 struct dlist *q,*r,*p;
 int number,k=1;
 p=start;
 printf (" (Insertion )Enter position of node: ");
 scanf ("%d",&number);
 if (number==1)
```

```
{
 q=(struct dlist*)malloc(sizeof(struct dlist));
 printf ("\n (Insertion) Enter the Number: ");
 scanf ("%d",&q->number);
  q->prev=NULL;
 q->next=start;
 start=q;
}
while (start!=NULL)
{
 if (++k==number)
  {
 q=(struct dlist*)malloc(sizeof(struct dlist));
  printf ("\n Enter the Number: ");
 scanf ("%d",&q->number);
 r=start->next;
 r->prev=q;
  q->next=r;
 q->prev=start;
 start->next=q;
 break;
  }
  else
 start=start->next;
  }
 if (number==1) start=q;
 else start=p;
}
void re_move ()
{
 struct dlist *q,*r,*p,*n;
 int number,c=0;
 printf ("\n (Deletion) Enter position of node: ");
 scanf ("%d",&number);
r=start;
if (number==0)
{
 p=start;
 free(p);
 start=start->next;
 start->prev=NULL;
}
 else
 while (r!=NULL)
  {
 c++;
 if (c==(number-1)) p=r;
```

```
if(c==number)
{
q=r;
free(q);
}
if(c==(number+1)) n=r;
r=r->next;
}
p->next=n;
}
```

```
OUTPUT
Enter Numbers (0 to stop): 1 2 3 4 5 6 7 0
(Insertion )Enter position of node: 3
Enter the Number: 8
Original List: 1 2 8 3 4 5 6 7
(Deletion) Enter position of node: 6
Original List: 1 2 8 3 4 6 7
```

6.26.2 Advantages of Doubly Linked List

1. The doubly linked list is bi-directional, i.e. it can be traversed in both backward and forward direction.
2. The operations such as insertion, deletion and searching can be done from both ends.
3. Predecessor and successor of any element can be searched quickly.
4. It is very helpful to implement arithmetic operations on large integer numbers.

6.26.3 Disadvantages of Doubly Linked List

1. It consumes more memory space.
2. There is large pointer adjustment during insertion and deletion of element.
3. It consumes more time for few basic list operations.

6.27 CIRCULAR DOUBLY LINKED LIST

A circular doubly linked list has both successor and predecessor pointers. Using the circular fashioned doubly linked list the insertion and deletion operation, which are little complicated in the previous types of linked list are easily performed. Consider the following Fig. 6.36:

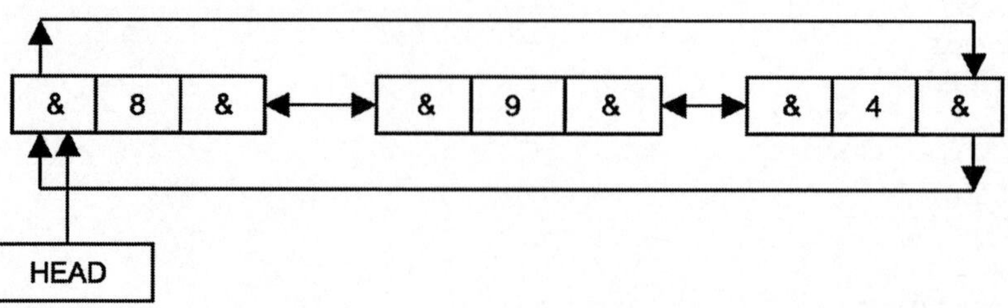

Figure 6.36 Circular doubly linked list

6.27.1 Insertion and Deletion Operation

The insertion operation is similar to what we have already learnt in previous types. The only difference is the way we link the pointer fields. Consider Fig. 6.37.

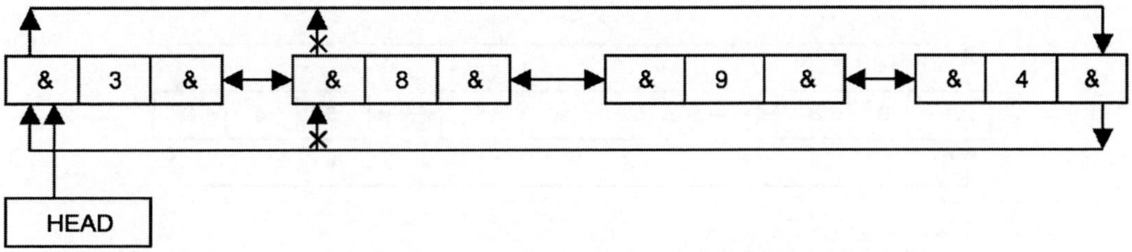

Figure 6.37 Inserting a node at the beginning

The × indicates that the previous links are destroyed. The pointer links from *ex-first node* are removed and linked to new inserted node at the beginning. The element 8 was previous first node and 3 is the new node inserted and becomes first node now after inserting it at the beginning.

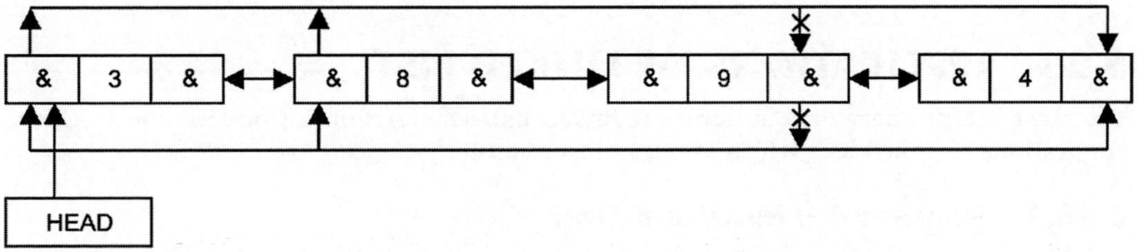

Figure 6.38 Inserting the node at the end

The × indicates, that the previous links are destroyed. The pointer links from *ex-last node* are removed and linked to new inserted node at the end. The address of last node is given to first node to form circular list. The node 9 was previously the last node but after insertion of the node at the end, newly inserted node is the last node. Fig. 6.39 shows the deletion of the node at beginning.

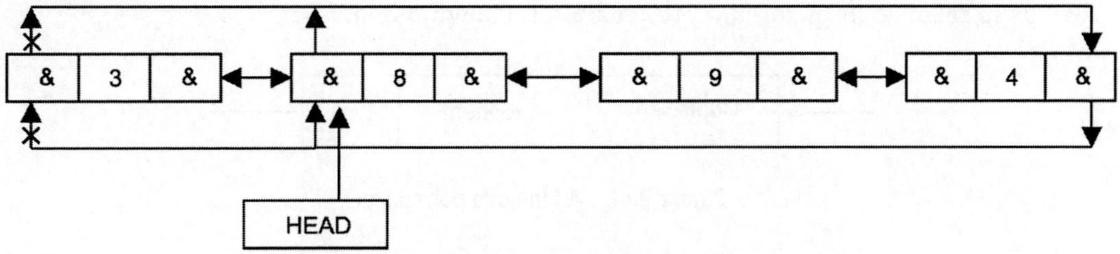

Figure 6.39 Deleting a node from the beginning

The × indicates that the previous links are destroyed. After deletion of the first node, the second node becomes first node. The pointer head also points to the newly appeared first node. Thus, when a node from the beginning is removed, the node followed by it will become the head node (first node). Accordingly, pointer adjustment is performed in the real application.

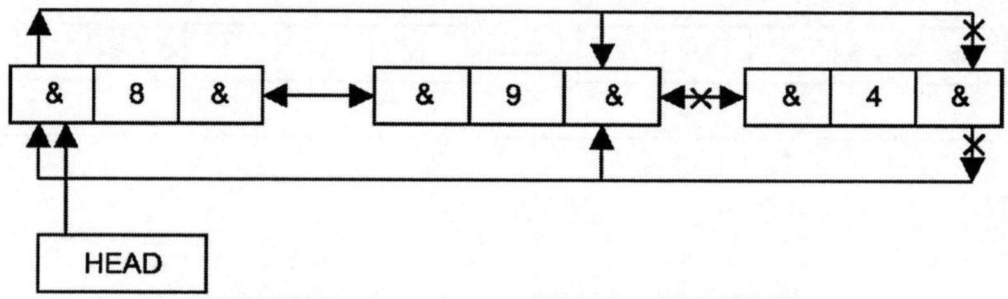

Figure 6.40 Deletion of the node at the end

The × as usual is the symbol destroying previous links. When the last node is removed, one node will be the last node and its links are established with the first node. The removal operation is shown in Fig. 6.40.

6.28 APPLICATIONS OF LINKED LIST

The most useful linear data structure is linked list. This section introduces you to a few applications of linked lists which are useful in computer science.

6.28.1 Polynomial Manipulation

A polynomial can be represented and manipulated using linear link list. Various applications on polynomials can be implemented with linked lists. We perform various operations such as addition, multiplication with polynomials. To get better proficiency in processing, each polynomial is stored in decreasing order. These arrangements of polynomial in series allow easy operation on them. Actually, two polynomials can be added by checking each term. The prior comparison can be easily done to add corresponding terms of two polynomials.

A polynomial is represented with various terms containing coefficients and exponents. In other words, a polynomial can be expressed with different terms, each of which comprises of coefficients and exponents. The structure of a node of linked list for polynomial implementation will be as follows. Its pictorial representation is shown in Fig. 6.41.

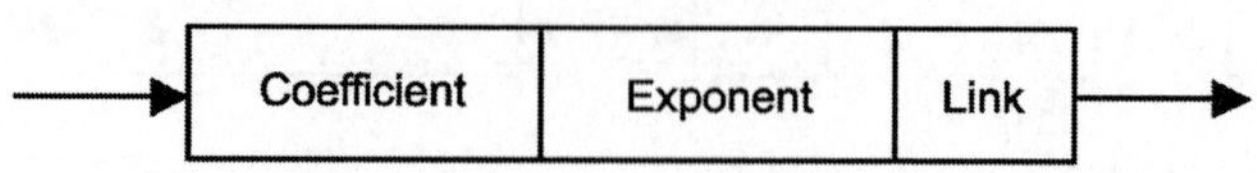

Figure 6.41 A term of a polynomial

The coefficient field contains the value of coefficient of the term. Similarly, the exponent field contains the value of exponent. As usual, the link field points to the term (next node).

The structure for the above node would be as follows:

```
struct poly
{
    double coeff;
    int exp;
    struct poly *next;
};
```

Consider a polynomial

$$P = P^8 + 5P^4 - 7P^2 + 6P$$

In this equation 1,5,7 and 6 are coefficients and exponents are 8,4,2 and 1. The number of nodes required would be the same as the number of terms in the polynomial. There are four terms in this polynomial hence it is represented with four nodes.

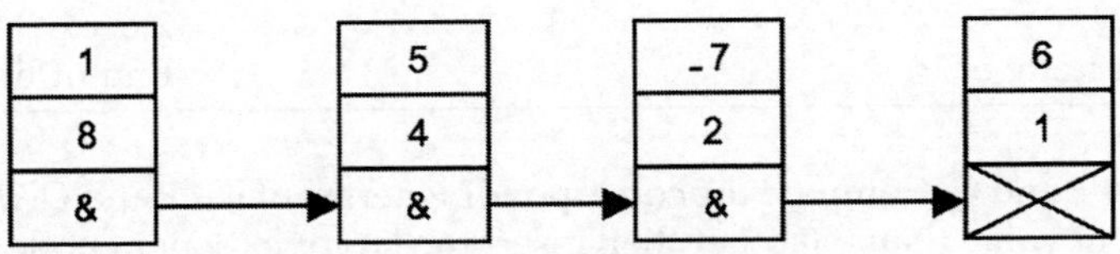

Figure 6.42 Polynomial representation

The top of every node represents coefficients of the polynomial, exponents are at the centre and the pointers are (*next*) at the bottom. The terms are stored in order of descending exponent in the linked list. It is assumed that no two terms have the similar exponents. Fig. 6.42 shows the polynomial.

Consider the following equations,

$$P = P^8 + 5P^4 - 7P^2 + 6P$$
$$Q = 2P^9 + 7P^5 - 3P^4 + 2P^3$$

The representation of the above two polynomials can be shown in Fig. 6.43.

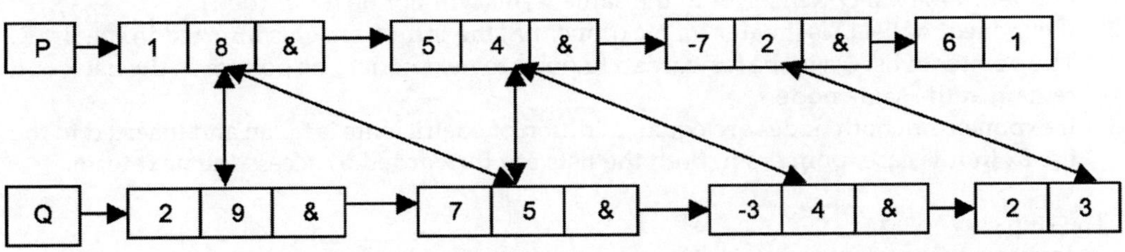

Figure 6.43 Addition of two polynomials

If the term is shown without coefficient then the coefficient is assumed to be 1. In case the term is without variable, the coefficient is zero. Such terms are not required to be stored in the memory. The arrow in the figure indicates that the two exponents are compared. Where the link of arrow is disconnected, exponent of both the terms is same. The term, which has no touch of any arrow, means it is the last node and inserted in the resulting list at the end. The arrow indicates two terms, which are compared systematically from left to right.

Table 6.1 Exponent

Exponent comparison from list P and Q	*List R (Inserted exponent)*	*Smaller exponent*
8<9	9	8 is carried forward
8>5	8	5 is carried forward
5>4	5	4 is carried forward
4= =4	4	No term is carried
	(Sum of coefficient is taken)	
2<3	3	2 is carried forward
1 is taken (last node of P)	1	End of linked list

Traverse the list *P* and *Q*. Compare the corresponding terms of list *P* and *Q*. In case one node has larger exponent value than the other then insert the larger exponent node in the third list and forward the pointer to next node of the list whose current term is inserted in the third list. The pointer of the list whose exponent is smaller will not be forwarded. The pointer of the lists forwarded only when the current nodes from the lists are inserted into the third list. Table 6.1 shows these operations.

If exponents are equal, add the coefficients and insert their addition in the third list. In this step, exponents from both the expressions are same, move the pointer to next node in both the list *P* and *Q*. Repeat the same process until one list is scanned completely.

`expo(P) = expo(Q)`.

The possible conditions can be stated as follows:

1. If exponent of list *P* is greater than corresponding exponent of list *Q*, insert the term of *P* into the list *R* and forward the pointer in list *P* to access the next term. In this case, the pointer in the list *Q* will point to the same term (will not be forwarded).
2. If exponent of list *Q* is greater than exponent *P*, the term from *Q* is inserted in the list *R*. The pointer of list *Q* will be forwarded to point to next node. The pointer in the list *P* will remain at the same node.
3. If exponents of both nodes are equal, addition of coefficients is taken and inserted in the list *R*. In this case, pointers in both the lists are forwarded to access the next term.

The steps involved,

1. Traverse the two lists (*P*) and (*Q*) and inspect all the elements.
2. Compare corresponding exponents *P* and *Q* of two polynomials. The first terms of the two polynomials contain exponents 8 and 9, respectively. Exponent of first term of first

polynomial is smaller than the second one. Hence 8<9. Here, the first exponent of list *Q* is greater than the first exponent of list *P*. Hence, the term having larger exponent will be inserted in the list *R*. The list *R* initially looks like as shown in Fig. 6.44(a).

Figure 6.44 (a)

Next, check the next term of the list *Q*. Compare it with the present term (exponent) of list *P*. The next node from *P* will be taken when current node is inserted in the list *R* because 8>5. Here, the exponent of current node of list *P* is greater that list *Q*. Hence, current term (node) of list *P* will be inserted in the list *R* and the list *R* becomes as Fig. 6.44 (b).

Figure 6.44 (b)

After moving to next node in list *P*, the exponent is 4, and exponent of *Q* is 5. Compare 4 with 5. Of course 4<5. Here, the term of list *Q* is greater than term of *P*. Therefore, the term of list, *Q* (7,5) will be inserted to list *R*. The list *R* becomes Fig. 6.44 (c).

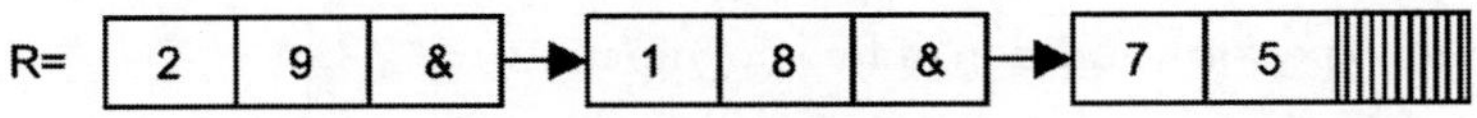

Figure 6.44 (c)

In this step a node from list *Q* is inserted and therefore, the pointer in the list *Q* will be forwarded and point to the term (–3,4) and from list *P* we have the current node (5,4). Compare exponent of these two terms. The condition observed here is 4==4. Here, exponents of both the terms are equal. Therefore, addition of coefficients is taken and result is inserted in the list R. The addition is 2 (5–3). The list *R* becomes as the Fig. 6.44 (d).

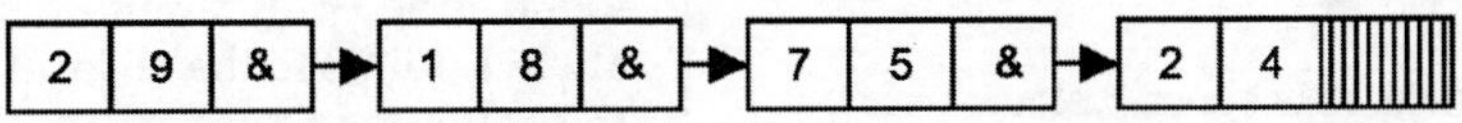

Figure 6.44 (d)

Move forward the pointers to next nodes in both the lists, since, the previous terms were having same exponents. The next comparison is 2<3. Here, the exponent of current node of list *Q* is greater than of *P*. The node from *Q* will be inserted to list *R*. The list *R* will be shown as Fig. 6.44(e).

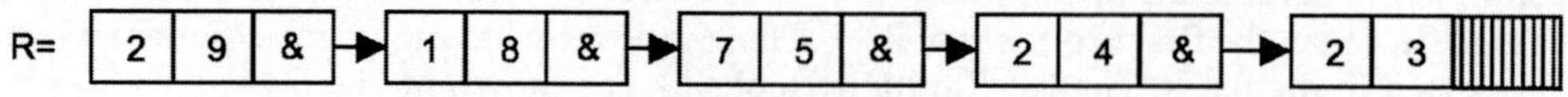

Figure 6.44 (e)

The list *Q* is completely scanned and reached to end. The remaining node from the list *P* will be inserted to list *R*. The list *R* is as Fig. 6.44(f).

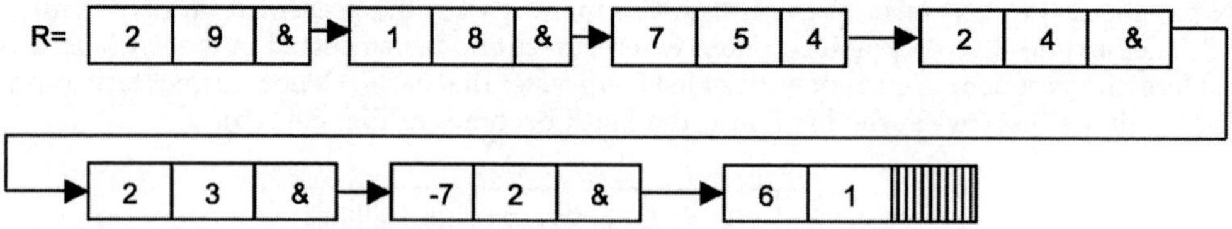

Figure 6.44 (f)

A program on the above is provided for understanding.

Example 6.35

Write a program to perform addition of two polynomials

Solution

```
# include <stdio.h>
# include <conio.h>
# include <malloc.h>
struct term
{
   float coef;
   int expn;
   struct term *next;
};
struct term *ployadd(struct term *, struct term *);
struct term *poly_in (struct term *);
struct term *insert(struct term *,float,int);
struct term *show (struct term *);

main ()
{
   struct term *t1,*t2,*t3;
   clrscr();
   t1=t2=t3=0;
   puts ("Polynomial (A): ");
```

Explanation In this program at the beginning three pointers *t1*, *t2*, and *t3* are declared and initialized to NULL (0). The value zero means NULL. The pointer *t1* and *t2* denotes address of polynomial *t1* and *t2* respectively. The pointer *t3* points to the added polynomial. The pointer *t3* always points to the term added. In case the polynomials are empty, the resulting polynomial will be empty. That is why we are returning NULL value through the pointer *t3*. The NULL value of *t3* indicates that the polynomial is empty.

```
    t1=poly_in(t1);
    puts ("Polynomial (B):");
    t2=poly_in(t2);
    t3=ployadd(t1,t2);
    puts ("Polynomial (A): ");
    show(t1);
    puts ("Polynomial (B): ");
    show(t2);
    puts ("Added Polynomial (C): ");
    show (t3);
}
struct term *poly_in(struct term *begin)
{
    int j,ex,n;
    float cof;
    printf ("\n Enter number of terms: ");
    scanf ("%d",&n);
    for (j=1;j<=n;j++)
    {
    printf ("Enter coefficient for term %d: ",j);
    scanf ("%f",&cof);
    printf ("Enter exponent for term %d:",j);
    scanf ("%d",&ex);
    begin=insert(begin,cof,ex);
    begin=insert(begin,cof,ex);
 }
 return begin;
 }
struct term *insert(struct term *begin,float co, int e_x)
 {
    struct term *pt,*temp;
    temp=(struct term*)malloc(sizeof(struct term));
    temp->coef=co;
    temp->expn=e_x;
    if (begin==0 || e_x>begin->expn)
    {
    temp->next=begin;
    begin=temp;
    }
    else
 {
    pt=begin;
    while (pt->next!=0 && pt->next->expn>e_x)
    pt=pt->next;
    temp->next=pt->next;
    pt->next=temp;
    if (pt->next==0) temp->next=0;
```

```
}
return begin;
}
struct term *ployadd(struct term *g1,struct term *g2)
{
struct term *t3=0,*p3, *temp;
if (g1==0 && g2==0) return t3;
while (g1!=0 && g2!=0)
{
   temp=(struct term*)malloc(sizeof(struct term));
      if (t3==0)
       {
       t3=temp;
       p3=t3;
       }
    else
       {
       p3->next=temp;
       p3=p3->next;
       }

       if (g1->expn>g2->expn)
       {
       temp->coef=g1->coef;
       temp->expn=g1->expn;
       g1=g1->next;
       }
       else   if (g2->expn>g1->expn)
       {
          temp->coef=g2->coef;
          temp->expn=g2->expn;
          g2=g2->next;
       }
       else if (g1->expn==g2->expn)
       {
          temp->coef=g1->coef+g2->coef;
          temp->expn=g1->expn;
          g1=g1->next;
          g2=g2->next;
       }
}
while (g1!=0)
{
  temp=(struct term*)malloc(sizeof(struct term));
  temp->coef=g1->coef;
  temp->expn=g1->expn;
  if (t3==0)
```

```
{
  t3=temp;
  p3=t3;
}
else
{
  p3->next=temp;
  p3=p3->next;
}
g1=g1->next;
}
while (g2!=0)
{
   temp=(struct term*)malloc(sizeof(struct term));
   temp->coef=g2->coef;
   temp->expn=g2->expn;
   if (t3==0)
   {
   t3=temp;
   p3=t3;
   }
   else
   {
   p3->next=temp;
   p3=p3->next;
   }
   g2=g2->next;
}
   p3->next=0;
   return t3;
}
struct term *show (struct term *pt)
{
   if (pt==0)
   {
   printf ("Empty\n");
   return 0;
   }
   while (pt!=0)
   {
   printf ("%.1fx^%d)+",pt->coef,pt->expn);
   pt=pt->next;
   }
   printf ("\b\b\bn");
   return 0;
}
```

```
OUTPUT
***
Polynomial (A):
Enter number of terms: 1
Enter coefficient for term 1: 2
Enter exponent for term 1:3
Polynomial (B):
Enter number of terms: 1
Enter coefficient for term 1: 2
Enter exponent for term 1:3
Polynomial (A):
2.0x^3)+
Polynomial (B):
2.0x^3)+
Added Polynomial (C):
4.0x^3)+
```

Both polynomials are traversed, i.e. each and every node is visited. The new node is inserted to the third polynomial and followed by it coefficient and exponent are assigned.

We have written a ladder of *if-else* conditions.

1. if *t1->expo > t2->expo*: In this case, the value of current node of *t1* is assigned to current node of *t3*. The polynomial *linked list (A)* is traversed and pointer *t1* will point to the next node.
2. If *t2->expo>t1->expo*: In this case, the value of current node of polynomial (*B*) is assigned to current node of *t3*. The node from polynomial is added hence, the linked list (*B*) is traversed and pointer *t2* will point to next node.
3. If (*t1->expo==t2->expo*): In this case, where terms of both polynomials are same, the coefficient of both terms are added and the resulting value is assigned to node of third list. Here, both the lists are traversed and pointer *t1* and *t2* will point to next node of polynomial (*A*) and (*B*).

The same addition of two polynomials can be done from the following example.

Example 6.36

Write a program to perform addition of two polynomials.

Solution

```
# include <stdio.h>
# include <conio.h>
# include <malloc.h>

struct poly
{
 float coef;
```

Explanation The logic of this program is same as program 6.35.

```
int expo;
struct poly *nterm;
};
int j,num;
struct poly begin;
void create_poly (struct poly *node)
{
char h;
begin.nterm=NULL;
node=&begin;
j=0;
printf ("\n Input n for end: ");
h=getchar();
while (h!='n')
{
node->nterm=(struct poly*) malloc(sizeof(struct poly));
node=node->nterm;
printf ("\n Enter coefficient value %d: ", j+1);
scanf ("%g",&node->coef);
printf ("\n Enter exponent value %d: ",j+1);
scanf ("%d",&node->expo);
node->nterm=NULL;
fflush(stdin);
printf ("\n Input n for end: ");
h=getchar ();
j++;
}
printf ("\n Total Nodes = %d",j);
}
void show ( struct poly *node )
{
node=&begin;
node=node->nterm;
while (node)
{
printf ("\n + %g", node->coef);
printf ("X^%d", node->expo);
node=node->nterm;
}
}
void main ()
{
struct poly *node=(struct poly*)malloc(sizeof(struct poly));
clrscr();
create_poly(node);
show(node);
getch();
```

```
}

OUTPUT
Input n for end:
Enter coefficient value 1: 4
Enter exponent value 1: 5
Input n for end:
Enter coefficient value 2: 9
Enter exponent value 2: 8
Input n for end: n
 Total Nodes = 2
+ 4X^5 + 9X^8
```

6.28.2 Linked Dictionary

In compiler, creation of the linked dictionary has an important role. In compiler, the organization and maintenance of dictionary holding names and their corresponding values are maintained in the linked dictionary. This linked directory is called *symbol table.* While designing compiler, two factors, i.e. time and memory space are considered.

The process of compiler designing has various steps. The memory space and speed of symbol table algorithm have opposite relationship. The construction and referencing is an important factor of linked dictionary. Construction means insertion of symbols with their values available. Referencing means, obtaining values from the table.

The ratio of estimated number of insertion to reference is significant factor. In symbol-tables, access retrieve time and insertion time are very much associated. The quick symbol table can be simply constructed if large memory space is available. When a reference is obtained from arithmetic value of character (forming name), each name is stored in a unique memory location.

The easiest way to access the symbol table is linear search method. Using simple linked list the symbols are organized in a sequence. The insertion can be easily done by adding symbols at the rear of the list. If any particular symbol is to be searched, by traversing each node the required element can be searched.

The symbol table can also be searched using binary search. All the entries in the symbol table are sorted in ascending order. A middle entry is spotted and its value is determined. A separate topic is given for search techniques in this book. However, this method has some drawbacks.

6.28.3 Addition of Long Positive Integers

The application of adding long positive integers can be solved using circular list. There is always a restriction or limitation in the programming language that every data type has a lower and upper limit. The variables of a particular data type can have the values as per the range. Some time, it is very essential if any problem to be solved is having maximum range, which exceeds the limit of the range. In order to add two long integers, below mentioned steps are followed:

1. The digits of the given numbers are individually traversed from left to right.
2. In parallel, i.e. corresponding digits and a carry from prior digits sums, are added.

6.28.4 Searching in a Linked List

Finding some specific element in a given set of elements is called searching. Assume, we have a linked list of 10 numbers. In order to search a particular number in the list, all the elements of list are visited and compared with the expected one. When the given number matches with some number, search process completes. Occurrence of a particular number in a list for number of times can also be found. In other words, we can find out for how many times a particular number exist in the list. A program is illustrated below on this point.

Example 6.37

Write a program to create a linked list of integers and search for a given element.

Solution

```
# include <stdio.h>
# include <conio.h>
# include <malloc.h>

struct node
{
   int data;
   struct node *next;
};
int j;
struct node begin;
void search(struct node*);
void create_list(struct node*);
void show(struct node *);
void create_list(struct node *node)
{
 int n=1;
 begin.next=NULL;
 node=&begin;
 j=0;
 printf ("\n Input integers (0 to stop):");
 while (n)
 {
 scanf ("%d", &n);
 if (n==0) break;
 else node->next=(struct node*) malloc(sizeof(struct node));
 node->data=n;
 node=node->next;
 node->next=NULL;
 fflush(stdin);
 }
 }
void search(struct node *node)
```

Explanation In this program a list is created with *create ()* function. The number, which is to be searched, is entered. In the *search ()* function the entered number is compared with the linked list elements. When equal number is found the number along with its position in the linked list is displayed. The *show ()* function is used to display all the linked list elements. Thus, through traversing and comparing elements search process is done.

```
{
 int node_num=0;
 int s_node;
 int flag=0;
 node=&begin;
 printf ("\n Enter number to be searched: ");
 scanf ("%d",&s_node);
 if (node==NULL)
 printf ("\n List is empty ");
 while (node)
 {
 if (s_node==node->data)
 {
 printf ("\n search is successful");
 printf ("\n Position of %d from beginning of the list: %d",s_node,node_num+1);
 node=node->next;
 flag=1;7
 }
 else
 node=node->next;
 node_num++;
 }
 if (!flag)
 {
 printf ("\n Search is unsuccessful");
 printf ("\n %d does not found in the list", s_node);
 }
 }
 void show (struct node * node)
 {
 node=&begin;
 while(node->next)
 {
 printf(" %d",node->data);
 node=node->next;
 }
 }
 void main ()
 {
 struct node *node=(struct node *) malloc (sizeof(struct node));
 clrscr();
 create_list(node);
 printf ("\n List: ");
 show(node);
 search(node);
 }
```

```
OUTPUT
Input integers (0 to stop):
1
2
3
4
5
9
7
5
0
List: 1 2 3 4 5 9 7 5
Enter number to be searched: 3
search is successful
Position of 3 from beginning of the list: 3
```

6.28.5 Sorting a Linked List

Example 6.38

Write a program to create linked list and sort the list in ascending order.

Solution

```
# include <stdio.h>
# include <conio.h>

struct node
{
 int value;
 struct node *next;
 };
    void create (void);
    void sort(void);
    void show (void);
    struct node *rear;
    int nodes;
    struct node *head;
    main ()
{
    clrscr();
    create();
    sort();
    show ();
}
void create ( )
```

Explanation In this program the *create()* function is used for inputting the elements into the linked list. The *sort()* is used to sort the linked list elements in ascending order. The *struct num* is used to store the linked list. The *show()* displays the sorted elements of linked list.

```
{
   struct node *item;
   printf ("Enter numbers( 0 to exit): ");
   if (head==NULL)
 {
   head=(struct node*)malloc(sizeof(struct node));
   scanf ("%d",&head->value);
   head->next=NULL;
   rear=head;
 }
 while (1)
 {
   item=(struct node *)malloc(sizeof(struct node));
   scanf ("%d",&item->value);

   if (item->value==0) break;
   item->next=NULL;
   rear->next=item;
   rear=item;
 }
}
void sort()
{
 int temp;
 struct node *nlink, *count;
 if (head==NULL)
 {
 printf ("List is empty");
 }
 nlink=head;
   for(;nlink->next!=NULL;nlink=nlink->next)
for(count=nlink->next;count!=NULL;count = count->next)
if(nlink->value>count->value)
{
temp=nlink->value;
nlink->value=count->value;
count->value=temp;
}
}
 void show ( )
 {
   printf ("\n Sorted list is: ");
   while (head!=NULL)
 {
   nodes++;
   printf (" %d ",head->value);
   head=head->next;
```

```
}
nodes=0;
}
```

```
OUTPUT
Enter numbers( 0 to exit): 12 1 2 34 5 65 4 0
Sorted list is: 1 2 4 5 12 34 65
```

Summary

This chapter presents the following points:

1. Series of linearly arranged numbers is a list. The list can be of basic data type or custom data type. The first element of the list is called HEAD and the last element TAIL.
2. Static implementation of list can be implemented using arrays. Examples have been illustrated on this point.
3. Pointers are used for implementation of linked list. The linked list is a major application of the dynamic implementation.
4. In the list of elements, for any location *n*, *(n–1)* is *predecessor* and *(n+1)* is *successor*. In other words, for any location *n* in the list, the left element is *predecessor* and the right element is *successor*.
5. The merging is a procedure in which two or more lists can be combined and third list is created.
6. A linked list is a dynamic data structure. It is an ideal technique to store data when user does not know in advance how many elements are to be stored. The dynamic implementation of list using pointers is also known as *linked list*.
7. *Singly linked list*: In this type of linked list two successive nodes of the linked list are linked with each other in sequential linear manner.
8. *Doubly linked list*: In this type of linked list the data structure holds two-pointer fields.
9. *Circular list*: In this list the first and last elements are adjacent. This type of list has neither end nor starting node.
10. *A circular doubly linked list*: In this type of linked list the structure field contains three fields. Two link fields and one data field.
11. *Creation*: The linked list creation operation involves allocation of structure size memory to pointer of the same structure.
12. *Traversing*: It is the procedure of passing through (visiting) all the nodes of the linked list from starting to end.
13. *Display*: The operation in which data field of every node is accessed and are displayed on the screen.
14. *Splitting of a linked list*: Once a singly linked list is created, it can be divided into many sub-lists. The technique is very simple. Put the NULL value in the node where you want to finish the first sub-list in the main list. Later, the next node will act as first node for the second sub-list.
15. *Doubly linked list*: Each node of the doubly linked list has two pointer fields and holds the address of predecessor and successor elements. These pointers enable bi-directional traversing, i.e. traversing the list in backward and forward direction.

16. *Circular doubly linked list*: A circular doubly linked list has both successor and predecessor pointers. In this type insertion and deletion operations are easily performed as compared to other type of linked lists.
17. *Polynomial manipulation*: The linked list is used for implementation of polynomial. The operations such as addition, multiplication etc., are performed. To get better proficiency in processing each polynomial is stored in decreasing order.
18. *Linked dictionary*: While compiling a program the linked dictionary has an important role. In compiler, the organization and maintenance of dictionary holding names and their corresponding values are maintained in the linked dictionary. This linked directory is called *symbol table*. While designing compiler, two factors, i.e. time and memory space are considered.

Exercises

A. Answer the following questions:

1. What is the static list? How is it implemented?
2. Explain traversal of static list.
3. What is predecessor and successor of an element in a list?
4. The first element does not have predecessor and the last element does not have successor in a list. Explain.
5. Explain insertion and deletion operation with the static list.
6. Explain merging operation of two lists.
7. Differentiate between static and dynamic list.
8. Explain the use of pointer head in the linked list.
9. Mention types of linked lists with explanation. On which basis are the linked lists classified?
10. Explain applications of linked list.

B. Select the appropriate options from the following:

1. The elements of static lists are stored in
   a. successive memory locations　　c. alternate memory locations
   b. random memory locations　　d. all of the above.
2. The elements of linked lists are stored in
   a. successive memory locations　　c. alternate memory locations
   b. random memory locations　　d. all of the above.
3. Name the function that is used for memory allocation in implementation of linked list
   1. malloc ()　　3. free()
   2. realloc()　　4. both (a) and (c).
4. If it is decided to create the linked list in C++, function that allocates memory is
   a. malloc ()　　c. delete
   b. new　　d. both (a) and (b).
5. The free() function is used to
   a. release the memory　　c. to unlink the fist and last node
   b. to unlink the node　　d. none of the above.
6. The pointer head points to the
   a. first node　　c. either first or last node
   b. last node　　d. none of the above.

7. This type of linked list does not have null value in the last node
   a. circular linked list
   b. singly linked list
   c. static list
   d. none of the above.
8. The first node of this type of linked list has NULL value
   a. doubly linked list
   b. doubly circular linked list
   c. singly linked list
   d. all of the above.
9. This type of linked list does not have first and last node
   a. circular linked list
   b. singly linked list
   c. doubly linked list
   d. static list.
10. When the malloc () function returns NULL value it means
    a. memory is not allocated
    b. memory is allocated but no data entered
    c. memory is allocated
    d. none of the above.
11. If memory is not allocated, what further action will you suggest?
    a. try again
    b. exit from the program
    c. both (a) & (b)
    d. continue the program.

C. Attempt the following programs:

1. Write a program to remove first and last node of the linked list.
2. Write a program to duplicate a linked list from other linked list. Remove all odd numbers from the new list and display both of the linked lists.
3. Write a program to create the linked list and remove all the duplicate elements of the list. The list should have unique elements.
4. Write a program to find successor of the given element in a linked list.
5. Write a program to create and display the elements of a circular linked list.
6. Write a program to terminate the program when malloc () returns to NULL.
7. Write a program to merge two linked list and display elements.
8. Write a program to swap first and last nodes of the linked list.
9. Write a program to create a linked list with integer elements and count the occurrence of given number in linked list.
10. Write a program to find the number of even and odd elements in a linked list.
11. Write a program to find the average value of elements of a linked list.
12. Write a menu driven program to perform the following operations on linked list:
    1. Create
    2. Insert
    3. Delete
    4. Display
    5. Exit.
13. Write a program to multiply two polynomials.
14. Write a program to create and display circular linked list containing five elements.
15. Write a program to find the minimum and maximum value from the linked list.

D. What will be the output of the following programs?

1.

```
main ()
{
   int sim[5]={0,1,2,3,4},j;
   for (j=4;j>0;j—)
   printf (" %d ",sim[j]);
}
```

2.

```
main ()
{
    int sim[]={0,1,2,3,4},j=3;
    clrscr();
    printf ("\n Predecessor of %d = %d",sim[j],
    sim[j-1]);
    printf ("\n Successor of %d = %d", sim[j],
    sim[j+1]);
}
```

3.

```
main ()
{
    int num[8]={1,2,3,4,5,6,7,8},j=0;
    clrscr();
    while (j<=7)
{
    if (j>=5)
    num[j]=num[j+1];
    j++;
}
j=num[j]=0;
while (j<8)
printf (" %d ",num[j++]);
}
```

4.

```
main ()
{
int num[8]={1,2,3,4,5,6,7,8},j=0,n=-5;
clrscr();
while (j<8)
{
    if (num[j++]==abs(n))
{
printf ("Elemenent found");
exit(0); } }
printf ("Element not found");

}
```

5.

```
# include <stdio.h>
# include <conio.h>
main ()

{
int array[6]={0},j,no1,no2;
clrscr();

printf ("\n Enter elements: " );
for (j=0;j<5;j++)
scanf ("%d",&array[j]);

printf ("\n Enter elements for insertion:-");
scanf ("%d %d",&no1,&no2);
for (j=5;j>=1;j—)
array[j]=array[j-1];

array[0]=no1;
array[6]=no2;

printf("\nList after insertion of elements\n");
for (j=0;j<=6;j++)
printf (" %d ", array[j]);
getch();
}
```

Chapter 7

Storage Management

Chapter Outline

7.1 INTRODUCTION

The fundamental purpose of any program is to manipulate data and its storage in the computer memory. Storage management consists of techniques that are used to manage the heap. Two memory management techniques are used for this purpose. They are:

1. Static storage management
2. Dynamic storage management.

Static Storage Management It is necessary to load the program into the memory before execution of a program. Before execution of a program, it is essential that the system should have enough memory. When program execution starts, it takes memory through operating system. Once the memory is allocated to the program, the memory allocated cannot be increased or decreased during program execution. The same memory cannot be used by other programs. All these are taken care of by the operating system. For example, an array is best example of static implementation in which the memory allocated is fixed in size.

Dynamic Storage Management The dynamic storage management allows the user to manage the memory during program execution. According to the request made by the program, memory can be allocated. In this technique, wastage of memory can be avoided. This is efficient for multiprogramming and single user environment, in which more than one program is executed simultaneously. The exact amount of memory needed for the programs can be estimated only during program execution. The operating system performs dynamic storage management. The linked list is an example of dynamic storage management. In linked list, we have noticed during program execution that when new node is created memory is allocated. Thus, depending upon the need of the user, any number of nodes can be created. Following are the techniques of dynamic memory management.

7.2 ALLOCATION TECHNIQUES

1. Fixed block allocation
2. Variable block allocation.

The variable block allocation is further divided into following types:

1. First fit
2. Next fit
3. Best fit
4. Worst fit.

De-allocation Techniques The different ways of de-allocation techniques are mentioned below:

1. Ordered de-allocation
2. Random de-allocation.

7.3 MEMORY REPRESENTATION

The free blocks of memory storage are nothing but a collection of non-contiguous memory blocks. They can be accessed in sequence by pointer from one block to another. The size of block depends on the method applied as given below.

7.3.1 Fixed Block Storage

This is a straightforward method in which, all the blocks are of identical size. The user can decide the size of the block. The operating system keeps a pointer called AVAIL. This pointer points to memory as shown in the Fig. 7.1.

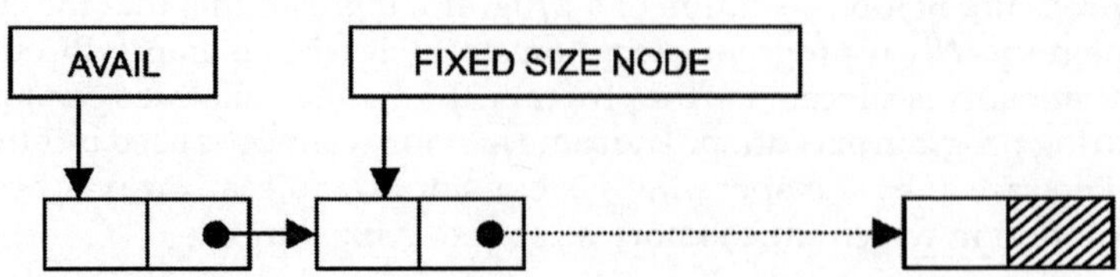

Figure 7.1 Free storage with fixed block memory

There are two functions *getnode ()* and *freenode ()*. Using these functions, the user program communicates with operating system. The *getnode ()* is used to obtain memory from the heap for storage of data. The argument passed denotes amount of memory required. When the user program makes a call to this function, a pointer to block in heap is returned after successful allocation otherwise returns NULL. The NULL value indicates that there is not enough memory available. The *returnnode ()* is opposite of the *getnode ()* function in which when a node is no longer needed its allocated memory is released and returned to pool as shown in Fig. 7.2.

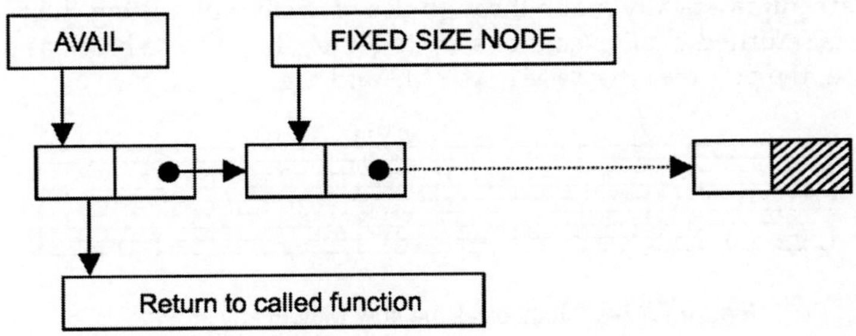

Figure 7.2 Obtaining memory block

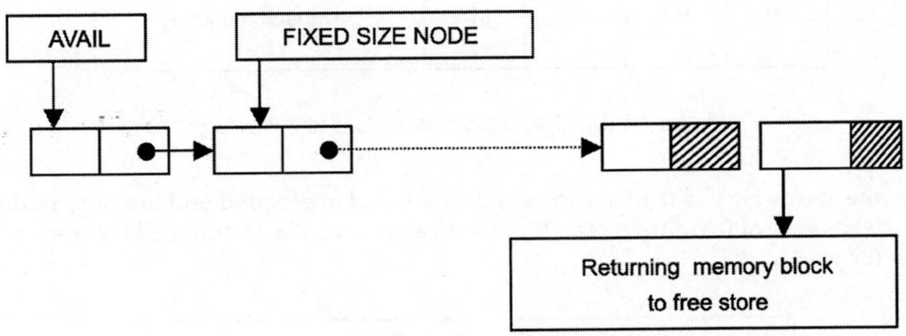

Figure 7.3 Mechanism of return node ()

Though the above method is straightforward, it consumes more memory. For example, the size of each block is 1 KB (1024 bytes) and the program requests the memory of 1.2 KB, in such a situation the memory allocated is 2 KB, hence, the extra memory allocated is of no use. If the size of the block is decreased, it reduces the program performance.

7.3.2 Variable Block Storage

We know that fixed size block method has a limitation, and this can be overcome by the use of variable block storage. The functions *getnode ()* and *freenode ()* suppose that the blocks of memory are ordered in ascending order according to their sizes. The node has an extra field that holds the size of block as per the Fig. 7.3. The function *getnode ()* returns a memory block which is more than or equal to the requested memory by the caller function.

In static storage management, memory blocks of fixed sizes are allocated for storing the programs whereas in many applications there is a need to have memory of different sizes. In *getnode ()* and *returnnode ()* function, we discussed that memory blocks of different sizes are present and blocks are connected with each other. However, in reality when there is no program in the memory, the whole memory is considered as a block. In this situation, the blocks of required sizes are automatically made through use of system by calling the functions many times. The blocks returned in all executions are together shaped as a block as per the Fig. 7.4 (a to d). Suppose, the pointer returns M1, M2, M3 and M4.

Figure 7.4 (a) Total block memory without any program

In the above Fig. 7.4 (a), no program is loaded and hence total block of memory is available.

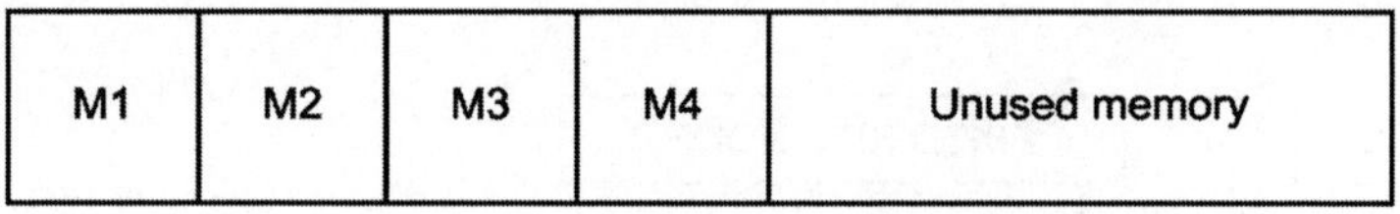

Figure 7.4 (b) Four programs are loaded in memory

As per the above Fig. 7.4 (b), four programs M1 to M4 are loaded and memory is allocated to them in sequence of their order. The Fig. 7.4 (b) also indicates the unused memory, which is available for use.

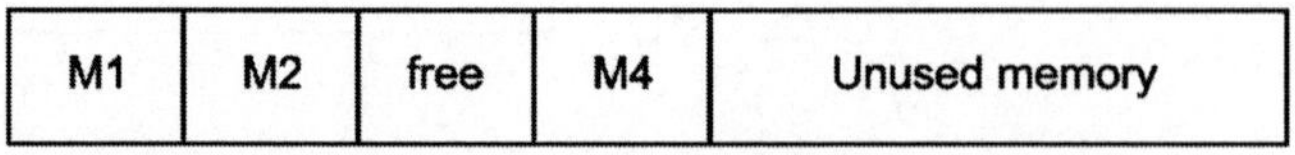

Figure 7.4 (c) Three programs and unused memory

The execution of programs M3 is completed and when it quits from the memory the space is returned to main storage. Here, blocks of variable sizes are generated.

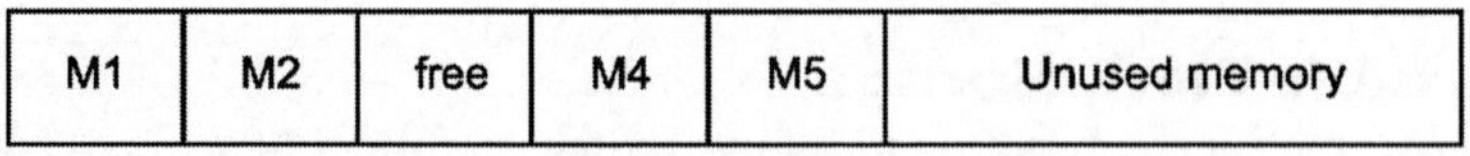

Figure 7.4 (d) Program and memory

Another program (M5) requests for memory and the memory needed is allocated to it. Thus, the dynamic memory management performs the following tasks:

1. It searches requested blocks of memory and allocates memory.
2. Supervises the released blocks of memory.
3. Combines the tiny blocks of memory to bigger blocks.

In order to provide the above services two memory management systems are used. They are (i) boundary tag system and (ii) buddy system.

7.4 BOUNDARY TAG SYSTEM

The boundary tag system is a resourceful memory system for dynamic memory management system. It works on a node structure as per the Fig. 7.5. In the node structure for a specified block, first and last words are set aside for block information. The *LL* and *RL* are pointers to predecessor and successor blocks from the current block. The argument *S* contains amount of free memory available. The *TAG* is flag field and stores values *0* (free) or *1* (engaged). There are two flag fields on the two boundaries of the block. Hence, the system is called boundary tag system. The filed *UPLINK* points to beginning of the same block. The uses of all the above fields are explained at appropriate situations. These systems sustain a circular linked list of free memory blocks. Using circular doubly linked implementation a block can be easily released. The header node is also used in the boundary tag system and holds the value zero in field *S* and *TAG*.

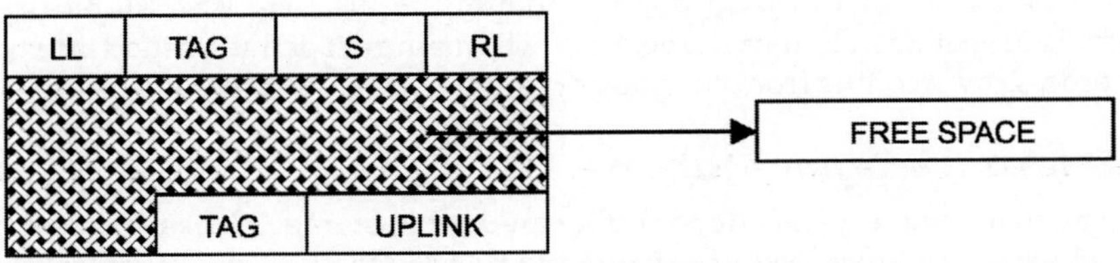

Figure 7.5 Node structure

7.5 STORAGE ALLOCATIONS

As discussed in the list structure, the request for memory block to system can be made in the following ways:

1. First-fit storage allocation
2. Best-fit storage allocation
3. Worst-fit storage allocation
4. Next-fit storage allocation.

7.5.1 First-fit Allocation

This is a straightforward way of memory allocation. In this method when a request is made, first available free blocks are searched. When a free block of memory is obtained, a pointer pointing to the same block is returned to call function. In this method, the memory allocated is always larger than the memory required. This process requires a minimum search for the needed size of memory. The first fit method allocates lowest memory addresses.

7.5.2 Best-fit Storage Allocation

In this type, the required memory and allocated memory are calculated. The memory is allocated in such a way that the need of memory and allocated amount of memory is nearly the same. For example, required memory is R and allocated memory is A and assume the difference is D. Then, D is very small. In the examples, so far we have observed that whenever memory is needed for a single node it is requested by the program using *malloc ()* function. Hence, our unit of memory is node. This technique reduces consumption of memory as the required memory and allocated memory is very close.

7.5.3 Worst-fit Storage Allocation

This method is opposite of best-fit method. Instead of finding a smaller block close to request size of block, this method searches the largest block and allocates it. The worst-fit allocation decreases the creation of small block as created in best-fit allocation.

7.5.4 Next-fit Storage Allocation

We have already learnt the first-fit allocation method and in this method searching starts from the beginning of the free list. In case of next fit storage allocation searching starts from the last allocation in the list. In this method pointer pointing to the free list is stored next to the allocation node. It is utilized to start the next call. The main goal of this method is to trim down the search process by recoiling from checking of smaller blocks, which is lengthy in execution.

7.5.5 External Fragmentation

Let us assume that a request is made for bulky amount of storage blocks and as soon as the request is released, the linked list of existing blocks are searched and if returned it means adjacent blocks are not merged into one. This also means that the average block size available is small and larger blocks are not available as per the request. In case if a request for a bigger block is accepted, it may possibly have to be ignored due to lack of a single block on the free list that is large enough, although the total amount of free storage is much greater than the requested storage amount. This process of decomposing the total available storage into a larger number of comparatively small blocks is known as external fragmentation.

7.5.6 Internal Fragmentation

It is possible to reduce external fragmentation to some extent by allocating a larger block than the requested size. It can be done by avoiding partition of a block into various parts. If we apply this method, it could happen that a request for storage is rejected due to the lack of blocks of the desired size. This can occur even if the amount of storage that is wasted is more than enough to fulfil the required amount. Internal fragmentation is nothing but dividing the total unused storage into available blocks. Further these blocks are allocated with some parts of these blocks remains unused, but not made availble to other programs. Fragmentation must be done cautiously as it is a main problem in dynamic memory management.

7.6 STORAGE RELEASE

The de-allocation of the memory is a very essential process and utmost care must be taken by the programmer to shun the wastage of memory. In static implementation of data structure the wastage of memory is more than that in the dynamic implementation. This topic is devoted for discussion of de-allocation of allocated memory, which is returned to free store. It is one type of re-cycling. The system sources allocated must be returned to the system if the program is not in use. This way the performance of the system is maintained.

We have observed in the boundary tag system that it inserts the block to the list of free blocks and merge recently inserted blocks with its neighbouring blocks.

7.7 BUDDY SYSTEM

The buddy system is the alternative storage management system. This system limits the sizes of the block to some fixed set of sizes. Till now we have learnt that the block sizes are fixed arbitrarily. The linked list keeps the size of blocks of buddy system to a restricted size. When a request is made for size S then the size X, which is the minimum of the fixed sizes but equivalent to or larger than S, is searched and block of size X is allocated.

In case if block of size S is not available, then a larger block is split into two sub-buddies (block). The blocks splitted are also of equal and fixed sizes. This procedure is repetitively done until a block of size X is formed. The restriction sizes in buddy system are as F_0, F_1 to F_M. According to the recurrence, the requirement of block sizes can be expressed by the following equation:

$$F_n = F_{n-1} + F_{n-g},\ g \leq n \leq M \qquad \text{.... (7.1)}$$

M is maximum size.

For given values of g and f

$$F_0 = V_0,\ F_1 = V_1, \ldots, F_{g-1} = V_{g-1}$$

If values of g=1 and F_0 =8 the block sizes are 8,16,32,64,128. These values can be obtained from Eq. 7.1. We can also observe that the block sizes are successive powers of two. The buddy system based on the above condition is called binary buddy system.

One more buddy system, which restricts the fixed sizes to the Fibonacci series sequence, is known as Fibonacci buddy system. The initial value is g=2 and F_0=8, F_1=13. The sizes of the blocks are 8,13,21,34,55,89. The values of F_0, F_1 and F_2 are depending according to the application.

When a request is made to get memory space to the system, the system searches for a block, which is closely equal to but not less than the requested memory block. When the above-described block is found it is immediately allocated, else next larger block in the list will be divided until the block of nearest size is found. On the contrary, when a block of memory is returned to the system (de-allocated), the returned block is pooled with another free block into larger free blocks.

In order to illustrate the above allocation and de-allocation methods, consider the fibonacci buddy system in which the restricted block sizes are 8,13,21,34,55,89 and 144. The 144 is the biggest possible block from the memory available. The Fig. 7.6 illustrates the allocation and de-allocation.

From Fig. 7.6 the following points are observed. In the beginning, the system keeps a free block of size 144. When a demand for memory comes for size 25, the system divides and creates two buddies of sizes 89 and 55, respectively. The second buddy, i.e. 55 is divided into two buddies as 21 and 34. The block of size 34 is closely nearest further and hence it is used for allocation as per Fig. 7.6.

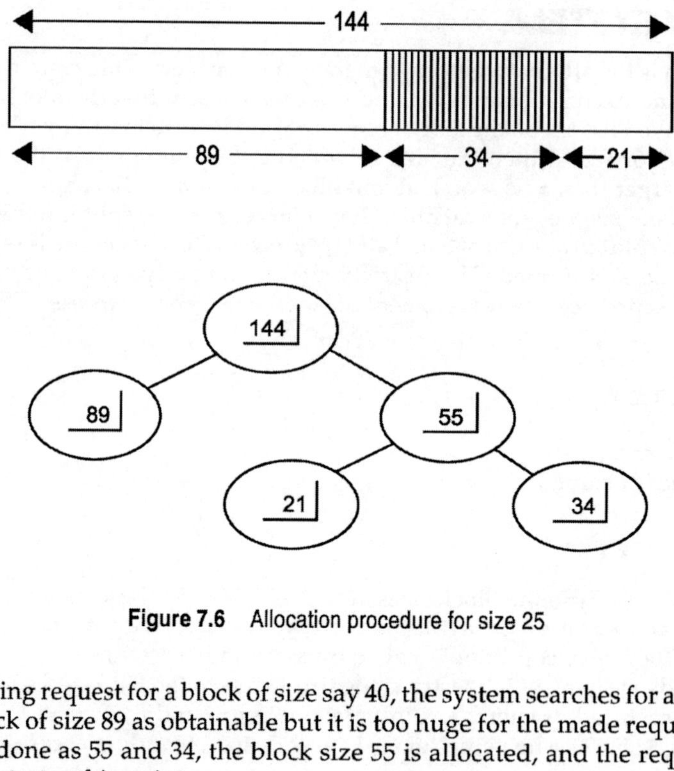

Figure 7.6 Allocation procedure for size 25

For a succeeding request for a block of size say 40, the system searches for a matching block and sets the block of size 89 as obtainable but it is too huge for the made request. That is why the partition is done as 55 and 34, the block size 55 is allocated, and the request is fulfilled. The Fig. 7.7 illustrates this point.

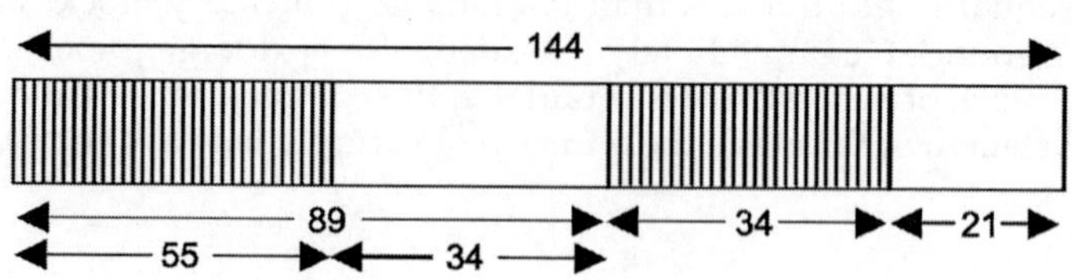

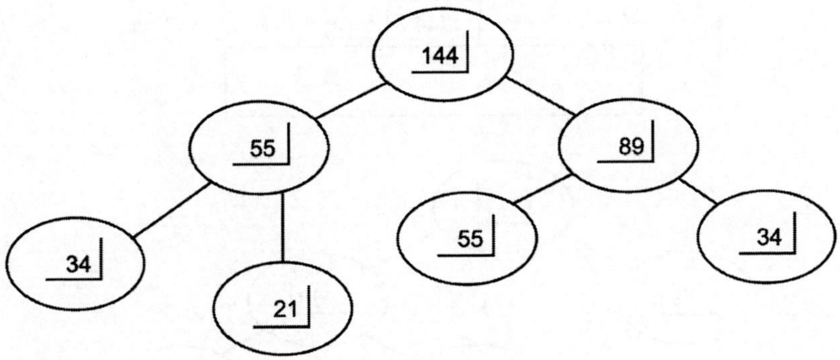

Figure 7.7 Allocation procedure for size 40

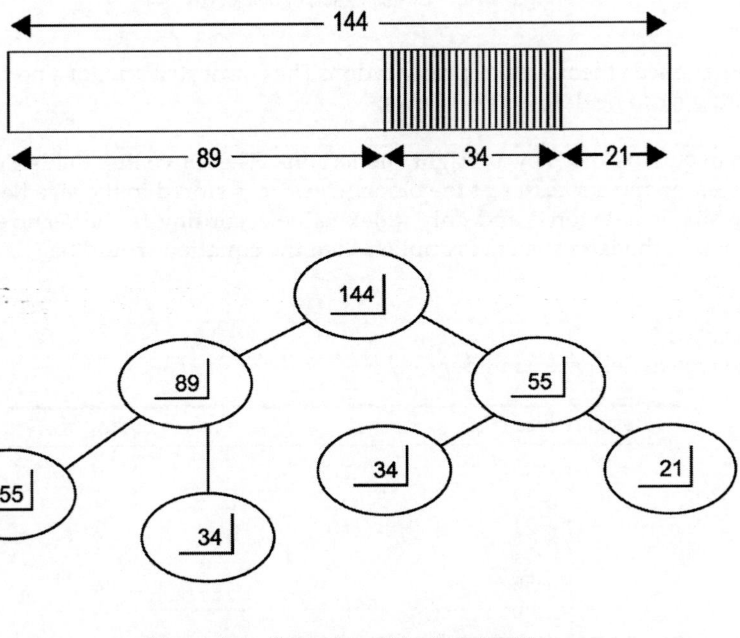

Figure 7.8 Releasing of block of size 55

Consider the situation if block of size 55 is de-allocated and returned to the system as shown in Fig. 7.8. The two buddies namely 55 and 34 are free buddies. These two free buddies come together and block of size 89 is formed. We know that the block 89 is a free buddy and the combination comes to the end of the procedure.

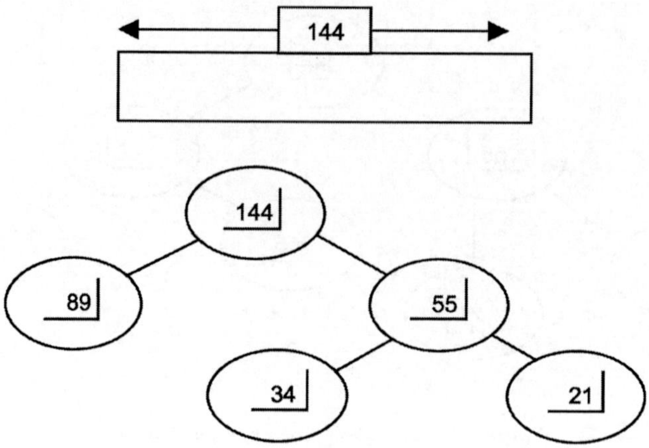

Figure 7.9 De-allocation of block size (34)

So far we have seen theoretical representation. The use of structure of a node to implement above operations can be defined as follows:

There are two fields and they are right and left link. These two link fields store the address of the predecessor and successor of the block. The size is stored in the size field. In the field, the absolute size is not stored and only index value according to the recurrence relation is stored. Suppose, Fibonacci system is applied then the equation would be,

$$F_N = F_{N-1} + F_{N-2} \qquad \text{....(7.2)}$$

Let F_0= 8 and F_1=13

The value of size field are as under

Absolute size (F_n)	*Sizes* (n)
F_0 =8	0
F_1=13	1
F_2=21	2
F_3=34	3
F_4=55	4
F_5=89	5

The field CODE is used to get information about the blocks, that is, whether the two blocks are buddies or not. The buddy property can be determined by the solution given by Hinds as follows:

Initially, the block is largest, then field CODE = 0

After partition of parent block, two blocks left and right are created. Then,

$CODE_L = CODE_P+1$

$CODE_R=0$

After combining these two buddies the ensuing block CODE field is one less as compared to its left buddy as follows:

$CODE_P = CODE_{L\text{-}1}$

By the following method, various partitions from biggest block to the smallest block can be created.

Depending upon the value of code field we can determine whether the block is left block or right block. When the value of CODE=0 then it is right block and if the value is greater than 0 then it is a left block (buddy). The code value denotes the number of splits of some larger block so far made by the buddy.

Consider two cases of allocation,

1. Best-fit strategy
2. Fibonacci buddy system.

According to Fibonacci buddy system, $FN = FN_{-1} + FN_{-2}$

Also,

$2 \leq n \leq M=6$ When $F_0=8$ and $F_1=13$

At the starting, the block of size 34 is allocated as shown in the Fig. 7.10 (a).

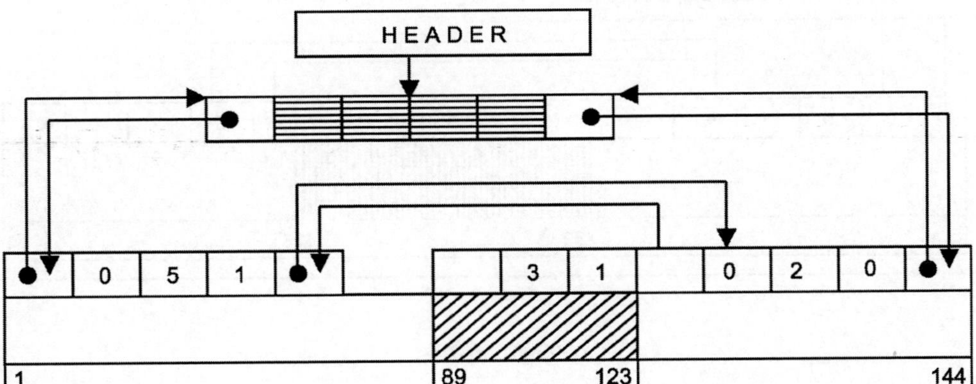

Figure 7.10(a)

Assume that the successive request is made for a block size 50. The system will search for the required closer block from header. When the block of size 89 is found which is larger than the requested one, partition is carried out. After partition, we get two buddies of 55 and 34 size. The block of size 55 is allocated as per the Fig. 7.10 (b).

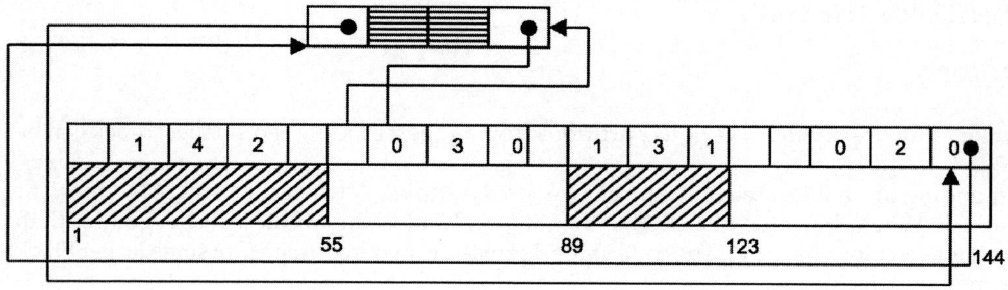

Figure 7.10(b)

When memory is not required it is released, i.e. the memory block allocated is returned to heap. Consider the following Fig. 7.10 (c).

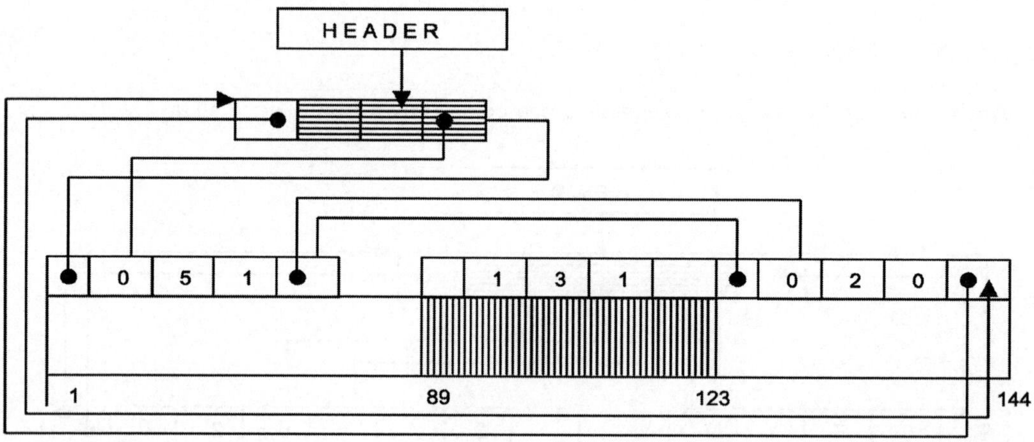

Figure 7.10(c)

When a block of size 34 is returned as shown in the Fig. 7.10 (c) the code of free block is one and hence it is a left buddy of any larger buddy. Its right corresponding block is free; they can be combined as shown in Fig. 7.10 (c). The size of newly formed block will be 55 and it is a free buddy. We can notice that it is a left buddy. One more combination can be done if we find its right corresponding block. Figs 7.10 (d) and 7.10 (e) show this block. This is the largest block and no further combinations are possible. Thus, de-allocation is complete.

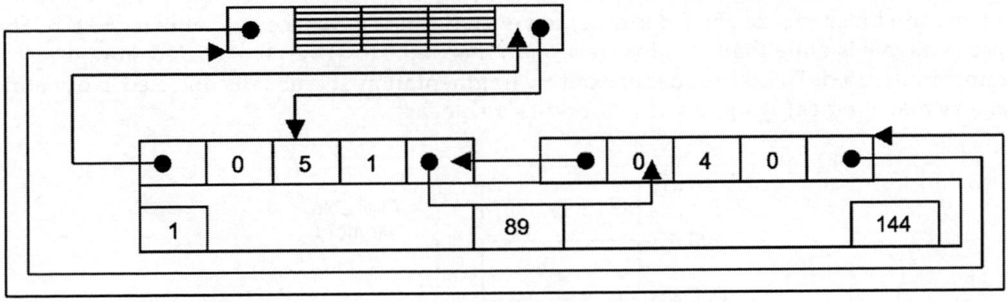

Figure 7.10(d)

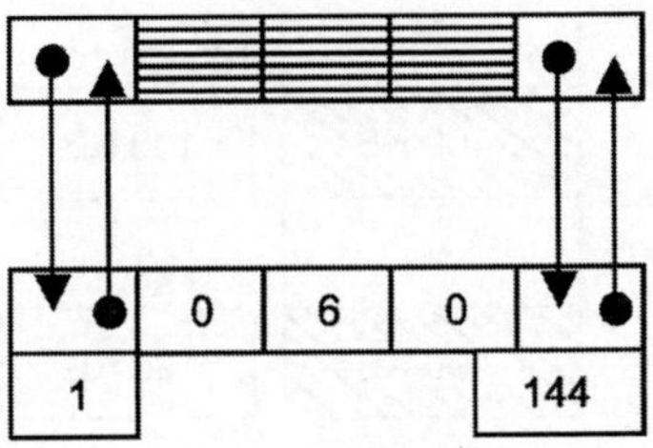

Figure 7.10(e)

7.8 BINARY BUDDY SYSTEM

After studying the buddy system now, it is time to turn to binary buddy system (BBS). The BBS is based on the recurrence relation given as follows:

$$FI = FI\text{-}1 + FI\text{-}1 \qquad \ldots(7.3)$$
$$1 \le I \le MAX$$

In the binary system, the block sizes are power of base 2. In this system the block of memory is accurately partitioned into two sections of fifty-fifty. This system also has one advantage that the base address of other buddy system can be easily computed, if the size along with base address of at least one buddy is available for the block of size 2^k. In this way when a block of memory is released, its amalgamation with its other matching part is straightforward.

7.9 COMPACTION

The part of free memory is mixed together with the dynamically used partitions throughout the memory and this is one of the critical problem in dynamic storage allocation. For example, consider the system whose memory picture is as per the Fig. 7.11. When all requirements for storage are of fixed size, then it is sufficient to link all unused available blocks together into an existing space list and the request received can be fulfilled. On the other hand, when storage requests received are of different sizes, it might be too expensive. For example, assume that a request for a block of size 256 KB is accepted even if total free space available is 360 KB. The space available is more than the storage amount needed. However, the needed storage space cannot be allocated. This is because of external fragmentation. It is usually detected in dynamic memory management systems with different size blocks.

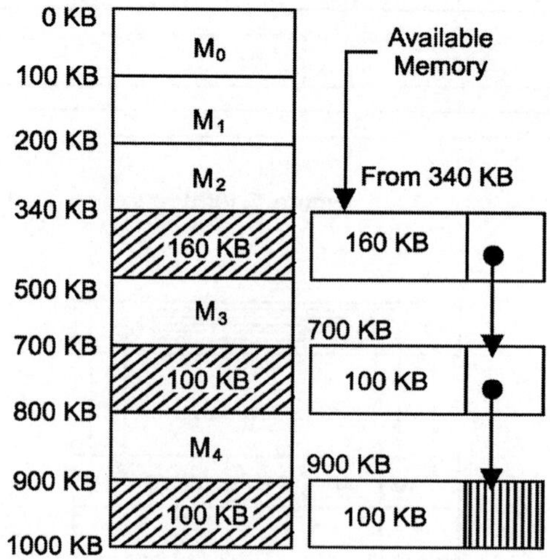

Figure 7.11 Dynamic partitioning of memory

We have already learnt in previous sections that combining of contiguous free portions when free blocks are returned is a technique frequently followed to decrease fragmentation and thus the amount of unused wasted memory is prohibited. Nevertheless, the above techniques are inclined to put off the impact moderately than to avert the problem. Comprehensive study provides the fact that after some time of operation, the system is likely to attain a status of constancy and maintain a rule which is called fifty per cent rule. This rule points out that the number of used and free blocks are same, i.e. 50% each. In addition, the study divulges that more or less one-third of memory is not used and wasted because of fragmentation. This is the case even if contiguous free areas are re- combined every time a block is returned. Furthermore, this type of implementation slows down execution speed of program as the system has a task of releasing and coalescing block at the same time during program execution.

When memory is fragmented, it can be re-allocated a few or entire portion into one last part of memory and consequently coalesce the small holes into one big free part. This practice of recovering memory storage is known de-fragmentation or compaction. Compaction mechanism is shifting of used blocks from one place in memory to other location. To accomplish this all the active processes are required to be suspended and in fact copied from one part of memory into a different part.

The process of memory compaction is possibly carried out whenever required. In some memory management methods, compact process is performed when a free portion of memory is available. In this way, gathering maximum of the free memory into one large portion takes place. A substitute way is to compact only when the request received cannot be fulfilled and system fails to allocate the memory. If the combined sizes of free portions of memory go above the requested amount of memory available, or else, free memory cannot satisfy the pending need in any case then compaction may not be useful.

There are two approaches:

1. Incremental compaction
2. Selective compaction.

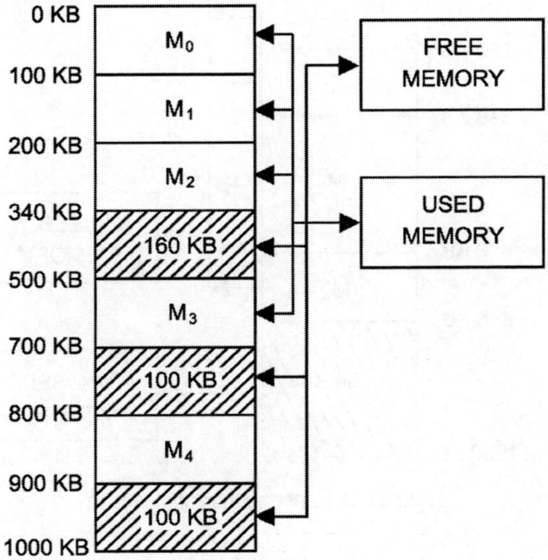

Figure 7.12 Actual memory

Incremental Compaction In this type every free block is moved into one end of the memory to compose a big hole. This procedure is very straightforward to apply but costly. The Fig. 7.13 shows incremental compaction.

Selective Compaction Selective compaction seeks for least number of free blocks, movement of which produces a larger free hole. The obtained hole may be at any place in the memory and need not be at the end of the memory. Fig. 7.14 shows a memory picture of selective compaction.

Through selective compaction, only by moving block M3 of size 200 KB from location 500 KB to the location 700 KB; continuing this way we can create the largest possible free holes of size 360 KB at the location 340 KB.

Therefore, time for shifting data is minimum. However, with the incremental method we have to move first the memory portion of the block M3 from 500 KB location to 340 KB location, then the memory content of the block M4 at 540 KB location. Therefore, here, total movement is

200 KB + 100 KB = 300 KB instead of 200 KB in selective method. Selective compaction approach is seldom applied because of the overhead in evaluating the option while selecting the most advantageous moving method. Time for selecting such block may be more than the time required to shift the block one-by-one at the end of the memory. Consequently, a more general approach to compaction is to reallocate all free blocks to one end of memory.

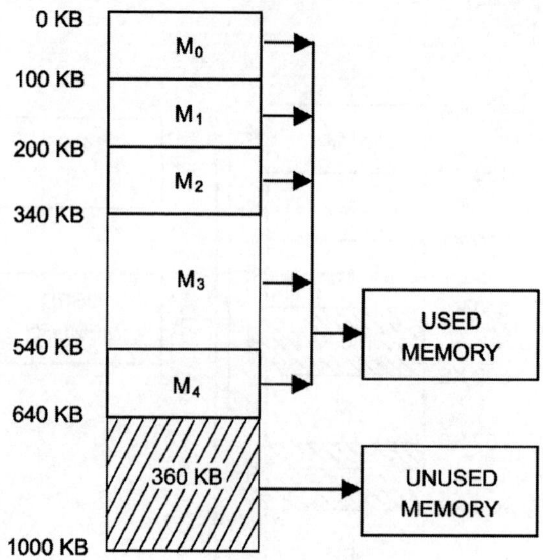

Figure 7.13 Incremental compaction

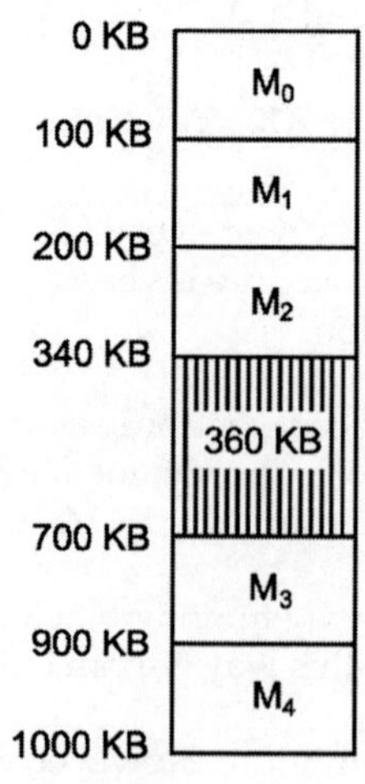

Figure 7.14 Selective compaction

7.9.1 Memory (Storage) Allocation

The operating system of the computer controls entire system resources and permits or denies the use of system resources by other programs. The other programs need to request the operating system for any requirement of memory. The operating system manages the entire process and allocates the memory to other programs. It performs the memory allocation using the following two systems:

Linked Allocation We know that a linked list is nothing but a sequence of nodes linked with the pointer. Every node has two parts, i.e. data field and link field. The data is stored in the data filed and link field stores address of next field.

Fixed Sized Partition Technique In this type memory space is partitioned into fixed sections and each block holds given memory. The size of the block is predetermined and cannot be modified at run time. If the program size is less than the block of memory, the memory more than the requirement remains unused. If the memory of the block is less than the program size, the program will not be executed.

7.9.2 Storage Pools

Storage pools mean every node present in memory. There are two ways to manage the pools:

Bit Tables/Paging Technique When all the nodes of the data structure are of identical size, this method is applicable. In this technique, every program is split into fixed size pages. Later, each page is sub-divided into fixed blocks of nodes known *page frames*. For example, memory size is 20 KB and every page frames needs 200 KB. The memory space divided as following table.

Page Frame	*Bit*
0	1
1	1
2	1
3	1
4	1
5	1
6	1
7	1
8	1
9	1

In the above table one shows free space and initially for page frame 0 to 9 the page frame status is zero. For example, five programs are to be executed and memory needed is as follows:

Program	*Memory needed*
Program –1	60 KB
Program –2	80 KB
Program –3	80 KB
Program –4	40 KB
Program –5	40 KB

For the preceding table the memory allocation will be as follows:

Program No.	Page No.	Part of page No.	Bit status (a)	Bit status (b)
1	0	0	0	1
1	1	1	0	1
2	0	2	0	0
2	1	3	0	0
2	2	4	0	0
3	0	5	0	1
3	1	6	0	1
3	2	7	0	1
4	0	8	0	0
5	0	9	0	0

In the above table, the bit status 1 specifies that all the nodes of the memory be already allocated to 1 to 5 programs. Assume, program 3 and 1 complete their execution and the memory engaged due to these programs is released. The status bit 2 points the altered bit status. The paging technique has some drawbacks and undergoes trouble for searching the best possible page frame size. In case the size of the program is larger and memory space allocated is more then memory is wasted. Similarly, if the page frame is small, the program has to undergo several partitions and it will be very tedious to match the frame with the required size. In paging technique, the entire program must be memory resident. In this situation, if program size is larger than available memory, the program will not be executed.

Demand Paging Method To overcome the limitations of the paging technique, demand paging method is followed. In this method, a large program is divided into small sizes of program segments and first page is then loaded in the memory. If few functions or statements of first pages, which are currently executed in the memory having relation with statements which are in next page, then the required page is loaded from disk to memory. In this procedure, the operating system can take part and transfer the required page to the disk and vice-versa. This is known as thrashing.

7.10 GARBAGE COLLECTIONS

Garbage collection means the de-allocation of unused memory. Deciding when to release the allocated memory is very simple. The memory de-allocation is done when the programmer requests by executing a specific function. Languages like Java have in-built garbage collection system. The function *free ()* in C and *delete* in C++ are used to release the memory. The garbage collection system checks the entire memory, marks the unused nodes and releases the memory associated with them.

The garbage collection consists of two steps:

Marking In this process, all the accessible nodes are marked and one field is kept for marking. The field is marked with true or false.

Collection In this process, memory allocated of all the nodes, which are not marked, are released.

The garbage collection is a complex procedure and has the following disadvantages:

1. The garbage collection technique is applied when there is not much space.
2. The garbage collection may not be helpful if the pointers associated with the list are not properly pointed.

However, the memory de-allocation is not as easy as it appears. The memory allocated during compile time can be freed easily. The memory allocated dynamically at run time can be de-allocated but some care must be taken. The dynamic structure such as linked list contains nodes, which are dynamically created and contains reference of next nodes.

Summary

In this chapter, the reader is exposed to the allocation and release of memory. Different techniques of allocation of memory are discussed. Memory is one of the precious resources and it is essential to manage it efficiently. Two methods are used for management of memory.

Static storage management When program execution starts, it takes memory through operating system. Once a memory is allocated to the program, the memory allocated cannot be increased or decreased during program execution.

Dynamic storage management The dynamic storage management allows the user to manage the memory during program execution. According to the request made by the program, memory can be allocated. Under dynamic memory management various techniques have been discussed in this chapter. The best-fit, first-fit and worst-fit memory management techniques have been briefed.

Exercises

A. **Answer the following questions:**
   1. What do you mean by static memory management? Explain in detail.
   2. Distinguish between the static and dynamic memory management techniques.
   3. Explain the various methods used to allocate memory under dynamic memory management.
   4. Explain the demand paging method.
   5. What is compaction?

Chapter 8

Trees

Chapter Outline

8.1 INTRODUCTION

In the previous chapters, we have studied various data structures such as arrays, stacks, queues and linked list. All these are linear data structures. In these data structures the elements are arranged in a linear manner, i.e. one after another. Tree is an equally useful data structure of non-linear type. In tree, elements are arranged in non-linear fashion. A tree structure means data is organized in branches. The following Fig. 8.1 is a sample tree.

A tree is a non-linear data structure and its elements are arranged in sorted order.

Tree has several practical applications. It is immensely useful in manipulating data and to protect hierarchical relationship among data. The fundamental operations such as insertion, deletion etc. is easy and efficient in tree data structure than in linear data structures. Fig. 8.2 represents family hierarchy, which keeps relations among them. The hierarchy gives relations between associates of family members. In this tree, node 'A' can be assumed as a parent of 'B' and 'C', 'D' and 'E' are the children of 'B'. 'F' is the child of 'C'. This tree represents the relation between the family members.

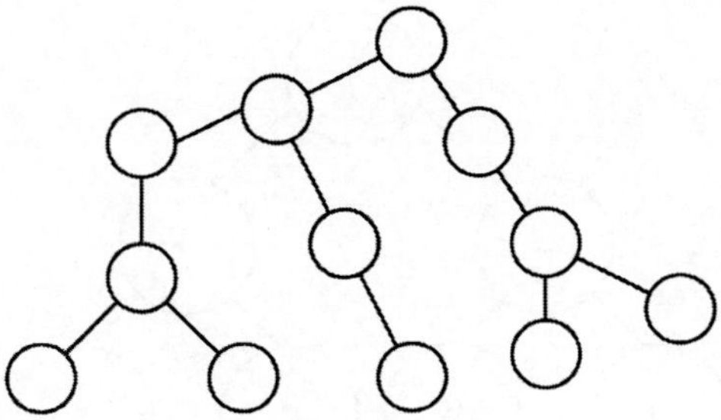

Figure 8.1 Sample tree

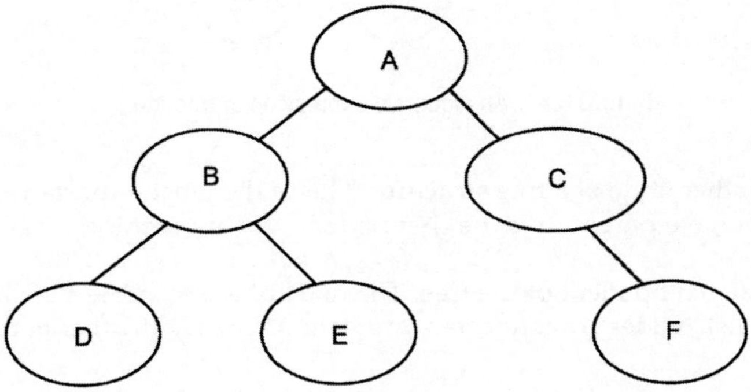

Figure 8.2 A family hierarchy in tree structure

For example, suppose the left side member is male and right side member is female. Then, various relations such as sister, brother, grandfather, grandmother can also be implied.

The algebraic expression can be represented with a tree. Consider the following example of an algebraic expression.

$Z=(J-K) / ((L^{*} M)+N)$

The operators of the above equation have different priority. The priority of the operators can be represented by the tree structure. The operators of high priority are at low level and operator and associated operands are represented in tree structure. The Fig. 8.3 illustrates the representation of an algebraic expression.

8.2 BASIC TERMS

Some of the basic concepts relevant to trees are described in this section. These are node, parents, roots, child, link, leaf, level, height, degree of node, sibling, terminal nodes, path length, and forest.

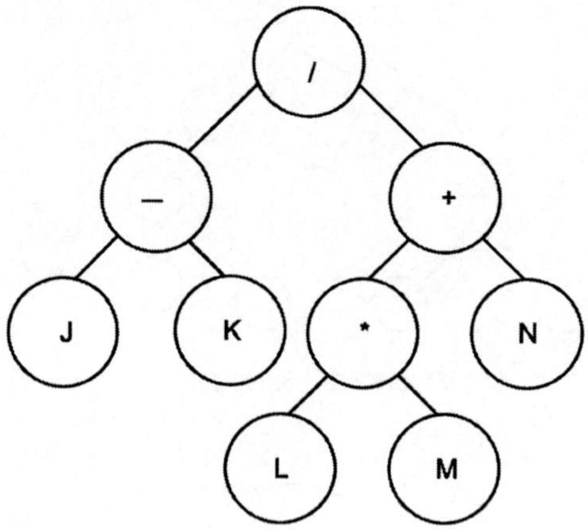

Figure 8.3 An algebraic expression in tree form

Root It is the mother node of a tree structure. This is the most important node of any tree. This node does not have parent. It is the first node in the hierarchical arrangement.

Node It is the main component of the tree. The node of a tree stores the data and its role is same as the linked list. Nodes are connected by means of links with other nodes. This is shown in Fig. 8.4.

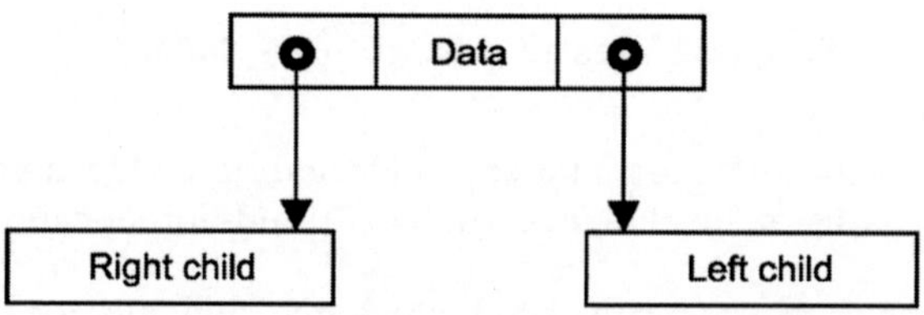

Figure 8.4 Right and left nodes of a tree

Parent It is an immediate predecessor of a node. In the Fig. 8.5 A is parent of B and C.

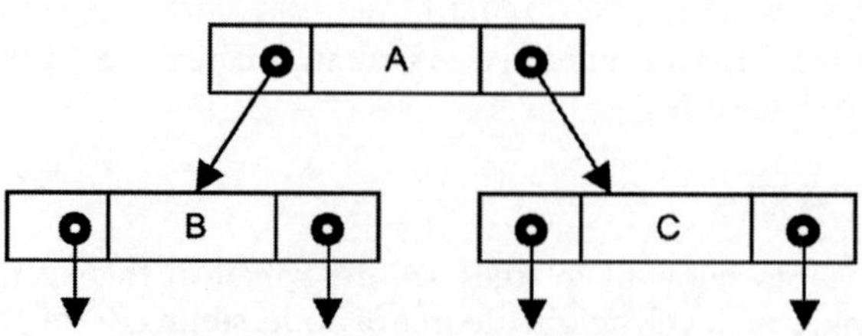

Figure 8.5 Parent nodes with child nodes

Child When a predecessor of a node is parent then all successor nodes are called child nodes. In Fig. 8.5, B and C are child nodes of A. The node at left side is called left child node and node at right side is called right child node.

Link The link is nothing but pointer to node in a tree structure. In other words, link connects the two nodes. The line drawn from one node to other node is called a link. Fig. 8.5 shows left and right child. Here, two links are shown from node A. More than two links from a node may be drawn in a tree. In a few textbooks the term edge is used instead of link. Functions of both of them are same.

Leaf This node is located at the end of the tree. It does not have any child hence it is called as leaf node. Here, 'H', 'I', 'F', and 'J' are leaf nodes in Fig. 8.6.

Level Level is a rank of tree hierarchy. The whole tree structure is levelled. The level of root node is always at 0. The immediate children of root are at level 1 and their immediate children are at level 2 and so on. If children nodes are at level n+1 then parent node would be at level n. The Fig. 8.6 shows the levels of tree.

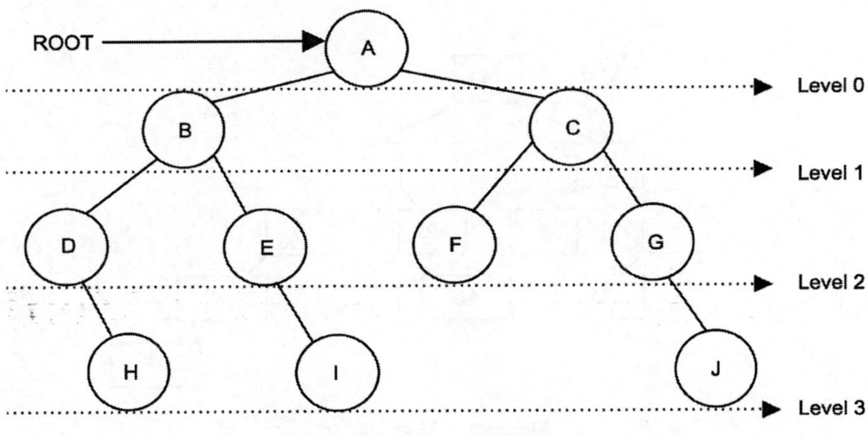

Figure 8.6 Levels of tree

Height The highest number of nodes that is possible in a way starting from the first node (root) to a leaf node is called the height of tree. In Fig. 8.6, the height of tree is 4. This value can be obtained by referring three different paths from the source node to leaf node. The paths A-B-D-H, A-B-E-I, and A-C-G-J have the same height. The height can be obtained from the number of levels, which exists in the tree. The formula for finding the height of the tree $h = i_{max} + 1$, where h is the height and i_{max} is maximum level of the tree. In the above Fig. 8.6 the maximum level of the tree is 3(i_{max}=3). By substituting the value into the formula the h will be 4. The term depth can be used in place of height.

Degree of a Node The maximum number of children that can exist for a node, is called as the degree of the node. In Fig. 8.6 the node A, B and C have maximum two Children. So, the degree of A, B and C is same and it is equal to 2.

Sibling The child nodes of same parent are called sibling. They are also called brother nodes. A, B and C nodes in the Fig. 8.6 have two child nodes. B and C are the siblings of the node A, whereas D and E are the siblings of the node B.

Terminal Node A node with degree zero is called terminal node or leaf. Fig. 8.6 shows 4 terminal nodes and they are H, I, F and J.

Path Length It is the number of successive edges from source node to destination node. In the above Fig. 8.6 the path length from the root node A to H is three because there are three edges.

Forest It is a group of disjoint trees. If we remove a root node from a tree then it becomes the forest. If we remove root node A then the two disjoint sub-trees will be observed. They are left sub-tree B and right sub-tree C.

Labelled Trees In the labelled tree the nodes are labelled with alphabetic or numerical values. The labels are the values allotted to the nodes in the tree. Fig. 8.7 shows the diagram of a labelled tree. Finally obtained tree is called as labelled tree.

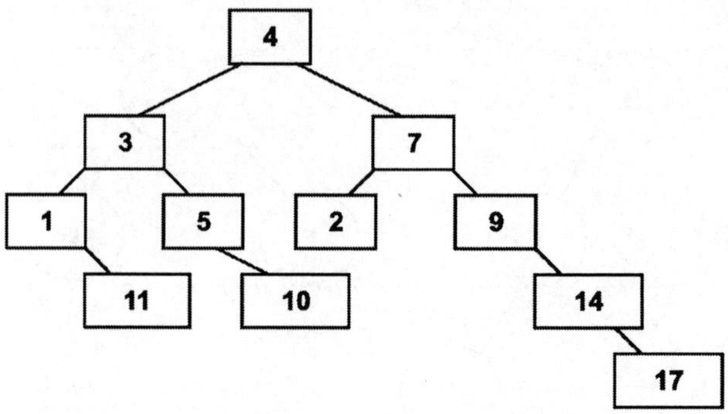

Figure 8.7 Labelled tree

The Fig. 8.7 shows the labelled tree having 11 nodes; root node is 4 and leaf nodes 11,10,17, and 2. The parent and children relationship between them is shown in Table 8.1.

Table 8.1 Parent and children relationship

Parent nodes	*Children nodes*
4	3,7
3	1,5
1	11
5	10
7	2,9
9	14
14	17

There is one more relationship, which is called left node left child and right node right child. This is useful for traversing the binary tree.

Table 8.2 Relationship between parent, left and right nodes

Parent node	*Left child*	*Right child*
4	3	7
3	1	5
1	–	11
5	–	10
7	2	9
9	–	14
14	–	17

Table 8.2 describes the relationship between the parents, left and right nodes, which is drawn from the Fig. 8.7. The '—' indicate that root node (parent) does not have child node. The 11,10 and 17 labelled nodes are the leaf nodes of the tree.

A program is provided based on the above relationships. It finds the number of nodes in a tree and leaf nodes.

Example 8.1

Write a program to find number of nodes and leaf nodes in the given tree.

Solution

```
#include<stdio.h>
#include<conio.h>
struct tree
{
long data;
struct tree *left;
struct tree *right;
};
int node=1,lev;
struct tree *bt=NULL;
struct tree *insert(struct tree*bt,long no);
void lev_count(struct tree*bt);
void node_count(struct tree*bt);

main()
{
 long no;
 clrscr();
   puts("Enter the nodes of tree in preorder: and 0 to quit");
   scanf("%ld",&no);
   while(no!=0)
```

Explanation This program contains three functions *insert()*, *lev_count()*, and *node_count()*. The *insert()* is used to insert the element into the binary tree. The *lev_count()* function is used to count the total leaf nodes of the binary tree. The global variable *lev* stores the total number of the leaf nodes. The function *node_count()* is initialized to count number of the nodes which are present in the binary tree. The global variable *node* is used to store the total number of nodes present in the tree.

```
 {
    bt= insert(bt,no);
    scanf("%d",&no);
 }
 node_count(bt);
 printf("The tree contains %d nodes\n",node);
 lev_count(bt);
 printf("\nThe tree contains %d leaf nodes\n", lev);
}
struct tree*insert(struct tree*bt,long no)
{
 if(bt==NULL)
 {
 bt=(struct tree*) malloc(sizeof(struct tree));
 bt->left=bt->right=NULL;
 bt->data=no;
 }
 else
 {
 if(no<bt->data)
 bt->left=insert(bt->left,no);
 else
 if(no>bt->data)
 bt->right=insert(bt->right,no);
 else
 if(no==bt->data)
 {
 puts("Duplicates nodes: Program exited");
 exit(0);
 }
 }
 return(bt);
}
void node_count(struct tree*bt)
{
 if(bt!=NULL)
 {
 if(bt->left!=NULL)
 {
    node++;
    node_count(bt->left);
 }
 if(bt->right!=NULL)
 {
    node++;
    node_count(bt->right);
 }
```

```
  }
 }
 void lev_count(struct tree*bt)
 {
  if(bt!=NULL)
  {
    if((bt->left==NULL)&&(bt->right==NULL))
    lev++;
  else
    lev_count(bt->left);
    lev_count(bt->right);
  }
 }
```

```
OUTPUT
Enter the nodes of tree in preorder: and 0 to quit
5 3 11 0
The tree contains 3 nodes
The tree contains 2 leaf nodes
```

8.3 BINARY TREES

A binary tree is a finite set of data elements. A tree is binary if each node of it has a maximum of two branches. The data element is either empty or holds a single element called root along with two disjoint trees called left sub-tree and right sub-tree, i.e. in a binary tree the maximum degree of any node is two. The binary tree may be empty. However, the tree cannot be empty. The node of tree can have any number of children whereas the node of binary tree can have maximum two children. Fig. 8.8 shows a sample binary tree.

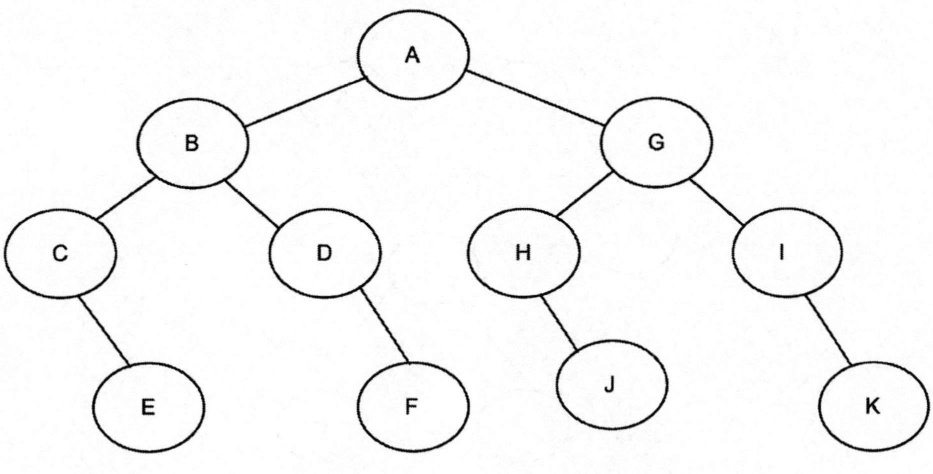

Figure 8.8 A sample binary tree

In Fig. 8.8, A is the root and B and G are its child nodes. The nodes B and G are non-empty nodes, hence they are called left successor and right successor of the root A. The node root without successor is called the terminal node of that root. In Fig. 8.8 the node E, F, J, and K are the terminal nodes.

The right tree is G and left tree is B. Next B has left tree C and right tree D. The right tree further has left tree H and right tree I. This will be continued up to last level.

8.4 COMPLETE BINARY TREE

A tree is called complete binary tree if each of its nodes has two children, except the last nodes. In other words, every non-terminal node of it must have both children except the last leaf nodes. So, at any level the maximum number of nodes is equal to 2. At level 0, there must be only one node and that is the root node. A at level 1 the maximum nodes must be 2. At level 3 the maximum nodes must be equal to 8. A complete binary tree can be obtained from Fig. 8.8.

The advantage of this complete binary tree is that one can very easily locate the position of the parent and also left and right child nodes of a complete binary tree.Left child node and right child nodes are located at 2N and 2N+1. Similarly, the parent node of any node would be at floor (N/2).

Parent of D would be floor (5/2)=2, i.e. B is the parent and its left and right child are 2*2=4 and 2*2+1=5. 4 and 5 are the C and D child nodes in Fig. 8.8.

8.5 STRICTLY BINARY TREE

When every non-leaf node in binary tree is filled with left and right sub-trees, the tree is called strictly binary tree. It is shown in Fig. 8.9.

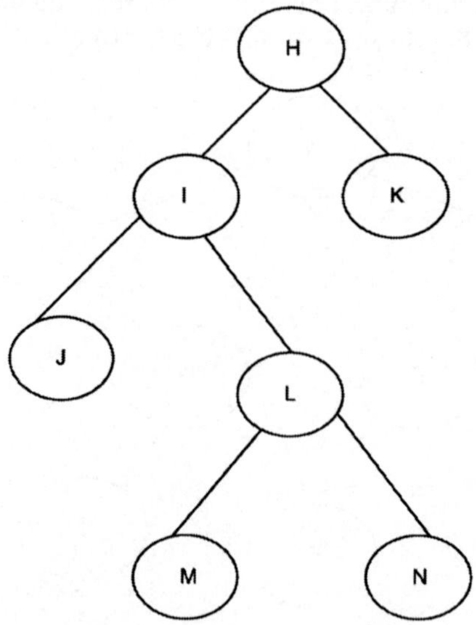

Figure 8.9 Strictly binary trees

In the strictly binary tree as shown in Fig. 8.9, L and I are non-terminal nodes with non-empty left and right sub trees.

8.6 EXTENDED BINARY TREE

When every node of a tree has either 0 or 2 children then such a tree is called extended binary tree or 2-tree. The nodes with two children are called internal nodes. The nodes without children are known as external nodes. At some places in order to identify internal nodes in figures 8.10 to 8.13 circles are used. To identify external nodes squares are used. The nodes in binary tree that have only one child can be extended with one more child. This extended binary tree can be used for implementing the algebraic equation because in the algebraic equation the left and right child nodes are operands and the parent of the child represents the operator.

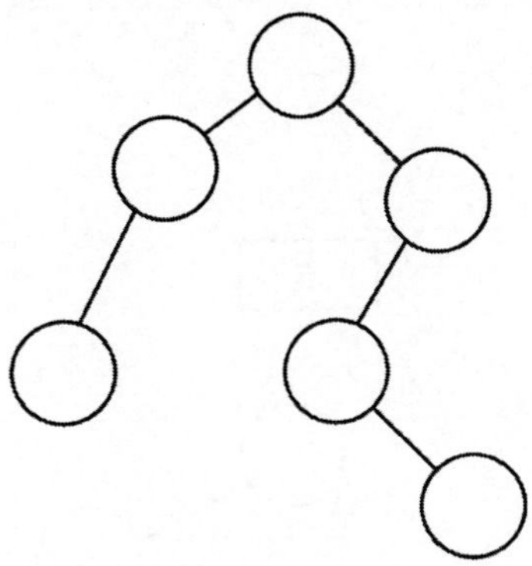

Figure 8.10 Binary tree

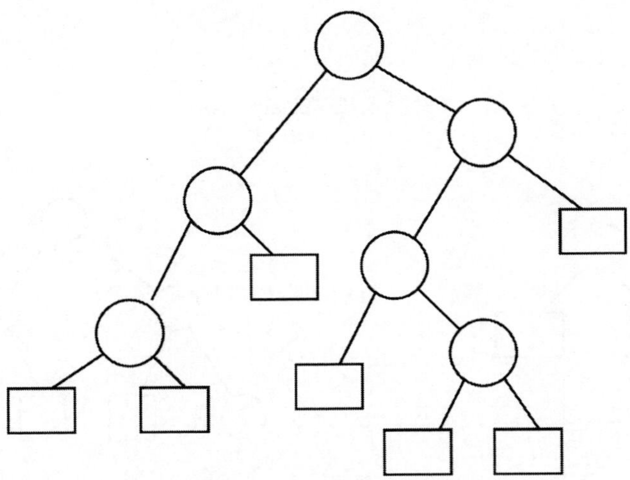

Figure 8.11 Extended 2-tree

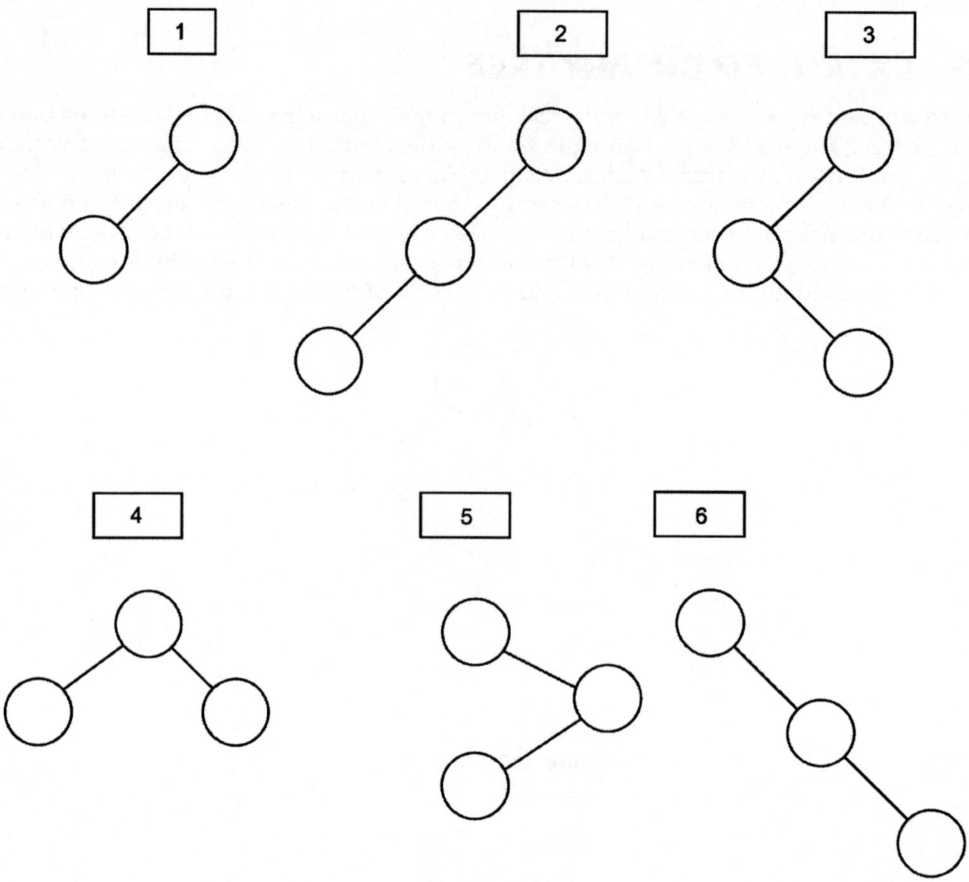

Figure 8.12 Binary trees

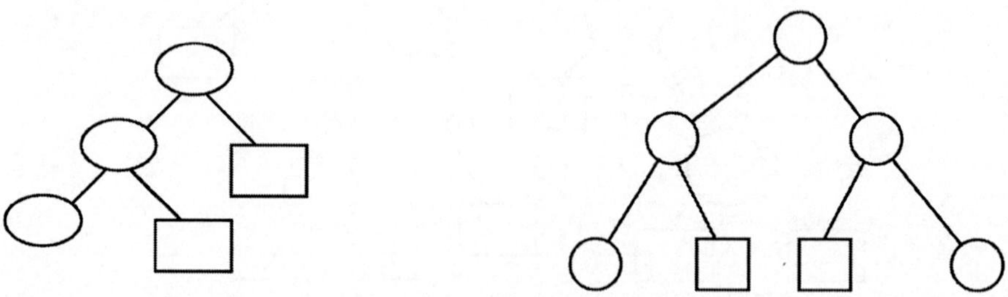

Figure 8.13 2-trees

8.7 BINARY TREE REPRESENTATION

Binary tree can be represented by two ways:

1. Array representation
2. Linked representation.

8.7.1 Array Representation of Binary Tree

In any type of data structure array representation plays an important role. The nodes of trees can be stored in an array. The nodes can be accessed in sequence one after another. In array, element counting starts from zero to (n–1) where n is the maximum number of nodes. In other words, the numbering of binary tree nodes will start from 0 rather than 1.

Assume an integer array. Its declaration is as follows:

```
int array tree[n];
```

The root node of the tree always starts at index zero. Then, successive memory locations are used for storing left and right child nodes. Consider the following Fig. 8.14,

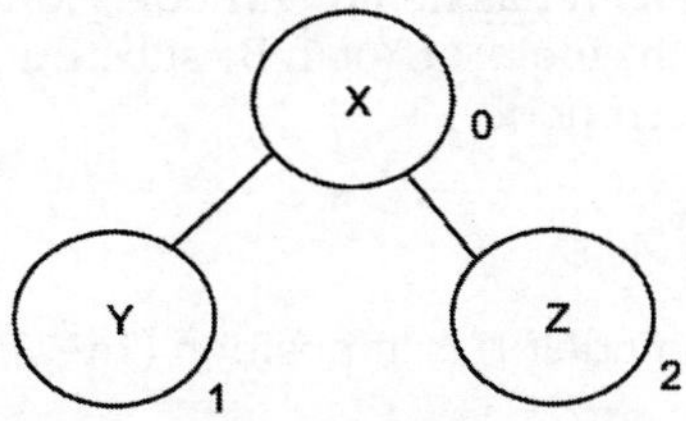

Figure 8.14 Array representation of tree

TREE[0] X
TREE[1] Y
TREE[2] Z

In the above figure, *X* is the root and *Y* and *Z* are children. *X* is father of child *Y* and *Z*. Consider the following Fig. 8.15 with one more level.

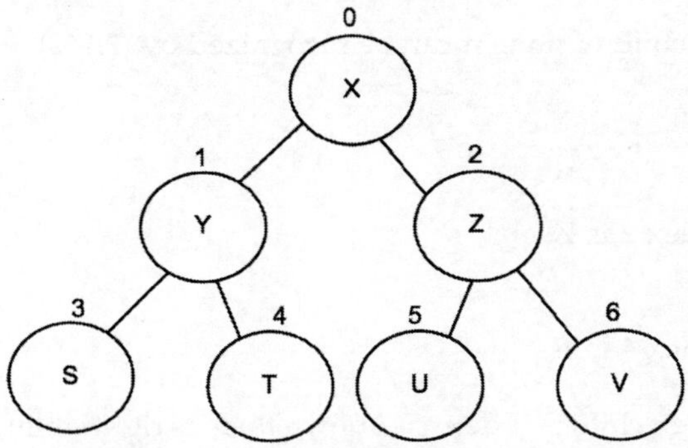

Figure 8.15 Array representation of a tree

The array representation with one more level would be as follows:

0	X
1	Y
2	Z
3	S
4	T
5	U
6	V

It is very easy in this representation to identify the father, left and right child of an arbitrary node. For any node n, $0 \leq n \leq (MAXSIZE - 1)$, the following can be used to identify the father and child nodes.

Father (n) The location of the father node can be identified in a given tree by using the ((n–1)/2) where n is the index of child node, provided that n! =0 (not equal to zero). In case if n=0, the said node is root node. It has no father node. Consider the node 3 in Fig. 8.15 i.e. S. The father of node S is Y and the index of Y is 1. By substituting these values in the equation we identify the index of the father node.

Floor ((3-1)/2)) i.e. (2/2)=1

Lchild(n) The left child of a node (n) is at position (2n+1).

1. Lchild(X) =lchild(0)
   =2 * 0+1
   =1
   The node with index 1 is Y.

2. lchild (Z) = lchild(2)
   = 2*2+1 = 5
   The node with index 5 is U.

rchild (n) The right child of node n can be recognized by (2n+2)

1. rchild (X)=rchild (0)
   = 2 * 0+2
   = 2
   The node with index 2 is Z.
2. rchild (Y): rchild(1)
   = 2 *1+2=4
   The node with index 4 is T.

Siblings In case the left child at index n is known then its right sibling is at (n+1). Likewise, if the right child at index n is known then is left sibling is at (n–1). The array representation is perfect for complete binary tree. However, this is not appropriate for other tree types and if we use array for their representation, it results in inefficient use of memory. Consider the binary trees shown in Figs 8.16(a) and 8.16(b).

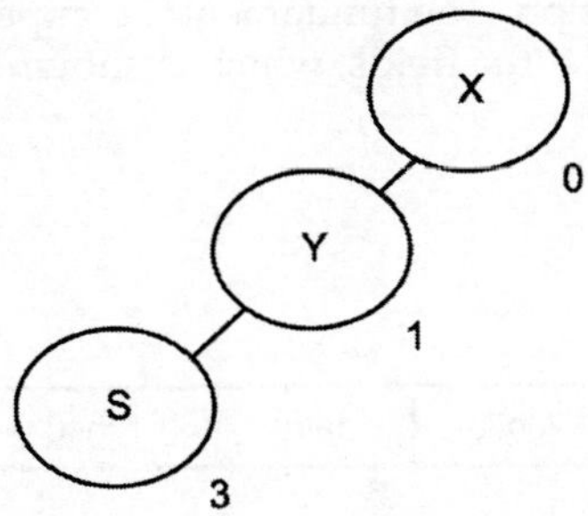

Figure 8.16(a) Left skewed binary tree

The above is skewed binary tree. Here, every left sub-tree again represents left sub-tree. Such type of binary tree is called left skewed binary tree. Similarly, right skewed binary tree is also present [See Figs 8.16(a) and 8.16(b)]. Fig. 8.17 shows array representation of left and right skewed trees.

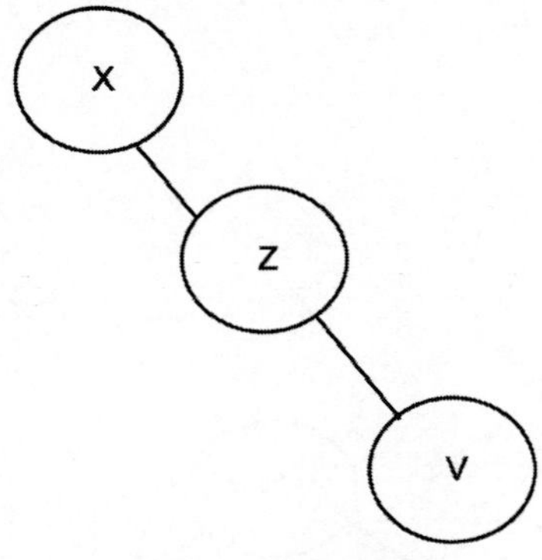

Figure 8.16(b) Right skewed binary tree

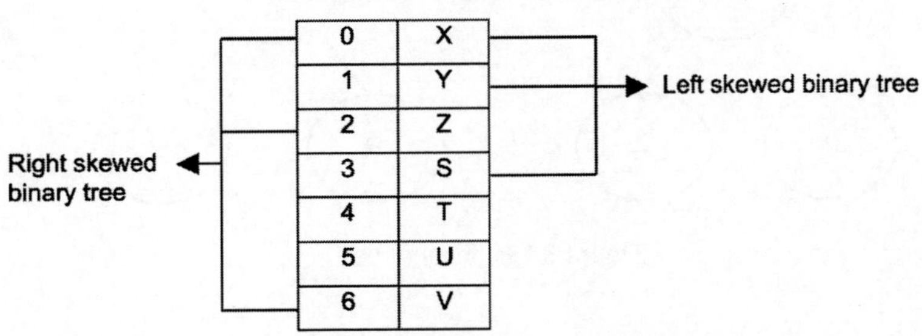

Figure 8.17 Left-right skewed binary tree

8.7.2 Linked Representation of Binary Tree

Another way of representation of binary tree is linked list, which is known to be more memory efficient than array representation. The fundamental component of binary tree is node. We know that the node consists of three fields, which is shown in Fig. 8.18.

- Data
- Left child
- Right child.

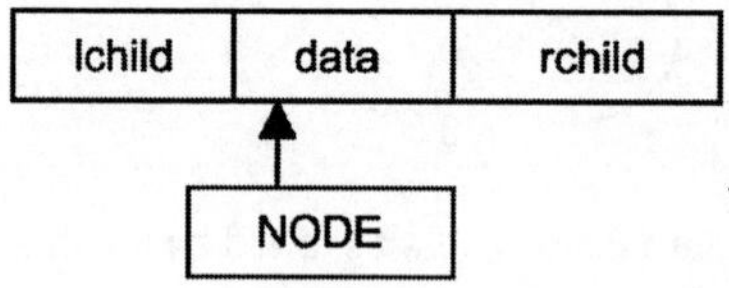

Figure 8.18 Link list representation of binary tree

We have already learnt about nodes in Chapter 6. The data field stores the given values. The lchild field is link field and holds the address of its left node. Similarly, the rchild holds the address of right node. The node can be logically represented as follows. Figs 8.19 and 8.20 show the linked list representation of binary tree.

```
struct node
{
    int data;
    struct node *rchild;
    struct node *lchild;
};
```

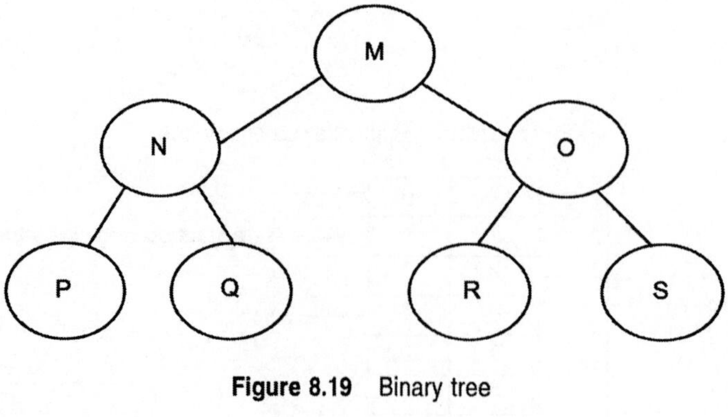

Figure 8.19 Binary tree

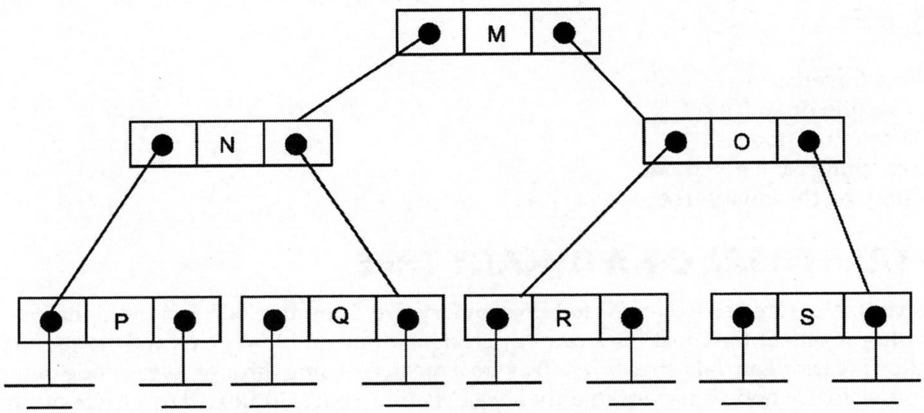

Figure 8.20 Linked list representation of binary tree

Binary tree has one root node and few non-terminal and terminal nodes. The terminal nodes are called leafs. The non-terminal nodes have their left and right child nodes. However, the terminal nodes are without child. While implementing this, fields of lchild and rchid are kept NULL. The non-terminal nodes are known as internal nodes and terminal nodes are known as external nodes.

8.8 OPERATION ON BINARY TREE

Following fundamental operations are performed on binary tree:

Create This operation creates an empty binary tree.

Make This operation creates a new binary tree. The data field of this node holds some value.

Empty When binary tree is empty, this function will return true else it will return false.

Lchild A pointer is returned to left child of the node. When the node is without left child, a NULL pointer is returned.

Rchild A pointer is returned to right child and if the node is without right child a NULL pointer is returned.

Father A pointer to father of the node is returned or else the NULL pointer is returned.

Sibling (Brother) A pointer to brother of the node is returned or else NULL pointer is returned.

Data Value stored is returned.

In addition to above mentioned operations, following operations can also be performed on binary tree:

1. Tree traversal
2. Insertion of nodes
3. Deletion of node
4. Searching for a given node
5. Copying the binary tree.

8.9 TRAVERSAL OF A BINARY TREE

Three parameters are needed for formation of binary tree. They are node, left and right sub-trees. Traversing is one of the most important operations done on binary tree and frequently this operation is carried on data structures. Traversal means passing through every node of the tree one by one. Every node is traversed only once. Assume, root is indicated by O, left sub-tree as L and right sub-tree as R. Then, the following traversal combinations are possible:

1. ORL - ROOT - RIGHT-LEFT
2. OLR - ROOT - LEFT-RIGHT
3. LOR - LEFT - ROOT- RIGHT
4. LRO - LEFT - RIGHT- ROOT
5. ROL - RIGHT - ROOT - LEFT
6. RLO - RIGHT - LEFT-ROOT

Out of six methods only three are standard and are discussed in this chapter. In traversing always right sub-tree is traversed after left sub-tree. Hence, the OLR is preorder, LOR is inorder and LRO is postorder.

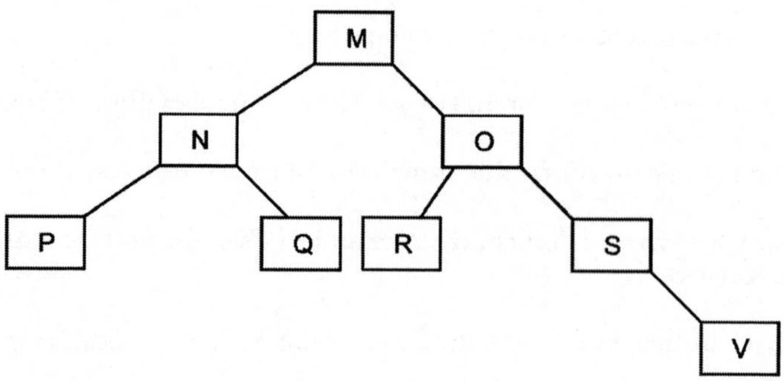

Figure 8.21 A model tree

The inorder representation of above tree is P-N-Q-M-R-O-S-V.

Traversing is a common operation on binary tree. The binary tree can be used to represent an arithmetic expression. Here, divide and conquer technique is used to convert an expression into a binary tree. The procedure to implement it is as follows.

The expression for which the following tree has been drawn is (X*Y)+Z. Fig. 8.22 represents the expression.

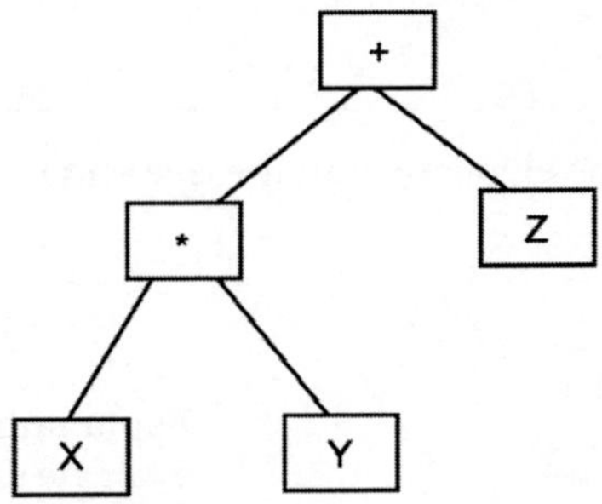

Figure 8.22 An arithmetic expression in binary tree form

Using the following three methods, the traversing operation can be performed. They are:

1. Preorder traversal
2. Inorder traversal
3. Postorder traversal.

All the above three types of traversing methods are explained below.

8.9.1 Inorder Traversal

The functioning of inorder traversal of a non-empty binary tree is as follows:

1. Firstly, traverse the left sub-tree in inorder.
2. Next, visit the root node.
3. At last, traverse the right sub-tree in inorder.

In the inorder traversal firstly the left sub-tree is traversed recursively in inorder. Then the root node is traversed. After visiting the root node, the right sub-tree is traversed recursively in inorder. Fig. 8.21 illustrates the binary tree with inorder traversal. The inorder traversing for the tree is P-N-Q-M-R-O-S-V. It can be illustrated as per Fig. 8.23.

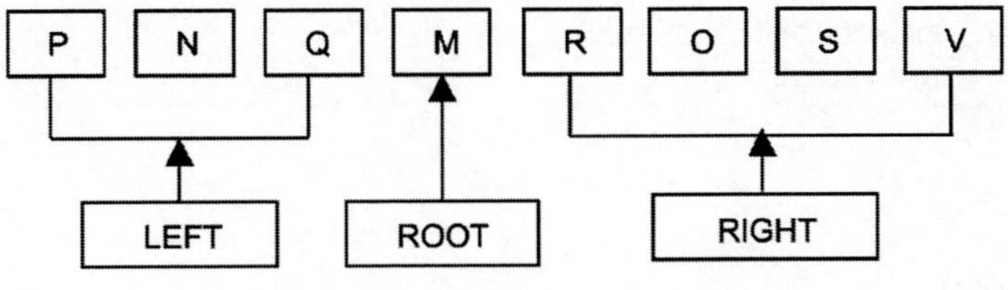

Figure 8.23 Inorder traversal

The left part constitutes P, N, and Q as the left sub-tree of root and R, O, S, and V are the right sub-tree.

Example 8.2

Write a program for inserting the elements into the tree and traverse the tree by the inorder.

Solution

```
#include<stdio.h>
#include<conio.h>
struct tree
{
long data;
struct tree *left;
struct tree *right;
};
struct tree *btree=NULL;
struct tree *insert(struct tree*btree,long digit);
void inorder(struct tree*btree);
main()
{
 long digit;
 clrscr();
    puts("Enter integers: and 0 to quit");
    scanf("%ld",&digit);
    while(digit!=0)
    {
    btree= insert(btree,digit);
    scanf("%d",&digit);
    }
    puts("Inorder traversing of btree:\n");
    inorder(btree);
}
struct tree*insert(struct tree*btree,long digit)
{
 if(btree==NULL)
  {
 btree=(struct tree*) malloc(sizeof(struct tree));
 btree->left=btree->right=NULL;
 btree->data=digit;
  }
  else
  {
 if(digit<btree->data)
 btree->left=insert(btree->left,digit);
  else
```

Explanation This program is used to evaluate the inorder of the given tree. The given binary tree is stored in **btree*. The elements are inserted by using the *insert()*. The inorder traversing, i.e. left, root and right is done by *inorder()*. The Fig. 8.24 illustrates the binary tree.

```
if(digit>btree->data)
btree->right=insert(btree->right,digit);
 else
if(digit==btree->data)
 {
puts("Duplicates nodes: Program exited");
 exit(0);
 }
 }
 return(btree);
}
void inorder(struct tree*btree)
{
if(btree!=NULL)
 {
 inorder(btree->left);
 printf("%4ld",btree->data);
 inorder(btree->right);
 }
}

OUTPUT
Enter integers: and 0 to quit
6 1 2 3 7 8 9 0
Inorder traversing of btree:
1 2 3 6 7 8 9
```

The inorder of binary tree is 1, 2, 3, 6, 7, 8, and 9 as shown in Fig. 8.24.

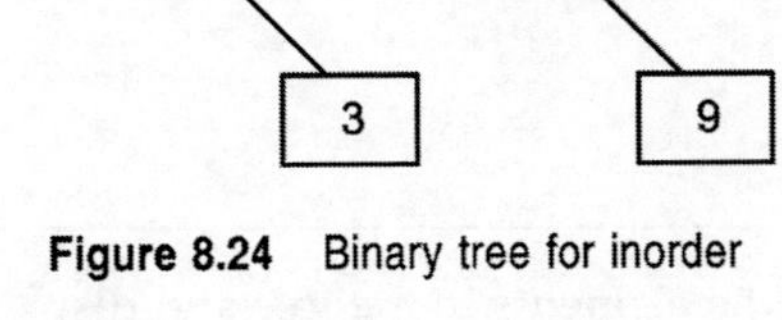

Figure 8.24 Binary tree for inorder

8.9.2 Preorder Traversal

The node is visited before the sub-trees. The following is the procedure for preorder traversal of non-empty binary tree.

1. Firstly, visit the root node (N).
2. Then, traverse the left sub-tree in preorder (L).
3. At last, traverse the right sub-tree in preorder R.

The preorder is recursive in operation. In this type, first root node is visited and later its left and right sub-trees. Consider the following Fig. 8.25 for preorder traversing.

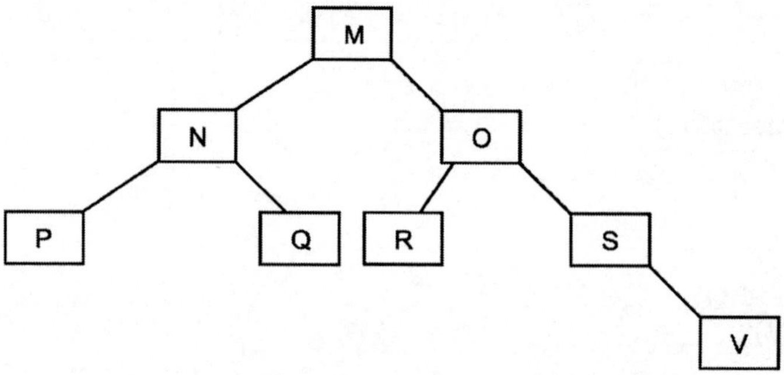

Figure 8.25 Tree for preorder traversal

The preorder traversing for Fig. 8.25 is M, N, P, Q, O, R, S, and V. This can also be shown in Fig. 8.26. In this traversing the root comes first and the left sub-tree and right sub-tree at last.

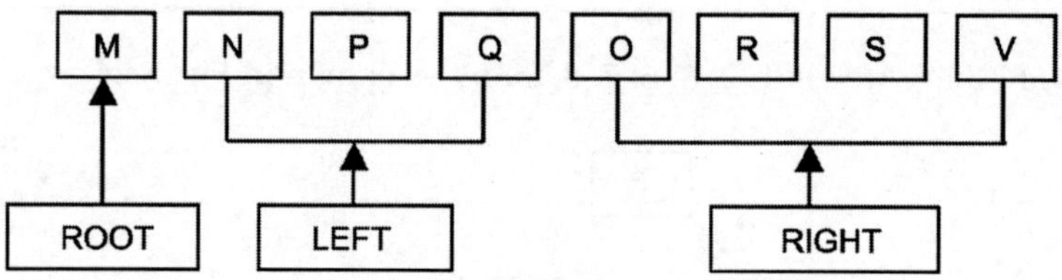

Figure 8.26 Preorder traversal

In the preorder the left sub-tree appears as N, P, and Q and right sub-tree appears as O,R,S, and V.

Example 8.3

Write a program for inserting the elements in the tree and display them in preorder.

Solution

```
#include<stdio.h>
#include<conio.h>
struct tree
```

```
{
long data;
struct tree *left;
struct tree *right;
};
struct tree *btree=NULL;
struct tree *insert(struct tree*btree,long digit);
void preorder(struct tree*btree);
main()
{
 long digit;
 clrscr();
    puts("Enter integers: and 0 to quit");
    scanf("%ld",&digit);
    while(digit!=0)
    {
    btree= insert(btree,digit);
    scanf("%d",&digit);
    }
    puts("Preorder traversing btree:\n");
    preorder(btree);
}
struct tree*insert(struct tree*btree,long digit)
{
 if(btree==NULL)
  {
 btree=(struct tree*) malloc(sizeof(struct tree));
 btree->left=btree->right=NULL;
 btree->data=digit;
  }
  else
  {
 if(digit<btree->data)
 btree->left=insert(btree->left,digit);
  else
 if(digit>btree->data)
 btree->right=insert(btree->right,digit);
  else
 if(digit==btree->data)
  {
 puts("Duplicates nodes: Program exited");
 exit(0);
  }
  }
 return(btree);
}
void preorder(struct tree*btree)
```

Explanation The program stores the binary tree in **btree* structure variable of the structure *tree*. By invoking the *insert()* the elements are inserted. The preorder traversing is done by using *preorder()*. Fig. 8.27 shows the **btree*, which is inserted in this program.

```
{
if(btree!=NULL)
 {
 printf("%4ld",btree->data);
 preorder(btree->left);
 preorder(btree->right);
 }
}

OUTPUT
Enter integers: and 0 to quit
5 2 1 7 0
Preorder traversing btree:
5 2 1 7
```

The preorder of the binary tree is 5, 2, 1, 7.

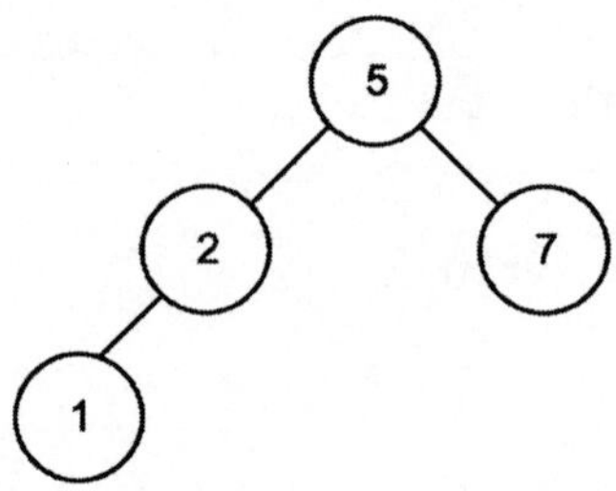

Figure 8.27 Binary tree

8.9.3 Postorder Traversal

In the postorder traversal the traversing is done firstly left and right sub-trees before visiting the root. The postorder traversal of non-empty binary tree is to be implemented as follows:

1. Firstly, traverse the left sub-tree in postorder style.
2. Then, traverse the right sub tree in postorder.
3. At last, visit the root node (N).

In this type, the left and right sub-trees are processed recursively. The left sub-tree is traversed first in postorder. After this, the right sub-tree is traversed in post order. At last, the data of the root node is shown. Fig. 8.28 shows the postorder traversal of a binary tree.

The postorder traversing for the above Fig. 8.28 is P, Q, N, R, V, S, O, and M. This can also be shown as in Fig. 8.29. In this traversing the left sub-tree is traversed first, then right sub-tree and at last root.

In the postorder the left sub-tree is P, Q and N and the right sub-tree is R, V, S and O.

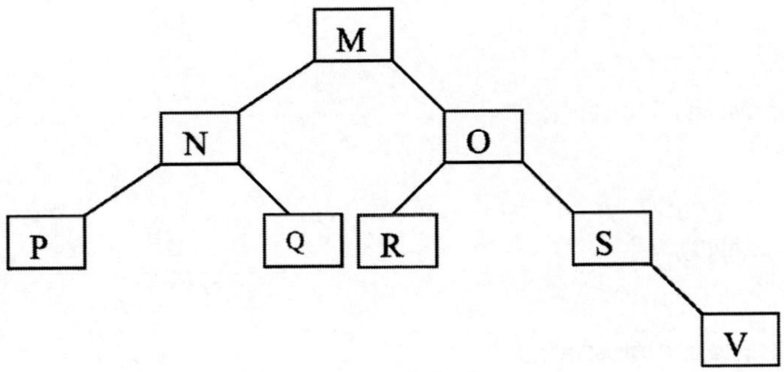

Figure 8.28 Tree for post order

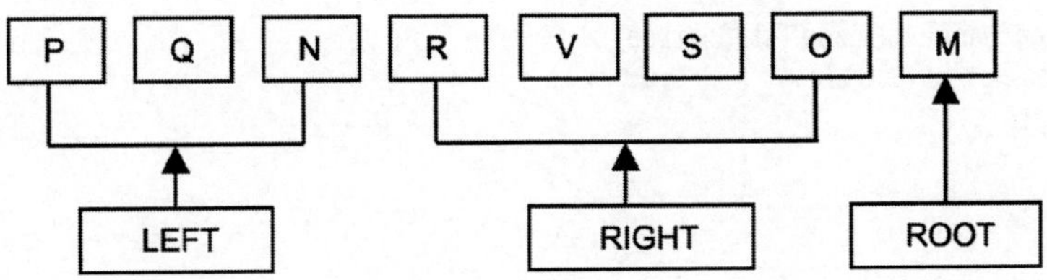

Figure 8.29 Postorder traverse

Example 8.4

Program for inserting the nodes in tree and traversing these nodes by using the postorder method.

Solution

```
#include<stdio.h>
#include<conio.h>
struct tree
{
long data;
struct tree *left;
struct tree *right;
};
struct tree *btree=NULL;
struct tree *insert(struct tree*btree,long digit);
void postorder(struct tree*btree);
main()
{
```

Explanation In this program, **btree* is used to store the binary tree. The **btree* is the structure variable of the structure *tree*. In this program the *insert()* is invoked to insert the elements in the **btree. postorder()* is used to traverse the binary tree in the post order manner. The Fig. 8.30 shows the btree which is inserted in the program.

```
 long digit;
 clrscr();
    puts("Enter integers: and 0 to quit");
    scanf("%ld",&digit);
    while(digit!=0)
    {
    btree= insert(btree,digit);
    scanf("%d",&digit);
    }
    puts("Postorder traversing btree:\n");
    postorder(btree);
}
struct tree*insert(struct tree*btree,long digit)
{
 if(btree==NULL)
 {
 btree=(struct tree*) malloc(sizeof(struct tree));
 btree->left=btree->right=NULL;
 btree->data=digit;
 }
 else
 {
 if(digit<btree->data)
 btree->left=insert(btree->left,digit);
 else
 if(digit>btree->data)
 btree->right=insert(btree->right,digit);
 else
 if(digit==btree->data)
 {
 puts("Duplicates nodes: Program exited");
 exit(0);
 }
 }
 return(btree);
}
void postorder(struct tree*btree)
{
if(btree!=NULL)
 {
 postorder(btree->left);
 postorder(btree->right);
 printf("%4ld",btree->data);
 }
}
```

```
OUTPUT
Enter integers: and 0 to quit
5 3 4 1 9 6 7 0
Postorder traversing btree:
1 4 3 7 6 9 5
```

The postorder traversing of the tree in Fig. 8.30 is 1, 4, 3, 7, 6, 9 and 5.

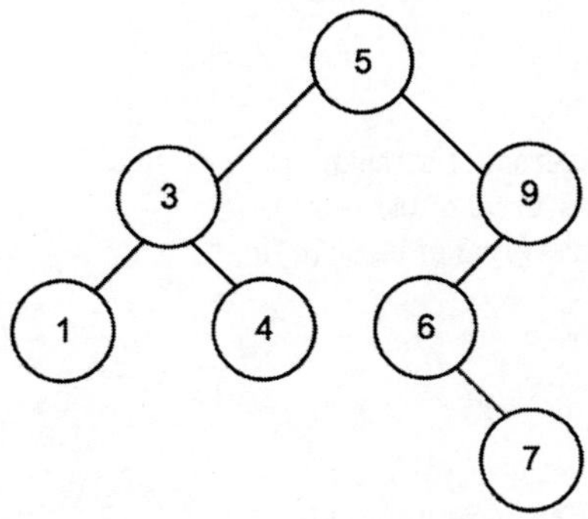

Figure 8.30 btree of the above program

Example 8.5

Write a menu-driven program for various traversals such as 1) inorder 2) preorder 3) postorder.

Solution

```
#include<stdio.h>
#include<conio.h>
struct tree
{
long data;
struct tree *left;
struct tree *right;
};
struct tree *btree=NULL;
struct tree *insert(struct tree*btree,long digit);
void inorder(struct tree*btree);
void preorder(struct tree*btree);
void postorder(struct tree*btree);

main()
{
 long digit;
 int ch;
```

Explanation This program uses the *switch()* and case for the menu-driven purpose, the structure tree is used to store the whole tree and the left and right pointer of the tree is used to maintain the left and right sub-tree. The function *inorder()* is used for displaying the tree in inorder and similarly, the *postorder()* and *preorder()* used for the traversing purpose. The tree, which is used in this program, is shown in Fig. 8.31.

```
 clrscr();
    puts("Enter integers: and 0 to quit");
    scanf("%ld",&digit);
    while(digit!=0)
    {
    btree= insert(btree,digit);
    scanf("%d",&digit);
    }
    while(1)
    {
    clrscr();
    printf(" 1] For Inorder traversal of btree\n");
    printf(" 2] For Preorder traversal of btree\n");
    printf(" 3] For Postorder traversal of btree\n");
    printf(" 4] For Exit\n");
    printf("Enter the choice:-");
    scanf("%d",&ch);
    switch(ch)
    {
    case 1: printf("The inorder traversing of tree\n");
            inorder(btree);
            getch(); break;
    case 2: printf("The preorder traversing of tree\n");
            preorder(btree);
            getch(); break;
    case 3: printf("The postorder traversing of tree\n");
            postorder(btree);
            getch(); break;
    default: exit(0);
    }
    }
    }
struct tree*insert(struct tree*btree,long digit)
{
 if(btree==NULL)
 {
 btree=(struct tree*) malloc(sizeof(struct tree));
 btree->left=btree->right=NULL;
 btree->data=digit;
 }
 else
 {
 if(digit<btree->data)
 btree->left=insert(btree->left,digit);
 else
 if(digit>btree->data)
 btree->right=insert(btree->right,digit);
```

```
 else
 if(digit==btree->data)
  {
 puts("Duplicates nodes: Program exited");
  exit(0);
  }
  }
 return(btree);
}
void inorder(struct tree*btree)
{
if(btree!=NULL)
 {
 inorder(btree->left);
 printf("%4ld",btree->data);
 inorder(btree->right);
 }
}
void preorder(struct tree*btree)
{
if(btree!=NULL)
 {
 printf("%4ld",btree->data);
 preorder(btree->left);
 preorder(btree->right);
 }
}
void postorder(struct tree*btree)
{
if(btree!=NULL)
 {
 postorder(btree->left);
 postorder(btree->right);
 printf("%4ld",btree->data);
 }
}
```

```
OUTPUT
Enter integers: and 0 to quit
5 3 1 4 11 8 12 0
1] For Inorder traversal of btree
2] For Preorder traversal of btree
3] For Postorder traversal of btree
4] For Exit
Enter the choice:-1
The inorder traversing of tree
1 3 4 5 8 11 12
```

```
1] For Inorder traversal of btree
2] For Preorder traversal of btree
3] For Postorder traversal of btree
4] For Exit
Enter the choice:-3
The postorder traversing of tree
1 4 3 8 12 11 5
```

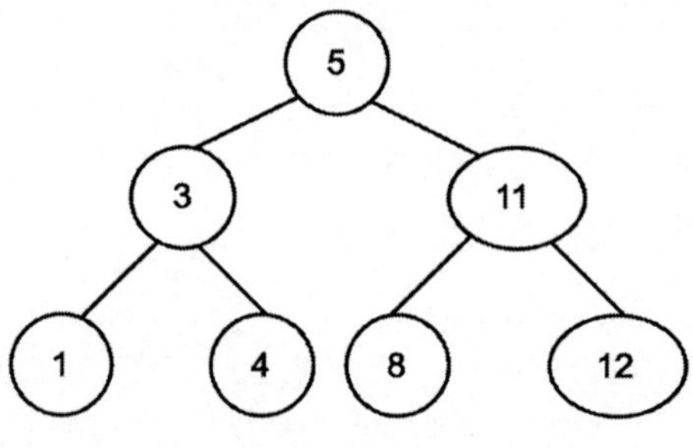

Figure 8.31 Tree representation

8.10 CONVERSION OF EXPRESSION INTO POSTFIX

The arithmetic expression can be converted from infix to postfix. Consider the following example:

(A+B)*(D/E)

In the conversion of the expression into binary tree the operator divides the expression into two parts, and on that basis the binary tree is formed. Always the operators are at the root nodes and the operands are at the leaf nodes.

In above expression at first the '*' operator divides the expression into the two parts, i.e. (A+B) and (D/E). The '*' is at the root of the tree.

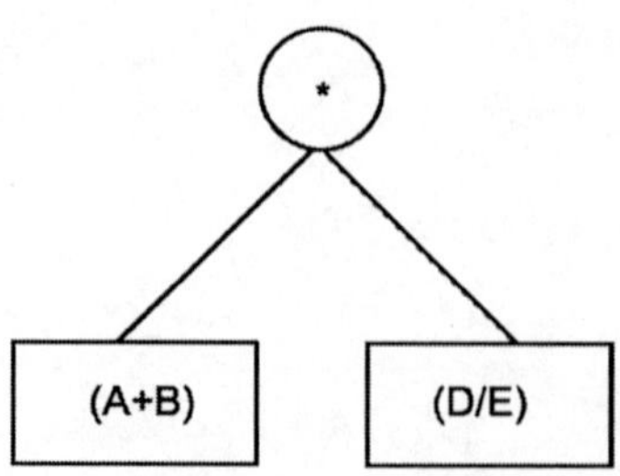

Figure 8.32 Expression in binary tree

Further, the (A+B) and (D/E) can be converted into the binary tree as shown below:

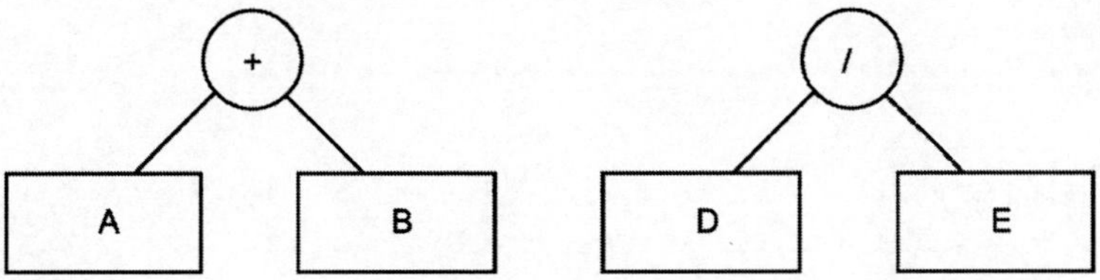

Example 8.1

Write a program to convert infix to postfix expression.

Solution

```
#include<stdio.h>
#include<conio.h>
#include<string.h>
char stack[50];
int top=-1;
void post(char inexp[]);
void push(char);
char pop();
int preced(char c);

main()
{
 char inexp[25];
 clrscr();
 printf("\nEnter the inexp expression:- ");
 scanf("%s",inexp);
 post(inexp);
 getch();
}
void push(char sy)
{
 if(top>=49)
 {
 printf("\nstack overflow");
 getch();
 }
 else
 {
 top=top+1;
 stack[top]=sy;
 }
}
```

```
char pop()
{
 char item;
 if(top==-1)
 {
 printf("\nStack is empty");
 getch();
 return 0;
 }
 else
 {
 item=stack[top];
 top--;
 }
 return(item);
}
int preced(char ch)
{
 if(ch==47)
 return(5);
 if(ch==42)
 return(4);
 if(ch==43)
 return(3);
 return(2);
}
void post(char inexp[])
{
 int len;
 static int index=0,pt=0;
 char oper,temp;
 char postf[40];
 len=strlen(inexp);
 push('#');
 while(index<len)
 {
 oper=inexp[index];
 switch(oper)
 {
 case '(': push(oper);
          break;
 case ')': temp=pop();
 while(temp!='(')
    {
    postf[pt]=temp;
     pt++;
    temp=pop();
    }
```

```
    break;
 case '+':
 case '-':
 case '*':
 case '/':
 case '^':
 while(preced(stack[top])>=preced(oper))
 {
    temp=pop();
    postf[pt]=temp;
    pt++;
 }
 push(oper);
 break;
 default: postf[pt++]=oper;
 break;
 }
 index++;
 }
 while(top>0)
 {
 temp=pop();
 postf[pt++]=temp;
 }
 postf[pt++]='\0';
 printf("\nThe expression into postfix:-");
 printf("%s",postf);
 }
```

```
OUTPUT
Enter the inexp expression:- (A+B)*(C/D)
The expression into postfix:-AB+CD/*
```

8.11 BINARY SEARCH TREE

A binary search tree is also called as binary sorted tree. Binary search tree is either empty or each node N of tree satisfies the following property:

1. The key value in the left child is not more than the value of root.
2. The key value in the right child is more than or identical to the value of root.
3. All the sub-trees, i.e. left and right sub-trees follow the two rules mentioned above.

Binary search tree is shown in Fig. 8.33.

In Fig. 8.33 number 7 is the root node of the binary tree. There are two sub-trees to root 7. The left sub-tree is 4 and right sub-tree is 8. Here, the value of left sub-tree is lower than root and value of right sub-tree is higher than root node. This property can be observed at all levels in the tree.

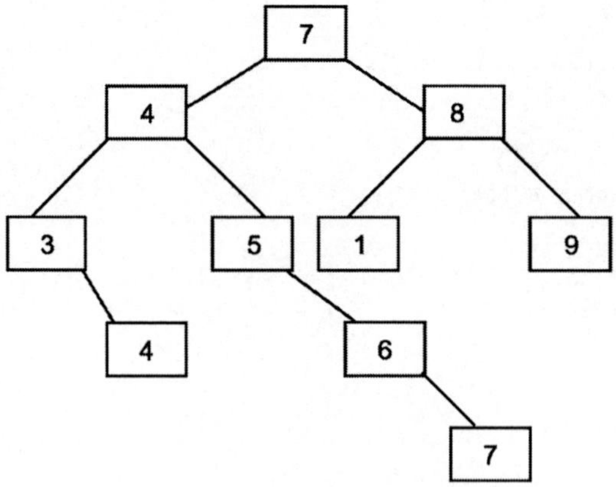

Figure 8.33 Binary search tree

8.11.1 Searching an Element in Binary Search Tree

The item which is to be searched is compared with the root node.If it is less than the root node then the left child of left sub tree is compared otherwise right child is compared. The process would be continued till the item is found. A program based on the above point is given below.

Example 8.5

Write a program to search an element from the binary tree.

Solution

```
#include<stdio.h>
#include<conio.h>
struct tree
{
long data;
struct tree *left;
struct tree *right;
};
int sn;
struct tree *bt=NULL;
struct tree *insert(struct tree*bt,long no);
void search(struct tree *bt, long sn);

main()
{
 long no;
 clrscr();
```

Explanation This program contains *struct tree* which is used to store the binary tree. The *insert()* function inserts the nodes into the binary tree. The *search()* function searches the number from the tree. The *fn* variable is used to store the number which the user will not find. The search function first compares the *fn* with the root node. If the value of *fn* is less than the root node then the function searches the number in the left sub-tree, else it finds the number in the right sub-tree.

```
    puts("Enter the nodes of tree in preorder: and 0 to quit");
    scanf("%ld",&no);
    while(no!=0)
    {
    bt= insert(bt,no);
    scanf("%d",&no);
    }
    printf("\nEnter the number to search:-");
    scanf("%d",&sn);
    search(bt,sn);
}

struct tree*insert(struct tree*bt,long no)
{
 if(bt==NULL)
  {
 bt=(struct tree*) malloc(sizeof(struct tree));
 bt->left=bt->right=NULL;
  bt->data=no;
  }
  else
  {
 if(no<bt->data)
 bt->left=insert(bt->left,no);
  else
 if(no>bt->data)
 bt->right=insert(bt->right,no);
  else
 if(no==bt->data)
  {
 puts("Duplicates nodes: Program exited");
 exit(0);
  }
  }
 return(bt);
}
void search(struct tree*bt, long fn)
{
 if(bt==NULL)
 puts("The number does not exit");
  else
 if(fn==bt->data)
 printf("The number %d is present in tree",fn);
  else
 if(fn<bt->data)
 search(bt->left,fn);
  else
```

```
search(bt->right, fn);
}
```

```
OUTPUT

Enter the nodes of tree in preorder: and 0 to quit
3 5 11 17 34 0
Enter the number to search:-17
The number 17 is present in tree
Enter the nodes of tree in preorder: and 0 to quit
3 5 11 17 34 0
Enter the number to search:-4
The number does not exit
```

8.11.2 Insertion of an Element in Binary Search Tree

Insertion of an element in binary search tree needs to locate the parent node. The element to be inserted in the tree may be on the left sub-tree or right sub-tree. If the inserted number is lesser than the root node then left sub-tree is recursively called, otherwise right sub-tree is chosen for insertion. A program based on the above notion is described below.

Example 8.1

Write a program to insert an element into the binary search tree.

Solution

```
#include<stdio.h>
#include<conio.h>
struct tree
{
long data;
struct tree *left;
struct tree *right;
};
int in;
struct tree *bt=NULL;
struct tree *insert(struct tree*bt,long no);
void inorder(struct tree *bt);

main()
{
 long no;
clrscr();
   puts("Enter the nodes of tree in preorder: and 0 to quit");
   scanf("%ld",&no);
   while(no!=0)
```

Explanation This program invokes a function *insert()* which inserts the node into the structure pointer object **bt*. Firstly, the nodes which are to be inserted are entered and then program calls *insert()* for insertion of new element. The new inserted element firstly checks with the root of the tree. If the number is lesser than the root node it is recursively checked with the nodes, which are present on the left sub-tree, otherwise right sub-tree. Appropriate position of parent node is found and the element is inserted. After insertion, elements are arranged in inorder using the *inorder()* and the same numbers are displayed on the screen.

```
{
bt= insert(bt,no);
scanf("%d",&no);
}
printf("Enter the number to insert:- ");
scanf("%d",&in);
bt=insert(bt,in);
printf("The inorder of tree after insertion of an element\n");
inorder(bt);
}
struct tree*insert(struct tree*bt,long no)
{
if(bt==NULL)
{
bt=(struct tree*) malloc(sizeof(struct tree));
bt->left=bt->right=NULL;
bt->data=no;
}
else
{
if(no<bt->data)
bt->left=insert(bt->left,no);
else
if(no>bt->data)
bt->right=insert(bt->right,no);
else
if(no==bt->data)
{
puts("Duplicates nodes: Program exited");
exit(0);
}
}
return(bt);
}
void inorder(struct tree *bt)
{
if(bt!=NULL)
{
inorder(bt->left);
printf("%d ",bt->data);
inorder(bt->right);
}
}
```

```
OUTPUT
Enter the nodes of tree in preorder: and 0 to quit
7 5 9 0
```

```
Enter the number to insert:- 2
The inorder of tree after insertion of an element
2 5 7 9
```

8.11.3 Traversing the Binary Search Tree

The binary search tree can be traversed similar to the binary tree by the inorder, preorder and postorder traversing methods.

Example 8.1

Program to traverse the binary search tree by using the inorder, preorder and postorder methods.

Solution

```
# include <stdio.h>
# include <conio.h>

struct rec
{
 int data;
 struct rec *left;
 struct rec *right;
};
struct rec *t1;
struct rec *insert(struct rec * t1, int data);
void inorder(struct rec *t1);
void preorder(struct rec *t1);
void postorder(struct rec *t1);

main()
{
int digit;
 clrscr();
 printf("\nEnter the t1 in pre order and 0 to quit\n");
 scanf("%d",&digit);
 while(digit!=0)
 {
 t1=insert(t1,digit);
 scanf("%d",&digit);
 }

 printf("\nThe preorder of the t1 is\n");
preorder(t1);

 printf("\nThe inorder of the t1 is\n");
inorder(t1);
```

Explanation The program first gets the binary search tree into the structure object *t1*. And the *insert()* is used to insert the element into the tree. The three functions *inorder()*, *preorder()* and *postorder()* are used to traverse the tree in appropriate manner.

```
printf("\nThe post order of the t1 is\n");
postorder(t1);
}
struct rec *insert(struct rec * t1, int digit)
{
if(t1==NULL)
{
t1=(struct rec *) malloc (sizeof(struct rec));
t1->left= t1->right=NULL;
t1->data=digit;
}
else
if(digit< t1->data)
t1->left=insert(t1->left,digit);
else
if(digit > t1->data)
t1->right=insert(t1->right, digit);
else
if(digit==t1->data)
{
printf("Duplicate node: program exited");
exit(0);
}
return(t1);
}
void inorder(struct rec *t1)
{
if(t1!=NULL)
{
inorder(t1->left);
printf("%d ",t1->data);
inorder(t1->right);
}
}
void preorder(struct rec *t1)
{
if(t1!=NULL)
{
printf("%d ",t1->data);
preorder(t1->left);
preorder(t1->right);
}
}
void postorder(struct rec *t1)
{
if(t1!=NULL)
{
```

```
postorder(tl->left);
postorder(tl->right);
printf("%d ",tl->data);
}
}
```

```
OUTPUT
Enter the tl in pre order and 0 to quit
3 2 4 0
The preorder of the tl is
3 2 4
The inorder of the tl is
2 3 4
The post order of the tl is
2 4 3
```

8.12 THREADED BINARY TREE

While studying the linked representation of a binary tree, it is observed that the number of nodes that have null values are more than the non-null pointers. The number of left and right leaf nodes has number of null pointer fields in such a representation. These null pointer fields are used to keep some other information for operations of binary tree. The null pointer fields are to be used for storing the address fields of higher nodes in tree, which is called thread. Threaded binary tree is the one in which we find these types of pointers from null pointer fields to higher nodes in a binary tree. Consider the following tree:

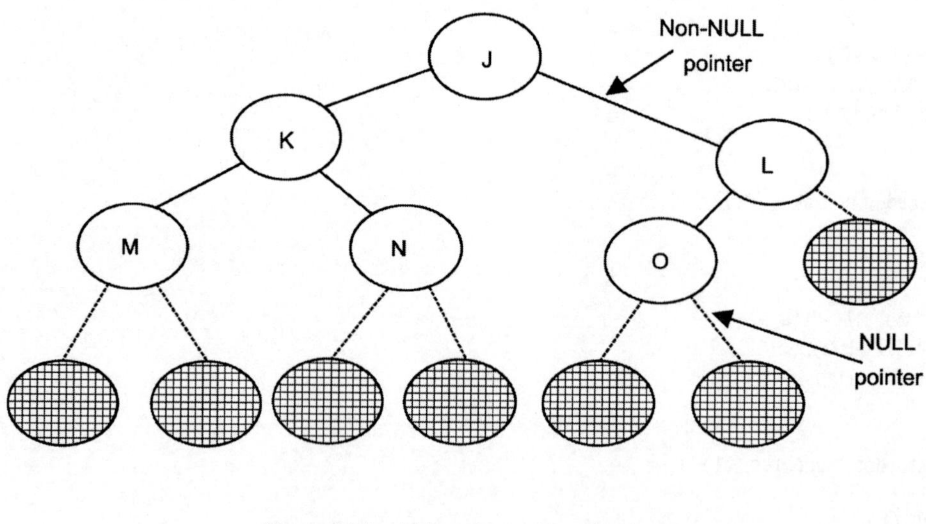

Figure 8.34 A binary tree with null pointers

In Fig. 8.34, in the binary tree there are 7 null pointers. These are shown with the dotted lines. There are total 12 node pointers out of which 5 are actual node pointers, i.e. non-null pointer (solid lines). For any binary tree having n nodes there will be (n+1) null pointers and 2n total pointers. All the null pointers can be replaced with appropriate pointer value known as thread. The binary tree can be threaded according to appropriate traversal method. The null pointer can be replaced as follows:

Threaded binary tree can be traversed by any one of the three traversals, i.e. preorder, postorder and inorder. Further, in inorder threading there may be one-way inorder threading or two–way inorder threading. In one way inorder threading the right child of the node would point to the next node in the sequence of the inorder traversal. Such a threading tree is called right in threaded binary tree. Also, the left child of the node would point to the previous node in the sequence of inorder traversal. This type of tree is called as left in threaded binary tree. In case both the children of the nodes point to other nodes then such a tree is called as fully threaded binary tree.

Fig. 8.35 describes the working of right in threaded binary tree in which one can see that the right child of the node points to the node in the sequence of the inorder traversal method.

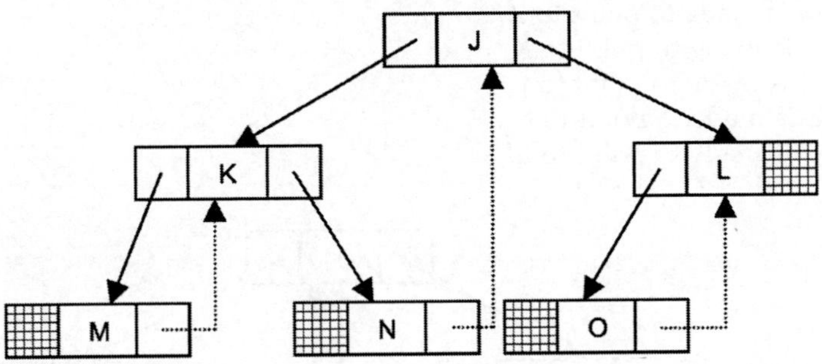

Figure 8.35 Right in threaded binary tree

The inorder traversal shown in the Fig. 8.35 will be as M-K-N-J-O-L. Two dangling pointers are shown to point a header node as shown below:

- rchild of M is made to point to K
- rchild of N is made to point to J
- rchild of O is made to point to L.

Similarly, the working of the left in binary threaded tree is illustrated in Fig. 8.36. In this case the left child of node points to the previous node in the sequence of inorder traversal.

As shown in Fig. 8.36, thread of N points to K. Here, K is the predecessor of N in inorder traversal. Hence, the pointer points to K. In this type of tree the pointers pointing to other nodes are as follows:

- lchild of N is made to point to K
- lchild of O is made to point to J.

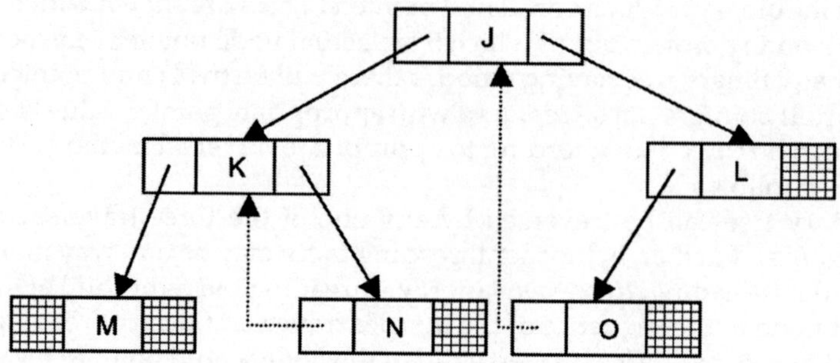

Figure 8.36 Left in threaded binary tree

Fig. 8.37 illustrates the operation of fully threaded binary tree. Right and left children are used for pointing to the nodes in inorder traversal method.

- rchild of M is made to point to K
- lchild of N is made to point to K
- rchild of N is made to point to J
- lchild of O is made to point to J
- rchild of O is made to point to L.

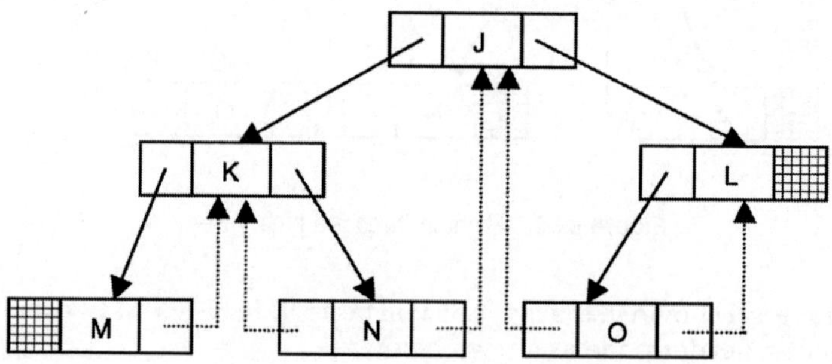

Figure 8.37 Fully threaded binary tree

Fully threaded binary tree with header is described in Fig. 8.38.

rchild of M is made to point to K
lchild of M is made to point to Header
lchild of N is made to point to K
rchild of N is made to point to J
lchild of O is made to point to J
rchild of O is made to point to L
rchild of L is made to point to Header.

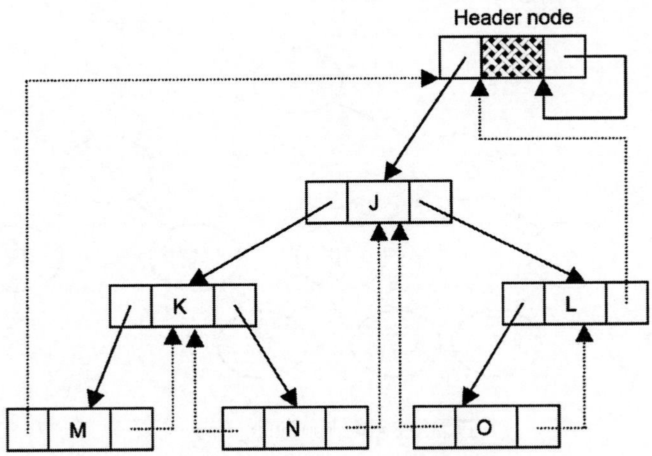

Figure 8.38 Fully threaded tree with header

The working of the fully threaded binary tree is illustrated in Fig. 8.38. In this case the left child of node points to the previous node in the sequence of inorder traversal and right child of the node points to the successor node in the inorder traversal of the node. In the previous two methods left and right pointers of the first and last node in the inorder list are NULL. But in this method the left pointer of the first node points to the header node and the right pointer of the last node points to the header node. The header node's right pointer points to itself, and the left pointer points to the root node of the tree. The use of the header is to store the starting address of the tree. In the fully threaded binary thread each and every pointer points to the other nodes. In this tree we do not find any NULL pointers.

In the Fig. 8.38 the first node in the inorder is M and its left pointer points to the left pointer of the header node. Similarly, the last node in the inorder is L and its right pointer points to the left pointer of the header.

In memory representation of threaded binary tree, it is very important to consider the difference between thread and normal pointer. The threaded binary tree node is represented in Fig. 8.39.

LTHREAD	DATA	RTHREAD

Figure 8.39 Representation of the node

Each node of any binary tree stores the three fields. The left field stores the left thread value and the right field stores the right thread value. The middle field contains the actual value of the node, i.e. data.

8.13 HEIGHT-BALANCED TREE

The efficiency of searching process in binary tree depends upon the method in which the data is organised. A binary tree is said to be completely balanced binary tree if all its leaves present at nodes of level h or h-1 and all its nodes at level less than h-1 contain two children.

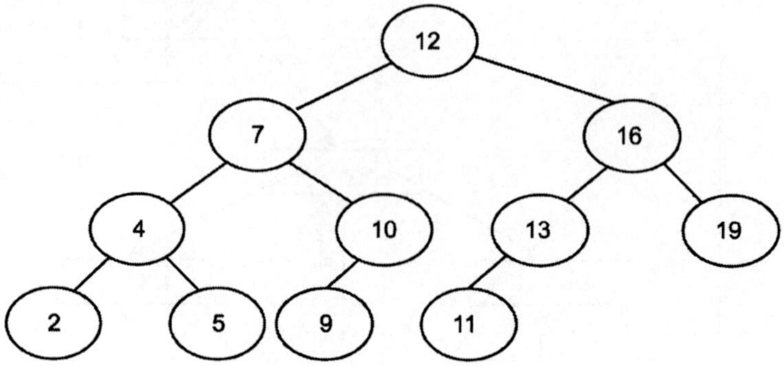

Figure 8.40 Full binary tree

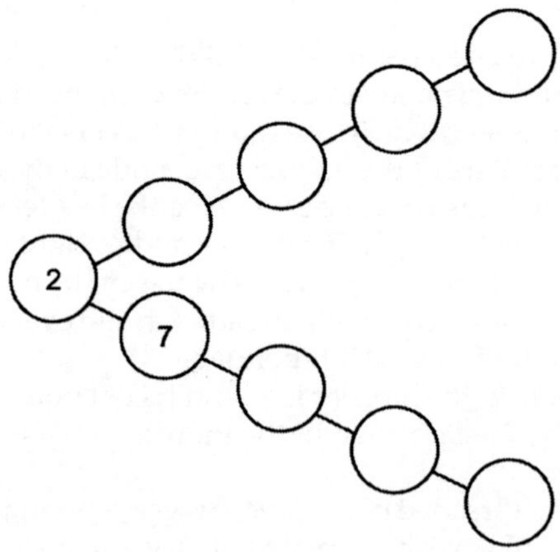

Figure 8.41 A degenerate binary tree

A tree is height balanced tree when each node in the left sub-tree varies from right sub-tree by not more than one.

A nearly height balanced tree is called an AVL. This form of tree is studied and defined by Russian mathematician G.M. Adel'son-Velskii and E.M. Landis in 1962.

We can conclude number of nodes might be present in a balanced tree having height h. At level one there is only one node, i.e. root. In every successive level the number of nodes increases i.e. 2 nodes at level 2, 4 nodes at level 3, and so on. There will be 2^{1-1} nodes at level 1. Thus, we can calculate total number of nodes from level 1 through level h-1 will be $1+2+2^2+2^3+.....+2^{h-2} = 2^{h-1} - 1$. The number of nodes at level h may be from 1 to 2h-1 nodes. The total number of nodes (n) of tree range from 2h-1 to 2h-1 or (2h-1-1+1).

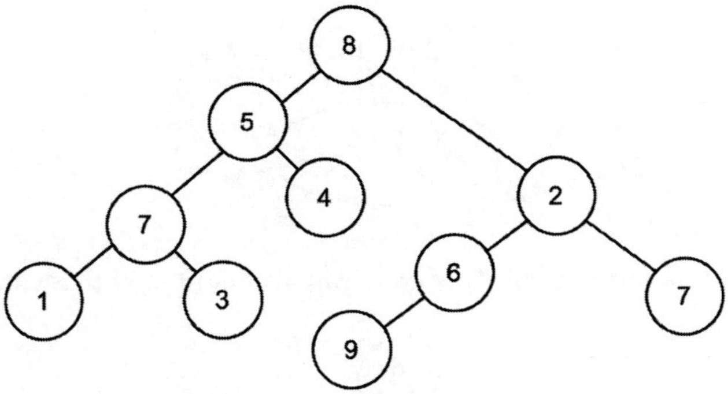

Figure 8.42 Completely balanced tree

An AVL tree should satisfy the following rules:

1. A node is known as left heavy if the longest path in its left child (left sub-tree) is longer than the longest path in right sub-tree.
2. A node is known as right heavy if the longest path in its right sub-tree is longer than left sub-tree.
3. A node is known as balanced if the longest path in left and right sub-trees are identical.

8.14 B-TREE (BALANCED MULTI-WAY TREE)

Binary search tree is, in general called multi-way search tree. The integer m is called the order of the tree. Each node should have maximum m children. If k ≤ m, where m is number of children, then node has accurately k-1 keys which divides all the keys into k number of sets. In case some sets are empty, the children are also empty.

The B-tree is also known as the balanced sort tree. The B-tree is used in external sorting. The B-tree is not a binary tree. While implementing B-tree following conditions are followed:

1. The height of the tree must be minimum.
2. There should be no empty sub-trees after the leaves of the tree.
3. The leaves of the tree should be at the same level.
4. All nodes excepting the leaves should have at least few children.

8.14.1 B-Tree Insertion

In B-tree insertion at first search is made where the new element is to be placed. If the node is suitable to the given element then insertion is straightforward. The element is inserted by using an appropriate pointer in such an order that number of pointers will be one more than the number of records. In case, the node overflows due to upper bound of node, splitting is mandatory. The node is divided into three parts. The middle part is passed upward. It will be inserted into the parent. Partition may spread the tree. This is because the parent into which element is to be inserted spilts into its child nodes. If the root is needed to be split, a new root is created with two children. The tree grows by one level.

Example: Consider the following B-tree of degree 4. It can be balanced in four ways. Here, each node holds elements. It also has four branches. Suppose, it has the following values:

1 5 6 2 8 11 13 18 20 7 9

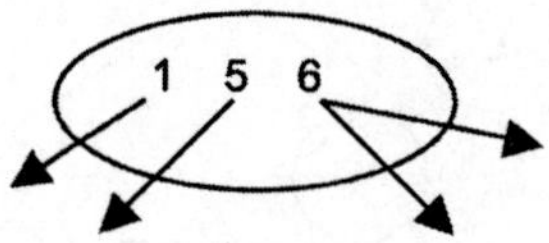

The value 1 is put in a new node. This node can also hold next two values.

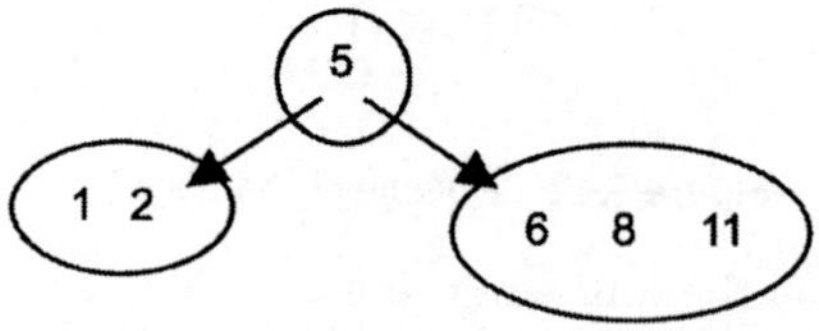

When value 2 (4th value) is put, the node is split at 5 into leaf nodes. Here, 5 is parent. The element 8 is added in leaf node. The search for its accurate position is done in the node having value 6. The element 8 also is present in the same node.

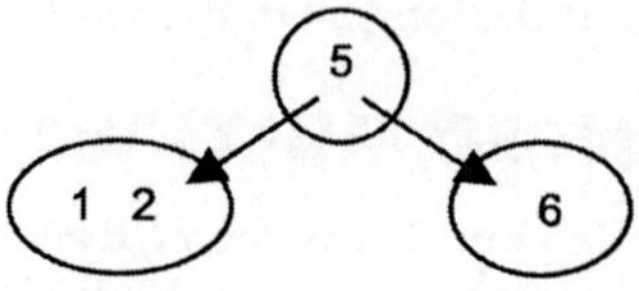

The element 13 is to be inserted. However, the right leaf node, in which 1 to 3 values have appropriate plane, is occupied. Hence, the node splits at median 8 and this moves it up to the parent.

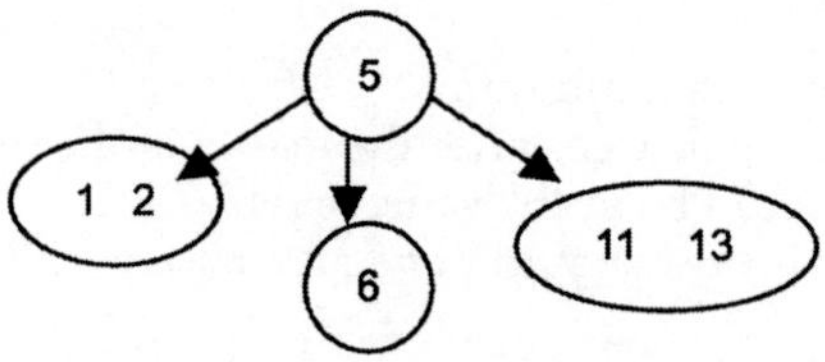

By following the above procedure the remaining nodes can be included. The final figure would be as follows:

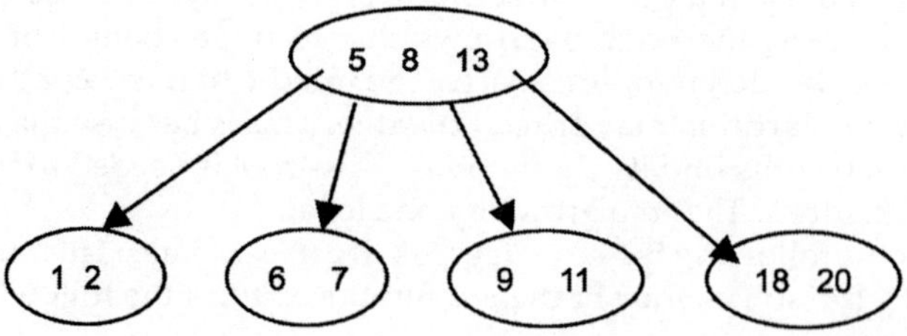

8.14.2 B-Tree Deletion

In B-Tree deletion the element which is to be deleted is searched. In case the element is terminal node, the deletion process is straightforward. The element with a suitable pointer is deleted.

If the element fixed for deletion is not a terminal node, it is replaced by its successor element. Actually, a copy of successor is taken. The successor is an element with higher value. The successor of any node which is not at lowest level, be a terminal node. Thus, deletion is nothing but removing of a particular element or record from a terminal node. While deleting the record the new node size is more than minimum, i.e. the deletion is complete. If the node size is less than minimum, an underflow happens.

Rearrangement is done if either of adjacent siblings has more than the minimum elements (records). For rearrangement, the contents of the node (only those nodes having less than minimum records) along with sorting out records from parent node are gathered. The central record is written back to the parent and left and right halves are written back to two siblings.

Concatenation is applied if the node with less than minimum number of records has no adjacent sibling. The node is combined with its neighbouring sibling and element is moved from its parent.

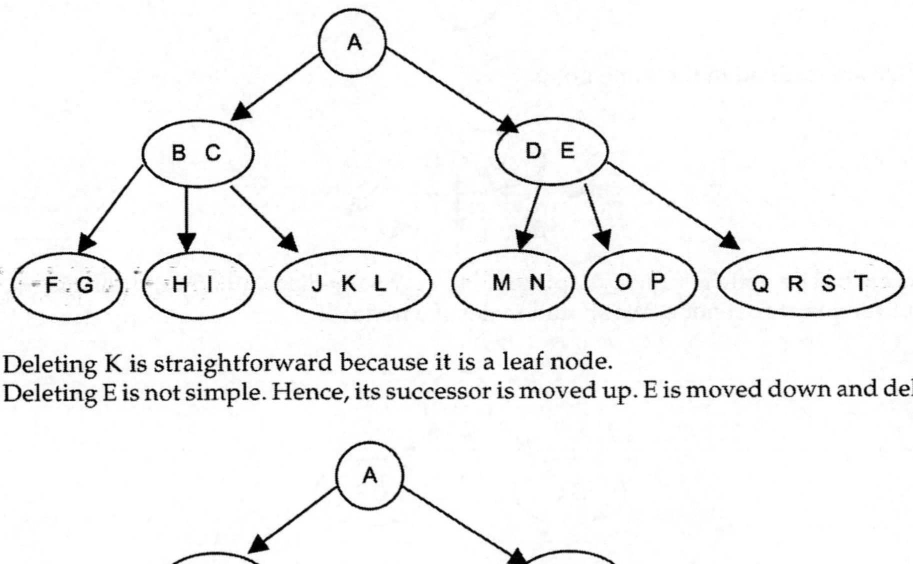

1. Deleting K is straightforward because it is a leaf node.
2. Deleting E is not simple. Hence, its successor is moved up. E is moved down and deleted.

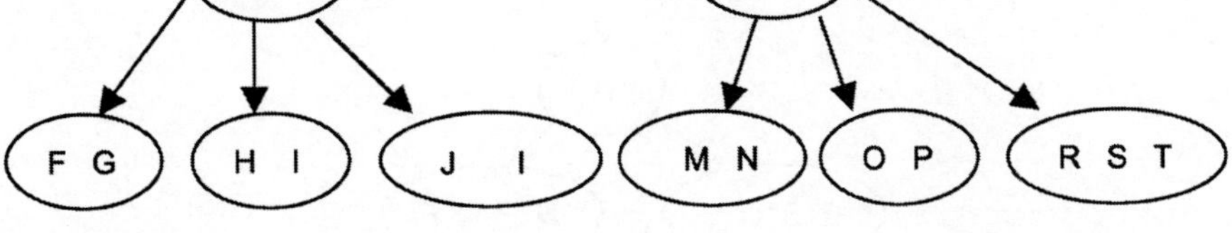

3. To delete P, the node has less than minimum numbers of keys. The sibling is carried. R moves up and Q moves down.

4. Deleting H, again node has less than minimum keys than required. The parent is left with only one key. Here, sibling cannot be applied. Hence, A, C, D and R form a new node.

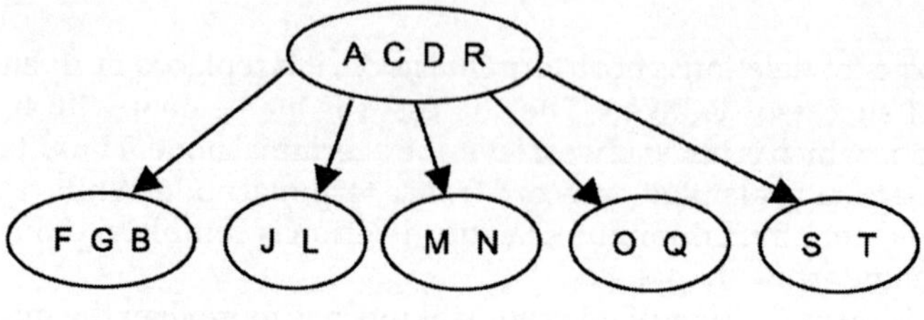

8.15 B-TREE OF ORDER 5

We can build a B-tree of order 5.

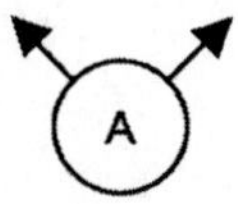

1. CDF are inserted in the same node.

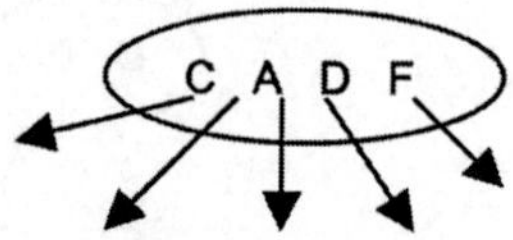

2. Insert B. The node is full. It is splitted. Here, A is median in BCADF. A is parent. The splitting is at root node. We should make one node.

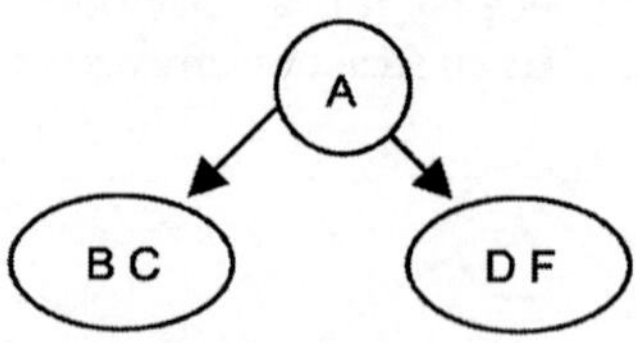

3. Again, insert P, Q, R, S.

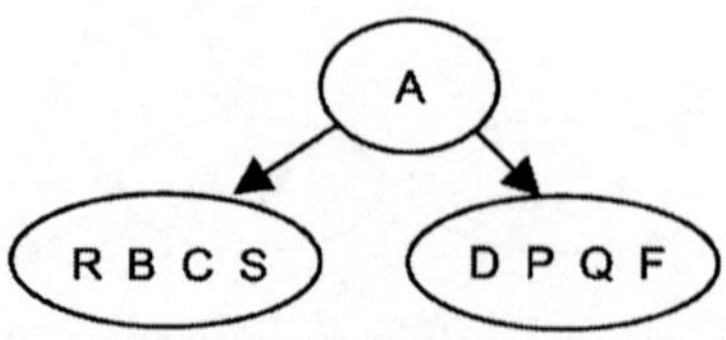

4. E can be added in DPQF and here Q is median.

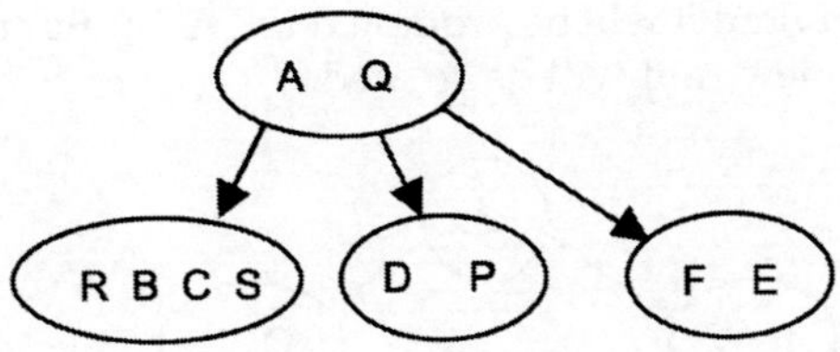

5. X and Y are entered after Q.

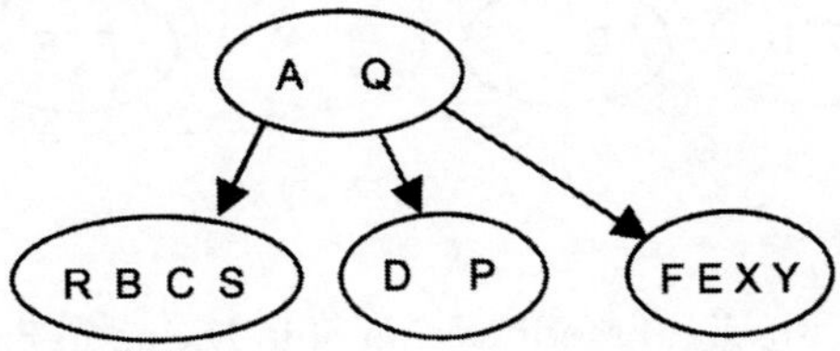

6. After addition of T.

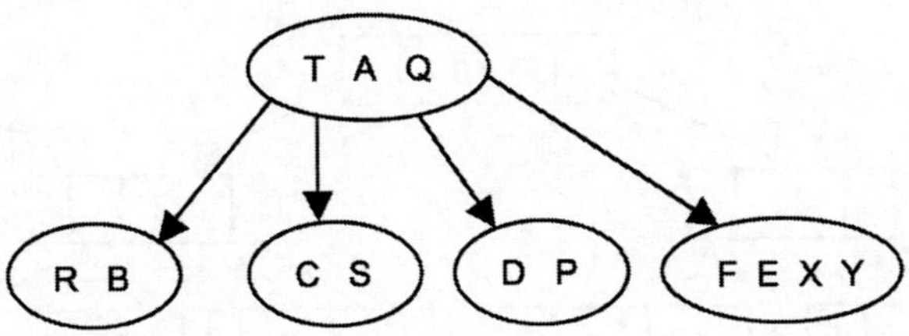

7. J, K are inserted.

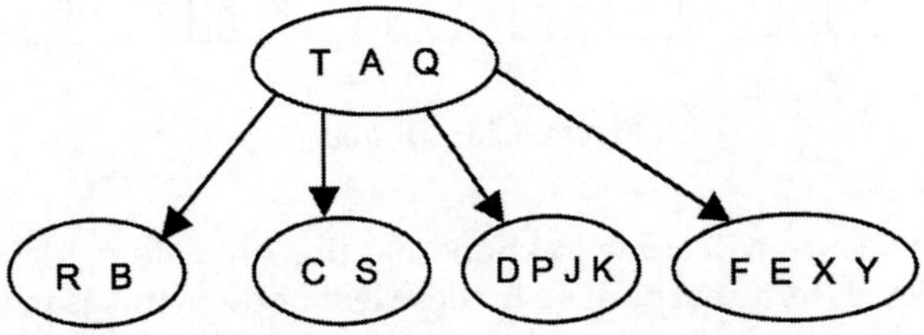

8. L can be added FEXY and X will be median.

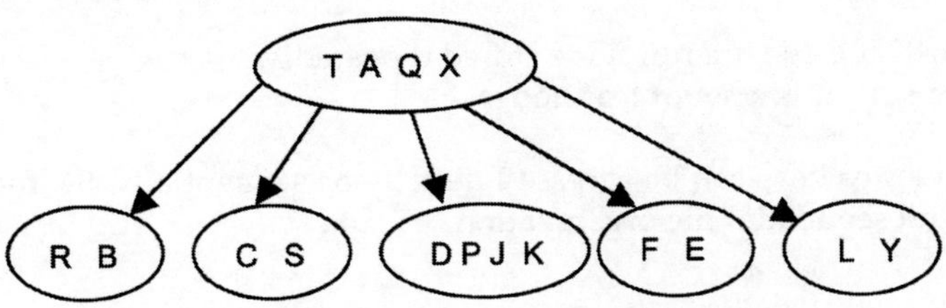

9. Z can be placed in DPJK and it will be promoted to TAQX. But this is also full and hence, the root will split and new root will be created.

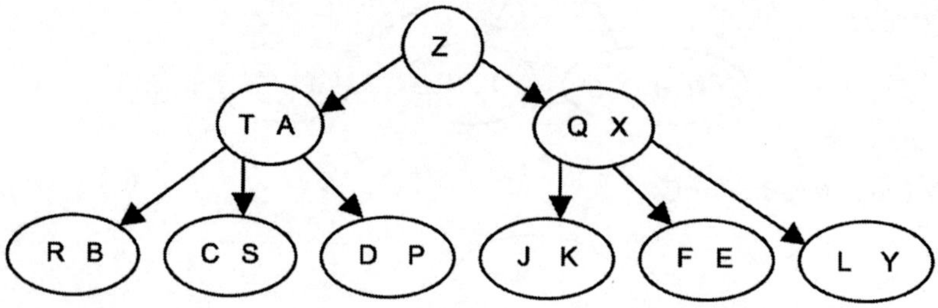

8.16 B+ TREE

A B+ tree can be obtained with slight modification of indexing in B tree. A B+ tree stores key values repeatedly. Fig. 8.43 shows B+ tree indexing.

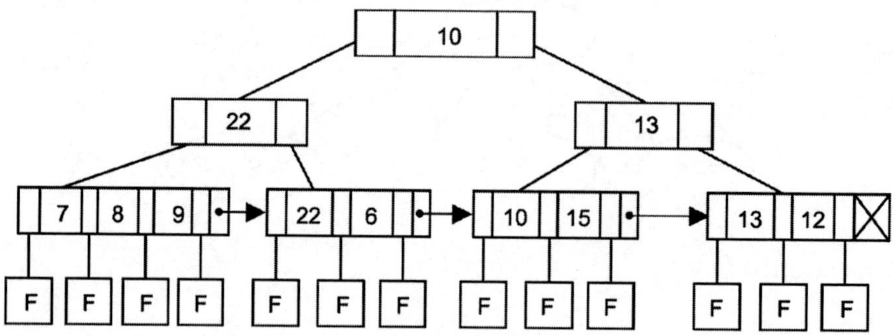

Figure 8.43 B+ tree

By observing Fig. 8.43, we will come to know that the key values 10, 22 and 13 are stored repeatedly in the last level (terminal nodes). In these leaf nodes a link is maintained so that the traversing can be done from the leaf node at the extreme left to the leaf node at the extreme right. B tree and B+ tree are same except the above differences.

Every leaf node of B+ tree has two parts:

1. **Index part** It is the interior node stored repeatedly.
2. **Sequence set** It is a set of leaf nodes.

The interior nodes or keys can be accessed directly or sequentially. B+ tree is useful data structure in indexed sequential file organization.

Exercises

A. Answer the following questions:

1. Explain trees and binary trees.
2. Give the properties of binary tree.
3. Explain the various types of binary trees.
4. Define the following terminologies of tree:
   (a) Height (b) Degree of a node (c) Siblings (d) Terminal node.
5. How are binary trees represented?
6. Give the working of binary trees.
7. What is meant by traversing? List the methods of node traversing. Explain briefly.
8. What are the differences between tree and graph?
9. What is binary search tree? How is an element searched?
10. Explain the procedure of insertion and deletion of data with binary search tree.

B. Select the appropriate option for each of the following questions:

1. Traversing means
   a. visiting all the nodes of the list
   b. shifting all the nodes at forward
   c. randomly accessing the elements
   d. none of the above.
2. Every tree structure must contain
   a. root node
   b. either left right branch with root node
   c. both left and right branches with root
   d. all of the above.
3. When every no-leaf node in binary tree has filled left and right sub-trees, the tree is called
   a. strictly binary tree
   b. complete binary tree
   c. binary search tree
   d. none of the above.
4. The last node of this binary tree contains two branches. Such a tree is called
   a. strictly binary tree
   b. complete binary tree
   c. extended binary tree
   d. none of the above.
5. The following sequence of the traversing is called
   Go to the root
   Traverse the left sub-tree
   Traverse the right sub-trees
   a. inorder
   b. postorder
   c. preorder
   d. pre-postorder.
6. The following sequence of the traversing is called
   Traverse the left sub tree in inorder
   Visit root node.
   Traverse the right sub tree in inorder.
   a. inorder
   b. postorder
   c. preorder
   d. pre-postorder.
7. The following sequence of the traversing is called
   Traversing the left sub-tree in postorder style.
   Traverse the right sub tree in postorder.

Visit the root node (N).

a. inorder
b. postorder
c. preorder
d. pre-postorder.

8. The tree given below is called as
   a. complete tree
   b. left-skewed binary tree
   c. right-skewed binary tree
   d. none of above.

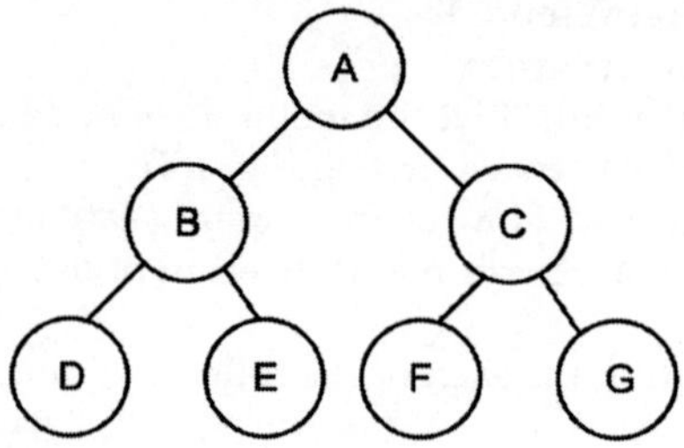

Consider the above figure for the following questions:

9. The tree contains ________level(s).
   a. one
   b. zero
   c. two
   d. none of the above.
10. Degree of the B node is
    a. one
    b. two
    c. three
    d. none of the above.
11. Height of the tree is
    a. two
    b. three
    c. four
    d. none of the above.
12. Siblings of B are
    a. F and G
    b. D and E
    c. A and C
    d. none of the above.
13. If root node 'A' is deleted then the left sub tree contains the elements
    a. C, F, and G
    b. B, D, and E
    c. A, B, and C
    d. none of the above.

C. Attempt the following programs:

1. Write a program to create tree structure, perform insert and delete operations.
2. Write a program to traverse the binary search tree with different traversal methods such as inorder, preorder and postorder.
3. Construct binary tree for the following data:
   Inorder: F E A C D G H B I
   Postorder: E F C D H I B G A
4. Construct the binary tree for the following:
   1.
   Inorder: 3 5 6 8 12 15 18 19
   Preorder: 12 5 3 6 8 18 15 19
   Postorder: 3 8 6 5 15 19 18 12

2.
Preorder: A E F D J H I G B C
Inorder: F E A H J I D B G C
3.
Inorder: 1 3 4 5 6 7 9 12
Postorder: 3 5 4 1 7 12 9 6

5. Determine the preorder, inorder and postorder of the following trees:

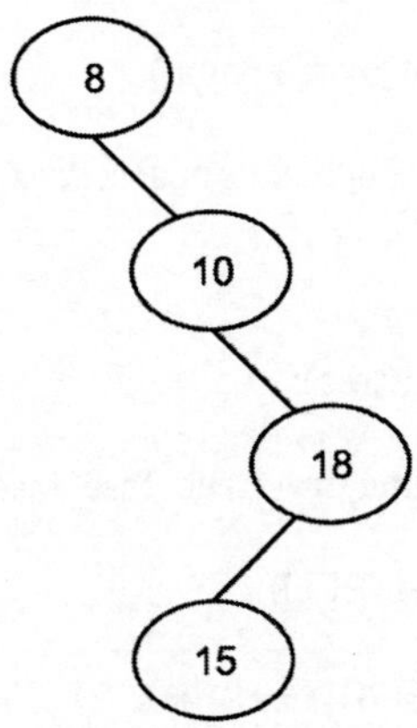

(1)

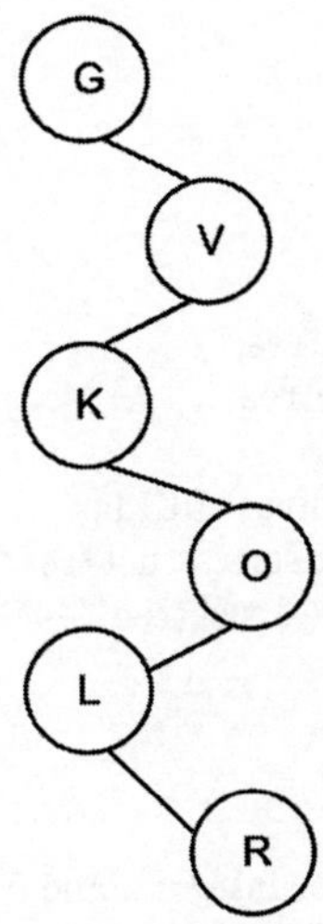

(2)

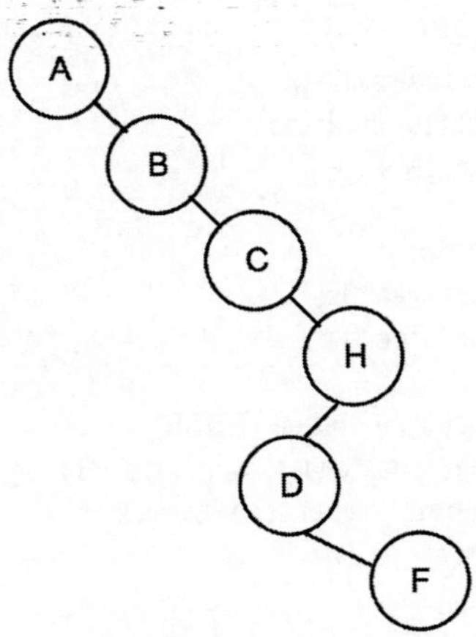

(3)

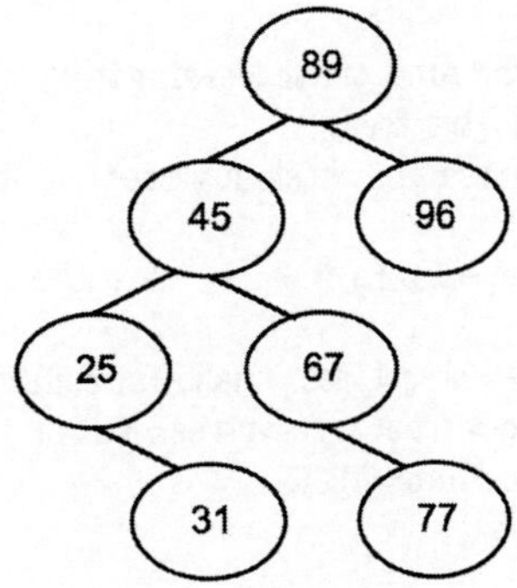

(4)

6. Write a C program to insert nodes into a binary tree and traverse them in preorder.
7. Write a program for finding the height of the tree.

8. Write a program to display all the nodes of the binary search tree and then insert data and display it along with the previous data of the tree.
9. Write a C program to search an element from the binary search tree.
10. Write a program for implementing binary tree traversal.

D. What is the output of each of the following programs?

1.

```
#include<stdio.h>
#include<conio.h>
struct tree
{
long num;
struct tree *ltree;
struct tree *rtree;
};
struct tree *btree=NULL;
struct tree *insert(struct tree*tree,long digit);
void func_trv(struct tree*tree);
main()
{
long digit;
clrscr();
   puts("Enter integers: and 0 to quit");
   scanf("%ld",&digit);
   while(digit!=0)
   {
   tree= insert(tree,digit);
   scanf("%d",&digit);
   }
   puts("func_trv traversing tree:\n");
   func_trv(tree);
struct tree*insert(struct tree*tree,long digit)
{
if(tree==NULL)
{
   tree=(struct tree*)malloc(sizeof(struct tree));
   tree->ltree=tree->rtree=NULL;
   tree->num=digit;
}
else
{
if(digit<tree->num)
tree->ltree=insert(tree->ltree,digit);
else
if(digit>tree->num)
tree->rtree=insert(tree->rtree,digit);
else
if(digit==tree->num)
{
puts("Duplicates nodes: Program exited");
exit(0);
}
}
return(tree);
}
void func_trv(struct tree*tree)
{
if(tree!=NULL)
{
func_trv(tree->ltree);
printf("%4ld",tree->num);
func_trv(tree->rtree);
}
}
```

2.

```
#include<stdio.h>
#include<conio.h>
struct tree
{
long no;
struct tree *ls;
struct tree *rs;
};
struct tree *btree=NULL;
struct tree *creat(struct tree*btree,long ele);
void fun1(struct tree*btree);
main()
{
long ele;
clrscr();
   puts("Enter integers: and 0 to quit");
   scanf("%ld",&ele);
   while(ele!=0)
```

```
    {
    btree= creat(btree,ele);
    scanf("%d",&ele);
    }
    puts("traversing by fun1 tree:\n");
    fun1(btree);
    }
struct tree*creat(struct tree*btree,long ele)
{
if(btree==NULL)
{
btree=(struct tree*) malloc(sizeof(struct tree));
btree->ls=btree->rs=NULL;
btree->no=ele;
}
else
{
if(ele<btree->no)
btree->ls=creat(btree->ls,ele);
else
if(ele>btree->no)
btree->rs=creat(btree->rs,ele);
else
if(ele==btree->no)
{
puts("Duplicates nodes: Program exited");
exit(0);
}
}
return(btree);
}

void fun1(struct tree*btree)
{
if(btree!=NULL)
{
printf("%4ld",btree->no);
fun1(btree->ls);
fun1(btree->rs);
}
}
```

3.

```
#include<stdio.h>
#include<conio.h>
struct tree
{
long data;
struct tree *left;
struct tree *right;
};
struct tree *bt=NULL;
struct tree *insert(struct tree*bt,long no);
void fun_t(struct tree*bt);
main()
{
long no;
clrscr();
    puts("Enter integers: and 0 to quit");
    scanf("%ld",&no);
    while(no!=0)
    {
    bt= insert(bt,no);
    scanf("%d",&no);
    }
    puts("traversing btree by fun_t:\n");
    fun_t(bt);
}
struct tree*insert(struct tree*bt,long no)
{
if(bt==NULL)
{
bt=(struct tree*) malloc(sizeof(struct tree));
bt->left=bt->right=NULL;
bt->data=no;
}
else
{
if(no<bt->data)
bt->left=insert(bt->left,no);
else
if(no>bt->data)
bt->right=insert(bt->right,no);
else
if(no==bt->data)
{
puts("Duplicates nodes: Program exited");
exit(0);
}
}
return(bt);
}
void fun_t(struct tree*bt)
{
```

```
if(bt!=NULL)
{
fun_t(bt->left);
fun_t(bt->right);
printf("%4ld",bt->data);
}
}
```

4.

```
#include<stdio.h>
#include<conio.h>
struct tree
{
long data;
struct tree *left;
struct tree *right;
};

struct tree *bt=NULL;
struct tree *insert(struct tree*bt,long no);
void fun1(struct tree*bt);
void fun2(struct tree*bt);
void fun3(struct tree*bt);
main()
{
long no;
clrscr();
    puts("Enter integers: and 0 to quit");
    scanf("%ld",&no);
    while(no!=0)
    {
    bt= insert(bt,no);
    scanf("%d",&no);
    }
    puts("fun1 traversing bt:\n");
    fun1(bt);
    puts("\nfun2 traversing bt:\n");
    fun2(bt);
    puts("\nfun3 traversing bt:\n");
    fun3(bt);
}
struct tree*insert(struct tree*bt,long no)
{
if(bt==NULL)
{
bt=(struct tree*) malloc(sizeof(struct tree));
bt->left=bt->right=NULL;
bt->data=no;
}
else
{
if(no<bt->data)
bt->left=insert(bt->left,no);
else
if(no>bt->data)
bt->right=insert(bt->right,no);
else
if(no==bt->data)
{
puts("Duplicates nodes: Program exited");
exit(0);
}
}
return(bt);
}
void fun2(struct tree*bt)
{
if(bt!=NULL)
{
fun2(bt->left);
fun2(bt->right);
printf("%4ld",bt->data);
}
}
void fun1(struct tree*bt)
{
if(bt!=NULL)
{
printf("%4ld",bt->data);
fun1(bt->left);
fun1(bt->right);
}
}
void fun3(struct tree*bt)
{
if(bt!=NULL)
{
fun3(bt->left);
printf("%4ld",bt->data);
fun3(bt->right);
}
}
```

5.

```
#include<stdio.h>
#include<conio.h>
struct tree
{
long num;
struct tree *left;
struct tree *right;
};
int sn;
struct tree *bt=NULL;
struct tree *place(struct tree*bt,long digit);
void fun_s(struct tree *bt, long sn);
main()
{
long digit;
clrscr();
    puts("Enter the nodes of tree in preorder:
    and 0 to quit");
    scanf("%ld",&digit);
    while(digit!=0)
    {
    bt= place(bt,digit);
    scanf("%d",&digit);
    }
    printf("\nEnter the number:-");
    scanf("%d",&sn);
    fun_s(bt,sn);
}

struct tree*place(struct tree*bt,long digit)
{
if(bt==NULL)
{
bt=(struct tree*) malloc(sizeof(struct tree));
bt->left=bt->right=NULL;
bt->num=digit;
}
else
{
if(digit<bt->num)
bt->left=place(bt->left,digit);
else
if(digit>bt->num)
bt->right=place(bt->right,digit);
else
if(digit==bt->num)
{
puts("Duplicates nodes: Program exited");
exit(0);
}
}
return(bt);
}
void fun_s(struct tree*bt, long sno)
{
if(bt==NULL)
puts("Number does not found");
else
if(sno==bt->num)
printf("Number %d is found",sno);
else
if(sno<bt->num)
fun_s(bt->left,sno);
else
fun_s(bt->right, sno);
}
```

Chapter 9

Graph

Chapter Outline

9.1 INTRODUCTION

Graphs are frequently used in every walk of life. Every day we come across various kinds of graphs appearing in newspapers or television. The countries in a globe are seen in a map. A map depends on the geographic location of the places or cities. As such, a map is a well-known example of a graph. In the map, various connections are shown between the cities. The cities are connected via roads, rail or aerial network. How to reach a place is indicated by means of a graph. Using the various types of the links the maps can be shown.

Fig. 9.1 illustrates a graph that contains the cities of India connected by means of road. Assume that the graph is the interconnection of cities by roads. As per the graph, Mumbai, Hyderabad and Kolkata are directly connected to all the other cities by road. Delhi is directly connected to Mumbai, Hyderabad, and Kolkata. Delhi is connected to Chennai via Hyderabad.

Generally, we provide the address of our office/residence to a stranger who is not aware of our address and location of city. At this juncture we use the graph for the easiest representation of our residential location. Fig. 9.2 shows the location of place by graph. By using the graph any stranger can easily find location. For example, a pilgrim wishes to reach the Gurudwara in Nanded. The path is shown in the figure for reaching the Gurudwara. The devotee has to reach the destination via Shivaji statue, Mahatma Gandhi statue and then Gurudwara as per the graph. Once a map is provided, any stranger can reach any destination by using appropriate conveyance.

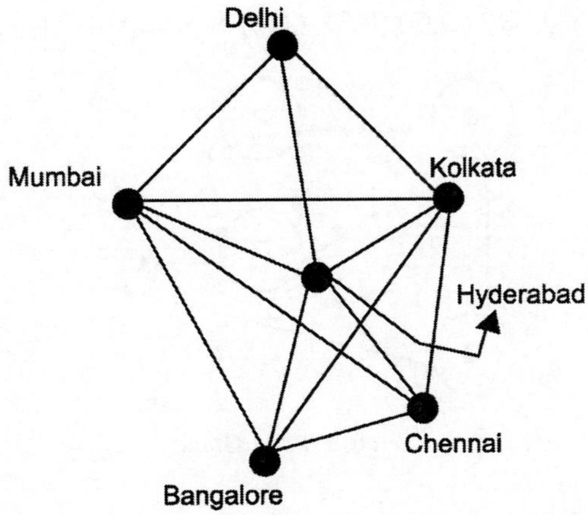

Figure 9.1 Map representation of connection of cities

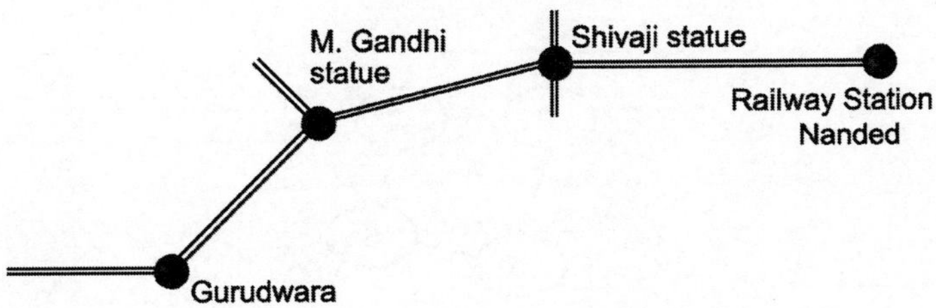

Figure 9.2 Representation of a map

In Fig. 9.2, four places are connected by road links. In the graph the road links are called as edges and the places are called as vertices. The graph is a collection of the vertices and the edges, hence a map is treated as graph. The following section describes the graph and relevant theories.

Like tree, graphs are nonlinear data structures. Tree nodes are arranged hierarchically from top to bottom like a parent is placed at the top and child as successor at the lower level. Tree has some specific structure whereas graph does not have a specific structure. It varies from application to application.

9.2 GRAPH

A graph is set of nodes and arcs. The nodes are also termed as *vertices* and *arcs* are termed as *edges*. The set of nodes as per the Fig. 9.3 is denoted as {O, P, R, S, Q}. The set of arcs in the following graph are {(O,P), (O,R), (O,Q), (R,S), (Q,S)}. Graph can be represented as,

G= (V,E) and V(G)= (O, Q, P, R, S) or group of vertices.

Similarly, E(G)= ((O,P), (O,R), (O,Q),(R,S),(Q,S)) or group of edges.

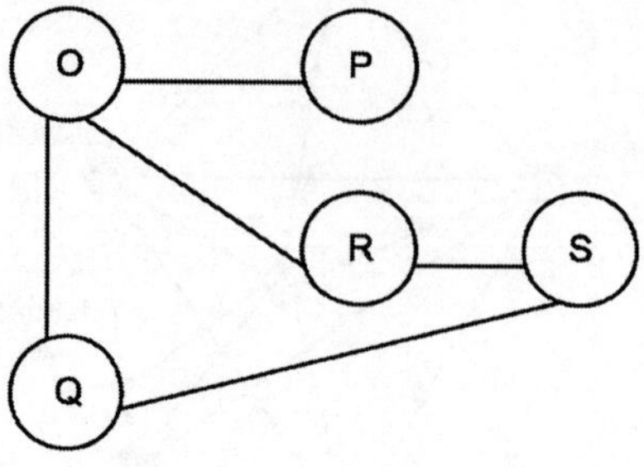

Figure 9.3 Graph

A graph is linked if there is pathway between any two nodes of the graph, such a graph is called *connected graph* or else, it is *non-connected graph.* Fig. 9.4 and 9.5 are connected and non-connected graphs, respectively. In both the figures four nodes are depicted. In the latter all the nodes are not connected by links whereas in the former case all the nodes are joined by paths or links.

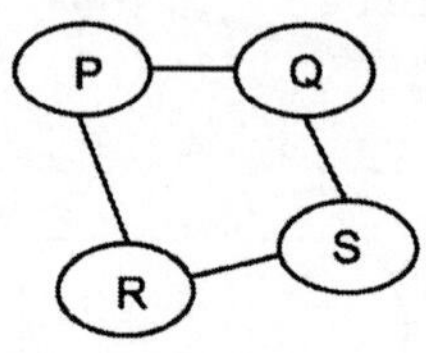

Figure 9.4 Connected graph

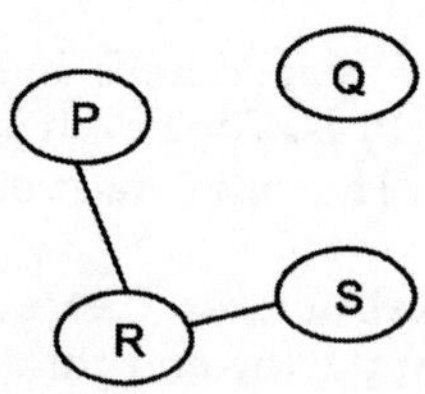

Figure 9.5 Non-connected graph

Undirected Graph A graph containing unordered pair of nodes is termed as *undirected graph.*

The vertices are {A, B, C, D} and edges are {(A, B), (A, D), (A, C), (B, D), (B, C), (D, C)}. The graph has four nodes and six edges. This type of graph is known as completely connected network, in which every node is having out going path to all nodes in the network. For a complete network the number of links =N (N–1)/2, where N is the number of vertices or nodes. In the Fig. 9.6 N is 4. By substituting its value the number of edges obtained will be equal to 6.

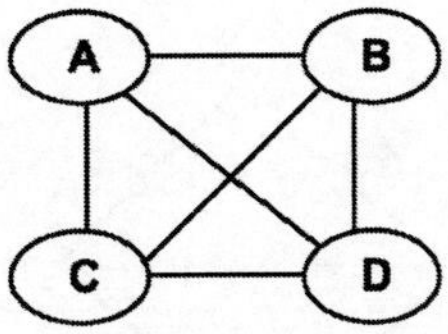

Figure 9.6 Undirected graph

Directed Graph This kind of graph contains ordered pairs of vertices. For example, graph vertices are {A,B,C,D,E} and edges are {(A,B),(B,D),(C,D)(C,A), (C,E), (E, A) }. Fig. 9.7 represents a graph having five nodes and six edges.

A direction is associated with each edge. The directed graph is also known as digraph.

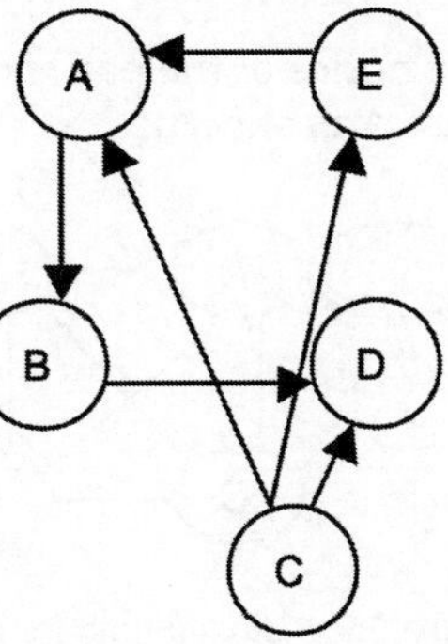

Figure 9.7 Directed graph

V(G) = {A, B, C, D, E} and
group of directed edges = {(A,B), (B,D), (C,D)(C,A), (C,E), (E, A)}.

9.3 TERMINOLOGIES OF GRAPH

Weighted Graph A graph is supposed to be weighted if its every edge is assigned some value which is greater than or equal to zero, i.e. non-negative value. The value is equal to the length between two vertices. Weighted graph is also called as network. Weighted graph is shown in Fig. 9.8.

Adjacent Nodes When there is an edge from one node to another then these nodes are called adjacent nodes.

Incidence In an undirected graph the edges v0 , v1 is incident on nodes. In a direct graph the edge v0, v1 is incident from node v0. It is incident to node v1.

Path A path from edges u_0 to node u_n is a sequence of nodes u_0, u_1,u_2, u_3...u_{n-1}, u_n. Here, u_0 is adjacent to u_1, u_1 is adjacent to u_2 and u_{n-1} is adjacent to u_n.

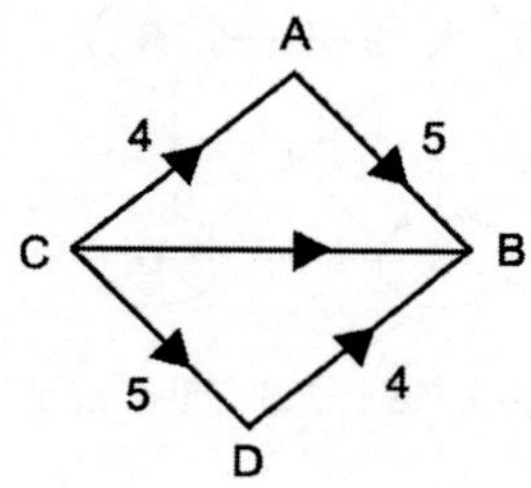

Figure 9.8 A weighted graph

Length of Path Length of path is nothing but total number of edges included in the path from source node to destination node.

Closed Path When first and last nodes of the path are same, such path is known as closed path. In Fig. 9.9 closed path at node A is shown.

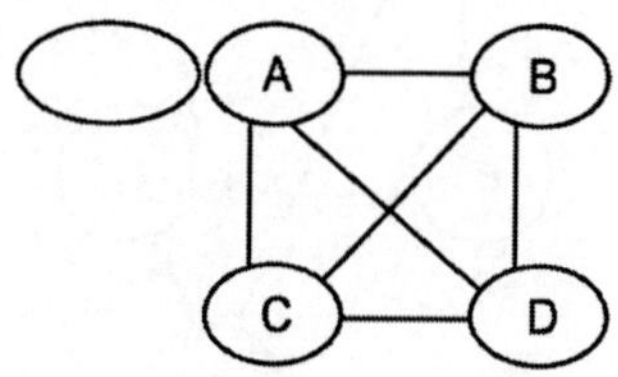

Figure 9.9 Closed path for node A

Simple Path In this path all the nodes are different with an exception that the first and last nodes of the path can be similar.

Cycle Cycle is a simple path. The first and last nodes are same. In other words, a closed simple path is a cycle. In a digraph a path is known as cycle if it has one or more nodes. The starting node is connected to the last node. In an undirected graph a path is called cycle if it has at least three nodes. The starting node is connected to last node. In the following figure path ACDBA is a closed path. Example of a cycle is shown in Fig. 9.10.

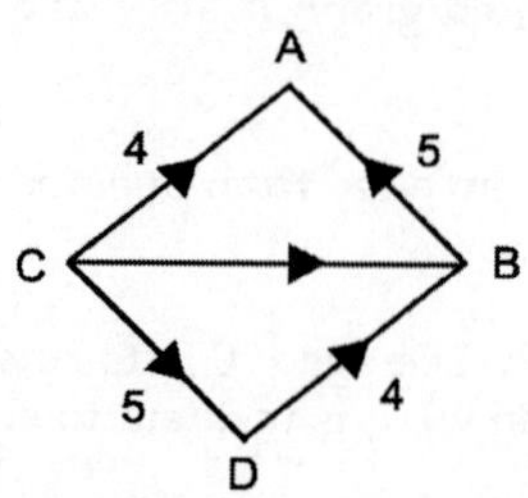

Figure 9.10 Example of a cycle

Cycle Graph A graph having cycle is called cycle graph. In this case the first and last nodes are the same. A closed simple path is a cycle. This is same as closed path shown in Fig. 9.10.

Acyclic Graph A graph without cycle is called acyclic graph. Examples of acyclic graphs are shown in Fig. 9.11.

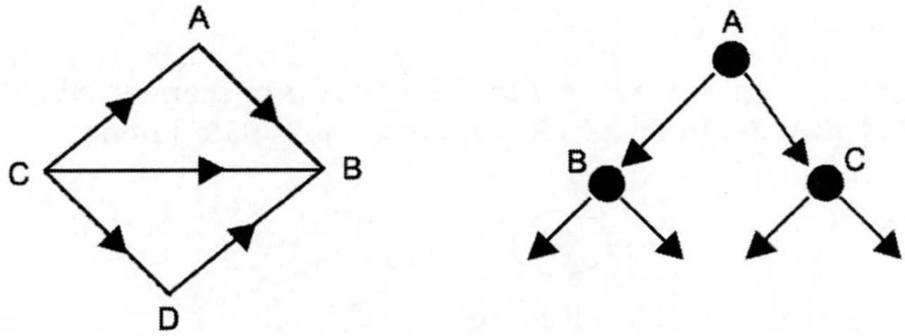

Figure 9.11 Acyclic graphs

Dag A directed acyclic graph is called dag after its acronym (reduction). Fig. 9.12 is a graph showing the dag.

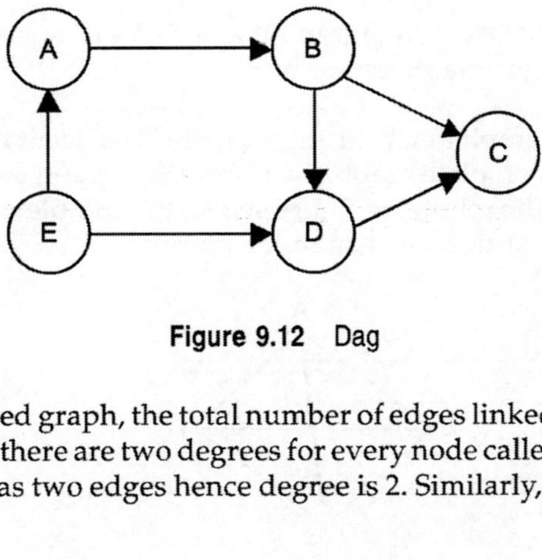

Figure 9.12 Dag

Degree In an undirected graph, the total number of edges linked to a node is called degree of that node. In a digraph there are two degrees for every node called indegree and outdegree. In the above Fig. 9.12, E has two edges hence degree is 2. Similarly, D has degree three and so on.

Indegree The indegree of a node is the total number of edges coming to that node. In Fig. 9.12, C is receiving two edges hence, the indegree is two.

Outdegree: The outdegree of a node is the total number of edges going outside from that node. In the above Fig. 9.12 the outdegree of D is one.

Source A node, which has only outgoing edges and no incoming edges, is called a source. The indegree of source is zero. In Fig. 9.12 the node E is the source since it does not have any incoming edges. It has only the outgoing edges.

Sink A node having only incoming edges and no outgoing edges is called sink node. Node C in Fig. 9.12 is a sink node because it has only incoming edges but no outgoing edges.

Pendant Node When indegree of node is one and outdegree is zero then such a node is called pendant node.

Reachable If a path exists between two nodes it will be called reachable from one node to other node.

Isolated Node When degree of node is zero, i.e. node is not connected with any other node then it is called isolated node. In Fig. 9.13 B node is the isolated node.

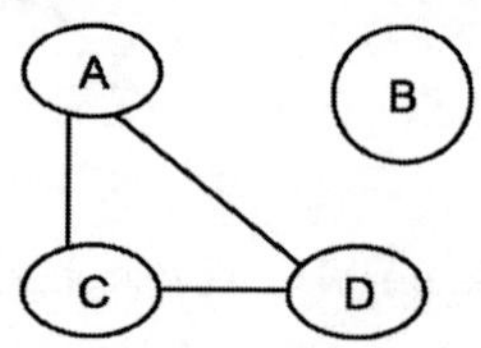

Figure 9.13 Isolated node

Successor and Predecessor In digraph if a node V_0 is adjacent to node V_1 then V_0 is the predecessor of V_1 and V_1 is the successor of V_0.

Complete Graph The graph in which any V_0 node is adjacent to all other nodes present in the graph is known as a complete graph. An undirected graph contains the edges that are equal to edges= n(n–1)/2. The following figure shows the complete graph.

The 'n' is the number of vertices present in the graph.

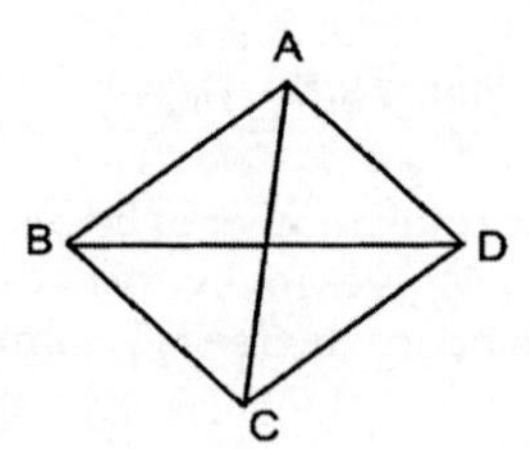

Articulation Point On removing the node the graph gets disconnected, then that node is called the articulation point.

Biconnected Graph The biconnected graph is the graph which does not contain any articulation point.

Multigraph A graph in which more than one edge is used to join the vertices is called multigraph. Edges of multigraph are parallel to each other.

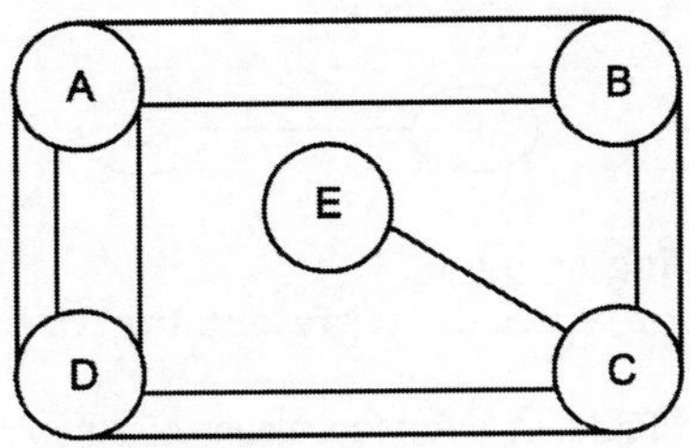

Figure 9.14 Multigraph

Fig. 9.14 shows the multigraph in which one can see the parallel edges between A and D, D and C, B and C, and A and B.

Regular Graph Regular graph is the graph in which nodes are adjacent to each other i.e. each node is accessible from any other node.

9.4 GRAPH REPRESENTATION

The graph can be implemented by linked list or array. Fig. 9.15 illustrates a graph and its representation and implementation is also described.

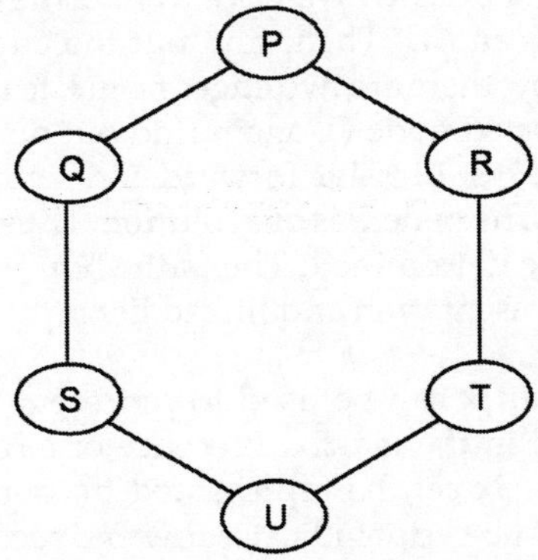

Figure 9.15 Model graph

Different possibilities of graph representations are dependent on two cases:

1. If there is no edge between two nodes.

There is no edge between nodes P and Q.

2. If there is an edge between any two nodes.

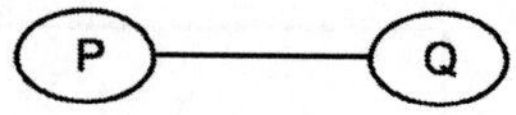

The nodes P and Q are having an edge.
Hence, following Table 9.1 provides the representation of the graph (Fig. 9.15).

Table 9.1 Representation of a graph

Nodes	*P*	*Q*	*R*	*S*	*T*	*U*
P	×	✓	✓	×	×	×
Q	✓	×	×	✓	×	×
R	✓	×	×	×	✓	×
S	×	✓	×	×	×	✓
T	×	×	✓	×	×	✓
U	×	×	×	✓	✓	×

As per the table 9.1, there is an edge in between the nodes P and Q, P and R, and there is no edge between nodes P and S. The symbol ✓ indicates existence of edge and × indicates absence of edge between two nodes.

From the above table one can predict the path to reach a particular node. For example, initial node is P and the destination node is U. We have to find the path to reach node U from P.

There is no edge between P and U. Then, find out the edge for nearest node in forward direction. By observing, we know there are two edges from P to Q and P to R. We can select either Q or R. Suppose, we have selected node Q, again find out next nearest successive node to Q by observing column Q. The next successive forward node will be S. Then, refer column S and it provides two edges Q and U. The node U is our solution. Thus, by using the above table, paths between any two nodes can be determined. The path should be P-Q-S-U. The graph can be represented by sequential representation and linked list representation.

Adjacency Matrix The matrix can be used to represent the graph. The information of adjacent nodes will be stored in the matrix. Presence of edges from a particular node can be determined easily. The matrix can be represented by two-dimensional array. In a two-dimensional array [][], the first sub-script indicates row and second, column. For example, there are five nodes in the graph then the 0th row indicates node1 and so on. Likewise, column represents node1, node2, and so on. For example, consider a two-dimensional array.

```
Nodes[j][k]
```

1 indicates presence of edge between two nodes j and k.
0 indicates absence of an edge between two nodes j and k.

Thus, the matrix will contain only 0 and 1 values.

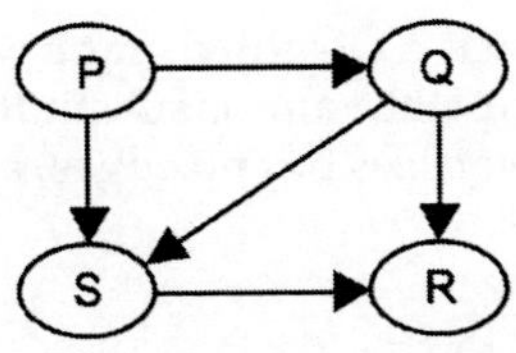

Figure 9.16 An example of graph

The matrix for the graph given in Fig. 9.16 would be

Matrix X =

	P	Q	R	S
P	0	1	0	1
Q	0	0	1	1
R	0	0	0	0
S	0	0	1	0

In the above matrix ,Mat[0][1]=1, which represents an edge between node P and Q. Entry of one in the matrix indicates that there is an edge and 0 for no edge. Thus, adjacency is maintained in the matrix X. One can also represent the undirected graph with adjacency matrix. Fig. 9.17 is an undirected graph.

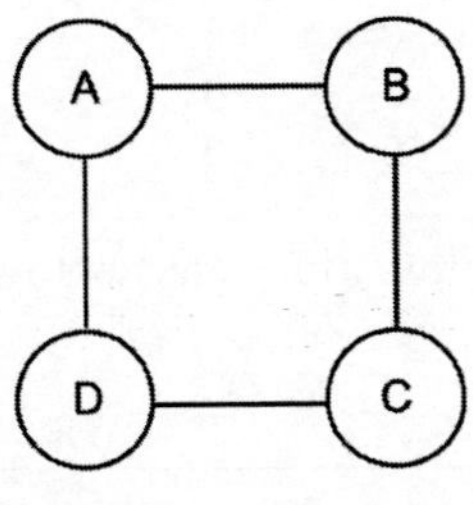

Figure 9.17 Undirected graph

The adjacency matrix for the above graph would be as follows:

Matrix X =

	A	B	C	D
A	0	1	0	1
B	1	0	1	0
C	0	1	0	1
D	1	0	1	0

The above matrix is symmetric since x[i][j]= x[j][i].

In undirected graph the sum of row elements and column elements is the same. The sum represents the degree of the node. In this matrix the sum of any row or any column is 2, which is nothing but the degree of each node is 2.

We can also represent in the same way a weighted graph with adjacency matrix. The contents of the matrix will not be only 0 and 1 but the value is substituted with the corresponding weight.

For a null graph, that contains n vertices but no edges, all the elements of such null graph in an adjacency matrix are 0.

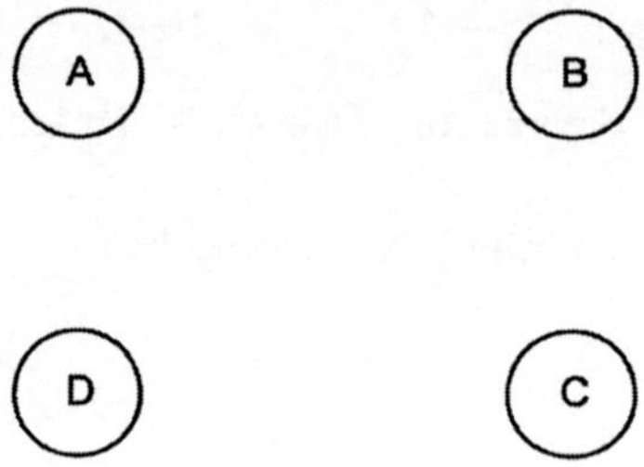

Figure 9.18 Null matrix

Fig. 9.18 represents the null graph and the adjacency matrix is as follows:

		A	B	C	D
	A	0	0	0	0
X =	B	0	0	0	0
	C	0	0	0	0
	D	0	0	0	0

A program on adjacency of a graph is illustrated below.

Example 9.1

Write a program to demonstrate adjacency of graph

Solution

```
#include <stdio.h>
#include <conio.h>

main()
{
 int me,j=1,k,beg,num, des;
 int adj[20][20]={( 0,0)};
 char g_type;
 clrscr();
 printf("\nEnter number of nodes : ");
 scanf("%d",&num);
 printf("Enter type of graph,(d)irected or (u)ndirected: ");
 g_type=getch();
```

Explanation In this program maximum edges are calculated by using formula. If the graph is directed type, the formula is *me=num*(num-1);* where, num is the total number of nodes. When the graph is undirected then the formula is *me=num*(num-1)/2.*

```
 fflush(stdin);
if(g_type=='u') me=num*(num-1)/2;
else          me=num*(num-1);
 while (j<=me)
 {
   printf("\n Enter edges %d ( 0  to exit ): ",j);
   scanf ("%d %d",&beg,&des);

   if((beg==0) && (des==0))  break;

   if ( beg > num  || des > num || beg<=0 || des<=0)
   {
      printf("Invalid edges !\n");
       j--;
   }
   else
   {
      adj[ beg ][ des ]=1;
     if( g_type== 'u')
        adj[beg][des]=1;
       if(g_type=='u')
           adj[des][beg]=1;
       }

        j++;
   }
   printf ("\n  The adjency of matrix is  : \n");

   for (j=1;j<=num;j++)
   {
      for (k=1;k<=num;k++)
      printf (" %d ",adj[j][k]);
      printf ("\n");
    }
   return 0;
}
```

```
OUTPUT
Enter number of nodes: 5
Enter type of graph,(d)irected or (u)ndirected: u
Enter edges 1 ( 0  to exit ): 1 1
Enter edges 2 ( 0  to exit ): 2 1
Enter edges 3 ( 0  to exit ): 2 2
Enter edges 4 ( 0  to exit ): 0 1
Invalid edges !
Enter edges 4 ( 0  to exit ): 1 2
Enter edges 5 ( 0  to exit ): 0 0
```

```
The adjency of matrix is:
1 1 0 0 0
1 1 0 0 0
0 0 0 0 0
0 0 0 0 0
0 0 0 0 0
```

After computing maximum edges, the user is prompted to enter edges. When 0,0 are entered the while loop is terminated. When the entered edges are greater than num and less than or equal to zero, message *"Invalid edges"* is displayed. Otherwise, adj[beg][des]=1.

9.4.1 Adjacency List

Two lists are maintained for adjacency of list. The first list is used to store information of all the nodes. The second list is used to store information of adjacent nodes for each node of a graph.

In case a graph comprises of N nodes, then two lists are to be prepared.

1. First list keeps the track of all the N nodes of a graph.
2. The second list is used to keep the information of adjacent nodes of each and every node of a graph. As such there will be N lists that would keep the information of adjacent nodes.

Header node is used to represent each list, which is assumed to be the first node of a list. Fig. 9.19 represents a header node.

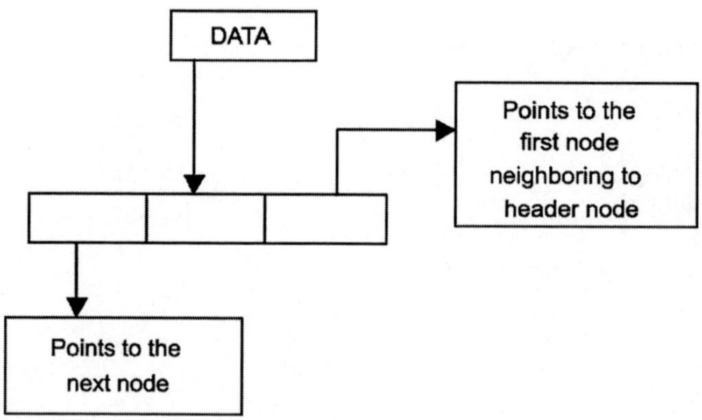

Figure 9.19 Header node

```
struct node
{
   struct * next
   int num;
   struct edge *aj;
};
```

Structure of an Edge Fig. 9.20 is the representation of an edge.

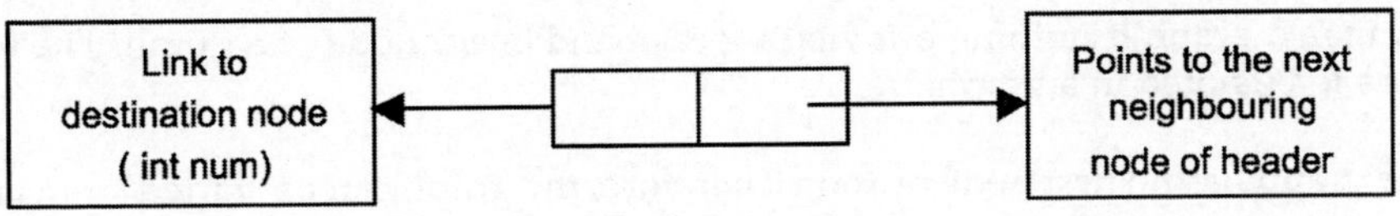

Figure 9.20 An edge of graph

```
struct edge
{
   int num;
   struct edge *ptr;
};
```

Consider a graph cited in Fig. 9.21.

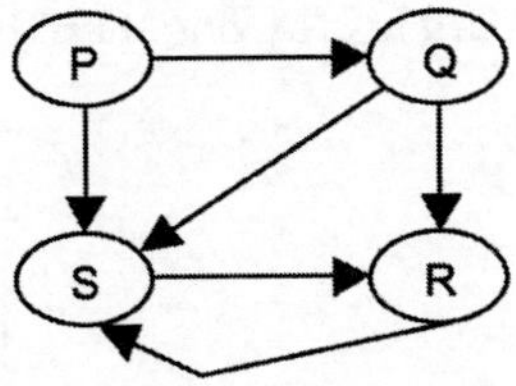

Figure 9.21 An example of graph

Adjacency list for the above graph would be given in Fig. 9.22.

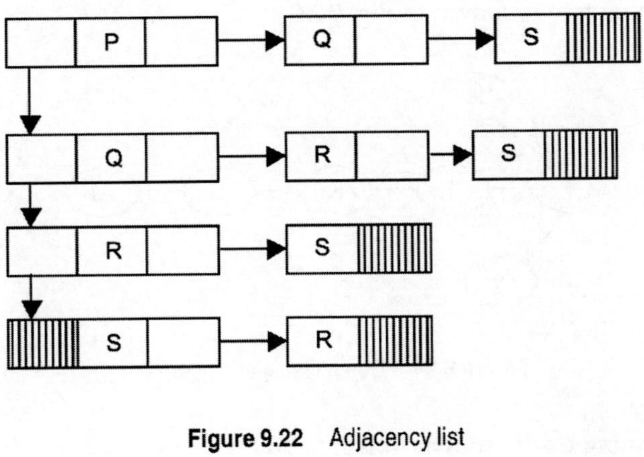

Figure 9.22 Adjacency list

9.5 TRAVERSAL IN GRAPH

Traversing in a graph is nothing but visiting each and every node of a graph. The following points are to be noted in a graph:

1. The graph has no first node or root. Therefore, the graph can be started from any node.
2. In graph, only those nodes are traversed which are accessible from the current node. For complete traversing of graph, the path can be determined by traversing nodes step by step.
3. In the graph, the particular node can be visited repeatedly. Hence, it is necessary to keep the track of the status of every node whether traversed or not.
4. In graph to reach a particular node, more paths are available.

Two techniques are used for traversing nodes in a graph. They are depth first and breadth first. These techniques have been elaborated in detail in the following sections.

9.6 SPANNING TREES

A spanning tree is an undirected tree, containing only those nodes that are necessary to join all the nodes in the graph. The nodes of spanning trees have only one path between them. In spanning trees, the number of edges are less by one than the number of nodes (see Fig. 9.23).

Figure 9.23 Spanning trees

Depth first spanning tree is shown in Fig. 9.24.

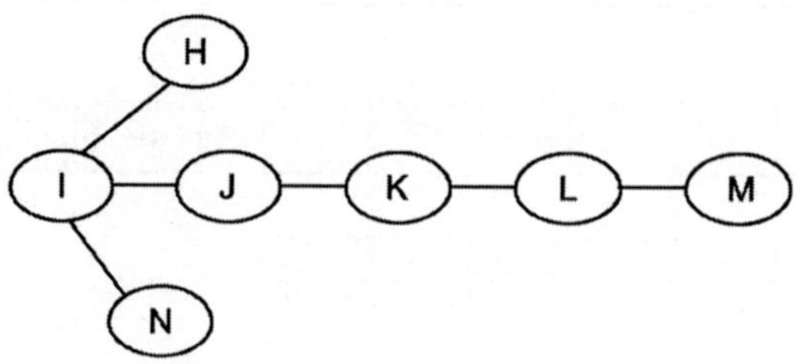

Figure 9.24 Depth first spanning tree

Breadth first spanning tree is shown in Fig. 9.25.

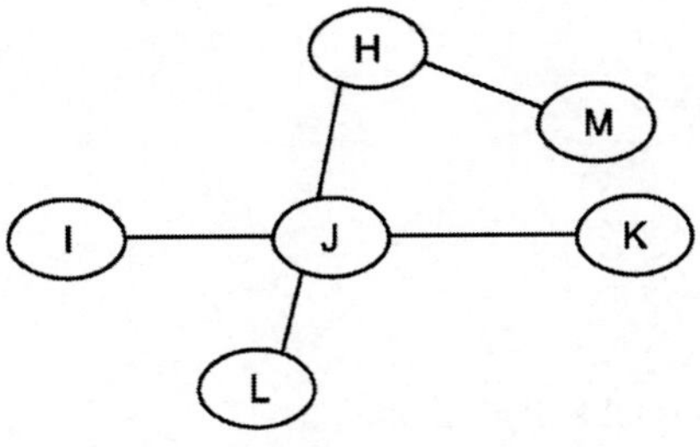

Figure 9.25 Breadth first spanning

Weighted Graph When the edges of the graph contain positive values as weight it is known as weighted graph or network.

Prim's Algorithm In this algorithm, the traversing can start from any node and addition can be done in spanning tree according to the weight of the edge. For example, we start with node n1, and then the next step is to check the entire connecting path to that node and find out which path has minimum weight. Thus, the nodes with minimum weight are added in Prim's algorithms. Here, while program implementation it is essential to know the weight of the edge. For example, we have two edges e1 and e2 with weights 3 and 5. The edge e1 has minimum weight than e2 and hence, e1 will be added to spanning tree.

Example 9.2

Write a program to create minimum spanning tree using Prim's algorithm.

Solution

```
#include<stdio.h>
# include <conio.h>
#include <process.h>

struct prim
{
   int pred_sor;
   int stat;
   int distance;
};
struct node {   int x; int w; };
int adjc[10][10],num;

int main()
{
   int y=1,wt,counter;
   struct node trees[10];
```

Explanation In this program the structure prim is defined as follows:

```
struct prim
{
   int pred_sor;
   int stat;
   int distance;
};
struct node {int x; int w;};
```

```
    void create (void );
    void show (void );
    int m_tree(struct node*, int*);
    clrscr();
    create();
    printf("Adjacency of Matrix  : ");
    show();
    counter=m_tree(trees,&wt);
    printf("Weight of spanning trees is : %d\n", wt);
    printf("Edges to be included in spanning trees : ");

    while(y<=counter)
    {
        printf("%d->",trees[y].x);
        printf("%d\num",trees[y].w);
        y++;
    }
return 0;
}
void create()
{
    int y=1,m_edge,start,end,wt;
    printf("Enter number of vertices : ");
    scanf("%d",&num);
    m_edge=num*(num-1)/2;
    while (y<=m_edge)
    {
        printf("Enter node %d( 0 to Exit) : ",y);
        scanf("%d %d",&start,&end);
        if((start==0) && (end==0))  break;
        printf("Enter weight of this node : ");
        scanf("%d",&wt);
        if( start > num || end > num || start<=0 || end<=0)
        {
            printf("Wrong  node!\n");
            --y;
        }
        else
        {
            adjc[start][end]=wt;
            adjc[end][start]=wt;
        }
    y++;
    }
    if(y<num-1)
    {
        printf("Spanning tree not possible\n");
```

```
        exit(0);
    }
}

void show()
{
    int y=1,p;
    while (y<=num)
    {
        for(p=1;p<=num;p++)
        printf("%3d",adjc[y][p]);
        printf("\n");
        y++;
    }
}

int m_tree(struct node trees[10],int *wht)
{
    struct prim p_ion[10];
    int y=1,mm,counter,cur;
    int perm(struct prim *);
    int uu,vv;
    wht=0;
    while(y<=num)
    {
        p_ion[y].pred_sor=0;
        p_ion[y].distance = 9999;
        p_ion[y].stat = 0;
        y++;
    }

    p_ion[1].pred_sor=0;
    p_ion[1].distance = 0;
    p_ion[1].stat = 1;
    cur=1;
    counter=0;
    while( perm(p_ion) != 1 )
    {
        for(y=1;y<=num;y++)
        {
            if ( adjc[cur][y] > 0 && p_ion[y].stat == 0 )
            {
                if(  adjc[cur][y] < p_ion[y].distance )
                {
                    p_ion[y].pred_sor = cur;
                    p_ion[y].distance = adjc[cur][y];
                }
```

```
            }
        }
        mm=9999;
        for(y=1;y<=num;y++)
        {
            if(p_ion[y].stat == 0 && p_ion[y].distance < mm)
            {
                mm = p_ion[y].distance;
                cur=y;
            }
        }
        p_ion[cur].stat=1;
        uu=p_ion[cur].pred_sor;
        vv=cur,counter++;
        trees[counter].x=uu;
        trees[counter].w=vv;
        *wht=*wht+adjc[uu][vv];
    }
    return (counter);
}
int perm(struct prim p_ion[10])
{
    int y=1;
    while(y<=num)
      if( p_ion[y++].stat == 0 )
      return 0;
    return 1;
}
```

```
OUTPUT
Enter number of vertices : 5
Enter node 1( 0 to Exit) : 1 1
Enter weight of this node : 5
Enter node 2( 0 to Exit) : 1 1
Enter weight of this node : 3
Enter node 3( 0 to Exit) : 0 0
Spanning tree not possible
```

The function *create ()* is used to compute maximum edges. The *m_tree ()* function is used to calculate the edges. The *show ()* function is used to display the nodes.

9.6.1 Breadth First Search

This is one of the popular methods of traversing graph. This method uses the queue data structure for traversing nodes of the graph. Any node of the graph can act as a beginning node. Using any node as starting node, all other nodes of the graph are traversed. To shun repeated visit to the same node an array is maintained which keeps status of visited node.

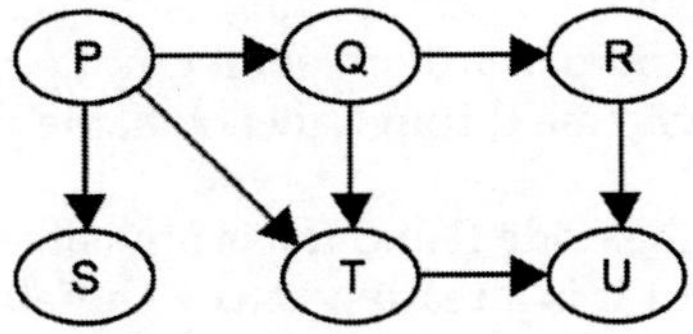

Figure 9.26 A model graph

Take the node P of Fig. 9.26 as a beginning node. Initially, the node P is traversed. After this, all the adjacent nodes of P are traversed, i.e. Q, T and S. The traversal of nodes can be carried in any sequence. For example, the sequence of traverse of nodes is Q, S and T. The traversal will be

P Q S T

First, all the nodes neighbouring Q are traversed, then neighbouring nodes of S and finally T are taken into account. The adjacent node of Q is R and T is U. Similarly, the adjacent node of T is U and S does not have any adjacent node. Hence, in this step the traversal now should be in the following way:

P Q S T R U

Now, the new nodes obtained are R and U after traversing. The new adjacent node of R is U and U node does not have any adjacent node. Node U has been visited in the previous case hence it must be ignored in this step.

9.6.2 Depth First Search

In this method, also a node from graph is taken as a starting node. Traverse through all the possible paths of the starting node. When the last node of the graph is obtained and path is not available from the node; then control returns to previous node. This process is implemented using stack.

Consider the following graph shown in Fig. 9.27

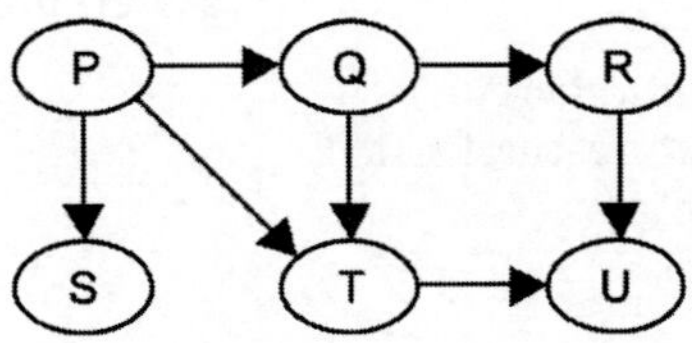

Figure 9.27 A model graph

Consider, P as starting node. Then, traverse the node adjacent to P and we will get Q and then R (adjacent to Q) and U (adjacent to R). The traversal will be

P Q R U

The search is always carried in forward direction. After reaching to U, we reach the end of the path and further movement in forward direction is not possible. Hence, the controls go to the previous node and again traverse through the available paths for non-traversed nodes.

In reverse direction, we get the node R and it has unvisited node. Hence, Q is taken and it gives T. The node T gives U, but it is already visited. Therefore, control in reverse direction checks all the nodes. It takes P and it gives node S. The sequence of traversal will be

P Q R U T S

The following program explains both the above procedures.

Example 9.3

Write a program to demonstrate breadth first search and depth first search.

Solution

```
#include<stdio.h>
#include <conio.h>
# include <process.h>
#define num 21

int aj[num][num],tra_sed[num],count;
int main()
{
   int j,x,select;
   int show (void),create(void),dfs(int);
   int dfs_rsn(int),bfs(int),adj_edg(int);
   void nodes(void);
   clrscr();
   create();
   for (;;)
   {
      printf("1.Adjacency of matrix\n");
      printf("2. Depth First Search with stack\n");
      printf("3. Depth First Search with recursion\n");
      printf("4. Breadth First Search\n");
      printf("5.Adjacent vertices\n");
      printf("6. Elements\n");
      printf("7. Quit\n");
      printf("Enter option : ");
      scanf("%d",&select);
      switch(select)
      {
```

Explanation In this program following user defined functions are defined to perform various tasks. *Create ()* function when executed prompts user to enter number of edges and corresponding edge values. When user enters edges, maximum edges are calculated. For complete details of the procedure read the topic depth first search. The function *adj_edg ()* calculates the edges. The function *bfs ()* performs breadth first search. For details, refer the topic breadth first search illustrated in the same topic.

```
        case 1:
          printf("Adjacency of Matrix\n");
          show();
          break;
        case 2:
          printf("Enter Beginning node for Depth First Search : ");
          scanf("%d",&x);
          for(j=1;j<=count;j++)
          tra_sed[j]=0;
          dfs(x);   break;
        case 3:
          printf("Enter Beginning node for Depth First Search : ");
          scanf("%d",&x);
          for(j=1;j<=count;j++)
          tra_sed[j]=0;
          dfs_rsn(x); break;
        case 4:
        printf("Enter Beginning node for Breadth First Search : ");
          scanf("%d", &x);
          for(j=1;j<=count;j++)
          tra_sed[j]=0;
          bfs(x);
          break;
        case 5:
          printf("Enter node to search adjacent vertices : ");
          scanf("%d", &x);
          printf("Adjacent Vertices : ");
          adj_edg(x);
          break;
        case 6:
          nodes();
          break;
        case 7:
          exit(0);
        default:
          printf("Invalid selection\n");
          break;
        }
    }
}
create()
{
    int j,m_edges,start,target;
    printf("Enter number of nodes : ");
    scanf("%d",&count);
    m_edges=count*(count-1);
    for(j=1;j<=m_edges;j++)
```

```
    {
        printf("Enter edge %d( 0 0 to quit ) : ",j);
        scanf("%d %d",&start,&target);
        if((start==0) && (target==0))
            break;
        if( start > count || target > count || start<=0 || target<=0)
        {
            printf("Invalid edges try again !\n");
            --j;
        }
        else   aj[start][target]=1;
    }
return 0;
}
show()
{
    int j;
    for(j=1;j<=count;j++)
    {
        for(j=1;j<=count;j++)
            printf("%5d",aj[j][j]);
        printf("\n");
    }
return 0;
}
dfs_rsn(int x)
{
    int j;
    tra_sed[x]=1;
    printf(" %d ",x);
    for(j=1;j<=count;j++)
    if(aj[x][j]==1 && tra_sed[j]==0)
    dfs_rsn(j);
return 0;
}
dfs(int x)
{
    int j,stack[num],TOP=-1,popve;
    TOP++;
    stack[TOP]=x;
    while (TOP>=0)
    {
        popve=stack[TOP];
        TOP--;
        if( tra_sed[popve]==0)
        {
            printf("%d ",popve);
```

```
            tra_sed[popve]=1;
        }
        else
            continue;
        for(j=count;j>=1;j--)
        {
            if( aj[popve][j]==1 && tra_sed[j]==0)
            {
                TOP++;
                stack[TOP]=j;
            }
        }
    }
return 0;
}
bfs(int x)
{
    int j,fr,re;
    int queue[20];
    fr=re= -1;

    printf("%d ",x);
    tra_sed[x]=1;
    re++;
    fr++;
    queue[re]=x;

    while(fr<=re)
    {
        x=queue[fr];
        fr++;
        for(j=1;j<=count;j++)
        {
            /* Check for adjacent unvisited nodes */
            if( aj[x][j]==1 && tra_sed[j]==0)
            {
                printf("%d ",j);
                tra_sed[j]=1;
                re++;
                queue[re]=j;
            }
        }
    }
return 0;
}
adj_edg(int x)
{
```

```
    int j;
    for(j=1;j<=count;j++)
    if(aj[x][j]==1)
    printf("%d ",j);
    printf("\n");
return 0;
}
void nodes()
{
    int j;
    for(j=1;j<=count;j++)
        tra_sed[j]=0;
    for(j=1;j<=count;j++)
    {
        if(tra_sed[j]==0)
            dfs_rsn(j);
    }
    printf("\n");
}
```

```
OUTPUT
Enter number of nodes : 5
Enter edge 1( 0 0 to quit ) : 1 1
Enter edge 2( 0 0 to quit ) : 2 2
Enter edge 3( 0 0 to quit ) :  1 5
Enter edge 4( 0 0 to quit ) : 0 0
1. Adjacency of matrix
2. Depth First Search with stack
3. Depth First Search with recursion
4. Breadth First Search
5. Adjacent vertices
6. Elements
7. Quit
Enter option : 1
Adjacency of Matrix
  1  1  0  0  0
```

Summary

1. In this chapter graph theory is described. Also, its implementation is illustrated with numerous examples.
2. A graph is a set of nodes and arcs. The nodes are also termed as *vertices* and *arcs* are termed as *edges*.
3. A graph is linked if there is a pathway between any two nodes of the graph, such a graph is called *connected graph* or else it is *non-connected graph.*
4. The graph can be implemented by linked list or array.

5. Explanation on adjacency matrix is provided in the form of matrix. The information of adjacent nodes can be stored in the matrix. Presence of edges from a particular node can be determined easily. The matrix can be represented by two-dimensional array. In two-dimensional, *array [][]* the first subscript.
6. Traversal in a tree is also explained in this chapter. The node can be visited repeatedly. Hence, it is necessary to keep the track of node as to whether it has been visited or not.
7. Spanning tree is discussed in detail. Two methods have been elaborated together with examples. Breadth first and depth first spanning trees have been illustrated in detail.

Exercises

A. Answer the following questions:
   1. What do you mean by edges and vertices of a graph?
   2. Define the following terms applicable to a graph:
      a. Degree
      b. Dag
      c. Indegree
      d. Outdegree
      e. Cycle.
   3. Distinguish between the directed and undirected graphs.
   4. What do you mean by complete graph?
   5. Explain traversing of a graph.
   6. Distinguish between the breadth first and depth first traversals in a graph.
   7. Describe spanning trees.
   8. How are graphs implemented in computer memory?
   9. Distinguish between the tree and graph.
   10. Define the following terms in a graph:
      a. Source
      b. Sink
      c. Isolated node
      d. Articulation point.

B. Select the appropriate options for each of the following questions:
   1. The header is used to point
      a. first node of the list
      b. last node of the list
      c. NULL value
      d. none of the above.
   2. Traversing means
      a. visiting all the nodes
      b. shifting all the nodes at forward
      c. randomly accessing the elements
      d. none of the above.
   3. Graph is a
      a. linear data structure
      b. nonlinear data structure
      c. none of the above.
   4. Graph contains
      a. edges
      b. arcs
      c. edges and arcs
      d. none of the above.
   5. The indegree of a node is
      a. the total number of edges coming to that node
      b. the total number of edges leaving from that node
      c. the total number of edges coming and leave to that node
      d. None of the above.

6. The directed graph is also called
   a. trigraph
   b. digraph
   c. none of the above.
7. Length of path is nothing but
   a. total number of edges included in the path from source to destination node
   b. total number of edges included in the path from destination to source
   c. none of the above.
8. When first and last nodes of the path are same such a path is known as
   a. open path
   b. closed path
   c. none of the above.
9. A directed acyclic graph is called
   a. dag
   b. acycle
   c. none of the above.
10. When a degree of node is zero then the node is called
    a. group node
    b. isolated node
    c. none of the above.
11. Traversal in graph is
    a. to visit only few nodes of a graph
    b. to visit all nodes of a graph
    c. none of the above.

C. Attempt the following program:
1. Write a program to demonstrate breadth first search and depth first search.
2. Write a program to demonstrate spanning tree.
3. Write a program to count the number of nodes of a graph.
4. Write a program to count the indegree and outdegree of every node of a graph.
5. Write a program to find the number of source nodes in a graph.
6. Write a program to find the number of sink nodes in a graph.
7. Write a program to find the successors and predecessors of each node in a graph.
8. Write a program to find the number of isolated nodes in a graph.
9. Find the adjacency matrix for the graph given below:

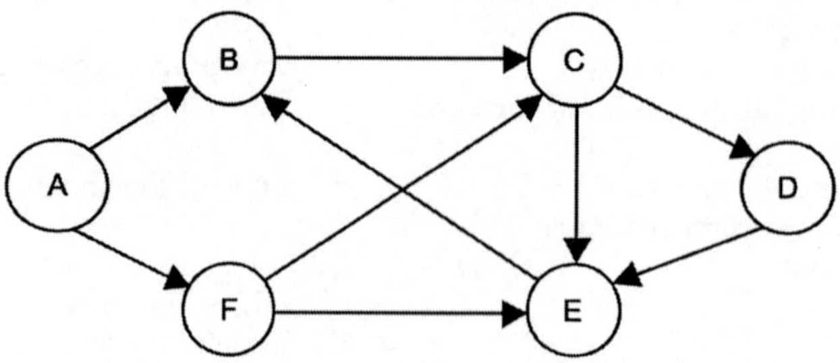

Chapter 10

Sorting

Chapter Outline

10.1 INTRODUCTION

In our daily life, we keep the information in particular order. This helps in accessing any part of it easily. Likewise, in database programs, large data is maintained in the form of records. It would be very difficult if data or records were unsorted. It is very boring to find a particular record if data or records are randomly stored. The process of sorting is essential for database applications.

Sorting is a process in which records are arranged in ascending or descending order. A group of fields is called record. For example, consider the following structure:

```
struct employee
{
   char *name;
   int age;
   float height;
} s;
```

We are familiar with the above declarations and definitions. The object *s* contains three fields as described in the structure. The database is a collection of such fields. Each record contains the above fields, and it may vary depending upon the structure defined. The sorting can be done or any one or a combination of one or more fields. Suppose, we sort the records based on name. Then, the field `name` will be the key field. A record is quickly searched in a sorted database. Thus, sorting is a very useful concept of data structure.

10.2 SORTING

As already defined in the previous section sorting is a process in which records are arranged in ascending or descending order. In real life we come across several examples of sorted information. For example, in telephone directory the names of the subscribers and their phone numbers are written in alphabetial order. The records of the list of these telephone holders are to be sorted by their names. By using this directory, we can access the telephone number and address of the subscriber very easily.

Bankers or businesspersons sort the currency denomination notes received from customers in the appropriate form. Currency denominations of Rs 1000, 500, 100, 50, 20, 10, 5, and 1 are separated first and then separate bundles are prepared.

While we play the cards, initially the cards appear random but we keep them in ascending or descending order. In most of the offices the officials keep the files in a specific order for tracing them easily in future. Even at our homes, many times we keep the utensils in particular order such as increasing or decreasing height size. This helps us in accessing a particular item without difficulty. The sort method has great impact on data structures in our dally life.

For example, consider the five numbers 5, 9, 7, 4, 1.

The above numbers can be sorted in ascending or descending order.
The representation of these numbers in

Ascending order (0 to n): 1 4 5 7 9
Descending order (n to 0): 9 7 5 4 1

Similarly, alphabets can also be sorted.
Consider the alphabets B, A, D, C, E. These can be sorted in ascending or descending order.

Ascending order (A to Z): A B C D E
Descending order (Z to A): E D C B A.

10.3 INSERTION SORT

In insertion sort the element is inserted at appropriate place. For example, consider an array of n elements. In this type, swapping of elements is done without taking any temporary variable. The greater numbers are shifted towards the end of the array and smaller are shifted to beginning. Here, a real life example of playing cards can be cited. We keep the cards in increasing order. The card having least value is placed at the extreme left and the largest one at the other side. In between them the other cards are managed in ascending order.

Consider an example of playing cards. The playing cards having values 4, 6, 2, 1, 8 can be sorted according to the method described above, as

Fig. 10.1 illustrates the insertion sort.

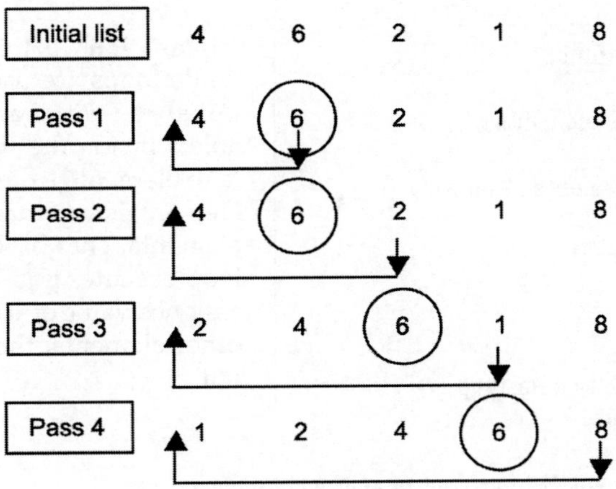

Figure 10.1 Insertion sort

The process of insertion sort can be explained with following steps:

- Get the random integer list. In the above example the list contains elements 4, 6, 2, 1, 8.
- In the first pass the initial key is defined as 6 and compared with 4. As 6 is larger than 4 hence the position of 6 remains as it is.
- In the second pass element 2 is compared with the initial key 6 and 4 and 2 are placed appropriately. That is, its position is now at first.
- In the pass three the elements 1 is compared with the earlier three elements and placed appropriately. Its position is shown in Fig. 10.1.
- In the pass 4 the last element 8 is compared with the initial key and it is found greater hence it is placed on the right side of 6.

The final sorted list appears as 1, 2, 4, 6, 8.

Thus, in the insertion sort we are actually finding the proper place for the element to insert with respect to the key.

Here, a program is provided on insertion sort.

Example 10.1

Write a program to sort array elements using insertion sort.

Solution

```
#include <stdio.h>
#include <conio.h>
```

```
main()
{
   int nums[20],p=0,q=1,r,num;
   clrscr();
   printf("Enter number of elements : ");
   scanf("%d",&num);
   printf ("\n Enter %d elements : ",num);
   while (p<num)
    scanf("%d", &nums[p++]);
   while(q<num)
   {
       r=nums[q];
       for(p=q-1;p>=0 && r<nums[p];p--)
       nums[p+1]=nums[p];
       nums[p+1]=r;
           printf(" Element %d inserted in appropriate place ",r);
       p=0;
       while (p<num)
       printf("%d ", nums[p++]);
       printf("\n");
       q++;
   }
   printf("Sorted elements are : ");
   for (p = 0; p < num; p++)
   printf("%d ", nums[p]);
}
```

Explanation In this program, the nested while loops are used. The variable *q* is initialized with 1 and *p* with 0. The variable *r* inside the while loop is used to take elements from array and the same element is compared with remaining elements. The *'for'* loop inside the while loop executes if *p>=zero* and *r* (recently assigned value of array element) less than other elements, the insertion is carried out.

```
OUTPUT
Enter number of elements: 5
Enter 5 elements: 4 6 2 1 8
Element 6 inserted in appropriate place 4 6 2 1 8
Element 2 inserted in appropriate place 2 4 6 1 8
Element 1 inserted in appropriate place 1 2 4 6 8
Element 8 inserted in appropriate place 1 2 4 6 8
Sorted elements are: 1 2 4 6 8
```

Example 10.2

Write a program to sort given list of elements by using insertion sort. Use pointer.

Solution

```
#include <stdio.h>
#include <conio.h>
main()
{
int ls[5],limit,*pt,p=0,q=0,tem;
```

```
pt=&ls[0];
clrscr();
printf("How many numbers would you like to sort?-");
scanf("%d",&limit);
printf("Enter %d elements:-",limit);
while(q<limit)
scanf("%d",&ls[q++]);
for(q=1;q<limit;q++)
{
tem=*(pt+q);
for(p=q-1;p>=0 && tem<*(pt+p);p--)
*(pt+p+1)=*(pt+p);
*(pt+p+1)=tem;
}
printf("Sorted elements are:- ");
for (p = 0; p <limit; p++)
printf("%d ", ls[p]);
}
```

Explanation In this program, the limit for the array is made available with variable limit. The variable **pt* is used for storing the starting address of the array element. With address location list is sorted by using the insertion sort method.

```
OUTPUT
How many numbers would you like to sort?-4
Enter 4 elements:-12 3 1 2
Sorted elements are:- 1 2 3 12
```

Time Complexity of Insertion Sort in Worst Case

Consider an example to sort the 5 elements 9, 8, 7, 6 and 5. The comparisons are shown in the different passes in Fig. 10.2.

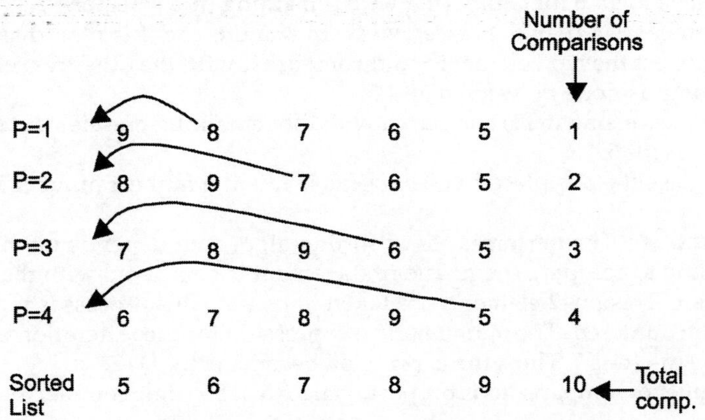

Figure 10.2 Insertion sort in worst case

The number of comparisons in worst case can be calculated by referring to Fig. 10.2. The comparisons in the different passes are made as follows:

1. In pass =1 only one comparison is made between the elements 9 and 8.
2. Pass =2 contains the two comparisons the element 7 is compared with 9 and 8.
3. Three comparisons are made in the pass=3. The element 6 is compared with 7, 8 and 9.
4. Four comparisons are made in the pass=4. The element 5 is compared with 6, 7, 8 and 9.

The total comparisons in the sorting method in worst case = 1+2+3+4=10.
Thus, theoretically f(n) = n(n–1)/2 =5(5–1)/2=10.
Practical values of comparisons are equal to the theoretical value.

10.4 SELECTION SORT

The selection sort is nearly the same as exchange sort. Assume, we have a list containing n elements. By applying selection sort, the first element is compared with all remaining (n–1) elements. The smallest element is placed at the first location. Again, the second element is compared with remaining (n–2) elements. If the item found is lesser than the compared elements in the remaining (n–2) list then the swap operation is done. In this type, entire array is checked for the smallest element and then swapped.

Fig. 10.3 illustrates the process of sorting elements by selection sort. In each pass, one element is sorted and kept at the left. Initially, the elements are temporarily sorted and after next pass, they are permanently sorted and kept at the left. Permanently sorted elements are covered with squares and temporarily with circles. Element inside the circle "O" is chosen for comparing with the other elements marked in a circle and sorted temporarily. Sorted elements inside the square "□" are shown.

Consider the elements 2, 6, 4, 8, and 5 for sorting under selection sort method.

1. In pass 1, select element 2 and check it with the remaining elements 6, 4, 8, and 5. There is no smaller value than 2, hence the element 2 is placed at the first position.
2. Now, select element 6 for comparing with remaining (n–2) elements, i.e. 4, 8, and 5. The smaller element is 4 than 6. Hence, we swap 4 and 6 and 4 is placed after 2.
3. Again, we select the next element 6 and compare it with the other two elements 8 and 5 and swapping is done between 6 and 5.
4. In the next pass element 8 is compared with the remaining one element 6. In this case, 8 is swapped with 6.
5. In the last pass the 8 is placed at last because it is the highest number in the list.

Time Complexity The performance of sorting algorithm depends upon the number of iterations and time to compare them. The first element is compared with the remaining n–1 elements in pass 1. Then, n–2 elements are taken in pass 2. This process is repeated until the last element is encountered. The mathematical expression for these iterations will be equal to (n–1)+(n–2)+ ... +(n– (n–1)). Thus, the expression become n*(n–1)/2.

Thus, the number of comparisons is proportional to (n^2). The time complexity of selection sort is O (n^2).

Comparison with Other Methods 1. This method requires more number of comparisons than quick sort, tree sort. 2. It is easier to implement than other methods such as quick sort, tree sort. 3. The performance of the selection sort is quicker than bubble sort.

Pass \ No.	1	2	3	4	5
1	2	6	4	8	5
2	2	6	4	8	5
3	2	4	6	8	5
4	2	4	5	8	6
5	2	4	5	6	8
SList	2	4	5	6	8

Figure 10.3 Selection sort

Example 10.3

Write a program to sort elements of an array using selection sort.

Solution

```
#include <stdio.h>
# include <conio.h>
main()
{
   int nums[15],p=0,q,r,num,t,small;
   clrscr();
   printf("How many elements to sort ? : ");
   scanf("%d",&num);

   printf("Enter %d elements : ":,num);

   while (p<num)
   scanf("%d", &nums[p++]);
   for(p=0;p<num-1;p++)
   {
      small = p;
      for(r=p+1;r<num;r++)
      if(nums[small] > nums[r])
      small = r ;
      if( p != small )
      {
```

Explanation This program of selection sort uses nested loops. Using nested loops array elements are compared with one another. The value of loop variable *p* is assigned to variable *small.* The inner loop executes from *(p+1)* to *num,* in which the number present at array position *nums [small]* if greater than nums[r], the location indicated by r is assigned to small. The next *if ()* block carries swapping of elements. Thus, all array elements are compared and necessary swapping is done.

```
        t = nums [p];
        nums[p] = nums[small];
        nums[small] = t ;
      }
      printf("\nAfter %d pass elements are :  ",p+1);
      q=0;
      while (q< num)
      printf(" %d ", nums[q++]);
   }
   printf("\nSorted elements are: ");
   p=0;
   while( p < num)
   printf("%d ", nums[p++]);
}
```

```
OUTPUT
How many elements to sort? : 5
Enter 5 elements:  8 6 4 2 5
After 1 pass elements are: 2  6  4  8  5
After 2 pass elements are :   2  4  6  8  5
After 3 pass elements are :   2  4  5  8  6
After 4 pass elements are :   2  4  5  6  8
Sorted elements are: 2 4 5 6 8
```

10.5 BUBBLE SORT

Bubble sort is a commonly used sorting algorithm. In this type, two successive elements are compared and swapping is done if the first element is greater than the second one. The elements are sorted in ascending order. It is easy to understand but it is time consuming.

Bubble sort is an example of exchange sort. In this method repetitively comparison is performed between the two successive elements and if essential swapping of elements is done. Thus, step-by-step entire array elements are checked. It is different from the selection sort. Instead of searching the minimum element and then applying swapping, two records are swapped instantly upon noticing that they are not in order.

The Fig. 10.4 illustrates the exchange sort.

Let us consider the elements 9, 5, 1, 4, and 3 for sorting under bubble sort.

1. In pass 1, first element 9 is compared with its next element 5. The next element is smaller than the 9. Hence, it is swapped. Now, the list is 5,9,1,4,3 again the 9 is compared with its next element 1 the next element is smaller than the 9 hence swapping is done. The same procedure is done with the 4 and 3 and at last we get the list as 5,1,4,3,9.
2. In pass 2, the elements of pass 1 are compared. The first element 5 is compared with its next element 1.5 and 1 are swapped because 1 is smaller than 5. Now, the list becomes 1,5,4,3,9. Next, 5 is compared with element 4. Again, 5 and 4 are swapped. This process is repeated until all successive elements are compared and if the succeeding number is smaller than the present number then the numbers are swapped. The final list at the end of this pass is 1,4,3,5,9.

3. In pass 3, the first element 1 is compared with the next element 4. The element 4 is having the higher value than the first element 1, hence they remain at their original positions. Next, 4 is compared with the subsequent element 3 and swapped due to smaller value of 3 than 4.
4. At last, the sorted list obtained is 1,3,4,5,9.

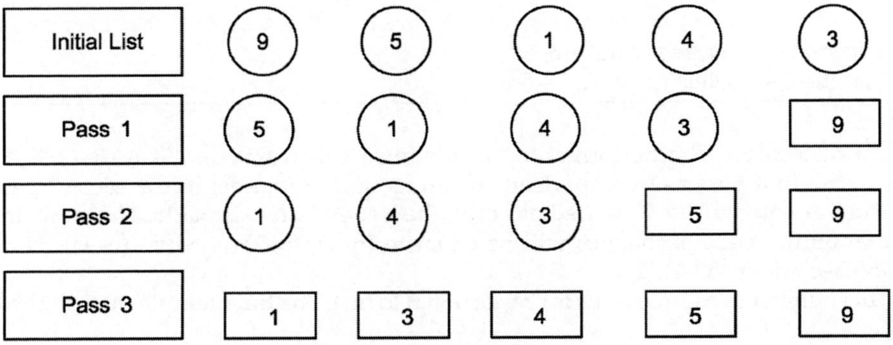

Figure 10.4 Bubble sort

Example 10.4

Write a program to sort a given array by using the bubble sort.

Solution

```
#include<stdio.h>
#include<conio.h>
main()
{
 int a[5],i,j,temp;
 clrscr();
 printf("Enter the elements of an array : ");
 for(i=0;i<5;i++)
 scanf("%d",&a[i]);
   for(i=0;i<5;i++)
    {
    for(j=i;j<4;j++)
   {
        if(a[i]>a[j+1])
        {
          temp=a[i];
          a[i]=a[j+1];
          a[j+1]=temp;
        }
   }
```

Explanation In this program an array of five elements is declared. The variable *j* and *i* are loop variables. The variable *i* is used in the outer loop and *j* is used in the inner loop. The 'if' statement checks the number, it compares every current element denoted by *ith* location with (*j+1*)th element. If the number ith is greater, it is assigned to temp. The smaller number is assigned to *ith* location and temp (holds larger number) assigned to (*j+1*)th location. Thus, by exchange elements are sorted.

```
}
  printf("Sorted elements in ascending order : ");
  for(i=0;i<5;i++)
  printf(" %d ",a[i]);
 }
```

```
OUTPUT
Enter the elements of an array: 9 5 1 4 3
Sorted elements in ascending order:  1 3 4 5 9
```

Time Complexity The performance of bubble sort in worst case is n (n–1)/2. This is because in the first pass n–1 comparisons or exchanges are made; in the second pass n–2 comparisons are made. This is carried out until the last exchange is made. The mathematical representation for these exchanges will be equal to (n–1)+(n–2)+ ... +(n– (n–1)). Thus, the expression becomes n*(n–1)/2.

Thus, the number of comparisons is proportional to (n^2). The time complexity of bubble sort is 0 (n^2).

10.6 QUICK SORT

It is also known as partition exchange sort. It was invented by CAR Hoare. It is based on partition. Hence, the method falls under divide and conquer technique. The main list of elements is divided into two sub-lists. For example, a list of X elements are to be sorted. The quick sort marks an element in a list called as pivot or key. Consider the first element J as a pivot. Shift all the elements whose value is less than J towards the left and elements whose value is greater than J to the right of J. Now, the key element divides the main list into two parts. It is not necessary that selected key element must be in the middle. Any element from the list can act as key element. However, for best performance preference is given to middle elements. Time consumption of the quick sort depends on the location of the key in the list.

Consider the following example in which five elements 8,9,7,6,4 are to be sorted using quick sort. The Fig. 10.5 illustrates it.

Consider pass 1 under which the following iterations are made. Similar operations are done in pass 2, pass 3, etc.

In iteration 1 the first element 8 is marked as pivot one. It is compared with the last element whose value is 4. Here, 4 is smaller than 8 hence the numbers are swapped. Iteration 2 shows the swapping operation.

In the iteration 3 and 4, the position of 8 is fixed. In iteration 2, 8 and 9 are compared and swapping is done after iteration 2.

In iteration 3, 8 and 6 are compared and necessary swapping is done. After this, it is impossible to swap. Hence, the position of 8 is fixed. Because of fixing the position of 8 the main list is divided into two parts. Towards the left of 8 elements smaller than 8 are placed and towards the right greater than 8 are placed.

Towards the right of 8 only one element is present hence there is no need of further swapping. This may be considered under pass 2.

However, towards the left of 8 there are three elements and these elements are to be swapped as per the procedure described above. This may be considered under pass 3.

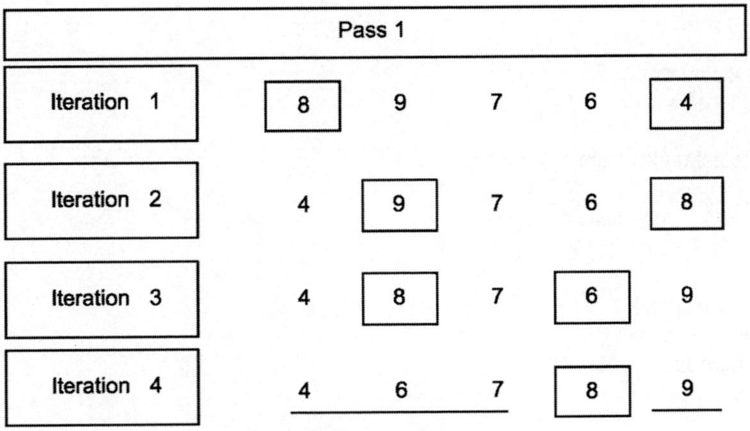

Figure 10.5 Quick sort

Example 10.5

Write a program to sort the array elements using quick sort.

Solution

```
#include<stdio.h>
#include <conio.h>

main()
{
   int nums[15],num,j=0;
   int q_sort(int *,int,int);
   int show(int *,int,int);
   clrscr();
   printf("Enter the number of elements : ");
   scanf("%d",&num);
   printf ("\n Enter %d elements : ",num);
   while (j<num)
      scanf("%d",&nums[j++]);
      q_sort(nums,0,num-1);
   printf("Sorted list is :\n");
   show(nums,0,num-1);
}
q_sort(int items[],int lower,int upper)
{
   int key,temp,l,r,key_placed=0;
   int show(int *,int,int);
   l=lower;
```

Explanation In this program the functions *q_sort ()* and *show ()* are defined. In *q_sort ()* elements are passed by value and address. The base address of an array nums is passed to function *q_sort ()*. The variable *num* holds total number of elements. The *q_sort ()* function is invoked recursively. In the first execution of *q_sort ()*, value 0 is taken as lower key and *(n–1)* is taken as upper key. If value of lower is greater than upper, the *q_sort ()* function terminates. The value of upper variable is assigned to *r*. The value of *r* is decremented continuously until it reaches to key value. When the value of variables key and *r* are same the key is placed to one and the while loop is terminated. The *'if ()'* statement carries swapping if element positioned at value key is greater than element positioned at value r. The same procedure is carried out when key is placed at one and swapping is carried out.

```
    r=upper;
    key=lower;
    if(lower>=upper) return 0;
    while(key_placed==0)
    {
        while( items[key]<=items[r] && key!=r)
         r--;
        if( key==r )    key_placed=1;
        if( items[key] > items[r] )
        {
            temp=items[key];
            items[key]=items[r];
            items[r]=temp;
            key=r;
        }
         while( items[key]>=items[l] && l!=key ) l++;
        if(key==l) key_placed=1;
        if( items[key] < items[l] )
        {
            temp=items[key];
            items[key]=items[l];
            items[l]=temp;
            key=l;
        }
    }
    printf(" * Key Placed is %d -> ",items[key]);
    show(items,lower,upper);
    printf("\n");

    q_sort(items,lower,key-1);
    q_sort(items,key+1,upper);
return 0;
}
show(int items[],int lower,int upper)
{
 while(lower<=upper)
 printf("%d ",items[lower++]);
  return 0;
}
```

```
OUTPUT
Enter the number of elements: 5
Enter 5 elements: 8 9 7 6 4
* Key Placed is 8 -> 4 6 7 8 9
* Key Placed is 4 -> 4 6 7
* Key Placed is 6 -> 6 7
Sorted list is : 4 6 7 8 9
```

Time Complexity The efficiency of quick sort depends upon the selection of pivot. The pivot can bifurcate the list into compartments. Sometimes, the compartments are having the same sizes or dissimilar sizes. Assume a case in which pivot is in the middle. Thus, the total elements towards left of it and right are equal. We can express the size of list with the power of 2. The mathematical representation for the size is $n=2^s$. The value of s can be calculated as $\log_2 n$.

After the first pass is completed there will be two compartments having equal number of elements, i.e. n/2 elements are on the left side as well as right side. In the subsequent passes, four portions are made and each compartment contains n/4 elements. In this way, we will be proceeding further until the list is sorted. The number of comparisons in different passes will be as follows:

Pass 1 will have n comparisons. Pass 2 will have 2*(n/2) comparisons. In the subsequent passes will have 4*(n/4), 8*(n/8) comparisons and so on. The total comparisons involved in this case would be 0 (n)+0 (n)+0 (n)+ ... +s. The value of expression will be 0 (n log n). Thus, time complexity of quick sort is 0 (n log n).

Comparison with Other Methods

1. This is the fastest sorting method among all.
2. It is somewhat complex, so little difficult to implement than other sorting algorithms.

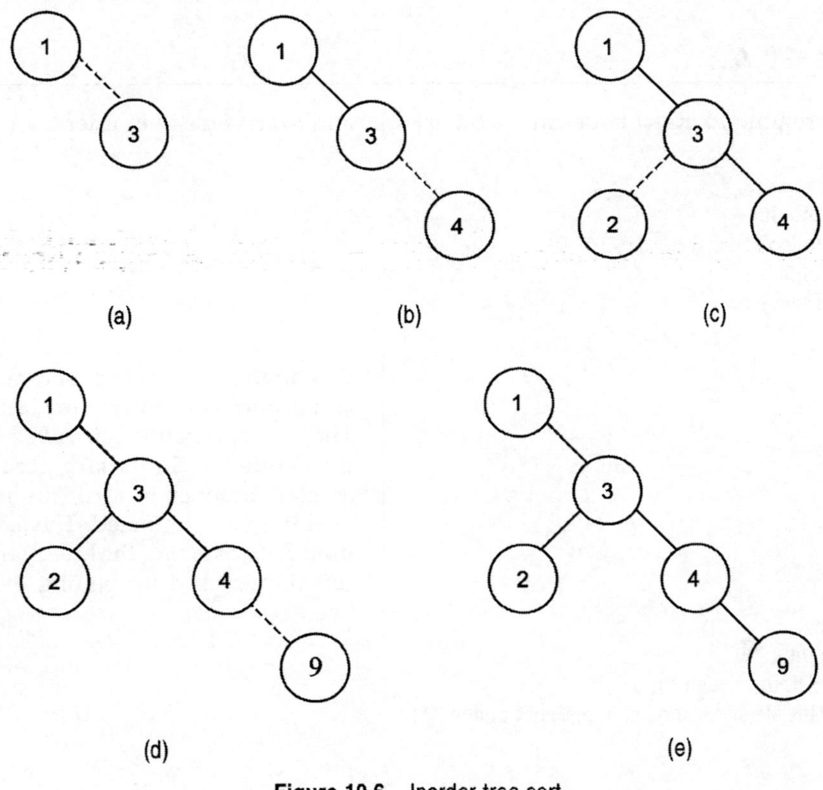

(a) (b) (c) (d) (e)

Figure 10.6 Inorder tree sort

10.7 TREE SORT

In binary tree, we know that the elements are inserted according to the value greater or less in between node and the root in traversing. If the value is less than traversing node, insertion is done at left side. If the value is greater than traversing node, it is inserted at right side. The elements of such tree can be sorted. This sorting involves creation of binary tree and then in order traversing is done. Few examples are illustrated based on the tree such as inorder tree and heap sort.

Consider the list containing elements 1, 3, 4, 2, 9 for sorting. Fig. 10.6 illustrates the inorder sort.

1. At first, element 1 is inserted in the tree as root node and element 3 is inserted at right to the root because the inserted node is larger than the root. Fig. 10.5 (a) explains it.
2. The element 4 is inserted at the right of the node 3 because it is larger than it. Insertion of element 4 is shown in Fig. 10.5(b).
3. As per Fig. 10.5 (c) element 2 is inserted at the left of the node 3 due to lesser value.
4. At last, the element 9 is inserted at right of the node 4. This is shown in Fig. 10.5 (d).
5. The final binary tree is shown in Fig. 10.5 (e). Using the inorder traversing the sorted list is obtained.

Example 10.6

Write a C program to insert nodes into a binary tree and to traverse in inorder.

Solution

```
# include <stdio.h>
# include <malloc.h>
# include <conio.h>
# include <process.h>

struct nodes
{
  int data;
  struct nodes *ls;
  struct nodes *rs;
}*tree;

main()
{
   int number;
   int insert (int);
   int inorder(struct nodes *);
   int search(int ele,struct nodes **p,struct nodes **l);
    tree=0;
   clrscr();
```

Explanation In this program, *insert()* and *inorder()* are user defined functions. The *insert()* function is invoked to insert the value in the binary tree. When entered number is zero, the insertion operation is terminated. The *inorder()* is used for traversing the binary tree. This function is used for getting the sorted list.

```
printf("Enter the numbers and 0 to exit :-");
while(1)
 {
  scanf("%d",&number);
   if (number==0)
     break;
  insert(number);
 }
printf("Inorder of the tree is as:-");
inorder(tree);
}
insert(int ele)
{
 struct nodes *t,*father,*m_loc;
 search(ele,&father,&m_loc);
 if(m_loc!=0)
 {
  printf("Item already present");
   return 0;
  }
 t=(struct nodes *)malloc(sizeof(struct nodes));
  t->data=ele;
  t->ls=0;
  t->rs=0;
  if(father==0)
  tree=t;
  else
  if(ele<father->data)
    father->ls=t;
  else
    father->rs=t;
  return 0;
 }
inorder(struct nodes *pr)
{
 if(tree==0)
 {
  printf("Tree is empty");
   return 0;
  }
 if(pr!=0)
   {
      inorder(pr->ls);
      printf("%d  ",pr->data);
      inorder(pr->rs);
    }
   return 0;
```

```
}
search(int ele,struct nodes **p,struct nodes **l)
{
  struct nodes *pr,*p_s;
  if(tree==0)
   {
     *l=0;
     *p=0;
    return 0;
   }
  if(ele==tree->data)
   {
     *l=tree;
     *p=0;
    return 0;
   }
  if(ele<tree->data)
    pr=tree->ls;
  else
     pr=tree->rs;
  p_s=tree;
  while(pr!=0)
  {
   if(ele==pr->data)
    {
       *l=pr;
       *p=p_s;
        return 0;
     }
   p_s=pr;
   if(ele<pr->data)
   pr=pr->ls;
 else
     pr=pr->rs;
 }
 *l=0;
 *p=p_s;
  return 0;
}
```

OUTPUT
Enter the numbers and 0 to exit :-12 3 53 5 0
Inorder of the tree is as:-3 5 12 53

10.8 MERGING LIST

Merging is a process in which two lists are merged to form a new list. The new list is the sorted list. Before merging, individual lists are sorted and then merging is done. The procedure is very straightforward.

Consider a list of 9 elements. They are as follows:

21,12,34,3,7,11,9,23,4.

Pass 1: In merge sort, first the list is divided into pairs containing two elements each. These can be shown as follows. If numbers are even then exact pairs are done. In this case nine numbers are assumed for selection. So, 5 pairs are possible. They are as follows:

21 12   34 3   7 11   9 23   4

After division of the list into pairs sort the elements of each pair.

12 21   3 34   7 11   23 9   4

Pass 2: Merge the pairs after sorting in the first pass. The elements appear as follows:

12 21 3 34   7 11 23 9   4

Sort the elements of the above merged pairs. On sorting, the elements will be as follows:

3 12 21 34 7 9 11 23   4

Pass 3: Again, merge two groups as follows:

3 12 21 34 7 9 11 23   4

Sort the elements of the merge groups.

3 7 9 11 12 21 23 34   4

Pass 4: Merge the element 4 with the remaining element.

3 7 9 11 12 21 23 34 4

At last pass all elements get sorted.

3 4 7 9 11 12 21 23 34

A program on merge sort is provided for understanding.

Example 10.7

Write a program to create two-array list of integers. Sort and store elements of both of them in the third list.

Solution

```
# include <stdio.h>
# include <conio.h>
# include <math.h>

main ()
{
  int m,n,p,sum=0;
  int listA[5],listB[5],listC[10]={0};
  clrscr();
  printf ("\n Enter elements for first list : ");
  for (m=0;m<5;m++)
  {
    scanf ("%d",&listA[m]);
     if (listA[m]==0) m--;
    sum=sum+abs(listA[m]);
  }
    printf ("\n Enter elements for second list : ");
  for (n=0;n<5;n++)
  {
    scanf ("%d",&listB[n]);
     if (listA[n]==0) n--;
    sum=sum+abs(listB[n]);
  }
 p=n=m=0;
 m=m-sum;
 while (m<sum)
 {
   for (n=0;n<5;n++)
   {
     if (m==listA[n] || m==listB[n])
      listC[p++]=m;
     if (m==listA[n] && m==listB[n])
      listC[p++]=m;
   }
   m++;
 }
 puts (" Merged sorted list  : ");
 for (n=0;n<10;++n)
```

Explanation In this program three arrays *listA [], listB [] and listC []* are declared. Using for loop elements in *listA []* and *listB []* are declared. The sum of all ten elements entered in both the lists are taken in variable *sum.* The *while* and nested *for loop* checks corresponding elements of both the list.

a. If one of the corresponding elements is same, that element is stored in the *list[]* array.
b. If both the corresponding elements are same, they are stored in successive locations in the *listC [].*

```
printf (" %d ",listC[n]);
}
```

```
OUTPUT
Enter elements for first list : 1 5 4 -3 2
Enter elements for second list : 9 5 1 2 10
Merged sorted list :
-3 1 1 2 2 4 5 5 9 10
```

The value of *m* is initially zero. The sum obtained is again subtracted from m. This is because if negative numbers are entered, they are to be considered in the sorting. For example, the value of *sum*=20. In real execution, the sum may be different depending on integers entered.

Value of *m* would be m = -20 (as pre m = m-20 when m = 0)

Thus, in the while loop value of m varies from –20 to 20. In this range, all the entered elements are covered. The value of m changes from –20 to 20, i.e. –20,-19 upto +20 in ascending order. Thus, the same order is applied while saving element in *arrayC[]*.

Time Complexity f(n) represents the number of comparisons needed to sort an array consisting of n elements. In worst case in every *pass n* comparisons would be needed for sorting the elements. The algorithms require at most $\log_2 n$ passes.

Please note that this algorithm has the same order as that of heap sort. Also, for average case it is similar to quick sort.

10.9 HEAP SORT

In heap sort, we use the binary tree in which the nodes are arranged in specific prearranged order. The rule prescribes that each node should have bigger value than its child node. The following steps are to be followed in heap sort:

1. Arrange the nodes in the binary tree form.
2. Node should be arranged as per the specific rules.
3. If the inserted node is bigger than its parent node then replace the node.
4. If the inserted node is lesser than its parent node then do not change the position.
5. Do not allow entering nodes on right side until the child nodes of the left are fulfilled.
6. Do not allow entering nodes on left side until the child nodes of the right are fulfilled.
7. The procedure from step 3 to step 6 is repeated for each entry of the node.

Consider the numbers 56, 23, 10, 99, 6, 19, 45, 45, 23 for sorting using heap. Sorting process is illustrated in Fig. 10.7.

1. At first, we pickup the first element 56 from the list. Make it as the root node.
2. Next, take the second element 23 from the list. Insert this to the left of the root node 56. Refer the Fig. 10.7 (2).
3. Then, take the third element 10 from the list for insertion. Insert it to the right of the root node.

4. Take the fourth element 99. Insert it to the left side node 23. The inserted element is greater than the parent element, hence swap the 99 with 23. But the parent node 56 is smaller than the child node 99 hence 99 and 56 are swapped. After swapping 99 becomes the root node. This is shown in Fig. 10.7 (4) and (5).
5. Consider the next element 6 to insert in the tree. Insert it at left side . There exists left node, hence insert it to the right of the 56. Refer Fig. 10.7 (6).
6. Element 19 is inserted to the right side of the 99 because the left side gets full. Insert the element 19 to the right node 10. However, the parent element is lesser than the child, hence swaps the 19 with 10.
7. Now, element 45 is to be inserted at the right side of 19. However, the parent element is having the value lesser than the child element hence swap the 45 with 19. Refer the Fig. 10.7 (9) and (10).
8. Now, the right side is fully filled hence add the next element 45 to the left. The element 45 is inserted at the last node of the left, i.e. 23. However, the parent element is having the value lesser than the child element hence swap 45 with 23. Refer the Fig. 10.7 (11) and (12).
9. Insert the last element 23 to the left side node, i.e. 45. The left of the 45 is already filled hence insert the element 23 at the right of the 45. Refer the Fig. 10.7 (13).
10. At last, we get a sorted heap tree, as shown in Fig. 10.7 (13).

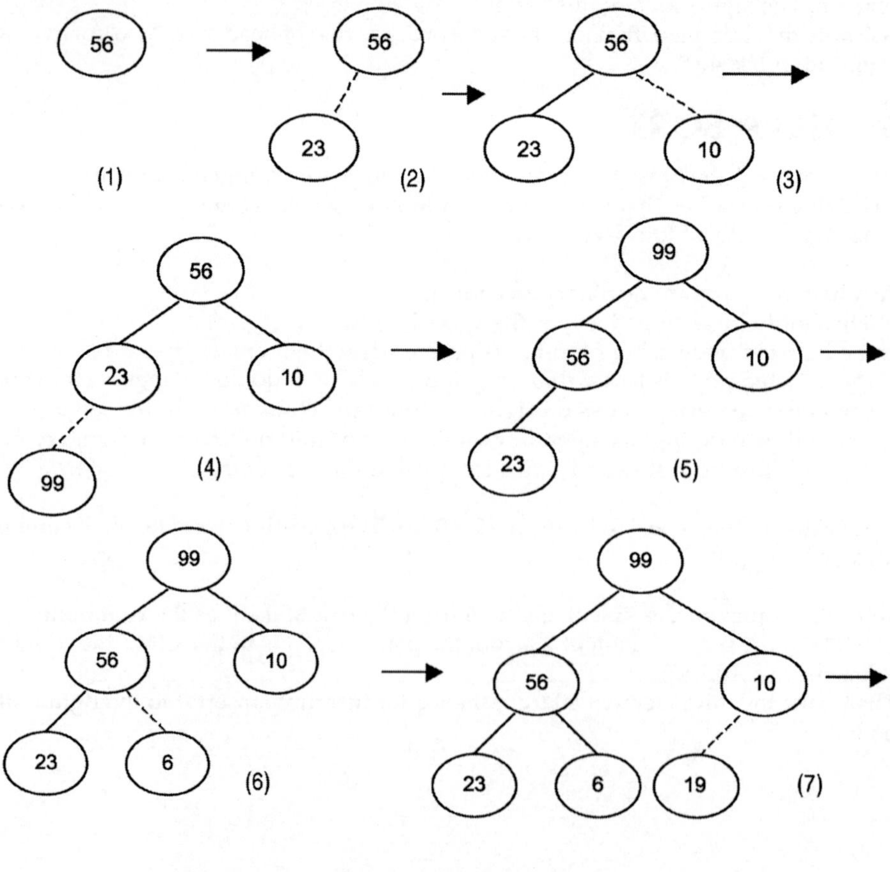

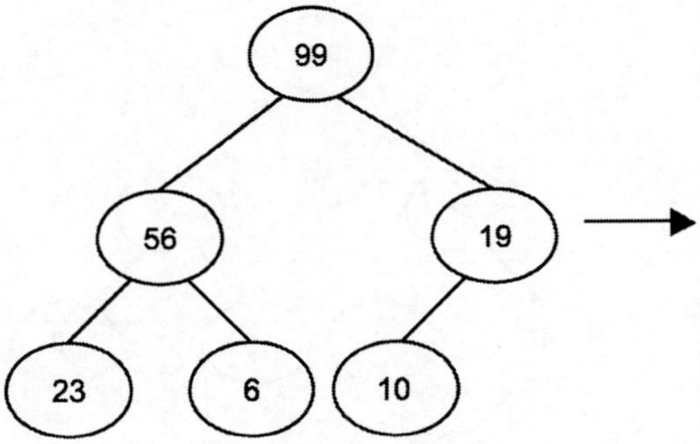
99
56
19
23
6
10

(8)

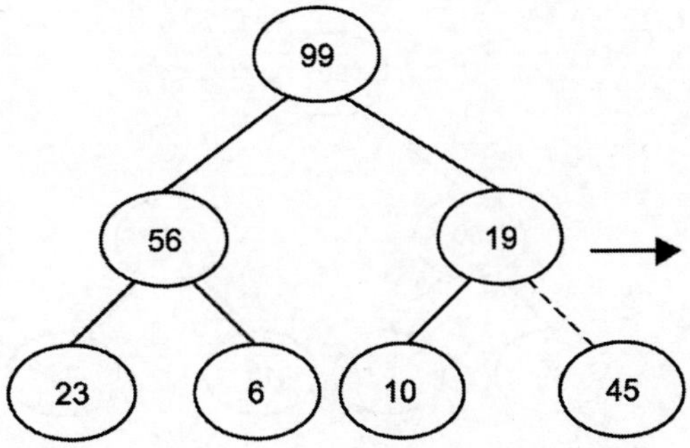
99
56
19
23
6
10
45

(9)

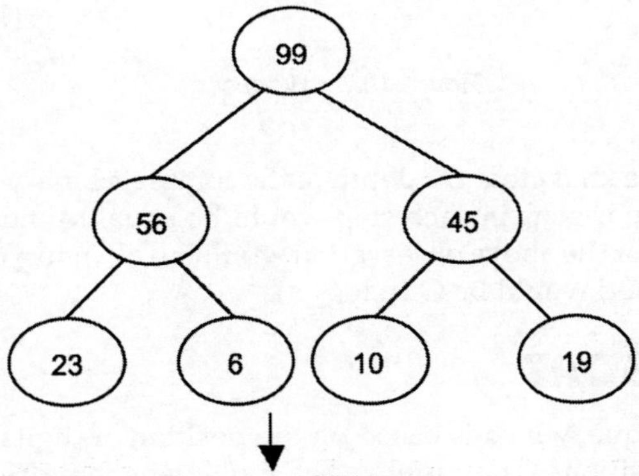
99
56
45
23
6
10
19

(10)

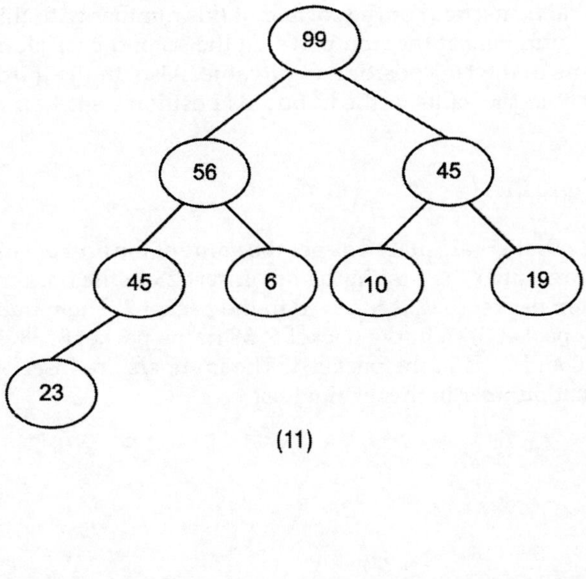
99
56
45
45
6
10
19
23

(11)

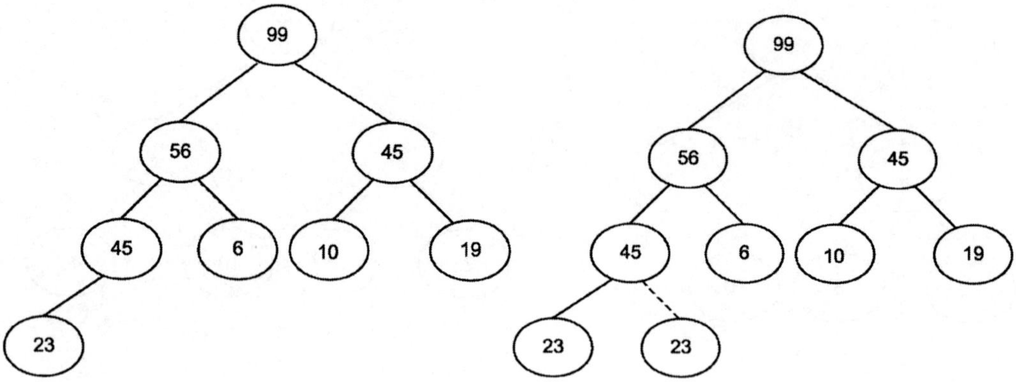

(12) (13)

Figure 10.7 Heap sort

Time Complexity We know that the depth of the complete binary tree is ($\log_2 n$). In worst case, the number of comparisons in each step would be equal to the depth of the tree. The number of comparisons for the above observation would be O (n $\log_2 n$). Thus, the number of comparisons in this method would be O (n $\log_2$ n).

10.10 RADIX SORT

The radix sort is a technique, which is based on the position of digits. The number is represented with different positions. The number has units, tens, hundreds positions onwards. Based on its position the sorting is done. For example, consider the number 456, which is selected for sorting. In this number 6 is at units position and 5 is at tens and 4 is at the hundreds position. 3 passes would be needed for the sorting of this number with this procedure. In the first pass, we place all numbers at the unit place. In the second pass all numbers are placed in the list with consents to the tens position digit value. Also, in the third pass the numbers are placed with consent to the value of the hundreds position digit.

For example:

23,46,12,34,45,49,58,38,10,21.

In the first pass, the numbers are placed as per the value of the unit position digit. First, take number 23, which is present at the first in the list. Insert 23 in the packet labelled 3. Second number 46 is inserted in packet 6. 12 is inserted in the packet 2. The number 34 is inserted in the packet 4. 45 in the packet 5, 46 in the packet 6, 58 in the packet 8, 38 is also in the packet 8, 10 is in the packet 0 and 21 is in the packet 1. The numbers are inserted in the packets as per the sequence of that number in the original list.

Table 10.1 Sorting the numbers on unit place digit

Pass									38	
1st	10	21	12	23	34	45	46		58	49
Packets for unit place	0	1	2	3	4	5	6	7	8	9

In first pass sort the elements as per the value of the unit place digit. The operation is shown in the above Table 10.1. After the first pass we get the following list as:

10,21,12,23,34,45,46,58,38,49.

Perform the second pass operation on the list, which is sorted list after the first pass. As per the values of the digit of the tens position, the place of the elements is fixed. At first, take the first element 10 of the list, which is obtained after the first pass. Insert 10 into the packet 1; insert 21 in the 2(second) packet. This procedure is repeated until the end of the list. In the second pass, the numbers are as:

Table 10.2 Sorting the numbers on ten's place digit

Pass					49					
		12	23	38	46					
2nd		10	21	34	45	58				
Packets for unit place	0	1	2	3	4	5	6	7	8	9

Table 10.2 shows the second pass for sorting the numbers. The sorted list after the second pass is as:

10,12,21,23,34,38,45,46,49,58.

By appropriately placing numbers, the sorted list of the items or elements is obtained. In this example of radix sort, two passes are required for complete sorting. The number of passes depends upon the length of the greatest number in the list. If the list contains the numbers greater than the 99, then the number of passes must be greater than 3 or equal to 3.

Example 10.8

Write a program to sort the given single digit numbers by using the radix sort.

Solution

```
#include<stdio.h>
#include<conio.h>

main()
{
static int bk[10][5],k1,k2,k3,k4,k5,k6,k7,k8,k9,k0,p;
int i,j,no_p,list[5],slist[5];
clrscr();
printf("Enter the one digit elements:-");
for(i=0;i<5;i++)
scanf("%d",&list[i]);
for(i=0;i<5;i++)
{
no_p=list[i]%10;
switch(no_p)
{
case 0: bk[0][k0++]=list[i];  break;
case 1: bk[1][k1++]=list[i];  break;
case 2: bk[2][k2++]=list[i];  break;
case 3: bk[3][k3++]=list[i];  break;
case 4: bk[4][k4++]=list[i];  break;
case 5: bk[5][k5++]=list[i];  break;
case 6: bk[6][k6++]=list[i];  break;
case 7: bk[7][k7++]=list[i];  break;
case 8: bk[8][k8++]=list[i];  break;
case 9: bk[9][k9++]=list[i];  break;
}
}
printf("The elements in table are:-");
printf("\n————————————————————————");
printf("\n\t\t\tElements");
for(j=0;j<10;j++)
{
printf("\nElements in bucket %d:-",j);
for(i=0;i<5;i++)
if(bk[j][i]>0)
{
printf("%3d",bk[j][i]);
slist[p++]=bk[j][i];
}
}
printf("\n————————————————————————");
printf("\nThe sorted numbers:-");
for(i=0;i<5;i++)
printf("%2d",slist[i]);
}
```

Explanation In this program the *list[]* is initialized to store the inputted numbers from the keyboard. The static int *bk[][]* is used to store the numbers in the buckets 0 to 9. The *k0* to *k9* are the variables, which are used to limit the buckets. The *no_p* variable stores the elements in buckets by the *switch()* control statement. At last, the sorted list is stored into the *slist[]*.

```
OUTPUT

Enter the one digit elements:- 1 6 8 3 6
The elements in table are:-
-----------------------------
                              Elements
Elements in bucket 0:-
Elements in bucket 1:-           1
Elements in bucket 2:-
Elements in bucket 3:-           3
Elements in bucket 4:-
Elements in bucket 5:-
Elements in bucket 6:-           6  6
Elements in bucket 7:-
Elements in bucket 8:-           8
Elements in bucket 9:-
-----------------------------
The sorted numbers:- 1 3 6 6 8
```

Example 10.9

Write a program to sort the given two digit numbers by using the radix sort. Use function.

Solution

```
#include<stdio.h>
#include<conio.h>
int l[5],flag=0;

main()
{
 int i,j;
 void place();
 clrscr();
 printf("Enter five elements with two digits:-");
 for(i=0;i<5;i++)
  scanf("%d",&l[i]);
 printf("\nThe first sorted table is");
 place();
 printf("\nFirst sorted list :-");
 for(i=0;i<5;i++)
 printf("%3d",l[i]);
  flag=2;
 getch();
 printf("\n\nThe final sorted table is");
 place();
 printf("\nFinal sorted list :-");
```

Explanation In this program function *place()* is used to sort the list. The variable *n* is used to store either the reminder or quotient. The modulus operator is used for finding the unit place and the divide operation for tens place. Then, these elements are stored in buckets by the *switch ()* control statement. After the first call of the *place ()* the first sorted list is stored into the *l[]* and after second call the final sorted list is placed into *l[]*.

```
 for(i=0;i<5;i++)
 printf("%3d",l[i]);
 getch();
}
void place()
 {
 int k1,k2,k3,k4,k5,k6,k7,k8,k9,k0;
 int a,p,q,r;
 int n,b[10][5]={0};
 k0=k1=k2=k3=k4=k5=k6=k7=k8=k9=a=0;
 while(a<5)
  {
   if(flag==2)
    n=l[a]/10;
   else
    n=l[a]%10;
   switch(n)
   {
     case 0: b[0][k0++]=l[a];  break;
     case 1: b[1][k1++]=l[a];  break;
     case 2: b[2][k2++]=l[a];  break;
     case 3: b[3][k3++]=l[a];  break;
     case 4: b[4][k4++]=l[a];  break;
     case 5: b[5][k5++]=l[a];  break;
     case 6: b[6][k6++]=l[a];  break;
     case 7: b[7][k7++]=l[a];  break;
     case 8: b[8][k8++]=l[a];  break;
     case 9: b[9][k9++]=l[a];  break;
   }a++;
  }
 r=0;
 for(p=0;p<10;p++)
  {
   if(b[p][0]!=0)
  printf("\nBucket %d contain:-",p);

   for(q=0;q<5;q++)
    if(b[p][q]>0)
    {
    printf("%3d",b[p][q]);
    l[r++]=b[p][q];
    }
  }
}
```

OUTPUT

Enter five elements with two digits:-99 12 11 48 10

```
The first sorted table is
Bucket 0 contain:- 10
Bucket 1 contain:- 11
Bucket 2 contain:- 12
Bucket 8 contain:- 48
Bucket 9 contain:- 99
First sorted list :- 10 11 12 48 99
The final sorted table is
Bucket 1 contain:- 10 11 12
Bucket 4 contain:- 48
Bucket 9 contain:- 99
Final sorted list :- 10 11 12 48 99
```

Time Complexity Number of comparisons require for radix sort algorithm in the worst case $f(n)=O(n^2)$ and in best case $f(n)= O(n \log_2 n)$.

10.11 PARTITION EXCHANGE SORT

The partition exchange sort is the sorting technique in which list of elements is divided into the two subparts. Using the pivot from the list makes the sublist of the list. The left part is called left sublist and the right part is called right sublist. On the sublist quick or the tree sort is performed and the two-sorted parts are prepared and combined.

For example, consider the following list:

24, 30, 27, 32, 11, 21, 19.

Assume the pivot key selected is 24 and the smaller numbers than pivot are shifted on its left side and remaining greater elements to the right of it. The element 24 divides the list in two parts. The Fig. 10.8 shows the partition exchange sort.

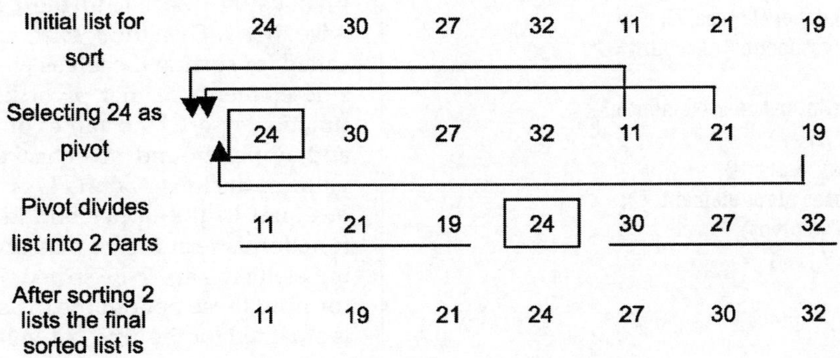

Figure 10.8 Partition exchange sort

After the swapping the elements towards left of the pivot:

11, 21, 19, 24, 30, 27, 32.

After removing 24 the two sublists become:

11, 21, 19 and 30, 27, 32.

The left and right parts after sorting:

11, 19, 21
27, 30, 32

After combining the two parts including the pivot key the sorted list becomes:

11, 19, 21, 24, 27, 30, 32.

Following program is presented on the same concept.

Example 10.10

Write a program to sort the elements by using the partition exchange sort.

Solution

```
#include<stdio.h>
#include<conio.h>

int q_sort(int items[],int lower,int upper);
main()
{
  int arr[7],ltree[7],rtree[7];
 int i=0,j,pivot,lcount=0,rcount=0;
 clrscr();
 printf("\nEnter the 7 elements:");
 for(i=0;i<7;i++)
   scanf("%d",&arr[i]);
 printf("Enter pivot element:-");
 scanf("%d",&pivot);
 for(j=0;j<7;j++)
 {
   if(arr[j]<=pivot)
    {
     ++lcount;
     ltree[lcount]=arr[j];
    }
   if(arr[j]>pivot)
```

Explanation In this program seven elements are inputted for sorting into the *arr[]*. After selecting the pivot key the elements whose values are lower than pivot key are placed into the *ltree[]* otherwise *rtree[]*. Then the *q_sort()* is resurvey called for sorting the left as well as right side elements of that pivot key. In the function *q_sort()* the values of the lower and upper bound are checked. If the value of the lower bound is greater than or equal to the upper bound than the function is terminated else the remaining elements are to be sorted. After performing these operations the sorted list is obtained for the *ltree[]* as well as *rtree[]*.

```
        {
          ++rcount;
          rtree[rcount]=arr[j];
        }
  }
 q_sort(ltree,0,lcount);
 for(j=0;j<lcount;j++)
 printf("%d ",ltree[j]);
 q_sort(rtree,0,rcount);
 for(i=0;i<rcount;i++)
 printf("%d ",rtree[i]);
}
int q_sort(int items[],int lower,int upper)
{
  int key,temp,l,r,key_placed=0;
  l=lower;r=upper;key=lower;
  if(lower>=upper)
    return 0;
  while(key_placed==0)
   {
    while( items[key]<=items[r] && key!=r)
      r--;
      if( key==r )
      key_placed=1;
      if( items[key] > items[r] )
      {
        temp=items[key];
        items[key]=items[r];
        items[r]=temp;
         key=r;
      }
     while( items[key]>=items[l] && l!=key )
      l++;
      if(key==l)
      key_placed=1;
      if( items[key] < items[l] )
      {
       temp=items[key];
       items[key]=items[l];
       items[l]=temp;
       key=l;
      }
   }
  q_sort(items,lower,key-1);
  q_sort(items,key+1,upper);
   return 0;
}
```

```
OUTPUT
Enter the 7 elements:- 24 30 27 32 11 21 19
Enter pivot element:- 24
11 19 21 24 27 30 32
```

Summary

This chapter deals with sorting and its implementations.

1. Sorting is a process in which records are arranged in ascending or descending order.
2. This chapter presents information on various sorting methods; each of them is illustrated with suitable example.
3. Insertion sort: In insertion sort the element is inserted at appropriate place. Here, a real life example of playing cards can be quoted. The cards are kept in increasing order. The card having least value is placed at the extreme left and the largest one at the other side. In between them the other cards are inserted in ascending order.
4. Selection sort: The selection sort is almost same as exchange sort. By applying selection sort, the first element is compared with remaining (n–1) elements. The smallest element is placed at the first location. Again, the second element is compared with remaining (n–2) elements. If the item found is lesser than the compared elements in the remaining n–2 list then the swap operation is done. In this type, entire array is checked for the smallest element and then swapped.
5. Bubble sort: Bubble sort is frequently used sorting algorithm. In this method, two successive elements are compared and exchanging is done if the first element is greater than the second one. The elements are sorted in ascending order.
6. Quick sort: It is also recognized as partition exchange sort. This method also falls under divide and conquer technique. The main list of elements is divided into two sub-lists. Any one element from the list is marked as pivot key in the quick sort. Now, the pivot key divides the main list into two parts. It is not necessary that selected key element must be at middle. Any element from the list can act as key element. However, for best performance preference is given to middle elements. Time consumption of the quick sort depends on the location of the key in the list.
9. Tree sort: Inorder and heap sort methods are elaborated under tree sorting. Inorder tree sorting method involves arranging the elements as per rules. In this method, firstly the left element of tree is chosen, then node and right node. The rule for heap sort prescribes that each parent node should have bigger value.
7. Heap sort: In heap sort, binary tree is used in which the nodes are arranged in specific prearranged order. The rule prescribes that each node should have bigger value than its child node. The heap sort process can be followed from the figure and example given in this chapter.
8. Radix sort: The radix sort is based on the position of digits. Based on the positions of digits sorting is done.
9. Partition exchange sort: The partition exchange sort divides the elements into the two subparts. A pivot is selected among the elements. The elements whose values are smaller than the pivot are shifted towards left of it. The right part has elements whose values are greater than the pivot.

Exercises

A. Answer the following questions:

1. What is sorting? How is sorting essential for data base applications?
2. Explain different types of sorting methods.
3. Distinguish between selection and exchange sort.
4. Explain the heap sort method.
5. How does the merge sort work?
6. How does radix sort work?
7. Explain the method of partition exchange sort.
8. Explain the insertion sort with its time complexity.
9. Compare the performance of selection and insertion sort.
10. How does the quick sort work? Explain with a suitable example.
11. Describe the working of tree sort.

B. Write following programs:

1. Apply selection sort on given ten numbers and sort them in ascending order.
2. Sort ten names of the students using merge sort.
3. Apply the quick sort to the given ten names and sort them in alphabetic order.
4. Write a program for sorting the given list by descending orders, using selection sort.
5. Apply tree-sorting method (inorder) on given ten numbers and arrange them in ascending order.
6. Write a program by using heap sort for sorting given numbers.
7. Apply partition sort on twelve numbers.
8. Write a program for sorting two digit numbers using radix sort.
9. Write a function for bubble sort.
10. Use selection sort method for sorting five numbers using pointers.
11. Write a program to sort 15 elements using bubble sort. Assume any suitable elements.
12. Write a program to sort the elements 2,32,45,67,89,4,3,8,10 in descending order using insertion sort.
13. Write a program to sort a given list of elements using tree sort.
14. Write a program to sort one digit number by using the radix sort method. Use pointer.
15. Write a program to sort the following numbers in ascending order using selection sort. 12,34,5,78,4,56,10,23,1,45,65.

C. Select the appropriate option for each of the following questions:

1. The process of arranging records in ordered manner is called
   a. sorting
   b. searching
   c. indexing
   d. none of the above.
2. In insertion sort, the shifting of numbers are:
   a. shift greater numbers at end and smaller at beginning of the array
   b. shift greater number at the middle and smaller at right
   c. shift smaller at the center and greater at beginning
   d. none of the above.
3. In this type of sort list is divided in two sub-lists:
   a. quick sort
   b. exchange sort
   c. merge sort
   d. none of the above.

4. The exchange sort is also called
   a. bubble sort
   b. merge sort
   c. shell sort
   d. none of the above.
5. In the bubble sort the sorting is done with comparing
   a. successive elements
   b. first and last elements
   c. last and middle elements
   d. none of the above.
6. In tree sort the elements are sorted with
   a. inorder traversing
   b. preorder traversing
   c. post order traversing
   d. none of the above.
7. Radix sort method is based on
   a. the positions of the digits
   b. the cubes of digits
   c. the squares of digits
   d. none of the above.
8. For sorting the elements with partition exchange sort which method is used?
   a. bubble sort
   b. quick sort
   c. heap sort
   d. none of the above.
9. In heap sort the numbers are initially arranged in
   a. ascending order
   b. descending order
   c. binary tree
   d. none of the above .
10. With merge sort number of list that can be sorted are
    a. one list
    b. more than one lists
    c. none of the above .

D. What is the output of each of the following programs?

1.

```
#include<stdio.h>
#include<conio.h>

main()
{
static int b[10][7],k1,k2,k3,k4,k5,k6,k7,k8,
k9,k0,p;
int i,j,no,l[7],sl[7];
clrscr();
printf("Enter elements <10:-");
for(i=0;i<7;i++)
scanf("%d",&l[i]);
i=0;
while(i<7)
{
no=l[i]%10;
switch(no)
{
case 0: b[0][k0++]=l[i];  break;
case 1: b[1][k1++]=l[i];  break;
case 2: b[2][k2++]=l[i];  break;
case 3: b[3][k3++]=l[i];  break;
case 4: b[4][k4++]=l[i];  break;
case 5: b[5][k5++]=l[i];  break;
case 6: b[6][k6++]=l[i];  break;
case 7: b[7][k7++]=l[i];  break;
case 8: b[8][k8++]=l[i];  break;
case 9: b[9][k9++]=l[i];  break;
}i++;
}
printf("The table is:-");
for(j=0;j<10;j++)
{
printf("\nBucket %d contain:-",j);
for(i=0;i<5;i++)
if(b[j][i]>0)
{
printf("%3d",b[j][i]);
sl[p++]=b[j][i];
}
}
printf("\nSorted list:-");
for(i=0;i<7;i++)
printf("%2d",sl[i]);
}
```

2.

```
#include <stdio.h>
#include <conio.h>
main()
{
int ns[5],p=0,q=1,temp;
clrscr();
printf ("\n Enter 5 elements : ");
while (p<5)
scanf("%d", &ns[p++]);
for(q=1;q<5;q++)
{
temp=ns[q];
for(p=q-1;p>=0 && temp<ns[p];p—)
ns[p+1]=ns[p];
ns[p+1]=temp;
}
printf("Sorted elements are : ");
for (p = 0; p < 5; p++)
printf("%d ", ns[p]);
}
```

3.

```
#include <stdio.h>
# include <conio.h>
main()
{
int p=0,q,r,num,t,small;
int arr[5]={ 12,23,1,4,2 };
clrscr();
for(p=0; p<4;p++)
{
small = p;
for(r=p+1; r<5;r++)
if(arr[small] > arr[r])
small = r ;
if( p != small )
{
t = arr [p];
arr[p] = arr[small];
arr[small] = t ;
}
}
printf("\nSorted elements are: ");
p=0;
for(p=0;p<5;p++)
printf("%d ", arr[p]);
}
```

4.

```
#include<stdio.h>
#include<conio.h>
main()
{
int arr1[5]={12,3,122,321,1},i,j,t;
clrscr();
for(i=0;i<5;i++)
for(j=i;j<4;j++)
if(arr1[i]>arr1[j+1])
{
t=arr1[i];
arr1[i]=arr1[j+1];
arr1[j+1]=t;
}
for(i=0;i<5;i++)
printf(" %d ",arr1[i]);
}
```

5.

```
# include <stdio.h>
# include <conio.h>
# include <math.h>
main ()
{
int m,n,p,sum=0,sl[10]={0};
int l1[5]={4,2,1,43,3},l2[5]={9,7,6,8,5};
clrscr();
for (n=0;n<5;n++)
{
sum=sum+l1[n];
}
for (n=0;n<5;n++)
{
sum=sum+l2[n];
}
p=n=m=0;
m=m-sum;
while (m<sum)
{
for (n=0;n<5;n++)
{
if (m==l1[n] || m==l2[n])
sl[p++]=m;
if (m==l1[n] && m==l2[n])
sl[p++]=m;
}
```

```
m++;
}
puts (" Merged sorted list : ");
for (n=0;n<10;++n)
printf (" %d ",sl[n]);
}
```

6.

```
#include <stdio.h>
#include <conio.h>
main()
{
int ns[5]={12,34,2,10,1},*pt,p=0,q=1,temp;
pt=&ns[0];
clrscr();
for(q=1;q<5;q++)
{
temp=*(pt+q);
for(p=q-1;p>=0 && temp<*(pt+p);p--)
*(pt+p+1)=*(pt+p);
*(pt+p+1)=temp;
}
printf("Sorted elements are : ");
for (p = 0; p < 5; p++)
printf("%d ", ns[p]);
}
```

7.

```
#include <stdio.h>
#include <conio.h>
int ns[5]={123,67,34,2,12};
main()
{
int p;
void sort();
clrscr();
sort();
printf("Sorted elements:- ");
for (p = 0; p < 5; p++)
printf("%d ", ns[p]);
}
void sort()
{
int q,p,temp;
for(q=1;q<5;q++)
{
temp=ns[q];
for(p=q-1;p>=0 && temp<ns[p];p—)
ns[p+1]=ns[p];
ns[p+1]=temp;
}
}
```

Chapter 11

Searching

Chapter Outline

11.1 INTRODUCTION

In our day-to-day life there are various applications, in which the process of searching is to be carried. Searching a name of a person from the given list, searching a specific card from the set of cards, etc., are few examples of searching.

A typical example where searching technique is applied is personal telephone diary. This diary is used to store phone/mobile numbers of friends, relatives, etc. For searching the phone number of a person one can directly search the number by using indexing in that diary. Quick search methods are to be adopted to search the data from the heap or large records. Two processes such as searching and sorting are essential for database applications.

In short, searching is a process in which a given record is searched from the set of records. Sorting is a process in which records are arranged in ascending or descending order. A group of field is called record. For example, consider the following structure:

```
struct employee
{
   char *name;
   int age;
   float  height;
} s;
```

We are familiar with the above declarations and definitions. The object *s* contains three fields as described in the structure. The database is a collection of such fields. Each record contains the above fields or may vary depending upon the structure defined. The sorting can be done on any one or combination of one or more fields. Suppose, we sort the records based on name. Then, the field *name* will be the key field. A record is quickly searched in a sorted database. Thus, sorting and searching are very useful concepts of data structure. This chapter aims to provide the information on searching and its techniques.

11.2 SEARCHING

Searching is a technique of finding an element from the given data list or set of the elements like an array, list, or trees. It is a technique to find out an element in a sorted or unsorted list. For example, consider an array of 10 elements. These data elements are stored in successive memory locations. We need to search an element from the array. In the searching operation, assume a particular element n is to be searched. The element n is compared with all the elements in a list starting from the first element of an array till the last element. In other words, the process of searching is continued till the element is found or list is completely exhausted. When the exact match is found then the search process is terminated. In case, no such element exists in the array, the process of searching should be abandoned.

In case the given element is existing in the set of elements or array then the search process is said to be successful as per Fig. 11.1. It means that the given element belongs to the array. The search is said to be unsuccessful if the given element does not exist in the array as per Fig. 11.2. It means that the given element does not belong to the array or collection of the items.

The complexity of any searching method is determined from the number of comparisons performed among the collected elements in order to find the element. The time required for the operation is dependent on the complexity of the operation or algorithm. In other words, the performance of searching algorithm can be measured by counting the comparisons in order to find the given element from the list. There are three cases in which an element can be found.

In the best case, the element is found during the first comparison itself. In the worst case, the element is found only in the last comparison. Whereas in the average case, number of comparisons should be more than comparisons in the best case and less than the worst case.

The searching can be classified into following types:

1. Linear search (sequential)
2. Binary search.

11.3 LINEAR (SEQUENTIAL) SEARCH

The linear search is a conventional method of searching data. The linear search is a method of searching a target element in a list sequence. The expected element is to be searched in the entire data structure in a sequential method from starting to last element. Though, it is simple and straightforward, it has serious limitations. It consumes more time and reduces the retrieval rate of the system. The linear or sequential name implies that the items are stored in systematic manner. The linear search can be applied on sorted or unsorted linear data structure.

Fig. 11.1 and 11.2 shows the searching by using the linear search method.

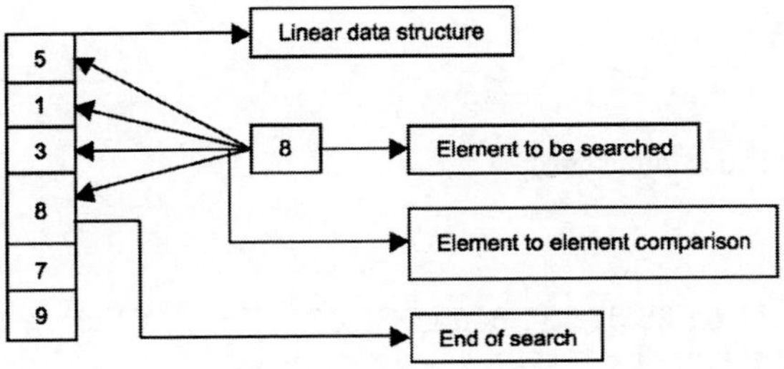

Figure 11.1

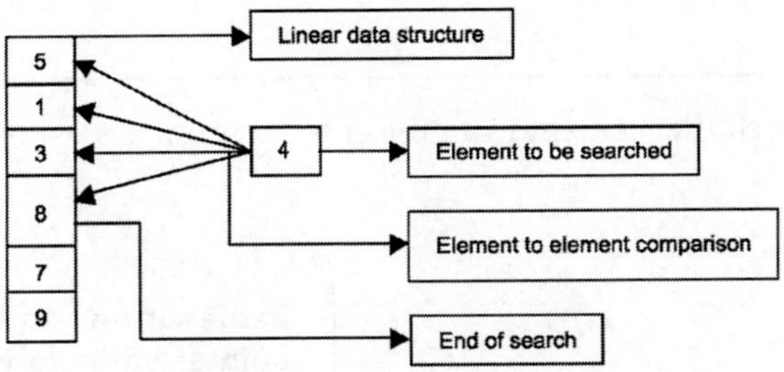

Figure 11.2 Unsuccessful search

Example 11.1

Write a program to search an element from the entered numbers. Also, indicate its position in case the element is found or unavailability.

Solution

```
#include <stdio.h>
#include<conio.h>
main()
{
int sn,arr[10],a;
clrscr();
printf("Enter ten elements:-");
for(a=1;a<=10;a++)
scanf("%d",&arr[a]);
printf("Enter the element to be searched:-");
scanf("%d",&sn);
a=1;
while(a<10)
{
  if(arr[a]==sn)
   {
  printf("The number %d is found %d location",sn,a);
   break;
   }
```

Explanation In this program the user enters ten elements by involving an array *arr[]*. The number, which is to be searched, is initialized with variable sn. By using the *for* loop ten elements are entered into the *arr[]*. By using the *while* loop the number is searched throughout the array and appropriate message is displayed.

```
   a++;
 }
if(arr[a]!=sn)
printf("The element %d is not found",sn);
}
```

```
OUTPUT
Enter ten elements:-12 34 64 23 67 123 346 45 30 19
Enter the element to be searched:-64
The number 64 is found 3 location
```

Example 11.2

Write a program to search the element from the entered numbers using the pointer.

Solution

```
#include <stdio.h>
#include<conio.h>
main()
{
  int sno,i;
  int ar[10],*list;
 clrscr();
  printf("Enter ten elements:-");
  for(i=1;i<=10;i++)
    scanf("%d",&ar[i]);
  printf("Enter the element to be searched:-");
 scanf("%d",&sno);
  list=&ar[1];
 for(i=1;i<=10;i++)
  {
  if(*list==sno)
    {
     printf("The number %d is found %d location",sno,i);
      break;
    }
   list++;
}
if(*list!=sno)
  printf("The element %d is not found",sno);
getch();
}
```

Explanation In this program **list* is a pointer variable which is used to store the address of the first element of the array. Ten elements are entered into the *arr[]* by using the *for* loop. First element address is stored into the **list* variable. By increasing the address, all elements of the array are accessed. If the match is found then message is displayed on screen.

```
OUTPUT

Enter ten elements:-12 44 23 122 45 67 78 56 65 90
Enter the element to be searched:-67
The number 67 is found 6 location
```

Example 11.3

Write a program to create a linked list and search a specific element from the linked list.

Solution

```
# include <stdio.h>
# include <conio.h>
# include <malloc.h>

struct link
{
  int num;
  struct link *next;
};
int j;
struct link begin;
void search(struct link*);
void create_list(struct link*);
void show(struct link *);
void create_list(struct link *link)
{
 int n=1,c=1;
 begin.next=NULL;
 link=&begin;
 j=0;
  printf ("\n Input integers (0 to stop) :\n");
 while (n)
 {
   printf("Enter the %d number:-",c);
   scanf ("%d", &n);
   if (n==0) break;
  else link->next=(struct link*) malloc(sizeof(struct link));

   link->num=n;
   link=link->next;
   link->next=NULL;
  fflush(stdin);
   c++;
}
}
void search(struct link *link)
{
 int node_num=0;
 int s_node;
 int flag=0;
 link=&begin;
```

Explanation In this program, the *struct link* is used to store linked list. List is created with *create ()* function. The number, which is to be searched, is entered. In the *search ()* function the entered number is compared with the linked list elements. When equal number is found the number along with its position in the linked list is displayed. The *show ()* function is used to display all the linked list elements. Thus, through traversing and comparing elements search process is done.

```
printf ("\n Enter number to be searched : ");
scanf ("%d",&s_node);
if (link==NULL)
printf ("\n List is empty ");
while (link)
{
 if (s_node==link->num)
 {
 printf ("\n search is successful");
  printf ("\n Position of %d from beginning of the list : %d",s_node,node_num+1);
  link=link->next;
  flag=1;
  }
  else
   link=link->next;
  node_num++;
  }
  if (!flag)
  {
  printf ("\n Search is unsuccessful");
   printf ("\n %d does not found in the list", s_node);
   }
   }
  void show (struct link * link)
   {
   link=&begin;
  while(link->next)
   {
  printf(" %d",link->num);
   link=link->next;
   }
 }
 void main ()
 {
 struct link *link=(struct link *) malloc (sizeof(struct link));
 clrscr();
 create_list(link);
  printf ("\n List :  ");
 show(link);
 search(link);
  }
```

```
OUTPUT
Input integers (0 to stop) :
Enter the 1 number:-12
Enter the 2 number:-23
Enter the 3 number:-34
```

```
Enter the 4 number:-45
Enter the 5 number:-56
Enter the 6 number:-76
Enter the 7 number:-0
List :  12 23 34 45 56 76
Enter number to be searched  : 34
search is successful
Position of 34 from beginning of the list : 3
```

11.4 BINARY SEARCH

The binary search approach is different from the linear search. Here, search of an element is not passed in sequence as in the case of linear search. Instead, two partitions of lists are made and then the given element is searched. Hence, it creates two parts of the lists known as binary search. Fig. 11.3 illustrates the operation of the binary search.

Binary search is quicker than the linear search. It is an efficient searching technique and works with sorted lists. However, it cannot be applied on unsorted data structure. Before applying binary search, the linear data structure must be sorted in either ascending or descending order. The binary search is unsuccessful if the elements are unordered. The binary search is based on the approach divide-and-conquer. In binary search, the element is compared with the middle element. If the expected element falls before the middle element, the left portion is searched otherwise right portion is searched.

The binary searching method is illustrated in Fig. 11.3.

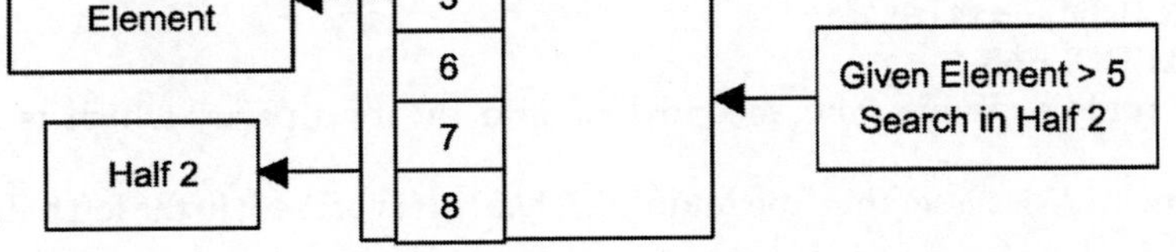

Figure 11.3 Binary search

Fig. 11.3 represents the operation of binary search. The total elements in the list are 8, and they are shown in the ascending order. In case the key element is less than 5 then searching is done in lower half otherwise in the upper half. The process of searching can be followed from the following Fig. 11.4.

Consider the array of seven elements. The array can be represented in Fig. 11.4(a). The elements of an array are 12, 14, 16, 19, 23, 27, and 31. Assume that we want to search the element 27 from the list of elements. The steps are as follows:

Arr[0]	Arr[1]	Arr[2]	Arr[3]	Arr[4]	Arr[5]	Arr[6]
12	14	16	19	23	27	31

Figure 11.4(a) Array in memory

1. The element 12 and 31 are at positions first and last, respectively.
2. Calculate the mid-value which is as
   MID=(FIRST+LAST)/2.
   MID = (0+6)/2.
   MID=3.
3. The key element 23 is to be compared with the mid-value. If the key is less than the mid then the key element is present in the first half else in the other half; in this case the key is on the right half. Hence, first is equal to middle+1.

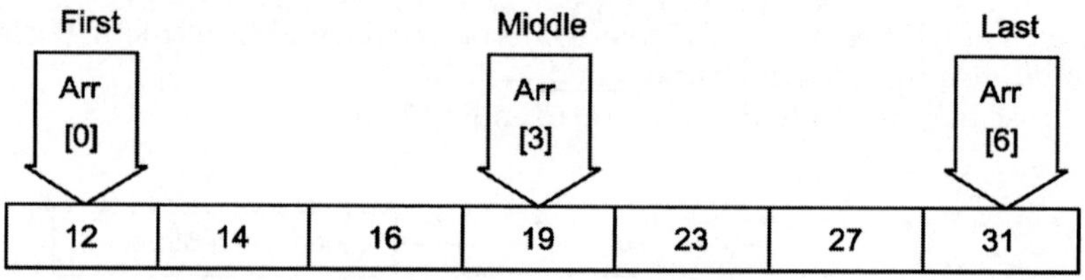

Figure 11.4(b) Calculating the middle at starting

4. Calculate the middle of the second half.
   MIDDLE=(FIRST+LAST)/2.
   MIDDLE = (4+6)/2
   MIDDLE=5.
5. Again, the middle divides the second half into the two parts, which is shown in Fig. 11.4(c).
6. The key element 23 is lesser than the middle 27, hence it is present in the left half (towards the left of 27).

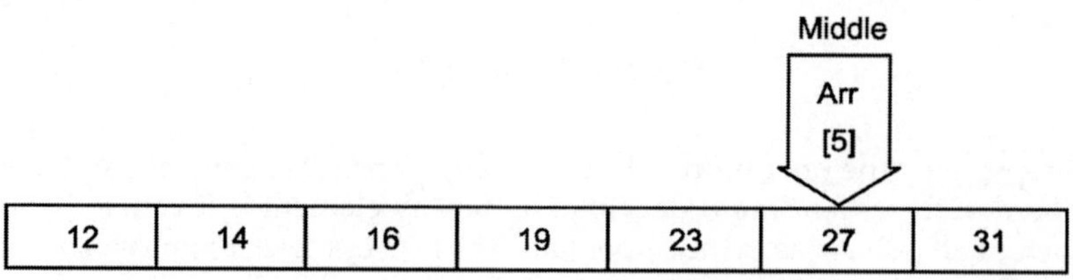

Figure 11.4(c) Finding element in second half

7. At last, the middle is calculated as
   MIDDLE =(FIRST + LAST)/2.
   MIDDLE=(4+4)/2.
   MIDDLE=4.
8. Now, the middle is 4 position and the middle element is 23. The key is searched successfully.

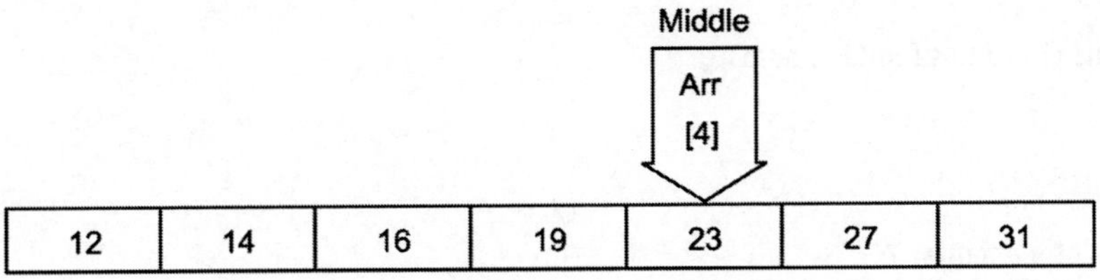

Figure 11.4(d) Result of searching

Based on the above concept an example is illustrated below.

Example 11.4

Write a program to sort an array elements using binary search.

Solution

```
#include <stdio.h>
#include <conio.h>

main()
{
  int items[20], s=0,e,n,j,num,mid;
  clrscr();

  printf ("\n Enter number of elements : ");
  scanf ("%d",&n);
  for (j=0;j<n;j++)
  {
    printf (" Enter element  %d : ",1+j);
    scanf ("%d",&items[j]);
  }

 printf ("\n Enter element to be searched :");
 scanf("%d",&num);
 e=n-1;
 mid=(s+e)/2;
 while (num!=items[mid] && s<=e)
 {
  if (num>items[mid])
   s=mid+1;
```

Explanation In this program an array *items[20]* elements is declared. The user is prompted to enter number of elements to be in the list. The numbers are entered through the keyboard. The variable *s* keeps track of the starting of list and the variable *e* keeps track of the end. The middle is calculated with the formula *mid=(s+e)/2;* If the sum of *(s+e)* is odd number then the result of division operation would be a float value. However, all the operands*(s,e)* of equation are integers, the float value is converted to lowest integer.

```
  else
  e=mid-1;
  mid=(s+e)/2;
 }
 if (num==items[mid])
  printf ("\n  %d found at position %d ",num,++mid);

 if (s>e) printf (" %d not found ", num);
 getch();
}
```

```
OUTPUT
Enter number of elements: 7
Enter element 1: 7
Enter element 2: 13
Enter element 3: 22
Enter element 4: 31
Enter element 5: 45
Enter element 6: 64
Enter element 7: 77
Enter element to be searched: 7
7 found at position 1
```

The above explanation is illustrated with the following figure, which is self-explanatory.

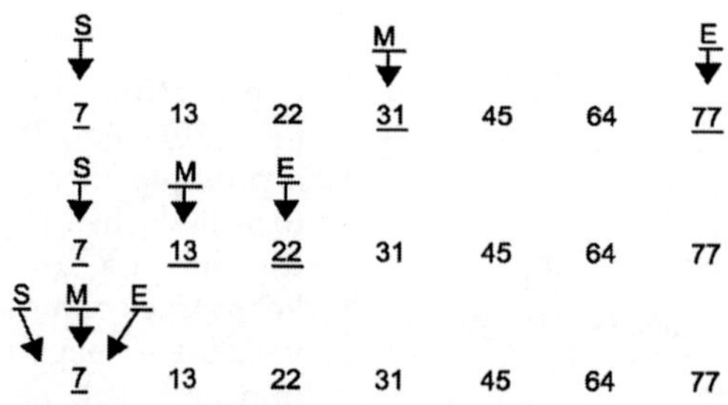

Example 11.5

Write a program to demonstrate binary search. Use character array and store 10 names.

Solution

```
#include<stdio.h>
#include<string.h>
#include<conio.h>

main()
{
   int beg=1,mid,end=10,i,flag=0,val;
   char name[15][10],fn[15];
```

Explanation This program prompts the user to enter ten names.They are stored in the *name [15][10]*, the *fn[15]* is used to store the name which we want to search. The program uses the binary search to search the entered name. In the search method the user must enter the list of name in ascending order. In this method first the *mid* is calculated by using *beg* and *end*.

```
  clrscr();
  printf("Enter 10 names :-\n");
  for(i=1;i<11;i++)
   scanf("%s",&name[i]);
  printf("\n\tEnter the name to search:-");
  scanf("%s",&fn);
  mid=(beg+end)/2;
printf("\n\tAt starting beg is %d, mid is %d & end is %d",beg,mid,end);
 while((strcmp(fn,name[mid]))!=0 && beg<=end)
  {
  val=strcmp(fn,name[mid]);
   if(val>0)
   {
   beg=mid+1;
   mid=(beg+end)/2;
  printf("\n\tmid is %d & beg is %d",mid,beg);
   }
   else
   {
   end=mid-1;
   mid=(beg+end)/2;
  printf("\n\tmid is %d & end is %d",mid,end);
   }
  }
 if(strcmp(fn,name[mid])==0){ flag=1; }
  if(flag==1)
 printf("\n\tThe name %s is traced successfully",fn);
  else
 printf("\n\tThe number %s is not traced",fn);
  getche();
  }
```

```
OUTPUT
Enter 10 names :-
ashish bhaskar deepak dinesh gajanan ganesh gopal govind raj ramash
Enter the name to search:-deepak
At starting beg is 1, mid is 5 & end is 10
mid is 2 & end is 4
mid is 3 & beg is 3
The name deepak is traced successfully
Enter 10 names :-
ashish bhaskar deepak dinesh gajanan ganesh goval govind raj ramesh
Enter the name to search:-amit
At starting beg is 1, mid is 5 & end is 10
mid is 2 & end is 4
mid is 1 & end is 1
mid is 0 & end is 0
The number amit is not traced
```

11.5 HASHING METHOD

Hashing technique is one of the complex searching techniques. In this section, we consider a class of search techniques whose search time is dependent on the number of entries available in the table. In this method, we fix the position of the key (element) into the table or the file, which is determined by the hash function. The function in which we use this key is known as hashing function.

For example, we want to search a number from the ten numbers of a file. Then, we must find the number throughout this range from the 1st number to 10th number. When we use the key for fixing its position in a table then the number can be searched very easily.

11.6 HASHING FUNCTION

In order to follow the operation of hashing function, consider an array that comprises a list containing some finite number of elements. Each element of it is a key. On performing operations on each key some value is obtained. The key is assigned to the index, which is having the appropriate value. The table is prepared with the keys called a hashing table.

Let us assume the following array that will hold the hash table:

12,22,32,17,19,28, 15,29,16,18,13,11.

Let us use the division method for the following hash table. We divide the key by '3' and the key is placed in the index based on the remainders obtained. The keys having equal remainders are placed in the same index. Any number divided by 3 always returnes 0,1, or 2. Hash table is prepared with three indices such as 0,1,2. All above keys are stored in these three indices as shown in Table 11.1.

Take the first key '12', divide it by '3' .The reminder is '0', hence insert it into the '0' index.

Then, take the next key '22' divide it by the '3', the reminder is '1'. Hence, insert the key in to the '1' index.

In the same way divide the key '32' by the 3, its reminder is 2. Place it into the '2' index in the table.

For the remaining elements, the same procedure is to be continued and by knowing reminders the numbers can be placed appropriately in the respective index table.

Table 11.1 explains hashing table.

Table 11.1 Hash table

Index	*Key*
0	12, 15, 18
1	22, 19, 28, 16, 13
2	32, 17, 29, 11

In short, the hashing function takes the key, and maps it to some index to the array. In our example, division function has been selected. The programmer can take any other function. This function maps several different keys to the same index. In the above table, key 12,15 and 18 are assigned to the index 0. While keys, 22,19,28,16 and 13 are placed in index 1. Keys 32,17,29 and 11 are in the index 2.

After preparation of the index table, it becomes easier to search the element from the list. One can use any searching method to search the element from the hashing table.

Consider the following program for preparation of an index using divide method.

Example 11.6

Write a program to prepare the hashing table. Enter the elements through the keyboard and map them in index. Use the division function.

Solution

```
#include<stdio.h>
#include<conio.h>
main()
{
int n[12],i0[12],i1[12],i2[12];
int rem,a=0,b=0,c=0,i,j;
clrscr();
printf("\nEnter the elements of array:-");
for(i=0;i<12;i++)
 scanf("%d",&n[i]);
for(i=0;i<12;i++)
{
  rem=n[i]%3;
 if(rem==0)
 {
   a++;
   i0[a]=n[i];
  }
 else
 {
  if(rem==1)
  {
   b++;
   i1[b]=n[i];
  }
  else
  {
   c++;
   i2[c]=n[i];
  }
 }
}
printf("\n\nThe Hashing Table is as follows\n");
printf("————————————————————\n");
printf("Index 0 :-");
for(j=1;j<=a;j++)
```

Explanation In this program the main array *'n[12]'* is declared having 12 elements. In addition to the above *i0[],i1[]* and *i2[]* arrays are initialized for storing the index. These arrays also accommodate 12 elements. In the above program, we calculate the hashing table by using the division method. The keys are divided by 3. Using the mod operation and the reminders are computed, they are placed in the appropriate index.

```
 printf("%5d",i0[j]);
printf("\nIndex 1 :-");
for(j=1;j<=b;j++)
 printf("%5d",i1[j]);
printf("\nIndex 2 :-");
for(j=1;j<=c;j++)
 printf("%5d",i2[j]);
printf("\n————————————————————");
}
```

```
OUTPUT
Enter the elements of array:-12 22 32 17 19 28 15 29 16 18 13 11
The Hashing Table is as follows
————————————————————
Index 0 :-  12  15  18
Index 1 :-  22  19  28  16  13
Index 2 :-  32  17  29  11
————————————————————
```

Some of the hashing methods that are commonly used are stated below.

11.7 DIVISION METHOD

The commonly used hashing method is the division method. In this hashing function, the integer key is divided by some number. The remainder value is taken as the hashing value. This method can be expressed as follows:

$H(k)=k(\text{mod } x)+1.$

In above equation the H(k) is the hashing function. In addition, the k is the key, which is to be used in hashing. The k(mod x) shows the result of division k by x.

In the above equation, the 'k' is the key and the 'x' is the size of list. We can take any value for the x.

For example, key is 25 and x=10

$H(25)=25(\text{mod } 10)+1 =5+1=6.$

Consider an example to prepare a hashing table and search the prompted number from the hashing table. Each number (key) is divided (mod operation) by 3. No addition of 1 is done after division. It is up to the user how to deal with the problem. The user can perform simply division operation and note down the remainders and place them in appropriate index. As such, there will be 3 indices. The following program illustrates this concept.

Example 11.7

Write a program for division method hashing, and find the given number from the hashing table.

Solution

```
#include<stdio.h>
#include<conio.h>
 main()
{
int  n[5],i0[5],i1[5],i2[5];
int num,rem,a=0,b=0,c=0,i,j;
clrscr();
printf("\nEnter the elements of array:-");
for(i=0;i<5;i++)
 scanf("%d",&n[i]);
for(i=0;i<5;i++)
{
  rem=n[i]%3;
  if(rem==0)
  {
    a++;
    i0[a]=n[i];
     }
  else
  {
   if(rem==1)
   {
    b++;
    i1[b]=n[i];
   }
   else
   {
    c++;
    i2[c]=n[i];
   }
  }
 }
 printf("\n\nThe Hashing Table is as follows\n");
 printf("——————————————————\n");

 printf("Index 0 :-");

 for(j=1;j<=a;j++)
  printf("%5d",i0[j]);

 printf("\nIndex 1 :-");
 for(j=1;j<=b;j++)
  printf("%5d",i1[j]);

 printf("\nIndex 2 :-");
```

Explanation In this program the main array '*n[]*' is declared. In it, five elements are declared. In addition to the above *i0[],i1[]* and *i2[]* arrays are also initialized for storing the index. In the program, we can calculate the hashing table by using the division method. The keys are divided by 3. Using the mod operation, the remainders are calculated and are placed in the appropriate index. The number, which is to be searched, is prompted through keyboard using variable num. The number is divided by 3 and after knowing the reminder; the particular index is searched for searching the element.

```
 for(j=1;j<=c;j++)
  printf("%5d",i2[j]);
 printf("\n------------------------");
printf("\nEnter the key to search:-");
scanf("%d",&num);
rem=num%3;
 if(rem==0)
 {
   for(j=1;j<=a;j++)
    if(num==i0[j])
      printf("\nThe position of the number is %d in the Index 0",j);
 }
 if(rem==1)
 {
     for(j=1;j<=b;j++)
    if(num==i1[j])
   printf("\nThe position of the number is %d in Index 1",j);
 }
 if(rem==2)
 {
   for(j=1;j<=c;j++)
   if(num==i2[j])
      printf("\nThe position of the number is %d in the Index 2",j);
 }
}
```

```
OUTPUT
Enter the elements of array:-4 11 5 17 23 12 10 13 6 21
The Hashing Table is as follows
------------------------
Index 0 :-  12   6  21
Index 1 :-   4  10  13
Index 2 :-  11   5  17  23
------------------------
Enter the key to search:-23
The position of the number is 4 in the Index 2
```

Example 11.8

Write a program to prepare hashing table by division method. Use functions and search number from the hashing table.

Solution

```
#include<stdio.h>
#include<conio.h>
main()
```

```
{
void show(int *a,int *nos);
int search(int gno,int *arr,int lim);
 int n[5],i0[5],i1[5],i2[5];
int num,rem,a=0,b=0,c=0,i,j;
clrscr();
printf("\nEnter the elements of array:-");
for(i=0;i<5;i++)
scanf("%d",&n[i]);
for(i=0;i<5;i++)
 {
  rem=n[i]%3;
 switch(rem)
  {
   case 0: a++; i0[a]=n[i]; break;
   case 1: b++; i1[b]=n[i]; break;
   case 2: c++; i2[c]=n[i]; break;
  }
 }
printf("\n\nThe Hashing Table is as follows\n");
printf("————————————————————\n");
printf("Index 0 :-");
show( &i0[1],&a);
printf("\nIndex 1 :-");
show(&i1[1],&b);
printf("\nIndex 2 :-");
show(&i2[1],&c);
printf("\n————————————————————");
printf("\nEnter the key to search:-");
scanf("%d",&num);
rem=num%3;
switch(rem)
 {
  case 0:
   printf("\nThe position of the number is %d in the Index 0",search(num,&i0[1],a));
    break;
  case 1:
   printf("\nThe position of the number is %d in Index 1",search(num,&i1[1],b));
    break;
  case 2:
   printf("\nThe position of the number is %d in the Index 2",search(num,&i2[1],c));
    break;
 }
}
void show(int *a,int *nos)
{
 int j;
```

Explanation In this program the division hashing method is used for storing the numbers. The *i0[],i1[],* and *i2[]* are three arrays, which are used for storing results. The variable *a, b, c* are used for storing the boundaries of the buckets. The function *show()* is used to display the elements of a bucket. Function *search()* is used for searching the given number into the three buckets. In function, *show()* the two arguments are passed and they are the address of bucket array and address of boundaries. Function *search()* contains three arguments address of bucket array, value of boundaries, and the given number to search.

```
 for(j=1;j<=*nos;j++)
  {
  printf("%5d",*a);
   a++;
  }
}
int search(int gno,int *arr,int lim)
{
int j;
for(j=1;j<=lim;j++)
if(gno==*arr)
return j;
else
arr++;
}
```

```
OUTPUT
Enter the elements of array:-12 34 65 23 10
The Hashing Table is as follows
-----------------------------
Index 0 :-  12
Index 1 :-  34  10
Index 2 :-  65  23
-----------------------------
Enter the key to search:-10
The position of the number is 2 in Index 1
```

11.8 MID-SQUARE METHOD

In mid-square method the key is multiplied with itself and middle digit is chosen as the address of that element in the hashing table. It is defined as follows:

$H(k)=(k*k)$

For example, if the key is $k=12$

$H(12)=(12*12)=144.$

In this example, the key is 12, its square is 144 and its middle digit is 4. Hence, 12 is placed in the hash table in the index 4 as index 4 is the address of 12. Similarly, for other keys the squares are calculated and mid digits are evaluated. Based on the mid digits the keys are placed in the appropriate index. Here, the mid digit obtained can be from 0 to 9. Hence, we may need up to 10 indices starting from index 0 through index 9.

For example, if the key is $k=10$

$H(10)=(10*10)=100$. Its middle digit is 0. Hence, number 10 would be placed in index 0. Similarly, the same procedure is adopted for all other numbers and they are placed in different indices based on the mid digit value.

Consider the following number for constricting the hashing table:

12,14,18,20,36,31,27,35,23,59.

Table 11.2 Table of key, square and mid

Key	Square	Mid	Key	Square	Mid
12	144	4	31	961	6
14	196	9	27	729	2
18	324	2	15	225	2
20	400	0	23	529	2
26	676	7	23	841	4

Figure 11.3 Hashing table using the mid-square method

Square	Mid	Key	Square
0	20	5	–
1	–	6	31
2	18, 27, 15, 23	7	26
3	–	8	–
4	12, 29	9	14

A program is prepared for hashing table using the mid-square method.

Example 11.9

Write a program to display the hash table, which is to be prepared by using the mid-square method.

Solution

```
#include<stdio.h>
#include<conio.h>
main()
{
int msarr[6]={18,21,29,27,12,11},ms1[6],ms2[6],ms3[6],ms4[6];
int a,i,m1,m2,m3,m4,smid;
int squ_mid(int);
void disp(int farr[],int count);
clrscr();
m1=m2=m3=m4=0;
printf("The numbers are as follows :-\n");
for(i=1;i<=7;i++)
printf("\t%d",msarr[i]);
for (a=1;a<7;a++)
```

```
{
smid=squ_mid(msarr[a]);
switch (smid)
 {
  case 1:
  { m1++; ms1[m1]=msarr[a]; break; }
  case 2:
  { m2++; ms2[m2]=msarr[a]; break; }
  case 3:
  { m3++; ms3[m3]=msarr[a]; break; }
  case 4:
  { m4++; ms4[m4]=msarr[a]; break; }
 }
}
printf("\n\nThe Hash Table with Mid-Square method is as follows");
printf("\n——————————————————\n");
printf("Index 1:-");
disp(ms1,m1);
printf("\nIndex 2:-");
disp(ms2,m2);

printf("\nIndex 3:-");
disp(ms3,m3);
printf("\nIndex 4:-");
disp(ms4,m4);
printf("\n——————————————————\n");
}
int squ_mid(int ele)
{
int squ=0,mid,n;
squ=ele*ele;
  for(n=0;n<2;n++)
   {
   mid=squ%10;
   squ=squ/10;
   }
return mid ;
}
void disp(int farr[],int count)
{
int a1;
for(a1=1;a1<=count;a1++)
printf("%5d",farr[a1]);
}
```

Explanation In this program the main array *'msarr[]'* having six elements are declared. In addition to the above *'m1[]'*, *'m2[]'*, *'m3[]'* and *'m4[]'* are initialized . These arrays are initialized for storing the index. Two functions are declared, they are *squ_mid();* and *dis()*. These two functions are initialized for finding the middle digit of the square and display the keys. By using the mod operator, the middle digit of the square number is calculated. After finding the middle digit they are displayed in the hash table.

OUTPUT

The numbers are as follows :-

```
21    29    27    12    11    64    0
The Hash Table with Mid-Square method is as follows
-------------------------
Index 1:-
Index 2:-  27  11
Index 3:-
Index 4:-  21  29  12
-------------------------
```

11.9 FOLDING METHOD

In the folding method, the key is divided into number of parts. The parts, of course, are dependent on the length of the key. All the parts are added together. If the carry results from this operation it is to be ignored and the number what remains behind after ignoring the carry is the address of key. By using this method, we fold the key hence this method is called as folding method.

For example,

1. If key k= 879987

Then, by using this method, we divide it into two parts like 879 and 987. They are added and then carry ignored and the number after ignoring the carry becomes the address of the key.

879 +987 = 1866. Its most significant digit is 1. Hence, after ignoring 1, the number that is left is 866 which is the address of the key.

2. If k=678897678

In this, key is divided into the 3 parts. They are 678, 897 and 678.

By adding, 678+897+678= 2253.

After ignoring last carry 2, the number that is left is 253. Therefore, 253 is the address of the key. Thus, the folding method is useful in converting multiword key into a single word. By applying hashing function, the key can be identified. The reader can develop a program on the topic.

11.10 LENGTH-DEPENDENT METHOD

One more hashing technique used is length dependent method. In this method, the length of the key is measured and the number is placed in the index table appropriately. Here, a simple program is made to search an element from the array. The program is self-explanatory. Length of an array and length of each element can be anything but some finite value can be taken.

Example 11.10

Write a program for searching an element by using the length dependent hash function. Display the hash table and search the element from the table.

Solution

```
#include<stdio.h>
#include<conio.h>

main()
{
 int arr[5],in1[5],in2[5],in3[5],in4[5],in5[5];
int a,i,len,i1,i2,i3,i4,i5,snum;
int length(int);
void disp(int farr[],int count);
void search(int sarr[],int n,int co);
clrscr();
i1=i2=i3=i4=i5=0;
printf("\nEnter the number of the elements:-");
for(i=1;i<=5;i++)
 scanf("%d",&arr[i]);
for (a=1;a<6;a++)
 {
  len=length(arr[a]);
  printf("\nThe length of %d is:-%d",arr[a],len);
  switch (len)
  {
   case 1:
   { i1++; in1[i1]=arr[a]; break; }
   case 2:
   { i2++; in2[i2]=arr[a]; break; }
   case 3:
   { i3++; in3[i3]=arr[a]; break; }
   case 4:
   { i4++; in4[i4]=arr[a]; break; }
   case 5:
  { i5++; in5[i5]=arr[a]; break; }
  }
}
 printf("\nThe Hash Table is as follows");
printf("\n————————————————————\n");
 printf("Index 1:-");
 disp(in1,i1);

 printf("\nIndex 2:-");
 disp(in2,i2);

 printf("\nIndex 3:-");
 disp(in3,i3);
 printf("\nIndex 4:-");
 disp(in4,i4);
```

Explanation As usual, the arrays are declared by using *arr[], in1[], in2[], in3[], in4[]* and *in5[]* each one having length of 5. By using *length()*, function length of each key is calculated and the keys are placed in the appropriate index. The number which is to be searched is inputted through the keyboard. Here, *snum* variable is declared. Its length is calculated by using the *length()*; and by knowing the length it is searched in the hash table.

```
 printf("\nIndex 5:-");
  disp(in5,i5);
 printf("\n——————————————————\n");
 printf("Enter the number to search;-");
 scanf("%d",&snum);
 len=length(snum);
 switch (len)
  {
   case 1:
   { search(in1,snum,i1); printf("in Index 1"); break; }
   case 2:
   { search(in2,snum,i2); printf("in Index 2"); break; }
   case 3:
   { search(in3,snum,i3); printf("in Index 3"); break; }
   case 4:
   { search(in4,snum,i4); printf("in Index 4"); break; }
   case 5:
    { search(in5,snum,i5); printf("in Index 5"); break; }
  }
}
int length(int ele)
{
int c=0,num;
while(ele>0)
{
 if(ele>=10)
 {
  ele=ele/10;
  c++;
 }
 else
 {
  c++;
  break;
 }
}
return c ;
}
void disp(int farr[],int count)
{
int a1;
for(a1=1;a1<=count;a1++)
printf("%5d",farr[a1]);
}
void search(int sarr[],int n,int co)
{
int a2;
```

```
 for (a2=1;a2<=co;a2++)
  {
   if(n==sarr[a2])
   {
   printf("The position of the number is %d ",a2);
   break;
   }
  }
}
```

```
OUTPUT
Enter the number of the elements:-1 12 123 12345 1234
The length of 1 is:-1
The length of 12 is:-2
The length of 123 is:-3
The length of 12345 is:-5
The length of 1234 is:-4
The Hash Table is as follows
-------------------
Index 1:-    1
Index 2:-   12
Index 3:-  123
Index 4:- 1234
Index 5:-12345
-------------------
Enter the number to search;-12345
The position of the number is 1 in Index 5
```

11.11 MULTIPLICATIVE HASHING FUNCTION

The name itself indicates that the function is having the multiplication operation in it. The multiplicative hashing function can be written as

H(key)=(b(c*key mod 1))+1.

In this hashing method, the key is multiplied with the number 'c'. The c is used in this function as a constant. After performing the mod of this product with 1 again multiplication operation with the number b is done and 1 is added. The number obtained is the index number for the placing the key.

Mainly, there are two types of searching methods used with hashing function. One is external searching and other is internal search. When the records are bulky then the records can be stored in the file and the file is stored on the disk, tape, etc. The record is outside of the computer memory. On that file the searching operation is to be performed. This searching operation is called as the external searching. Two techniques are used for the external search, one is hashing method and other is tree search method. In another case, when the records are shorter and in less numbers the same can be stored in the computer memory like array, list, etc. In general, the linear searching and binary search are used in the internal searching.

11.12 DIGIT ANALYSIS METHOD

Digit analysis method is the hashing function in which the analysis is done on the whole digits. In this method some digits of some positions of the number are taken out. Then, by making the reverse of the selected digits a value is obtained. The key is transferred to that location. Assume a key 348526917 and just select the digits at the 2, 5 and 7 position. They are as 1,2 and 8. By combining these digits we get a number 128 and after reversing the number have 821. Now, the key is transferred at the address location 821.

Summary

1. Searching is a technique of finding accurate location of an element in the given item list or set of the elements of an array, list, or trees.
2. If the given element is present in the collected elements or array then the search process is said to be successful. The search is said to be unsuccessful if the given element does not exist in the array.
3. The search method in which an element to be searched, is checked in the entire data structure in a sequential way from starting to end is called linear search.
4. Binary search is quicker than the linear search. However, it cannot be applied on unsorted data structure. This is the precondition. Before applying binary search, the linear data structure must be sorted in either ascending or descending order by using one of the sorted methods.
5. Hash is one of the complex searching techniques. In this method, the position of the key (element) is fixed into the table or the file, which is determined by the hash function. Division method is explained with a suitable example in this method. Other methods have also been discussed in detail.

Exercises

A. Answer the following questions:
   1. What is searching? How is the searching process essential for data base applications?
   2. Explain linear and binary search.
   3. Differentiate between linear and binary search.
   4. What are the different searching techniques known to you? Explain one of them in detail with a suitable example.
   5. Distinguish between the external and internal searching.

B. Select the appropriate option for each of the following questions:
   1. The process of finding a particular record is called
      a. sorting c. indexing
      b. searching d. none of the above.
   2. In this type of searching the records must be sorted
      a. linear search c. selection search
      b. binary search d. none of the above.

C. Write the following programs:

1. Write a program to find the given number in an array of 50 elements. Search how many times a given element exists in the list.
2. Write a program to demonstrate successful and unsuccessful search. Display appropriate messages.
3. Write a program to demonstrate binary search. Use character array and store 10 names. Find the given name.
4. Write a program to search with linear search the given name in string array of 10 names.

D. What is the output of following programs?

1.

```
#include <stdio.h>
#include<conio.h>
main()
{
   int n,b=1,a[5];
   clrscr();
   printf("Enter five elements:-");
   while(b<=5)
   { scanf("%d",&a[b]); b++; }
printf("Enter the element to be searched:-");
scanf("%d",&n);
b=1;
while(b<=5)
{
   if(a[b]==n)
{
printf("The number %d is found %d
location",n,b);
break;
}
   b++;
}
if(a[b]!=n)
   printf("The element %d is not found",n);
getch();
}
```

2.

```
#include <stdio.h>
#include<conio.h>
main()
{
   int no,j;
   int r[5],*pt;
clrscr();
printf("Enter five elements:-");
for(j=1;j<=5;j++)
scanf("%d",&r[j]);
printf("Enter the element to be searched:-");
scanf("%d",&no);
pt=&r[1];
j=1;
while(j<=5)
{
if(*pt==no)
{
printf("The number %d is found %d
location",no,j);
break;
}
pt++;
j++;
}
if(*pt!=no)
printf("The element %d is not found",no);
getch();
}
```

3.

```
#include <stdio.h>
#include <conio.h>
main()
{
int its[5], st=0,en=4,j,num,mid;
clrscr();
for (j=0;j<5;j++)
{
printf (" Enter element  %d : ",1+j);
scanf ("%d",&its[j]);
```

```
}
printf ("\n Enter element to be searched :");
scanf ("%d",&num);
mid=(st+en)/2;
while (num!=its[mid] && st<=en)
{
if (num>its[mid])
st=mid+1;
else
en=mid-1;
mid=(st+en)/2;
}
if (num==its[mid])
printf ("\n  %d found at position %d ",
num,++mid);
if (st>en)
printf (" %d not found ", num);
getch();
}
```

4.

```
#include<stdio.h>
#include<string.h>
#include<conio.h>
main()
{
int beg=1,mid,end=5,i,flag=0,val;
char name[5],fn;
clrscr();
printf("Enter name:-\n");
for(i=0;i<5;i++)
scanf("%c",&name[i]);
printf("\n\tEnter the name to search:-");
scanf("%s",&fn);
mid=(beg+end)/2;
printf("\n\tAt starting beg is %d, mid is %d &
end is %d",beg,mid,end);
while((strcmp(fn,name[mid]))!=0 && beg<=end)
{
val=strcmp(fn,name[mid]);
if(val>0)
{
beg=mid+1;
mid=(beg+end)/2;
printf("\n\tmid is %d & beg is %d",mid,beg);
}
else
{
end=mid-1;
mid=(beg+end)/2;
printf("\n\tmid is %d & end is %d",mid,end);
}
}
if(strcmp(fn,name[mid])==0)
flag=1;
if(flag==1)
printf("\n\tThe name %c is traced
successfully",fn);
else
printf("\n\tThe number %c is not traced",fn);
getche();
}
```

5.

```
#include<stdio.h>
#include<conio.h>
main()
{
int  n[10],bk0[5],bk1[5];
int rem,a=0,b=0,i;
clrscr();
printf("Enter ten numbers:-");
for(i=0;i<10;i++)
scanf("%d",&n[i]);
for(i=0;i<10;i++)
{
rem=n[i]%2;
switch(rem)
{
case 0: a++; bk0[a]=n[i];
break;
case 1: b++; bk1[b]=n[i];
break;
}
}
printf("\nIn 0 bkt total number are  :-%d",a);
printf("\nIn 1 bkt total number are  :-%d",b);
}
```

6.

```
#include<stdio.h>
#include<conio.h>
int  n[10]={1,2,9,8,4,6,7,5,3,10},b0[5],b1[5];
main()
```

```
{
void bucket();
clrscr();
bucket();
}
void bucket()
{
int r,a=0,b=0,i;
for(i=0;i<10;i++)
{
r=n[i]%2;
switch(r)
{
case 0: a++; b0[a]=n[i];break;
case 1: b++; b1[b]=n[i];break;
}
}
printf("\nThe elements of bucket 0 are  :-");
for(i=1;i<=a;i++)
printf("%3d",b0[i]);
printf("\nThe elements of bucket 1 are  :-");
for(i=1;i<=b;i++)
printf("%3d",b1[i]);
}
```

7.

```
#include<stdio.h>
#include<conio.h>
int arr[5]={2,9,4,7,10};
main()
{
int no,pos;
int search(int n);
clrscr();
printf("Enter number to search:-");
scanf("%d",&no);
pos=search(no);
if(pos==0)
printf("\nNumber is not found");
else
printf("\n%d number is at %d",no,pos);
}
int search(int n)
{
int i;
for(i=0;i<5;i++)
if(n==arr[i])
return(++i);
return 0;
}
```

Index